Theory and Practice of International Trade Linkage Models

ADVANCED STUDIES IN THEORETICAL AND APPLIED ECONOMETRICS
VOLUME 9

For a complete list of volumes in this series see final page of this volume.

Theory and Practice of International Trade Linkage Models

by

Alexander Italianer

1986 **MARTINUS NIJHOFF PUBLISHERS**
a member of the KLUWER ACADEMIC PUBLISHERS GROUP
DORDRECHT / BOSTON / LANCASTER

Distributors

for the United States and Canada: Kluwer Academic Publishers, 101 Philip Drive, Assinippi Park, Norwell, MA 02061, USA
for the UK and Ireland: Kluwer Academic Publishers, MTP Press Limited, Falcon House, Queen Square, Lancaster LA1 1RN, UK
for all other countries: Kluwer Academic Publishers Group, Distribution Center, P.O. Box 322, 3300 AH Dordrecht, The Netherlands

Library of Congress Cataloging in Publication Data

Italianer, Alexander.
Theory and practice of international trade linkage models.

(Advanced studies of theoretical and applied economics ; 9)
Bibliography: p.
Includes indexes.
1. Commerce--Econometric models. I. Title. II. Series.
HF1008.I85 1986 582'.0724 86-21804

ISBN 90-247-3407-X (this volume)
ISBN 90-247-2622-0 (series)

PRINTED IN THE NETHERLANDS

PREFACE

This book was mainly written while I stayed at the Catholic University of Louvain. Professor Anton P. Barten was the one who did not only give me a warm welcome in Louvain, but also supported my research with most valuable comments and constructive criticisms. In addition I benefitted from discussions with Erik Schokkaert, Denis de Crombrugghe and Jo Baras on various subjects, such as the small-sample correction of Chapter 9. The arduous task of transferring my neat handwriting into a readable typescript was excellently taken care of by Mrs. E. Crabbé and notably Mrs. F. Duijsens, even after working hours. Mrs. A. Molders prevented me of making serious abuse of the English language. My admiration for Carien, finally, is an exponential function of the patience and enthusiasm with which she supported my research.

Chapter 1 is a general introduction to the subject of linkage models, and it contains few mathematical elaborations. Chapters 2 to 4 use more, but elementary, mathematics, and treat several aspects related to the derivation, interpretation and estimation of linkage models. Chapter 2 deals with the theory of import allocation models, Chapter 3 treats the problem of defining and interpreting elasticities of substitution, while Chapter 4 is concerned with the econometric problems related to the estimation of multivariate models with linear restrictions, such as import allocation models. The core of the study is formed by the derivation, estimation and testing of a new (import) allocation model based on the CRESH aggregator function, in Chapters 5, 8 and 9 respectively. Chapters 6 and 7 describe the estimation method and the data corresponding to this model and therefore serve as background information. Chapter 10, finally, contains a summary and conclusions.

CONTENTS

CHAPTER 2 :

IMPORT ALLOCATION MODELS

CHAPTER 3 :

ON THE USE OF ELASTICITIES OF SUBSTITUTION

CHAPTER 5 :

A MODEL WITH PAIRWISE DIFFERING ELASTICITIES OF SUBSTITUTION

CHAPTER 6 :

ECONOMETRIC SPECIFICATION

CHAPTER 7 :
THE DATA

CHAPTER 8 :
ESTIMATION

CHAPTER 9 :

HYPOTHESIS TESTING

CHAPTER 10 :

CONCLUSIONS

CHAPTER 1 - THE LINKAGE SYSTEM

1.1. INTRODUCTION

Over the last fifteen years the already growing stock of econometric models has been enriched, one may say, by a substantial number of so-called *international linkage models*. An international linkage model may be defined as a set of two or more econometric models each of which contains at least one variable belonging to another model. The *models* are usually macro-economic models, and each individual model corresponds in general to a geographic region. Such a region may be a country or a group of countries, but might also be a province or any other geographic entity. The *variables* of one model appearing in another model are mostly related to international trade, as international trade is the major factor that links different geographical units, certainly if we restrict ourselves to those effects for which we have adequate quantitative information at our disposal. The expression "international" should of course be interpreted in a large sense, thus also representing "interregional", "interprovincial", *etc*.

Econometric models are in general held to be a stylized description of economic reality. International trade is a particular aspect of this reality. It is almost universally acknowledged that the economic prosperity which at least a large part of the world has known since 1945, and notably since the beginning of the sixties, may be ascribed to a considerable extent to the increase of international trade relative to the general level of economic growth. Between 1954 and 1982, the estimated value share of exports of goods and services in the Gross Domestic Product of the member countries of the Organisation for Economic Co-operation and Development increased from 11.6 % to 19.9 % [1].

Imports and exports of goods and services have not only been a source of economic growth themselves, their increased importance has also strengthened the way in which economic fluctuations are transferred from one country to another and *vice versa*. In short, they are one of the major factors behind a continually growing *interdependency* between the actors on the stage of the world economy. It was therefore inevitable that the importance of international trade in economic reality as a mainspring to growth and as a transmission mechanism for economic fluctuations should have its counterpart in econometric modelbuilding : this explains why international linkage models have taken such a lofty flight.

The *principle* of linking national macro-economic models is overly simple : the *exogenous* variables in each model relating to foreign trade should be made *endogenous*. Single national macro-economic models usually have the volume of exports exogenous or explained as a function of (exogenous) foreign demand, while the import price is also exogenous or determined again by exogenous foreign prices. The element which therefore makes such a set of models a truly international linkage model would be the explicit recognition in the models of the fact that a country's exports depend on the imports of other countries, and that similarly a country's import price is determined through the export prices of other countries. We should add immediately that this description is highly stylized. For instance, trade is not the only way by which country models may be linked : one might also consider migration or financial flows. But nevertheless the description may be considered sufficient to illustrate the distinction one should make between a set of independent country models and a true international linkage model.

Though the linking *principle* may be simple, its practical *implementation* seems, on the contrary, a far from trivial matter. The number of different approaches that may be found in the literature is almost equal to the number of international linkage models. This overwhelming variety of approaches is to a large extent due to empirical considerations that have guided modelbuilders in the construction of their international linkage models. Theoretical requirements derived both from economic and econometric theory often had to be abandoned in view of practical implementation of a linkage model.

The objects of this study are trade linkage models, and more particularly we analyze the interaction between trade linkage models in practice and the economic and econometric theory that relates to them.

That is, we will concentrate explicitly on the *trade linkage* part of international linkage models. Therefore, if we talk hereafter about linkage models, we are referring only to international trade and the way national economic models may be linked by means of an econometric model describing international trade. We will even restrict ourselves to the mechanism that links trade *flows*, discussing *price* linkage only briefly below.

Although we will touch upon a substantial number of aspects of the interactions briefly, the extensive field of study obliges us to consider at length only a limited number. More particularly, after a general overview of methods of trade linkage in this chapter, we will concentrate on the interactions concerning the so-called *import allocation models* in Chapter 2. These models have two important properties.

First, they may be derived using a model of (micro-economic) neoclassical optimizing behaviour including utility or production functions, or aggregator functions in short. This raises the question how the *substitution possibilities* between different trade partners as embodied in the aggregator function may be described adequately in terms of elasticities. This question on the use of price and substitution elasticities, whose interest extends beyond import allocation models alone, is discussed extensively in Chapter 3.

A second property of import allocation models and indeed of any allocation model concerns its *estimation*. An allocation model is a model which divides a pre-assigned total among given elements, be it total imports over trade partners, total consumer income over expenditure categories or whatsoever. For estimation this implies that the estimation procedure should take account of the fact that the fitted values of all elements should add up to the given total. As far as this requirement implies that the set of equations to be estimated should obey a linear adding-up restriction, the allocation model becomes a special case of the general model of which the equations should obey one or more linear restrictions. The special problems encountered in the estimation of such models with the method of maximum likelihood (which is a general method comprising other estimation methods as special cases) are therefore presented in Chapter 4.

Within the class of import allocation models, the models derived from the Constant-Elasticity-of-Substitution (CES) aggregator function play a predominant role. The hypotheses underlying these models are however extremely restrictive concerning the substitution possibilities between the products from the different trade partners supplying a given import market. This seems the only drawback of a model that otherwise may be empirically implemented in strict accordance with theoretical and econometric requirements. We will argue in section 1.5 that it should be tested empirically whether this CES import allocation model stands out against a more general specification that allows for less restrictive substitution possibilities. Moreover we will put forward that the success of such a test may depend on the conditions of the specific model-setting in which the test is performed, in particular the classification of the categories of traded goods that is used and the number of trade partners that are distinguished. A change in any of these conditions might influence the outcome of the test and therefore imposes, as it were, two meta-tests.

An import allocation model that allows for more general substitution possibilities than the CES model, but which nevertheless maintains the same advantages regarding its empirical implementation, is presented in Chapter 5. After its stochastic specification, in Chapter 6, a description of the data in Chapter 7 and standard estimations in Chapter 8, we use this model in Chapter 9 to test against the CES import allocation model. Apart from simple testing against the CES model, we also consider the meta-tests concerning the influence on the outcome of the ordinary test of the classification of the categories of goods and the number of trading partners. Finally the model is also used to provide a simple test of the justification of the separability assumption underlying the import allocation model.

1.2. SOME CONVENTIONS

Equations, assumptions, theorems, corollaries, figures, *etc.* will be numbered by section. They will only be preceded by their chapter number if they are referred to in another chapter than the one in which they originally appear.

Trade flows may be measured in current prices or in constant prices, and are everywhere assumed to be expressed in a common currency, the United States dollar. If we refer simply to "imports" or "exports" we will assume these flows to be in *constant* prices, unless otherwise indicated. Furthermore, we will in general mean by *total* imports or exports, the total over trade partners, and by *aggregate* imports or exports, the aggregate over all categories of commodities.

We will in general use capitals to indicate variables in current U.S. dollars and lowercase letters for variables in constant U.S. dollars, using for our estimations 1975 as the baseyear. Prices are usually prefixed by a "p".

Trade variables may have at most four dimensions, with four corresponding subscripts :

1) the category of goods, usually with subscript k;
2) the exporting country or region, usually with subscript i;
3) the importing country or region, usually with subscript j;
4) time, with subscript t.

If there is no danger of confusion, as many subscripts as possible will be deleted, but in any case one should be aware that despite of this simplification the variables *always* keep their four dimensions, unless otherwise indicated. For instance, m_{kijt}, imports in constant 1975 U.S. dollars by country j from country i of goods of category k at period t will usually be denoted by m_i, while the corresponding bilateral exports (from i to j) x_{kijt} will be denoted by x_j. Total imports of country j in constant 1975 U.S. dollars will in this way be denoted by m and total exports in constant

1975 U.S. dollars by x. If two subscripts are needed for the bilateral imports of exports (for instance for summations), total imports and exports will be denoted by m_j and x_i, and the bilateral imports and exports by m_{ij} and x_{ij}.

Summations or multiplications over country subscripts (which are usually i and j, and exceptionally h and l) will run from 1 to n, where n is the number of trading countries involved (we use *country* also to indicate regions). The commodity subscript k will run from 1 to g. We assume everywhere that the intratrade of the countries and regions is zero; consequently there is no harm in including the corresponding variables in the summations or multiplications. The corresponding price indices are simply assumed not to exist.

1.3. ELEMENTS OF A WORLD TRADE LINKAGE MODEL

In this section we consider the elements that in general compose the linkage part of an international linkage model. We also present some assumptions that are maintained throughout the rest of the study.

1.3.1. DATA FRAMEWORK

We will suppose for simplicity that our model describes the whole world, which is supposed to be divided in n countries and regions. Both will be referred to as *countries* for short. Their number n may vary but should at least be equal to 2.

Trade is taken to be divided into g categories of commodities, with g greater than or equal to 1. If g equals 1, we are considering *aggregate* trade, otherwise the g categories are assumed to have been defined as mutually exclusive according to some exhaustive classification, such as the Standard International Trade Classification (SITC) of the UNITED NATIONS (1961, 1975) or the NIMEXE classification of the COMMISSION OF THE EUROPEAN COMMUNITIES (1980).

Country models may in principle be linked through a number of channels, such as merchandise trade, services, primary income flows, financial flows, labour migration *etc.* [2)].

We will however make the following

ASSUMPTION 3.1 :

Throughout this study, we will only consider the linkage of country models through merchandise trade.

The consequence of this assumption is that the linkage model which we consider only consists of variables concerning imports and exports of goods (all assumed to be denominated in U.S. dollars). We make this assumption only for simplicity, such that if we talk about a *linkage model*, we only mean linkage by means of traded goods.

Next we define the trade variables that are determined in the linkage model, where we delete the time subscript

DEFINITION 3.1. :

m_{kij} : Imports of goods of category k by country j from country i in constant U.S. dollars; short notation : m_{ki}, m_{ij} or m_{i}

M_{kij} : Idem in current U.S. dollars; short notation : M_{ki}, M_{ij} or M_{i}

pm_{kij} : Idem, price index 1975 = 1; short notation : pm_{ki}, pm_{ij} or pm_{i} $(pm_{kij} = M_{kij}/m_{kij})$

m_{kj} : Total imports of goods of category k by country j in constant U.S. dollars; short notation : m_{k}, m_{j} or m

M_{kj} : Idem in current U.S. dollars; short notation : M_{k}, M_{j} or M

pm_{kj} : Idem, price index 1975 = 1; short notation : pm_{k}, pm_{j} or pm $(pm_{kj} = M_{kj}/m_{kj})$

x_{kij} : Exports of goods of category k from country i to country j in constant U.S. dollars; short notation : x_{kj}, x_{ij} or x_{j}

X_{kij} : Idem in current U.S. dollars; short notation : X_{kj}, X_{ij} or X_{j}

px_{kij} : Idem, price index 1975 = 1; short notation : px_{kj}, px_{ij} or px_{j} $(px_{kij} = X_{kij}/x_{kij})$

x_{ki} : Total exports of goods of category k by country i in constant U.S. dollars; short notation : x_{k}, x_{i} or x

X_{ki} : Idem in current U.S. dollars; short notation : X_{k}, X_{i} or X

px_{ki} : Idem, price index 1975 = 1; short notation : px_{k}, px_{i} or p_{x} $(px_{ki} = X_{ki}/x_{ki})$.

Remark : for any of these variables the subscript k will be replaced by the suffix g or G to indicate aggregate commodity trade.

In the definition of these variables concerning imports and exports we did not mention whether the variables were supposed to be measured free on board (fob) or including cost, insurance and freight (cif). If all variables are measured either fob or cif we would expect the world trade balance expressed in current U.S. dollars to be equal to zero. For, what are exports for one country are necessarily imports for another country, and if they are measured in the same way their sums should be equal on a world scale.

This however, is not the case in reality. In fact, not only the world trade balance but the whole world current balance do not equal zero. The fob trade balance discrepancy amounted to almost 2 % of the value of total world exports in 1980 [3]. Although this trade discrepancy is about half of the total discrepancy for invisibles, 2 % of world exports is still a considerable recording discrepancy, and it would be worth reducing it. VEIL (1982) attempted to do so, but in quantifying the main recording deficiencies he only succeeded, in spite of his considerable effort, to estimate the gaps due to the so-called timing asymmetry (the fact that recording of imports happens later than recording of exports [4]) and due to the exports of ships to open-registry countries. This left unexplained a relatively large part of the discrepancy (varying between 50 % and 80 % during the period 1969-1980). Errors due to differences of concept, differences in valuation, recording gaps, differences in methods of calculation *etc.* therefore still have to remain unknown [5].

The world trade balance is however only the tip of the iceberg, so to speak. As it is an aggregate figure which is composed of an almost infinite number of smaller pieces of information, errors contained in the latter may be much larger individually and cancel out against each other in the balance. Well known, for instance, are the differences between variables recorded from customs data, balance-of-payments data and National Accounts data concerning imports and exports. Another example are the negative cif-fob differences that may be observed if one analyzes individual bilateral trade flows.
This may be illustrated by our experience when analyzing a tape containing bilateral aggregate trade data, from the International Monetary Fund *Direction of Trade* Statistics, between 13 industrial countries and 5 zones

(dividing the rest of the world exhaustively). Over the period 1953-1980 we found that in 30 % of the total number of cases, recorded bilateral cif imports were smaller than the corresponding recorded bilateral fob exports. Considering only the trade between the 13 countries this percentage even amounted to 37 %.

We will circumvent the problem of recording discrepancies and the transition from cif to fob data by supposing that the import and export data are either both recorded cif or both recorded fob. In terms of the variables of Definition 3.1, this amounts to the following

ASSUMPTION 3.2 :

Throughout this study we assume that bilateral imports are equal to bilateral exports, *i.e.* :

$$M_{kij} = X_{kij} \qquad \text{all } k,\ i \neq j,$$

$$x_{kij} = m_{kij} \qquad \text{all } k,\ i \neq j.$$

With Definition 3.1 this assumption implies for the bilateral prices

$$pm_{kij} = px_{kij} \qquad \text{all } k,\ i \neq j. \tag{3.1}$$

The practical implication of Assumption 3.2 would be to use a set of bilateral trade data which are all recorded in the same way, such as only bilateral imports recorded cif or only bilateral exports recorded fob. The problem of how to transform in an actual model one set into the other would require explicit modelling of bilateral cif-fob margins, not to speak of recording discrepancies that trouble the credibility of the data on these margins. Given the actual state of data recording any elaborate approach is doomed to failure. If the margins (including the discrepancy) remain about constant over time relative to the flows to which they pertain, one may apply a constant transformation matrix [6], but that seems to be about the only viable way to treat the problem in a bilateral fashion [7].

Before we discuss the conceptual elements that may be of influence in a linkage model, we will first present a number of identities which should normally hold for the variables introduced in Definition 3.1. The most important one is that in the model the bilateral variables should add up to their totals per category of goods k

(3.2) $m_{kj} = \Sigma_i \, m_{kij}$ $\quad$ *all* j,

(3.3) $M_{kj} = \Sigma_i \, M_{kij}$ $\quad$ *all* j,

(3.4) $x_{ki} = \Sigma_j \, x_{kij}$ $\quad$ *all* i,

(3.5) $X_{ki} = \Sigma_j \, X_{kij}$ $\quad$ *all* i.

Summation over the categories of goods k should also give the totals for aggregate bilateral trade

(3.6) $mg_{ij} = \Sigma_k \, m_{kij}$ $\quad$ *all* $i \neq j$,

(3.7) $MG_{ij} = \Sigma_k \, M_{kij}$ $\quad$ *all* $i \neq j$,

(3.8) $xg_{ij} = \Sigma_k \, x_{kij}$ $\quad$ *all* $i \neq j$,

(3.9) $XG_{ij} = \Sigma_k \, X_{kij}$ $\quad$ *all* $i \neq j$.

Finally the summation over categories of goods and bilateral trade flows should result in aggregate total imports and exports

(3.10) $mg_j = \Sigma_i \, mg_{ij} = \Sigma_k \, m_{kj}$ $\quad$ *all* j,

(3.11) $MG_j = \Sigma_i \, MG_{ij} = \Sigma_k \, M_{kj}$ $\quad$ *all* j,

(3.12) $xg_i = \Sigma_j \, xg_{ij} = \Sigma_k \, x_{ki}$ $\quad$ *all* i,

(3.13) $XG_i = \Sigma_j \, XG_{ij} = \Sigma_k \, X_{ki}$ $\quad$ *all* i.

If these identities hold, they assure together with Assumption 3.2 that the world trade balance, both per individual category of goods and for aggregate trade, equals zero. This holds both in current and in constant prices

(3.14) $\Sigma_j\ m_{kj} = \Sigma_j\Sigma_i\ m_{kij} = \Sigma_i\Sigma_j\ x_{kij} = \Sigma_i\ x_{ki},$

(3.15) $\Sigma_j\ M_{kj} = \Sigma_j\Sigma_i\ M_{kij} = \Sigma_i\Sigma_j\ X_{kij} = \Sigma_i\ X_{ki},$

(3.16) $\Sigma_j\ mg_j = \Sigma_j\Sigma_k\ m_{kj} = \Sigma_k\Sigma_i\ x_{ki} = \Sigma_i\ xg_i,$

(3.17) $\Sigma_j\ MG_j = \Sigma_j\Sigma_k\ M_{kj} = \Sigma_k\Sigma_i\ X_{ki} = \Sigma_i\ XG_i.$

Furthermore the identities permit us, together with Definition 3.1, to see the way in which price increases in one country influence the prices in other countries by way of the transfer of export price changes into import prices. Consider for example the total import price of country j for commodities of category k, pm_{kj}. According to its definition it equals the ratio of the corresponding imports in current and constant prices. Using identities (3.2) and (3.3), Assumption 3.2 and the definition of px_{kij} we may derive

(3.18) $$\begin{aligned} pm_{kj} &= M_{kj}/m_{kj} \\ &= (\Sigma_i\ M_{kij})/(\Sigma_i\ m_{kij}) \\ &= (\Sigma_i\ X_{kij})/(\Sigma_i\ x_{kij}) \\ &= \Sigma_i(x_{kij}/\Sigma_h x_{khj})\ px_{kij}, \end{aligned}$$

which defines the total import price for commodity k as a weighted average of bilateral export prices with as weights the import shares of the exporting countries. Changes in price or cost conditions in an exporting country i that are translated into bilateral export price changes are clearly reflected in the import prices of its trade partners *j*. The exact determination of the bilateral trade flow prices is outside the scope of this study, however, and we will only touch upon it in the margin of other discussions.

The identities (3.2) - (3.13) provide a coherent framework for the trade variables : they should be valid for the data that are used in the model, but also for the values of the variables as produced by simulation.

Trade flow data alone may already be a rich source of information. Presently they are published by international institutions such as the United Nations, the International Monetary Fund or the Organisation for Economic Co-operation and Development. Their availability may be seen as one of the conditions favourable to the development of international linkage models. But this is a relatively recent phenomenon. The work of the LEAGUE OF NATIONS (1942) and BECKERMAN (1956) demonstrated already long ago the possibilities for economic analysis using international trade flow data.

1.3.2. CONCEPTUAL ASPECTS

Theoretical considerations concerning the conception of linkage models may be found in TAPLIN (1967), RHOMBERG (1970, 1973), WAELBROECK (1973), MAGEE (1975), BARTEN and d'ALCANTARA (1977), d'ALCANTARA and THEEUWES (1981), BIANCHI and RANUZZI (1981) and in the round-table discussion summarized by COURBIS (1981b). Together they provide an outline of the elements which an "ideal" linkage model might contain, even if we do not discuss yet the aspect of consistency related to the identities presented in the previous subsection. This subject will be taken up in subsection 1.4.3. below.

It should be brought up from the start that, in discussing the elements that possibly might appear in a linkage model, the model we have in mind is a *transmission* model. A transmission model explains the yearly or periodical changes in bilateral trade flows. This type of model should be contrasted with the *structural* model which aims at explaining the structure of world trade at a certain point in time, and which may be considered as being closer to the classical theories of RICARDO (1817), HECKSCHER (1919) and OHLIN (1933). This leads to cross-section estimations, while the transmission models are estimated on time series data or on pooled time series - cross-section data at most. Examples of structural models, which often include elements of gravitational models, may be found in SAVAGE and DEUTSCH (1960), TINBERGEN (1962), PÖYHÖNEN (1963a, 1963b), PULLIAINEN (1963), LINNEMAN (1966), WAELBROECK (1967), OLSEN (1971), AITKEN (1973), SIGNORA (1981) and DE VOS and BIKKER (1983), while a review may be found in LEAMER and STERN (1970, pp. 145-170). That elements of the structural models may appear in transmission models and *vice versa* is clear for example from DRAMAIS (1974/1975) or WAELBROECK (1967).

SIZE

It may be derived from the data framework set out in subsection 1.3.1. above that, *ceteris paribus*, the decisive elements for the *size* of any linkage model are the number of countries (trading partners) involved and the number of categories of commodities that are distinguished. Discussing possible set-ups for linkage models, TAPLIN (1967, p. 451) envisaged 10/12 regions and six categories of goods, these numbers being estimated at 20/30 regions and five categories of goods by RHOMBERG (1970, p. 7). An indication of the number of regions that is distinguished in models presently in use may be obtained if we look at the international linkage models reviewed in HELLIWELL and PADMORE (1984) [8]. By far the largest model is the one of FAIR (1981), containing models for 64 countries and the Rest of the World. Following are the Interlink model of the ORGANISATION FOR ECONOMIC CO-OPERATION AND DEVELOPMENT (OECD)(1979), with models for 23 countries and 8 regions and project LINK (BALL (1973), WAELBROECK (1976) and SAWYER (1979)), containing models for 25 countries and 4 regions. All other surveyed models had less than 20 country models. There clearly is a trade-off between the *number* of country models and their individual *size* : the country models of Fair and the OECD are relatively small in size, while those for project LINK are already more elaborate, and this also holds for the smaller models.

Of the models reviewed by Helliwell and Padmore that cover the whole world, only project LINK, the Interlink model and the Eurolink model describe disaggregate trade (in the four SITC categories 0+1, 2+4, 3, 5-9), *cfr.* GANA *et al.* (1979), SAMUELSON and KURIHARA (1980) and RANUZZI (1981). The other models describe only aggregate trade, *cfr.* AMANO *et al.* (1981a), HOWE *et al.* (1981), ITALIANER (1982a), WAELBROECK and DRAMAIS (1974), KOOYMAN (1981) and FAIR (1981). If one required from an ideal international linkage model that it discern at least 20 countries, about 4/5 categories of goods and if additionally the country models should be relatively elaborated, only project LINK and perhaps the Interlink model would meet these requirements (the Eurolink model describes only 4 countries and the Rest of the World), of the reviewed models.

In the present study we are not concerned with the country models and their degree of elaboration. But even if we leave this aspect out of consideration and formulate as a tentative standard for the size of a linkage model that it should distinguish about 20 countries and 4 or 5 categories of goods, this still turns out as a rather ambitious goal, given the moderate number of existing models that meets this criterion. Nevertheless we consider it a standard which is not excessively high. Any effort aimed at the construction of a linkage model should in principle be designed such that it would be applicable to a model of the size corresponding to this standard.

DEMAND AND SUPPLY

The traditional approach to linkage models has been *demand-oriented*. Trade flows, notably imports, were determined through an income/expenditure variable and relative prices. Notably the analogy between import allocation models, to be discussed more extensively in Chapter 2, and consumer demand systems has been exploited in empirical estimation, albeit that in import allocation models the income/expenditure variable is replaced by total imports.

Supply effects that are of importance on a domestic *import* market are twofold : there is the supply from domestic producers that tends to provoke import substitution, while there is also the foreign export supply. In a complete Walrasian equilibrium model equating demand and supply schemes, the supply shortages from the domestic side during a period of increased business activity would lead to an increased demand for imports. In the absence of a full equilibrium model such effects are usually introduced directly in the import demand equations by way of the degree of capacity utilization [9]. Furthermore, this is a way to deal with the cyclical trend decomposition of imports in the short run [10]. The degree of capacity utilization is generally included in the total import demand equation, but might in the absence of the latter also be introduced in the bilateral import demand equations [11]. The last approach should therefore not be applied to import allocation models which contain equations for both total imports and bilateral imports.

Export supply effects have been introduced in linkage models in two ways. The first approach is through the inclusion in import equations of *ad hoc* supply variables, the second is through the explicit introduction, next to an import demand equation, of an export supply equation, in this way creating a partial equilibrium model. In the *ad hoc* approach, two kinds of supply variables were usually introduced in the (bilateral) import equations [12] : *potential output* of the exporter and its *degree of capacity utilization*, possibly relative to those of competing countries [13]. Together these two variables represent competitive elements that may not be captured in the relative prices, such as technological innovations, export sales promotion efforts, delivery times, after-sales service, trade credit terms, the general ability to meet customer requirements *etc.* [14]. Most of these elements are assumed to be related to, and implicitly captured by, the potential output or production capacity, which therefore exerts a positive influence on export supply. If, however, an increased domestic demand starts to absorb part of the productive capacity, there is a tendency for less aggressive sales efforts, and bottlenecks may develop with a subsequent negative effect on delivery dates, whence loss on the export markets [15]. While the inclusion of production capacity and degree of capacity utilization as supply variables seemed justified for data which did not go beyond the first oil crisis in 1973-1974, doubt has been cast whether they have retained the same explanatory power since [16].

The introduction of an explicit *supply equation* next to a demand equation poses econometric problems, but such problems are no less present if there is only a demand equation. In the latter case it is well known that unless the export supply price elasticity is infinite, estimation by Ordinary Least Squares (OLS) of the demand equation (assuming it is linear) in the absence of a supply equation introduces simultaneity bias [17]. This same problem is also present if one specifies both a demand and supply equation, next to the textbook problem of identification which then may arise [18]. If one estimates the demand and supply equations separately by OLS (assuming the equations are linear), the estimates will be inconsistent [19]. Application of a single equation technique like Indirect Least Squares (ILS) removes the inconsistency. This is the reason why the supply equation often is renormalized as an export price equation [20]. The inconsistency might also be removed using techniques such as Instrumental Variables (IV) [21]. If one applies simultaneous-equation techniques to deal correctly with the simultaneous-equation bias, only the results of Full Information Maximum Likelihood (FIML) are invariant to the applied normalization, although other techniques such as Three-Stage Least Squares (3SLS) may also have this property if the equations are exactly identified [22].

The specification of export supply equations differs between specifications for *total* export supply or *bilateral* export supply, at least when there is a total export supply equation next to the bilateral supply equations; otherwise they will usually be explained in the same fashion. Whether it concerns aggregate or disaggregate trade makes less difference. As noted before, *total* export supply equations may be specified in structural form as real supply equations or in renormalized form as export price equations. Variables that play a role are the same as in the *ad hoc* equations described above, such as production capacity and the degree of capacity utilization. Key elements are, of course, exports and the export price either as dependent or independent variables, depending on whether one has a structural or renormalized form of the equation. Additionally the costs of domestic production, summarized in the GDP deflator or included separately through labour costs, the prices of material inputs and, in the long run, the costs of capital appear in the supply equation; compared to the export price, they determine the profitability of exports. A time trend might account for the differences between the rate of productivity growth in the export sector and the economy in general [23]. *Bilateral* export supply equations are usually specified as a function of total export supply (capacity) and the bilateral export price relative to the total export price [24]. This formulation may be derived in the framework of transformation functions, and the arguments of RANUZZI (1981, pp. 158-159) against inclusion of the export variable do not seem to hold water.

DISAGGREGATION

We saw in the paragraphs above concerning the size of linkage models that there were few existing linkage models that treated trade at any other than the aggregate level. To these models may be added the (non-estimated) Multilateral Exchange Rate Model (MERM) of the International Monetary Fund (IMF), describing trade in 6 categories of goods between 20 countries [25]. Despite the low number of disaggregated linkage models, there are sufficient arguments that warrant the use of such models. That their number has remained limited up to now must be ascribed to data problems; not so much in the field of international trade data but rather in the data for the national models which would have to be divided into branches matching the categories of trade in order to obtain a full articulation of the disaggregate trade effects. Although such models are constructed [26], the mere disaggregation of the linkage model may already be of sufficient interest in itself, however [27].

Disaggregation permits to distinguish influences that may be specific for individual categories of goods which would otherwise disappear in an aggregate trade study. Notably for the analysis of economic policy, the availability of disaggregated bilateral multipliers is very useful, *e.g.* for the effects of tariff rates, export credits *etc.* One might even consider policy questions regarding import quota, supply shortages, price rigidities *etc.* if a suitable framework for the analysis of disequilibria on bilateral markets were available, a desirable but presently remote tool of analysis [28]. Also the effects of stabilization policies may be traced more carefully as cyclical fluctuations find their way through the linkage system in a different manner for different categories of goods, notably for what concerns the timing of the effects in the short run and the long run [29]. The defective way in which the energy sector was introduced into international linkage models after the first and second oil crisis is a clear example of why there is a need for disaggregation in view of economic reality [30], and there is no reason why, in the near future, there would not be another crisis on the markets for raw materials. The same need for disaggregation could similarly be demonstrated in view of the policy questions regarding trade in automobiles, steel production quota *etc.*

In the context of international price transmission, one could furthermore think of a disaggregation to study price and wage developments in "open" and "sheltered" sector of the domestic economies, according to the so-called Scandinavian model [31)].

The final argument for disaggregation is a purely technical point concerning price elasticities, originally raised by ORCUTT (1950). He presented a list of five factors that could be a possible source of downward-biased price elasticities in international trade. One of the sources was simultaneity bias, which has been discussed already above. Another factor explained the low price elasticity of import demand as follows

> *"... it seems reasonable to assume that historical price changes have been largest for those goods that admittedly have low price elasticities of demand. Thus we expect raw material and agricultural prices to show a wider range of price fluctuations than do products in general. This means that most of the price changes in the historical price indices of imports lumped together were due to price changes of commodities with inelastic demands. Since these price changes were associated with only small quantity adjustments, the estimated price elasticities of all imports might well be low".*
>
> ORCUTT (1950, p. 125)

Although this argument must be judged in its historical context, and is conditional to the independency of price changes, it nevertheless illustrates the fact that aggregate data may display other elasticities than could be expected on the grounds of disaggregate results.

A technical analysis on the basis of this argument has been done by MAGEE (1975, pp. 206-207, 235-239) to demonstrate that a disaggregated approach is needed in order to be able to calculate the correct aggregate price elasticities.

DYNAMICS

As is well known, a number of factors may cause time lags between changes in independent variables and their effects on international trade flows. In the path-breaking studies of JUNZ and RHOMBERG (1965, 1973), five different lags are distinguished : recognition lags, decision lags, delivery lags[32], replacement lags and production lags. According to their findings, based on the combination of cross-section and time series data, price elasticities in international trade kept increasing in magnitude for three years following the year of the price change and declined afterwards, exerting significant effects on international trade for two more further years. As additional factors, BARTEN and d'ALCANTARA (1977) name expectations that would play a role in international trade and contracts of a certain duration that may cause parts of certain trade flows to be determined independently of changing external conditions for several years.

A serious problem concerning the use of lags in linkage models arises if the price indices that are used are based - as they often are - on *unit values*. These are obtained by dividing the value of goods crossing the border by their quantity. This price, however, may not be the current price at which the goods could be obtained : although many long-run contracts for quantities are implemented at day-prices, one sometimes uses the price negotiated at the time when the goods were contracted [33]. In particular the unit values of goods which have a long production lag (*e.g.* ships, aeroplanes) may suffer from this problem. Any inference concerning lag structures should therefore be considered with care if lags of unit values are involved.

FUNCTIONAL FORM

The discussion on the functional form in international trade has largely remained technical, concentrating on the advantages and disadvantages of specifications which are linear, loglinear or in logarithmic differences or relative first differences. Systematic comparisons of trade linkage methods are only quite recent and scarce, *cfr.* GANA *et al.* (1979), AMANO *et al.* (1981b), ITALIANER (1982a) and SARMA (1983). A round-table discussion on problems in the construction of multinational models at a conference in 1976 led COURBIS (1981a, p. 28) to conclude still

> "... *il convient maintenant - après la grande floraison de modèles de ce type depuis le début des années soixante-dix - de s'attacher desormais beaucoup plus à améliorer la spécification des relations ainsi que les méthodes d'estimation*".

As concerns the technical debate, the following points have been raised in the discussion. One of the essential differences between linear and loglinear specifications is their implication for *elasticities* : loglinear specifications provide in general constant elasticities, while a linear form gives elasticities which may change with the dependent variables. Notably the drastic fall in elasticities as imports rise has been called upon, next to empirical arguments, as one of the reasons for preferring loglinear total import equations rather than linear equations [34)]. To this argument is added that a loglinear total import equation assures that imports react in proportion to a rise and fall in the explanatory variables[35)]. A formulation in logarithmic differences then permits to calculate impact matrices directly [36)]. Also problems of heteroscedasticity may be avoided with a loglinear specification [37)]. The advantage of constancy of the elasticities has, however, been questioned as it might cause problems in the long run [38)]. Another drawback of a loglinear formulation with respect to a linear form, notably in the context of the import allocation models to be discussed later in Chapter 2, is that, of these two, only linear forms satisfy in general the adding-up condition [39)]. We will see later that this is true in general for these two forms but may in some cases be circumvented.

In GANA *et al.* (1979) the linkage models of KLEIN and VAN PEETERSSEN (1973) and HICKMAN and LAU (1973) are compared, together with the naive methods of constant value shares and constant quantity shares. The first approach, which estimates a total export equation, bears resemblance to the Linear Expenditure System (LES) developed by STONE (1954) in consumer demand theory. The bilateral import equations of the second method are based on a Constant-Elasticity-of-Substitution (CES) import quantity index, while the constant value share approach may be shown to be derived from the Cobb-Douglas function. The LES method performed the best for aggregate world trade, GDP, aggregate exports and aggregate trade balance predictions, while for commodity group SITC 5-9 (manufactures) the constant quantity share method performed the best for the prediction of exports and the CES model was the best for the prediction of imports, as well as for aggregate imports.

The approaches of KLEIN and VAN PEETERSSEN (1973) and HICKMAN and LAU (1973) were also compared by AMANO *et al.* (1981b), together with those of MORIGUCHI (1973), JOHNSON (1978) and SAMUELSON and KURIHARA (1980). On the basis of within-sample dynamic simulations, the Samuelson-Kurihara approach provided - on average - the best result for the prediction of total exports. The total import price and market shares were simulated with the best results for the Hickman-Lau approach.

To these results may be added those for the linkage model of the COMET model, *cfr.* d'ALCANTARA and ITALIANER (1981), as reported by ITALIANER (1982a). For all three elements of comparison, the last model turned out best or second-best when compared to the results of AMANO *et al.* (1981b), although the simulation exercises were not strictly comparable. Of these six approaches, the bilateral equations of d'ALCANTARA and ITALIANER (1981) and MORIGUCHI (1973) are reduced form equations derived from an equilibrium bilateral demand and supply framework [40)]. The approach of JOHNSON (1978) is an extended LES function for bilateral trade flows, while the approach of SAMUELSON and KURIHARA (1980) is a total export equation like that of Klein - Van Peeterssen.

SARMA (1983), finally, compared the one-year ahead predictive performance of total exports for the dynamic Hickman-Lau model, the static LES model, the naive constant value share approach and a total export equation with exports as a function of baseyear-weighted imports, relative prices and relative production capacities. On average, the constant value shares approach gave the best results.

The question of functional form is of most importance if *bilateral* trade flow equations are examined. As we will see below, a linkage model with a large number of countries and therefore a larger number of variables may inspire bilateral trade flow equations based on specific micro-economic neoclassical optimizing behaviour. The form of the aggregator (utility, production) function from which the equations are derived (if they are not derived in a flexible form or from duality theory) is decisive for the underlying substitution possibilities that are implied between the deliveries of the different trade partners : a simple aggregator function will in general limit the substitution possibilities more strongly than a more complex function. The aggregator function therefore constrains *a priori* the results that may be obtained from a simulation analysis of bilateral trade flows. In this respect, the strong assumptions underlying the CES approach of Hickman-Lau have usually only been accepted on the grounds that no better approach offering the same advantages from the point of view of theoretical consistency and estimation was available [41)]. The CES model will be treated more extensively below, and indeed the main empirical part of this study is devoted to the question of whether the CES model is not too restrictive regarding its implied substitution possibilities. We will see that there exist possible alternatives with the same advantages regarding consistency and estimation. The reasons why we focus specifically on the CES model are set out in subsections 1.4.6. and 2.3.1.

1.4. METHODS OF TRADE LINKAGE

After a discussion of the data framework and the conceptual elements that may be of importance for linkage models, we devote the present section to the characteristics that may be used in order to classify or at least distinguish different kinds of linkage models. In the first subsection we discuss the difference between global and bilateral linkage. Next we focus on total and import-export allocation models, consistent and inconsistent linkage and the difference between estimation-consistent linkage and simulation-consistent linkage. The final subsections concern methodological problems and the choice for a particular kind of linkage model.

1.4.1. GLOBAL AND BILATERAL LINKAGE

We will distinguish between *global* and *bilateral* linkage through the following

DEFINITION 4.1 :

An international linkage model is said to be linked by *bilateral linkage* if it contains bilateral trade flows such that bilateral imports by country j from country i explicitly determine bilateral exports from country i to country j or *vice versa*. Otherwise the model is said to be linked through *global linkage*.

This definition classifies linkage models which only contain *total* import and export equations as global linkage models. If constant import and/or export shares are used in the model, it may be both a global linkage model or a bilateral model, depending on how the shares are used. If they are used to calculate such variables as weighted foreign demand, weighted competitors' prices *etc.* which appear as auxiliary variables in other equations, the models are global linkage models. If the shares are used to calculate directly endogenous variables of the linkage model, such as exports being defined as a weighted average of imports using import shares, it will be assumed that there has to be an explicit explanation for the shares, and that we are therefore dealing with a bilateral linkage model. Assuming the shares to be constant is then a possible explanation, albeit a simple one. Although bilateral linkage models may consist of import share equations, their general characteristic is that bilateral trade flows *per se* are explained. Share models are a subset of the set of models so defined.

Global linkage has been called "direct linkage" by WAELBROECK (1973) and "world trade approach" by RANUZZI (1981). Bilateral linkage was named identically by WAELBROECK (1973), called "bilateral approach" by RHOMBERG (1973) and "bilateral direct linkage" by RANUZZI (1981). In contrast to these authors we employ however a large definition of bilateral linkage : we will also take it to comprise import allocation models, to be introduced below in subsection 1.4.2.

Global linkage models, thus in general containing only total import and export equations, were typically part of the seminal international linkage models such as those of NEISSER and MODIGLIANI (1953), POLAK (1953), BECKERMAN (1956) and MENNES (1967). However, also presently there exist a number of global linkage models, although they are in minority with respect to bilateral linkage models. In those cases, global linkage models seem to have been preferred to bilateral linkage models for a number of reasons. *First,* simply because the information which they contain is sufficient for the purposes of those who construct the model. That is, one may simply not be interested in the evolvement of the trade structure over time, and only in the development of total imports and exports. The essentials of the transmission mechanism may then be captured through global variables such as world trade. The seminal models mentioned above and models such as the General Equilibrium Model (CARRIN *et al.* (1980), WAELBROECK and GINSBURGH (1981)) or the METEOR model (KOOYMAN *et al.* (1977), KOOYMAN (1981)) may be expected to fall within this category. A *second* argument, much more widespread and prohibitive in nature, but as simple as the previous one, pertains to the everlasting data problem. For models which have more than one category of goods, a large number of countries, countries for which bilateral data are hard to come by or for which the handling of a large amount of (bilateral) data is not feasible or manageable for any reason, a global linkage system is the only remaining answer. For such models one may think of the IMF World Trade Model (DEPPLER and RIPLEY (1978), BOND (1979), RIPLEY (1980, 1981)) with 4 categories of goods and 18 countries, the OECD Interlink model (OECD (1979), SAMUELSON and KURIHARA (1980)) with also 4 categories of goods but 31 countries, the SIMLINK model (HICKS (1976)) with 14 categories of goods and 7 regions of developing countries, the LES export function of Project LINK (KLEIN *et al.* (1975), KLEIN (1976), the MARCO II model (GUILLAUME (1981)) and the Tsukuba-FAIS model (SHISHIDO *et al.* (1980, 1981)).

The last reason for the use of global rather than bilateral linkage models already indicates that most modelbuilders in principle have a preference for the latter and only switch to the former if they are more or less forced to do so. Indeed, the number of arguments for using bilateral linkage models exceeds its counterpart for global linkage models. A correct representation of the interdependency of world trade permits not only the correct application of weighting schemes in the calculation of synthetic variables, but is of foremost importance in the transmission of economic signals from one country to another. In particular, economic influences between closely tied economies such as the U.S. and Canada, the U.S. and Japan or the EEC countries are too important to be transmitted through global variables such as world trade in a total export equation. In short, bilateral linkage models provide in those cases the only correct way to measure the transmission effects that are obtained from the integration of national models. To these arguments is added the correct measurement of international trade policies such as tariff rate changes *etc.* Also, for an analysis of market shares in international trade, a bilateral linkage model seems indispensable.

Even at the time when the earlier global linkage models were constructed, there were already attempts at using aspects of the bilateral linkage model through constant import shares or the shares from the previous year, as demonstrated by the efforts of TYSZINSKI (1951), FLEMING and TSIANG (1956/1957), TIMS and MEYER-ZU-SCHLOCHTERN (1962), KUZNETS (1964), PHAN (1965) and WAELBROECK (1962, 1967). Bilateral trade linkage approaches based on constant shares do not necessarily have to perform badly with respect to other approaches, as is confirmed by the comparative studies of GANA *et al.* (1979), AMANO *et al.* (1980) and SARMA (1983). In the next subsection we turn to a more general discussion of bilateral linkage.

1.4.2. TOTAL AND IMPORT-EXPORT ALLOCATION

In a bilateral linkage model we are concerned with the explanation of bilateral trade flows. These may be measured in current or constant prices. In the last case, the absence of information on bilateral price and volume data usually leads to deflation of the value series by the *total* export price index of the exporting country. In doing so, one assumes that the exports of the particular category of goods are homogeneous with respect to destination and that the exporter sells this homogeneous product at the same price to every importer, the so-called assumption of *non-discriminatory pricing*. In reality, very few studies use bilateral trade flow price indices, and one is therefore in general forced to fall back on the use of total export prices or to use no deflation at all [42)].

The bilateral trade flow is usually explained as a function of an activity variable, (relative) prices and other independent variables. The activity variable pertains in general to the importing country, as most bilateral trade flow equations are estimated as bilateral import *demand* equations. But bilateral export *supply* equations do exist in the literature, and the activity variable may therefore also be related to the exporting country[43)]. If the bilateral trade flow equation is determined in an equilibrium bilateral demand and supply framework, activity variables of both the importing and exporting country may appear [44)]. According to the nature of the activity variable we will make a further distinction within the set of bilateral linkage models. We introduce therefore

DEFINITION 4.2 :

A bilateral linkage model will be called an *import* (and/or *export*) *allocation model*, if the activity variable represents total import demand (and/or total export supply). Otherwise the model will be called a *total allocation model*.

The import allocation model is called "structural approach" by RHOMBERG (1970), the "shares approach" by WAELBROECK (1973) and the "trade allocation model" by RANUZZI (1981).

Below the theoretical formulations for the import/export allocation model will be discussed more extensively, but here we may already state the basic ideas that lie behind its development. Seminal bilateral linkage models were usually total allocation models, such as the theoretical models of METZLER (1950) (one of the first bilateral linkage models) and ARMINGTON (1969a, 1969b, 1970a, 1970b, 1973) and the empirical models of the IMF (POLAK and RHOMBERG (1962), RHOMBERG and BOISSONNEAULT (1964), RHOMBERG and FORTUCCI (1964) and RHOMBERG (1968)) for 3 countries, and RESNICK (1968) for 6 countries. After 1970 the number of total allocation models declined relative to the number of import allocation models, although they have never really completely disappeared [45)]. The reason for their decline is the increasing *size* of the models. As there are a large number of trading partners, the number of price variables becomes large together with the other factors determining the bilateral imports, or exports for that matter. Any system of equations explaining the allocation of income or output over several domestic factors and all supplying trade partners would grow unduly large. It was therefore proposed, *e.g.* by TAPLIN (1967), to determine bilateral imports in two steps. In the first step the total amount of imports would be determined together with the allocation of income or output over domestic items, and in the second step total imports of each good would be allocated among the export suppliers. This procedure, whose theoretical foundations are treated more extensively below in Chapter 2, would considerably reduce the number of parameters to be estimated for the bilateral trade flow equations, because all domestic variables governing the choice between imports and domestic expenditures would no longer have to appear [46)]. It is therefore no surprise that the number of countries in total allocation models for which parameters were estimated econometrically, has never exceeded ten [47]. As the size of the models increased, the import allocation model became more popular as a consequence, without the assumption of separability - which makes it theoretically acceptable - being empirically tested or even challenged [48]. Testing it will be one of the purposes of the present study, therefore.

With the elimination of one problem, the other arises : in total allocation models total imports may simply be determined as the sum of bilateral imports from all trading partners. For import allocation models there is the additional problem that, imports being determined in a first stage, the bilateral imports should add up to this given total, thereby introducing the so-called *adding-up condition*, also to be discussed below in Chapter 2.

In the case of an *export* allocation model, there also is an adding-up condition that has to be fulfilled, completely analogous to the import allocation model. If the bilateral trade flow equation is the reduced form volume equation of an import allocation demand and export allocation supply model, the adding-up condition should hold with respect to the total import and export variables as far as they concern *actual* imports and exports, respectively. Usually, however, the total export variable is rather defined as export supply (capacity) [49], and the model therefore formally reduces to an import allocation model in those cases. In principle, an import-export allocation model which has to satisfy a double adding-up condition is feasible, but probably remote from econometric estimation.

1.4.3. CONSISTENT AND INCONSISTENT LINKAGE

The introduction of the adding-up problem in the previous subsection leads us to another characteristic which we may use to distinguish linkage models : the requirement of *consistency*. We will define it formally as

DEFINITION 4.3 :

A linkage model will be called *consistent* if its variables satisfy identities (3.2) - (3.13).

The identities (3.2) - (3.13) imply a number of characteristics that should be fulfilled in order to render a linkage model consistent. They assume for instance that the adding-up problem is solved because bilateral imports (exports) are required to add up to total imports (exports). Furthermore they guarantee, as we saw in equations (3.14) - (3.17), that the world trade balance equals zero. Because of Assumption 3.2 these properties hold regardless of the cif-fob margins, which are disregarded. In actual models sometimes account is taken of these margins through adjustment equations. In those cases we will nevertheless call the model consistent if, abstracting from these adjustments, the model satisfies the identities of Definition 4.3. Furthermore the definition is a large one : for instance, it implies for *global* linkage models that the only requirement is that the world trade balance should be zero, as no bilateral trade flows appear which would be subject to an adding-up condition with respect to total imports.

It is not always easy to detect whether a specific model in the literature is consistent or inconsistent, unless one is able to consult a full list of all the equations which make up the model or explicit information in the text concerning the presence or not of consistency. Any statements *we* make on a model's consistency should therefore be taken as best guesses, pending any supplementary information.

Models that are *inconsistent* on the basis of this kind of evidence (and therefore with a general disclaimer in mind) are the Eurolink model (RANUZZI (1981)), the IMF World Trade Model (DEPPLER and RIPLEY (1978), RIPLEY (1980, 1981), BOND (1979)), the OECD Interlink model (OECD (1979), SAMUELSON and KURIHARA (1980), SAMUELSON (1978)), the LINK Project (KLEIN *et al.* (1975), KLEIN (1976, 1981)), the MARCO II model (GUILLAUME (1981)), the models of MARWAH (1976), MENNES (1967) and the early model of NEISSER and MODIGLIANI (1953), the METEOR model (KOOYMAN *et al.* (1977), KOOYMAN (1981)) and the Tsukaba-FAIS model (SHISHIDO *et al.* (1980, 1981)). Next we turn to the consistent linkage models.

1.4.4. ESTIMATION-CONSISTENT LINKAGE AND SIMULATION-CONSISTENT LINKAGE

We will in general distinguish two ways in which a linkage model may be made consistent. The first is to include the consistency in the econometric specification of the estimating form of the equations in the form of adding-up conditions *etc.* The other is to impose consistency in the simulation stage. The last method will be assumed to be in use 1) if in the allocation of a given total such as total imports, one element is designated the residual, such as for instance imports from the Rest of the World being calculated as the difference between given total imports and the sum of the other bilateral imports 2) if residuals are allocated in an arbitrary fashion over given elements, such as a world trade surplus being allocated proportionally over imports, the excess of total imports over the sum of bilateral imports being allocated over bilateral imports *etc.* 3) if any other more or less arbitrary method is employed to obtain consistency, such as for instance the RAS method to adjust given elements of the world trade matrix, *i.e.* the complete matrix of bilateral trade flows [50)].

The first method to obtain consistency will be called *estimation - consistent linkage,* the second method will be given the name *simulation - consistent linkage.* With estimation - consistent linkage, the consistency problem finds its solution in a natural way, while with simulation consistency there is always some arbitrariness involved in achieving this goal. A residual in a world balance may in an extreme case be due, for instance, to the misspecification of one *single* equation, and allocating it to all equations simultaneously is not justified in such a case.

In import allocation models, *simulation consistency* is usually one of two types. For the first type, imports from the Rest of the World are calculated as a residual in order to obtain consistency. Examples are the COMET II model (BARTEN (1971, 1981), BARTEN and d'ALCANTARA (1976), BARTEN *et al.* (1976), the Interplay model (PLASMANS (1982, 1984)) and the model of EZAKI (1978) as described in AMANO *et al.* (1980). Errors are therefore arbitrarily accumulated in the residual. The second type is the one that applies an adjustment, either multiplicative or additive [51)], to all bilateral variables, be they in the form of import shares or in the form of bilateral imports. TAPLIN (1973), for example, applies a normalization to the shares, SAMUELSON and KURIHARA (1980) modify the shares using the RAS method, MORIGUCHI (1973) allocates the residual of the sum of the import shares and 1, and in the COMET III model the bilateral imports are proportionally adjusted (ITALIANER (1982a)).

Estimation-consistent linkage models will be discussed further if we regard the adding-up condition in more detail in Chapter 2.

1.4.5. METHODOLOGICAL PROBLEMS

Methodological problems in international linkage models relate to problems of data, specification and estimation. The feasability of the construction of any linkage model is determined by the availability of the *data* which are needed for it. We touched already on some of the problems that are encountered in this stage. Data should be disaggregated according to the correct classifications for goods and trading countries, bilateral price data may be lacking and price data may have to be calculated as unit value indices incorporating additional errors. The cif-fob margins should be dealt with, and should have a correct sign on a bilateral basis. They may have to be decomposed in margins according to sources of measurement differences, such as transportation lags, different valuations, exports to ships of open-registry countries, recording gaps, differences in methods of calculation *etc*. For a correct representation of prices tariff rates, which are not included in cif import prices, might also be included [52).]

Even if a satisfactory set of data is available, the estimation of a given specification may not be feasible, so there has to be an interaction between *specification* and *estimation*, notably in models with a large number of countries. In such a model one may decide that the number of countries is too large to specify any bilateral relationships at all. In that case one has to solve in a preferably non-arbitrary way the consistency problem. Similarly one might also reduce the number of parameters to be estimated by means of the choice of the functional form. A first reduction of parameters may be obtained if one employs the assumption of separability of domestic expenditure items and imports, and if one is therefore authorized to use an import allocation model. In order to deal correctly with the adding-up problem this may lead to a relatively simple linear specification to avoid any method of simulation consistency, although other solutions to the adding-up problem might be suggested, as will be seen in subsection 2.2.4.

A simple functional form of the import allocation model may reduce even further the number of parameters to be estimated but may at the same time also severely reduce the generality of substitution patterns embodied in a less restrictive specification. Here one has to deal with the number of parameters which may still be estimated freely without too drastic a loss of degrees of freedom in estimation. The freedom which all these restrictions leave for experimenting with functional forms should lead, according to L.R. Klein in COURBIS (1981b, p. 247), to a better specification of equations and model structure instead of creating new and larger models.

1.4.6. THE CHOICE OF A LINKAGE MODEL

In the previous subsections we have defined a number of characteristics that apply to linkage models. In this subsection we will ask along the lines of these characteristics if any linkage model in terms of a choice between characteristics is to be preferred. This choice will be decisive for the particular kind of linkage models which we will further analyze in Chapter 2.

In fact, our choice for a certain number of characteristics has already been hinted at in the discussions per characteristic, so we may be brief in those cases. Before entering into the discussion, it should be stated that our point of departure is that the kind of linkage model we will choose should be able to deal with a considerable number of countries and categories of goods at the same time; otherwise we could be tempted to choose an attractive model that does not have a general application.

The choice between *global* and *bilateral* linkage is largely inspired by the arguments already put forward in subsection 1.4.1 : correct transmission of economic fluctuations, possibility for detailed analysis of bilateral trade effects, analysis of substitution patterns and so forth. Unless there are severe reasons that inhibit the use of a bilateral linkage model (such as manageability), this model has to be preferred, with the additional exception of those cases in which one simply may not be interested in the value-added that is generated by the bilateral linkage model as compared to the global linkage model.

Another choice which is immediately clear is the one between *consistent* and *inconsistent* models. Obviously consistency has to be preferred because without it the resulting model produces results that are mutually incompatible. Of the consistent models, a model which imposes consistency in a natural rather than an arbitrary or asymmetrical way should be preferred, therefore pointing to estimation *consistency* rather than simulation *consistency*.

What remains then is the choice between *total allocation* and *import allocation* models. The former have the advantage that they have virtually no consistency problem, while for the import allocation models the adding-up problem has to be solved in an estimation-consistent way in order to remain attractive. On the other hand, once this problem is solved, the latter have the advantage that a number of variables pertaining to the allocation of income or output between domestic and foreign outlays no longer appears in the bilateral import equations of an import allocation system, thereby strongly reducing the number of explanatory variables and making room for more trading partners, so to speak. This advantage is confirmed empirically by the fact that total allocation models have never been estimated for models distinguishing more than 10 countries, which may be contrasted, for instance, with the import allocation model of HICKMAN and LAU (1973) which was estimated for 27 countries.

The final choice for the model to be further analyzed as the most interesting and as having wide possibilities of application therefore becomes the *estimation-consistent import allocation model*, which we take up in the next chapter.

1.5. A SLUICE

This last section of the chapter is intended as a sluice between the rather general treatment of linkage models considered so far and the more detailed analysis of certain subjects in the rest of this study. After summarizing this chapter we select a number of subjects which in our view should receive detailed attention, and put them in the coherent framework of an outline for the rest of this study. This finally leads to the hypotheses that will be tested.

1.5.1. SUMMARY

After the introduction and the presentation of some conventions, the first important section of this chapter discussed the elements of a world trade linkage model. We started with a *data framework* within which we could situate the trade variables of the discussed linkage models. The data framework also included a number of identities with respect to the world trade balance, bilateral imports adding up to total imports *etc.* Next we reviewed the *conceptual elements* that *a priori* would be candidate to play a role in a hypothetical linkage model. In particular we discussed the size of a linkage model, the treatment of demand and supply, the aspect of disaggregation, the introduction of dynamics and the choice of a functional form. Correspondingly we presented and discussed in the following section four *characteristics* with which one may distinguish linkage models : global versus bilateral linkage, total versus import-export allocation, consistent versus inconsistent linkage and finally estimation-consistent versus simulation-consistent linkage. Concentrating on the *methodological* problems, the largest problem still seems to be, given an available data set, to find a sufficiently good specification that, at least in the framework of import allocation models, satisfies the adding-up condition. On the basis of the four characteristics mentioned above, we finally made a *choice* as to the most interesting and adequate form of linkage, which we argued to be the *estimation-consistent import allocation model.*

1.5.2. OUTLINE OF THE REST OF THE STUDY

In subsection 1.4.6. we already argued our choice for the estimation-consistent import allocation model as the class of linkage models that should be preferred. This implies therefore that the rest of this study will be mainly occupied with subjects that are closely related to this type of linkage models. It does not mean, however, that our findings are completely constrained to such an already rather limited field of study. Notably the discussions in Chapters 3 and 4 are of a very general nature and may be applied to a larger part of economic and econometric theory than the mere specification and estimation of estimation-consistent import allocation models alone. After a further theoretical and empirical analysis of import allocation models in Chapter 2, our main preoccupations will concern two aspects of estimation-consistent import allocation models. The first aspect is their *estimation,* the second concerns, in a large sense, the notion of *substitution.*

As an example of what will concern us with *estimation,* we may consider the Constant-Elasticity-of-Substitution (CES) model, whose estimation we will discuss in Chapter 2. There we will see that the fact that the CES model should satisfy the adding-up condition leads to a system with a singular covariance matrix. We know from the literature that such a problem may usually be solved by deleting one equation from the system of equations [53)]. But we will also see that the best estimation method - in the sense of the absence of *a priori* restrictions on the covariance matrix - would be the method of maximum likelihood. And if the CES model becomes involved in hypothesis testing - as it will be -, we will need the value of the (log) likelihood function. But we do not know much about the influence on the value of the likelihood function of deleting an equation : does it matter which equation is deleted ? In Chapter 4 we will deal with this question and the question of whether parameter estimates depend on the deleted equation(s) in a very general framework, *viz.* we analyze the problem for the set of nonlinear models which should obey one or more linear restrictions on the functional form. The CES model with the adding-up restriction is one member of this set of models, but only a special case : the problem may also be applied to numerous other systems of equations. Each time we will have to answer for such models the question of whether the parameter estimates and the value of the likelihood function depend on the equations which are deleted in order to avoid a singular covariance matrix. Necessary and sufficient conditions that provide an answer to these questions are treated extensively in Chapter 4, therefore, and we will apply these general results to the specific cases of the models which we will estimate ourselves, including the CES model.

Apart from this theoretical chapter on the maximum likelihood estimation of constrained models and Chapter 2 on import allocation models, the rest of this study will evolve around the notion of *substitution*. In both consumption theory and production theory, any pair of bilateral imports of a specific category of goods may be characterized as substitutes or complements. In any estimation-consistent import allocation model derived from neoclassical optimizing behaviour, the form of the partial aggregator function (import quantity index) determines the substitution possibilities or the pattern of substitution, and we would like to characterize this substitution pattern in terms of an *elasticity* that somehow gives a measure of the degree of substitution which is possible. However, in the case of a partial aggregator function with more than two elements (supplying countries in our case), the conceptually attractive notion of *elasticity of substitution* as it may be used in the case of two inputs is no longer defined unequivocally. Several definition can be put forward and there is no natural choice to make between them that stands out clearly against the others. Therefore, although it seems very important to be able to describe the substitution possibilities in an estimation-consistent import allocation model, we are faced with the annoying situation that there is no unique measure to do so. The range of possibilities and the possible choice among them is therefore treated in Chapter 3. It will be clear that concepts of elasticities of substitution apply not only to import allocation models, but also extend their use, among others, to the theories of consumption and production. Chapter 3 is therefore, like Chapter 4, of more than a specific interest to import allocation models alone.

Even if we lack a unique concept of elasticity of substitution, it is not difficult to see that the pattern of substitution implied by the CES model (which will be presented in subsection 2.3.1) is extremely simple : we will see that there is only one relative price effect which is identical for each bilateral import demand equation. This single price effect corresponds to one single constant elasticity of substitution applying to each pair of bilateral imports on a given market. At the same time, the CES model is however rather popular when compared to the other estimation-consistent import allocation models presented in subsection 2.3.2. Not least, as we may surmise, because of the simple method by which it was apparently estimated by HICKMAN and LAU (1973), although we will see in subsection 2.3.1 that this method bears contradictory elements and delivers inefficient estimators. Also the fact that the number of parameters to be estimated increases about linearly with the number of countries which are distinguished may have contributed to its popularity. We will see however that the least arbitrary and correct way of estimating the CES model would be through the use of the method of maximum likelihood. Therefore any other estimation-consistent import allocation model that also has a relatively small number of parameters may be as attractive, even if it also has to be estimated by the method of maximum likelihood. The development of such an equally attractive model (from the point of view of estimation) is the subject of Chapters 5 and 6. Instead of a model with one distinct price effect, such as the CES model, we will however propose an estimation-consistent import allocation model which resembles the CES model, but which generates n^2 different price effects from n parameters, where n is equal to the number of supplying countries, and which therefore possesses a substitution pattern which is far more general than that of the CES model. It is not the most general substitution pattern that one might imagine, for example from flexible functional form models, but such models on the other hand become intractable because of the number of parameters to be estimated : in their standard form the number of parameters increases quadratically with the number of exporting countries that are distinguished. The model thus developed will be used for three purposes in the remaining chapters. The first is to estimate it on a data set for 1963-1980 and to analyze the resulting estimation results. The estimation results will also be used to analyze the empirical performance of different functional forms (linear, loglinear or logartihmic differences) as well as of different *a priori* specified covariance matrices. After a description of the available dataset in Chapter 7, these estimations are given in Chapter 8. The second purpose is to test the assumption of weak separability that is a pre-requisite for the derivation of any import allocation model, as will be derived in Chapter 2. The final goal is to test the model against the CES model, and to see additionally whether the outcome for this test is influenced in a certain direction if the conditions under which the tests are held are modified in one direction. The hypotheses involved for the second and third objectives are discussed in subsection 1.5.3, while the actual test results are contained in Chapter 9. In particular, the third objective is of importance to see whether, and under which conditions, the very simple substitution pattern of the CES model remains valid as a hypothesis against a more general model : if it is valid under general conditions, it may be a confirmation and validation of its popularity, despite the simple substitution effects which it encompasses. Chapter 10, finally, contains conclusions and suggestions for further research.

1.5.3. THE HYPOTHESES

The hypotheses may be divided into two parts. The first part consists of a hypothesis to test the weak separability assumption underlying any import allocation model, and the second part consists of testing the CES model against our more general model under different circumstances regarding the definition of the categories of goods and the trading partners.

WEAK SEPARABILITY

For the testing of the hypothesis of weak separability, we do not employ a general test, such as those sometimes performed with flexible functional form models. We start to use the CRESH function, which we will introduce in Chapter 5 to derive our estimation-consistent import allocation model, as the aggregator function from which a *total* allocation model per category of goods may be derived, which is nothing but a re-interpretation of our import allocation model extended to include domestically produced products. On this aggregator function we next impose weak separability of domestic inputs and imports, per category of goods. This implies a number of restrictions on the parameters of the total allocation model, which may then be estimated with and without these restrictions. A comparison of the values of the two likelihood functions under the two different estimations permits one then to draw statistical inference regarding the hypothesis of weak separability.

CES VERSUS GENERAL MODEL

The testing of the CES model against our more general model is simple in principle : we estimate our model, which may be considered as a generalization of the CES model, with and without the restrictions on the parameters which imply the CES model as a special case, and compare the resulting values of the likelihood function to derive a likelihood ratio test statistic. Although we will make such simple tests, there is one drawback to them : they are "local" in the sense that the test results hold only for the specific classification of goods that we have employed and for the specific kind and number of trading partners that are distinguished. This leads us to the interesting question of whether it is possible to predict on *a priori* grounds if a change in a certain direction of any of these two conditions changes the test outcome in a systematic way. For instance, would the CES model be more firmly rejected [54)] with few or with many trade partners ? Or : would the CES model be more strongly rejected if the classification of goods is at a low or high level of aggregation ? *A priori* considerations on these two influences, which would lead to the superposition of "meta-hypotheses" concerning the possible direction of the significance of rejection/acceptation of the "CES-hypothesis" as one of the two conditions goes in a certain direction, will occupy the rest of this subsection.

NUMBER OF TRADE PARTNERS

Let us first remember that the CES import allocation model is based upon the assumption that the elasticities of substitution (ES) between bilateral imports from two trading partners on a given market are *equal* and *constant*. The more general model, it will be seen, has *different* ES among each pair of trade partners, no matter how one defines the concept of multifactor ES. The last assertion also holds for the CES case, because the different concepts of ES then become equal. For the moment we will however simply assume that such a meaningful concept exists, and leave aside the question which concept to choose. Then we will consider the testing of a CES model with n trading partners (against our more general model) versus testing the same CES model with $n-1$ trading partners (which are assumed to be a mutually exclusive exhaustive partition of the n partners) [55]. We are then looking for any *a priori* reasons why we would expect the one test to be closer to a rejection of the CES model than the other. This may be done applying the following argument.

Suppose the ES are a measure of the physical possibility of substitution between the goods supplied by any two trade partners, and consider the ES of the two trade partners that were "merged" in order to obtain the $n-1$ trade partners. Under fairly general conditions it is then reasonable to assume that each ES involving this merged trade partner will be approximately equal to some weighted average of the corresponding ES involving the two merged trade partners individually, the weights depending on the import share of each trade partner. In other words, the physical substitution possibilities between goods supplied by the merged partner and any other partner are then an average of those between the same other partner and the merged partners individually. Then it is likely that the *variability* of the ES in the case with $n-1$ partners is smaller than with n partners, at least if one takes into account the import shares of the different partners.

In Chapter 9 we will illustrate this argument with an analytical example, but let us for the time being assume that it is true. Then the variability of the ES in our general model with *n-1* partners will consequently be smaller than in the model with *n* partners. *A fortiori*, the result of a test of the CES model against our model will also undergo this influence, and we are led to the *ex-ante* expectation or meta-hypothesis that the CES model will be less significantly rejected if the number of trade partners in the model decreases : because if the number of trade partners in the model decreases, the more general model comes closer to the CES model as the variability of its ES decreases. The empirical verification of this meta-hypothesis will be carried out in Chapter 9.

CLASSIFICATION OF GOODS

Now that we have considered changes in the number of trade partners, we direct our attention to changes in the classification of the categories of goods and how the concept of ES may play a role in the analysis of the influence of the classification on the outcome of tests on the CES model.

Let us first recall that, given a certain classification of the categories of goods, a test of the CES model against our more general model should be carried out on the import allocation models for *all* categories at the same time. In other words, we should consider their combined likelihood. Assume again the existence of a meaningful concept of multifactor ES and interpret the ES as measures of the physical substitution possibilities between the goods supplied by any pair of partners. Furthermore the number of partners is taken to be fixed. Then we analyze the expected change in the results of testing the CES model against our more general model if we change the classification of the categories of goods.

Unlike the analysis of changes in the number of trade partners, there are now two effects that play, and they play in directions opposite to each other. And unlike the analysis of changes in the number of trade partners, we will not be able to illustrate our arguments with an analytical example. The arguments should therefore be accepted intuitively. Before we go into them, however, it should be defined which changes in the classification of the categories of commodities are allowed such that two different classifications may be compared. Therefore we introduce the notion of *comparability*, defined as

DEFINITION 5.1 :

Two classifications of categories of goods are *comparable*, if the elements of one classification are a partitioning into mutually exclusive and exhaustive subsets of the elements of the other classification.

Comparability therefore rules out two different classifications with the same number of categories of goods, but also other pairs of classifications. Consider an example with the following four goods

A - Agricultural goods
E - Energy goods
C - Cars
M - Other manufactured products

Use furthermore the "+" sign to indicate aggregated categories of goods, *e.g.* $C + M$ is the category of manufactured products. Then, for instance, the classifications $\{A, E, C + M\}$ and $\{A, E, C, M\}$ are comparable because the first classification in an exhaustive partition into mutually exclusive subsets of the second classification. Examples of pairs of classifications that are not comparable are $\{A + C, E + M\}$ and $\{A + M, E + C\}$ or $\{A + C, E + M\}$ and $\{A, E, C + M\}$. The last pair is a clear example of the case where the number of categories are not equal, but where the two elements of the first classification can not be obtained as a partitioning of the three elements of the second classification.

Having defined the comparability between pairs of classifications, we turn to the differences between variability of the ES in two comparable classifications, and their implications for the significance of rejecting (accepting) the CES model. But first we will order two comparable classifications using the notion of degree of detail.

DEFINITION 5.2 :

Let there be two comparable classifications. The classification with the largest number of categories of goods is said to have the highest *degree of detail*, or be the most detailed of the two.

We may then distinguish two forces that determine the ES, interpreted as physical substitution measures, between the imports of two partners in a given classification. One of these is the product homogeneity, and the other the degree of specialization.

The *product homogeneity* will increase if a classification becomes more detailed : consider for example the chain manufactured products - transport equipment - automobiles [56)]. Not only will the ES between the suppliers of these goods increase if the classification becomes more detailed, but at the same time the different ES will become closer as the functional purposes of goods delivered by different exporters become more equal.

Assuming a positive correlation between the inequality of the ES and the significance with which the CES model is rejected against our more general model, the effect of product homogeneity therefore establishes the partial meta-hypothesis that for any two comparable classifications the CES model will be more valid (or less significantly rejected), in general, for the classification which is more detailed than the other.

Opposite the positive effect of a more detailed classification of categories of goods on the validity of the CES model stand the effects of the *degree of specialization* in international trade. Consider the chain all products - manufactured products - transport equipment - automobiles. Let the classification into categories of goods define only one category : the category of the aggregate of all commodities. Then it is reasonable and even tautological to assume that all suppliers on a particular import market produce this category of goods [57)]. Henceforth, with this classification, each exporter is able in principle to supply a substitute for the goods sold by other suppliers on that market because there is no distinction whatsoever between different kinds of goods.

However, as soon as the classification defines more than one category of goods, one or more of the suppliers may have been specializing such that within one or more of the categories its products necessarily have to be considered as bad substitutes in the sense that its ES within those groups becomes very small (using an interpretation of "small" ES as bad physical substitutes). Obvious examples for the category "manufactured products" are those developing countries that depend largely on trade in agricultural goods and raw materials, while for more detailed categories other examples are not hard to think of.

An increasingly more detailed classification is therefore tantamount to more inequality of ES due to the physical constraints on substitution implied by an increasing degree of specialization.

Because of the opposite direction of the effects of product homogeneity and the degree of specialization, we are not led, as with the changing number of trade partners, to posit any meta-hypothesis that predicts whether the CES model will be more significantly rejected or not if the degree of detail of the classification of categories of goods changes. We will therefore leave it open as a matter to be determined empirically. Also this verification will take place in Chapter 9.

FOOTNOTES TO CHAPTER 1

1) Calculated from OECD (1984), using 1975 exchange rates.

2) For examples of linkage other than through merchandise trade, *cfr.* RHOMBERG and BOISSONNEAULT (1964), HELLIWELL *et al.* (1973), HELLIWELL (1974), BOND (1979), HALTTUNEN and WARNER (1979a, 1979b), HOWE *et al.* (1981), HIERONYMI (1983), HOLTHAM (1984). A tremendous effort in the field of data was made by WOOLLEY (1965).

3) *Cfr.* VEIL (1982, p. 52).

4) *Cfr.* also HEMPHILL (1980).

5) For a detailed analysis of sources of trade balance discrepancies, *cfr.* YEATS (1979).

6) *Cfr.* SAMUELSON (1973) or RHOMBERG (1970, p. 11).

7) A more simple solution is to apply the constant cif-fob adjustments of total imports to all bilateral imports, *cfr.* TAPLIN (1973, pp. 200-202).

8) Other reviews of currently existing trade linkage models and their predecessors may be found in TAPLIN (1967), COURBIS (1981a) and HICKMAN (1982).

9) *Cfr.* GREGORY (1971), SIEBRAND (1972), RHOMBERG (1973, p. 19), BIANCHI and RANUZZI (1981, p. 191). For a full-equilibrium approach see ARTUS and RHOMBERG (1973).

10) *Cfr.* MAGEE (1975, pp. 188-192, 211-214).

11) *Cfr.* d'ALCANTARA and THEEUWES (1981). If there is no behavioural total import equation, this implies that total imports are defined through an identity.

12) That is, if one excludes a trend which may be introduced to capture effects that cause a systematic shift in the demand function.

13) *Cfr.* SIEBRAND (1972), SAMUELSON (1973), WAELBROECK and DRAMAIS (1974) or KHAN and ROSS (1975). MORIGUCHI (1973) includes a trend-fitted export supply variable.

14) *Cfr.* GREGORY (1971, p. 31).

15) *Cfr.* STEUER *et al.* (1966), MINTZ (1967), and ARTUS (1973) for evidence concerning the effects of an increase in domestic demand on delivery dates and subsequently on exports.

16) *Cfr.* SAMUELSON and KURIHARA (1980, p. 2).

17) *Cfr.* RAO and MILLER (1971, ch. 8), for a theoretical treatment and MAGEE (1975, pp. 181-184) for empirical evidence.

18) *Cfr.* MALINVAUD (1980, pp. 595-600) or MADDALA (1977, ch. 11).

19) An example is GÉRACI and PREWO (1982).

20) Examples are RHOMBERG and BOISSONNEAULT (1964, pp. 104-105) and RANUZZI (1981, pp. 169-172). In d'ALCANTARA and ITALIANER (1981) a reduced form bilateral import flow equation was estimated, based on the work of BARTEN and d'ALCANTARA (1977).

21) *Cfr.* MAGEE (1975, p. 183).

22) *Cfr.* MADDALA (1977, pp. 482-484). Examples of simultaneous estimation may be found in GOLDSTEIN and KHAN (1978) in the context of aggregate total trade and in ITALIANER (1982b) for disaggregated bilateral trade flows.

23) Total export supply equations may be found in RHOMBERG and BOISSONNEAULT (1964), GOLDSTEIN and KHAN (1978) and GERACI and PREWO (1982); bilateral supply equations in a model without total supply equations may be found in d'ALCANTARA and THEEUWES (1981), ARTUS and RHOMBERG (1973) or ARTUS and McGUIRK (1981).

24) Examples are BARTEN and d'ALCANTARA (1977) and GERACI and PREWO (1982).

25) *Cfr.* ARTUS and RHOMBERG (1973) and ARTUS and McGUIRK (1981).

26) *Cfr.* d'ALCANTARA and ITALIANER (1982).

27) *Cfr.* ITALIANER and d'ALCANTARA (1983).

28) For an attempt to include disequilibrium situations in a flexible manner in macro-economic models, see SIEBRAND (1979).

29) *Cfr.* BIANCHI and RANUZZI (1981).

30) *Cfr.* ITALIANER (1982a) for the example of the COMET model.

31) For an overview, see VAN POECK (1979).

32) For empirical evidence on delivery lags, *cfr.* ARTUS (1973).

33) *Cfr.* KRAVIS and LIPSEY (1971) for other disturbances in the use of unit values as price indices in international trade. Furthermore see KEMP (1962) for the consequences of measurement errors in unit value indices when they are used as deflators of value series and thus appear both on the left-hand side and right-hand side of an equation.

34) *Cfr.* KHAN (1974) or KHAN and ROSS (1977).

35) *Cfr.* KHAN (1974, p. 680).

36) *Cfr.* COURBIS (1981b, pp. 244-245).

37) *Cfr.* RANUZZI (1981, pp. 157-158).

38) *Cfr.* COURBIS (1981b, p. 243).

39) *Cfr.* THEIL (1971). Linear forms are not the only ones which satisfy the adding-up condition, though. Consider share equations of the form $w_i = f_i(.)/\Sigma_k f_k(.)$. Then these equations will automatically add up to one. They are not loglinear, however.

40) For the proof of this assertion concerning Moriguchi, *cfr.* AMANO *et al.* (1980, p. 7).

41) *Cfr. e.g.* KIRKPATRICK (1983, p. 11).

42) Apart from the present study, bilateral prices were used by RANUZZI (1981), GERACI and PREWO (1982) and VIAENE (1982), where the latter provided in VIAENE (1983) also evidence against the appropriateness of the non-discrimination assumption. Furthermore, the Interplay model uses bilateral price indices that were constructed using a quadratic programming problem. *Cfr.* PLASMANS (1982, 1984).

43) One of the rare examples of separately estimated bilateral export supply equations is GERACI and PREWO (1982).

44) Examples of equilibrium bilateral demand and supply models are in ARTUS and RHOMBERG (1973), ARTUS and McGUIRK (1981), d'ALCANTARA and ITALIANER (1981), RANUZZI (1981) and the model of MORIGUCHI (1973) as discussed in AMANO *et al.* (1980).

45) *Cfr.* the models of MORISHIMA and MURATA (1972), THORBECKE and FIELD (1974), the IMF MERM model building forth on the work of Armington (ARTUS and RHOMBERG (1973), ARTUS and McGUIRK (1981)), the Multi-country Model (MCM) of the Federal Reserve System (HOWE *et al.* (1981)), GERACI and PREWO (1982) and VIAENE (1982, 1983).

46) The same reasoning may be applied, *mutatis mutandis,* to derive the export (supply) allocation model.

47) *Cfr.* the models of footnote 45. The MERM covers 20 countries, but does not contain parameters estimated for the equations as they are specified in the model.

48) An exception is WINTERS (1984b).

49) *Cfr.* d'ALCANTARA and ITALIANER (1981), GERACI and PREWO (1982), and the discussion of MORIGUCHI (1973) in AMANO *et al.* (1980).

50) The RAS method, developed originally by STONE and BROWN (1964) for Input-Output matrices, consists of multiplying iteratively all rows and columns of an initial matrix by varying factors until they both add up to their given row totals and column totals. For each row (column) the multiplicative factor is defined as the given row (column) total divided by the row (column) total after the previous multiplication. With a given starting matrix, this is a convergent procedure with a unique solution, subject to a given normalization, *cfr.* BACHARACH (1965).

51) For a general treatment of additive adjustments, *cfr.* DON (1982).

52) For examples of bilateral import prices including tariff rates, *cfr.* GERACI and PREWO (1982) and VIAENE (1982).

53) *Cfr. e.g.* BARTEN (1969).

54) Formally : would the test stand a lower level of significance.

55) We assume that the classification of goods remains fixed in between the two experiments.

56) We assume everywhere that chains of comparable classifications consist of classifications that are built up according to a meaningful criterion. In our case the most useful criterion would start off from the *needs* that are fulfilled by the goods entering into the categories of goods. Goods of one category should all satisfy the needs corresponding to that category.

57) That is, we depart from the existing suppliers on that market, therefore disregarding aspects such as barriers to entry.

CHAPTER 2 - IMPORT ALLOCATION MODELS

2.1. INTRODUCTION

In the previous chapter we argued that among the possible kinds of linkage models the estimation-consistent import allocation model should be preferred. The present chapter will analyze in more detail this type of linkage model.

In section 2.2 we treat the microeconomic theoretical foundations of the import allocation model. We discuss the concept of aggregator function, introduce different notions of separability and treat the problem of aggregation over commodities. As a last theoretical aspect we discuss the adding-up condition, and present several solutions to satisfy this condition in the case of import allocation models derived from linear homogeneous import quantity indices or partial aggregator functions.

Section 2.3 is next devoted to a discussion of empirical estimation-consistent import allocation models. We pay most attention to the import allocation model derived from a Constant-Elasticity-of-Substitution (CES) import quantity index, first derived and estimated by HICKMAN and LAU (1973). This CES import allocation model has been the most widespread of estimation-consistent import allocation models and may therefore be considered as the current mainstream for this kind of linkage models. In particular we will pay attention to its merits with regard to theoretical attractiveness and empirical estimation.

Section 2.4, finally, contains a summary and some concluding remarks.

2.2. THEORETICAL CONSIDERATIONS

2.2.1. THE AGGREGATOR FUNCTION

In a national accounting framework, imports are subtracted from the sum of the components that constitute final demand in order to obtain Gross Domestic Product (GDP), or perhaps Value Added if one works on a sectoral basis. This treatment of imports indicates that they are by definition one of the inputs in the production process, and they could therefore be regarded as ordinary production factors like labour or capital. In reality this view should be shaded. It certainly holds for the large amounts of imports that are intermediary in the production process and which account for a large part of international trade, but there are additionally also a number of categories of tradable goods which directly satisfy the needs of final demand, such as investment goods or consumer goods. This distinction is of importance in applying the neoclassical cost-minimizing or utility-maximizing framework to a system including these variables. In the former case imports could be factors of a production function, in the latter case they could be elements of a utility function. For a general treatment of import allocation models it is however not necessary to specify whether we work in production theory or in consumer theory in order to derive import demand functions. We will therefore start with a general function, which we will call after DIEWERT (1976, 1982) *aggregator function*, in which imports play a role, and which may take the form of a production function or utility function when needed. For the moment we simply assume that this function represents the (technical or psychological) preferences of the national economy regarding expenditures on domestic factors (which may be production factors or consumer expenditure items) and imported goods.

Before we proceed any further we have to analyze the nature of the imports that take a place in the aggregator function. In our data framework of subsection 1.3.1, we distinguished bilateral imports by three subscripts (apart from a subscript t for time) : the category of goods, the exporter and the importer. The importer corresponds to the national economy or *market* which we consider, while the category of *goods* refers to categories of automobiles, television sets, computers and so forth. One may however wonder why we should make a distinction in the aggregator function between a category of goods supplied by one country or another. We will however take the view, first propagated by ARMINGTON (1969a), that no matter how detailed the category of goods may be, the same goods supplied by different countries are *imperfect substitutes* and therefore each deserve a separate place in the aggregator function, like those supplied by the domestic market [1]. It has become customary to call a category of goods supplied by one particular country a *product*, as opposed to goods of a *kind*. Thus if the *kind* of goods under consideration on the French market is the category of computers, computers supplied by Japan and Germany on that market are different *products*, distinguished as they are by their place of production.

The aggregator function on market j (of which we delete the subscript) therefore is composed of domestic inputs $z_1, \ldots, z_p$ and all products supplied by other countries m_{ki} for categories of goods $k = 1, \ldots, g$ and suppliers $i \neq j = 1, \ldots, n$. We will represent the aggregator function as the following real-valued function $f(.)$

$$(2.1) \qquad y = f(z_1, \ldots, z_p, m_{11}, \ldots, m_{1n}, \ldots, m_{g1}, \ldots, m_{gn}).$$

The regularity properties of the aggregator function are stated in the following

ASSUMPTION 2.1 :

The aggregator function defined in (2.1) is twice continuously differentiable, strictly quasi-concave and has decreasing positive marginal products.

Classical optimization using this aggregator function leads to demand functions for the domestic inputs $z_1, \ldots, z_p$ and the bilateral imports $m_{11}, \ldots, m_{1n}, \ldots, m_{g1}, \ldots, m_{gn}$ in terms of all their prices and possibly other variables such as income or production, depending on the nature of the aggregator function.

2.2.2. SEPARABILITY

It is exactly the property that all prices appear in all demand equations which makes their practical implementation in a linkage model with many countries unduly restrictive, even if we are only considering aggregate trade. It is exactly this property, therefore, which has led to the development of the import allocation model with bilateral imports on a market of a category of goods depending only on total imports and the prices of other products of the same kind. To derive this model mathematically, the aggregator function must have a special form. In order to discuss such forms, we must introduce the notion of *separability*.

Consider a real-valued function $f(.)$ with the properties of Assumption 2.1 and n arguments, gathered in the vector $x = [x_1, \ldots, x_n]'$, and denote the first and second partial derivatives of $f(.)$ by f_i and f_{ij}, respectively [2]. The elements are assumed to be quantities in an aggregator function, and therefore should not be confused with the export variables of Definition 1.3.1. To the quantities correspond n prices, gathered in the vector $p = [p_1, \ldots, p_n]'$. Call the set of indices $N = \{1, \ldots, n\}$. Partition this set into r mutually exclusive and exhaustive subsets $N_1, \ldots, N_r$, a partition which we shall call R. Then we start with the definition of weak separability as [3]

DEFINITION 2.1 :

The function $f(.)$ is *weakly separable* with respect to the partition R if the marginal rate of substitution *(MRS)* between any two elements x_i and x_j from any subset N_s, $s = 1, \ldots, r$, is independent of the quantities of elements outside N_s, *i.e.*

$$\frac{\partial}{\partial x_k}(f_i/f_j) = 0 \qquad \text{for all } i, j \in N_s, \text{ and } k \notin N_s.$$

As proved by GOLDMAN and UZAWA (1964), this condition is necessary and sufficient for the aggregator function to be of the form $f(\bar{x}^1, \ldots, \bar{x}^r)$, where the *partial aggregator function* $\bar{x}^s$ is a function of the elements of N_s only for all s. In the context of production theory weak separability was called *independence* by SOLOW (1955/1956), and is sometimes still referred to as such [4)].

The next definition of importance is that of strong or additive separability.

DEFINITION 2.2 :

The function $f(.)$ is said to be *strongly* or *additively separable* with respect to the partition R if the *MRS* between any two elements is independent of the quantity of any element in any third group, *i.e.*

$$\frac{\partial}{\partial x_k}(f_i/f_j) = 0, \qquad i \in N_s, \; j \in N_{s'}, \; k \notin N_s \cup N_{s'} .$$

As proved by GOLDMAN and UZAWA (1964), this condition is necessary and sufficient for the function $f(.)$ to be of the form $f(\bar{x}^1 + \ldots + \bar{x}^r)$, where the partial aggregator function $\bar{x}^s$ is a function of the elements of N_s only for all s.

Finally we introduce the definition of weak homothetic separability.

DEFINITION 2.3 :

The function $f(.)$ is said to be *weakly homothetic separable* with respect to the partition R if it can be written in the form $f(\bar{x}^1, \ldots, \bar{x}^r)$, where $\bar{x}^s$ is a function of the elements of N_s only for all s, and if $\bar{x}^1, \ldots, \bar{x}^r$ are each homothetic [5)].

Two forms of partitioning have received attention in the literature on linkage models. ARMINGTON (1969a) emphasized the separability of the aggregator function in different *kinds of goods*, using the assumption of independence or weak separability, as it is now usually called, to partition the arguments of the function into groups each corresponding to a different category of goods. Elements of each partial aggregator function were then the quantities of that good provided domestically or from different foreign suppliers. The separability assumption therefore served to eliminate the effects of quantities of different kinds of goods on each other, with such effects being conserved between the *products* of each category, including products produced domestically and abroad.

The second kind of partition, proposed in the context of aggregate trade by BARTEN (1971), makes a distinction between products produced *domestically* or *abroad*. This kind of partition is a true theoretical basis for the import allocation model, as Armington's partition leads in principle to a total allocation model, as demonstrated by its use for the Multilateral Exchange Rate Model of the IMF (ARTUS and RHOMBERG (1973), ARTUS and McGUIRK (1981)). Nevertheless, Armington's merit is that he has introduced the notion of a product distinguished by place of production, and in combination with Barten's partition applied to several goods we may propose a partition of the aggregator function, first, like with Armington, into different categories of goods and second, as with Barten, a further partitioning of each category of goods in domestic and foreign components, thus deriving import allocation models per category of goods in the spirit of both Armington and Barten.

In the usual derivation of import allocation models, Barten's contribution is normally neglected and reference is only made to Armington. We feel that this misrepresents the true state of affairs, and that the import allocation model *per se*, if ascribed to a single author, should rather be written on the name of Barten than Armington.

2.2.3. THE AGGREGATION PROBLEM

In general the aggregation problem refers to aggregation over individuals (households, individual firms) or to aggregation over goods and services (such as production factors, consumer goods), goods or commodities for short. Here we will deal with the latter, and more specifically in the context of international trade. Hence if we refer to *aggregation* here, we will do so with respect to aggregation over goods.

The results of research on aggregation have mainly been used in the context of consumer theory, production theory and international trade analysis. Although the principles of aggregation are therefore rather general, a major part of its theory has been developed in the context of consumer budgeting, when STROTZ (1957, 1959) and GORMAN (1959) through results in this field revived the seminal work on functional structure that was developed earlier independently by LEONTIEF (1947) and SONO (1945). We have already seen above that ARMINGTON (1969a) and BARTEN (1971), also independently, recognized the use of aggregation theory for the derivation of linkage models.

Generally speaking, aggregation refers to the situation where we exchange part of the information that is available for the solution of the problem at hand for an improvement in tractability, as we have already discussed above for the import allocation model. The *loss of information* usually applies to the conjunction of a set of quantities or prices of commodities into a single aggregate or a smaller set of quantity and price indices. The *aggregation problem* refers to the fact that we want the aggregation to be consistent, *i.e.* that

> *"the use of information more detailed than that contained in the aggregate would make no difference to the analysis of the problem at hand."*
>
> GREEN (1964, p. 3).

In applied analysis, one usually starts with a lowest level of aggregation with quantities and prices that are indices themselves. In order to remain consistent, one has to assume that there exists an ordering on this level that allows neo-classical optimization. We will maintain this hypothesis throughout [6)].

In the following we use the consumer budgeting terminology, but we should keep in mind that the results apply equally well to production and international trade theory.

The elementary commodities defined at the lowest level of aggregation can be grouped in a number of ways (as we saw above for the groupings of ARMINGTON (1969a) and BARTEN (1971)), but if we introduce what is now commonly known as the *two-stage budgeting procedure*, we can derive meaningful conditions for consistent aggregation on the utility (aggregator) function. In the two-stage budgeting procedure, introduced by STROTZ (1957) and GORMAN (1959), we assume that a consumer unit, given all prices, first allocates its income to certain budget branches, like food, clothing, housing *etc*. Next, the budget for each branch is spent on the different commodities in that branch, without being dependent on purchases in other branches. This procedure would be *consistent* [7], if the quantities of the individual commodities that are purchased this way are the same as when the consumer unit would have allocated its budget directly to individual commodities. In the context of linkage models this procedure may be compared to a first-stage decision between domestic and foreign purchases, and a second-stage decision how to allocate the foreign purchases among the different suppliers (exporting countries).

It was first pointed out by LAU (1969) that this discussion of consumer budgeting in fact confuses the two different notions of *budgeting* and *decentralization*, whereas they are also permeated by a third one, *price aggregation*.

The first notion is the budgetability of the consumer's income : the fact that he can allocate his income to different budget categories. The second is the decentralization of the category incomes : the possibility for the consumer to allocate optimally category expenditures knowing only intra-category prices. More formally we define budgetability as [8]

DEFINITION 2.4 :

A preference ordering is called *budgetable* if there exist functions θ^s, $s = 1, \ldots, r$, with images

$$m^s = \theta^s(p, y), \qquad \text{all } s,$$

where y is total expenditure and m^s is expenditure on group s for all s.

This notion is clearly an almost trivial concept. Decentralization, on the other hand, is characterized by the following

DEFINITION 2.5 :

The preferences are characterized by *decentralizability* if there exist r vector-valued functions ϕ^s such that

$$x^s = \phi^s(p^s, m^s), \qquad s = 1, \ldots, r,$$

where x^s and p^s are vectors of the elements of x and p that correspond to the elements of N_s only for all s.

For linkage models this definition would guarantee the existence of an import allocation model with bilateral imports being a function of total imports and the bilateral prices.

A third concept related to the two-stage budgeting procedure is the notion of price aggregation, *i.e.* can the first-stage allocation be carried out knowing category price indices, but not knowing the prices of individual goods in the category ? This issue was raised by GORMAN (1959). Formally we make the following

DEFINITION 2.6 :

The situation of *perfect price aggregation* prevails if there exist linear homogeneous functions $\Pi^1, \ldots, \Pi^r$, such that the income allocation functions θ^s can be written as follows

$$m^s = \tilde{\theta}^s(\Pi^1(p^1), \ldots, \Pi^r(p^r), y), \quad s = 1, \ldots, r,$$

where the price vectors p^s, $s = 1, \ldots, r$ have elements corresponding to the elements of N_s only for all s.

Because, as we will see below, weak separability is a necessary and sufficient condition for decentralizability, the utility (aggregator) function can in that case be written as a function of the category quantity indices or partial aggregator functions. In the case of perfect price aggregation, the product of such a quantity index and its corresponding price index Π^s does not necessarily equal the optimal expenditure m^s on that category. At the lowest level of aggregation, the price and quantity of each "elementary" commodity, though they may be indices themselves, exhibit the property that their product equals expenditure on that elementary commodity. In order to justify the first-stage of the two-stage budgeting procedure as a single maximization problem, GREEN (1964) required that the product of the category price index Π^s and the category quantity index or partial aggregator function μ^s should equal the optimal expenditure m^s on that category. This we shall call the case of additive perfect price aggregation. Formally, we employ the following

<u>DEFINITION 2.7</u> :

Preferences are characterized by *additive perfect price aggregation* if, in addition to the price indices defined in Definition 2.6, there exist quantity indices $\mu^1, \ldots, \mu^r$, such that

$$\Pi^s(p^s)\ \mu^s(x^s) = m^s\ , \qquad s = 1, \ldots, r\ .$$

If this condition is satisfied, it is possible to formulate a first-stage optimization problem in which the consumer maximizes utility with respect to the composite commodities $\mu^1, \ldots, \mu^r$, subject to the budget constraint

$$\text{(2.2)} \qquad \Sigma_s\ \Pi^s(p^s)\ \mu^s(x^s) = y.$$

Before we turn to the necessary and sufficient conditions in terms of separability related to the concepts of budgetability, decentralizability and price aggregation, we first present the class of preferences used by GORMAN (1959) in his proofs. Let $v(.)$ be the indirect utility (aggregator) function. Then we have the following

DEFINITION 2.8 :

The indirect utility function is said to have the *Gorman polar form*, if it can be written as

$$v(p, y) = \Psi(y/\Pi(p)) + \Lambda(p),$$

where $\Psi(.)$ is strictly increasing, $\Pi(.)$ is linear homogeneous and $\Lambda(.)$ is homogeneous of degree zero.

If we refer in the following to a strongly or weakly separable utility (aggregator) function $f(.)$ with the Gorman polar form, we mean that the partial aggregator functions have the following form

$$\mu^s(p^s, m^s) = \Psi^s(m^s/\Pi^s(p^s)) + \Lambda^s(p^s) , \quad s = 1, \ldots, r. \tag{2.3}$$

Next we present in the form of theorems the different necessary and/or sufficient conditions for the different concepts introduced in the definitions above, and using the definitions of separability already given in the previous subsection.

THEOREM 2.1 (LAU (1969)) :

If $f(.)$ is continuous, strictly quasi-concave, non-decreasing and strictly increasing in one ordinate, $f(.)$ is budgetable.

This implies that the utility (aggregator) function is budgetable, even if it has no specific structure but merely satisfies the maintained regularity properties (and even less) of Assumption 2.1.

THEOREM 2.2 (GORMAN (1959)) :

Weak homothetic separability with respect to the partition R implies perfect price aggregation.

THEOREM 2.3 (GORMAN (1959)) :

Strong separability with respect to the partition R with the Gorman polar form implies perfect price aggregation.

<u>THEOREM 2.4</u> (GORMAN (1959)) :

If *f(.)* is weakly separable with respect to the partition *R*, perfect price aggregation implies either weak homothetic separability or strong separability with partial aggregator functions restricted by the Gorman polar form.

Theorems 2.2 - 2.4 imply that, if the utility (aggregator) function is weakly separable, there exist necessary and sufficient conditions for perfect price aggregation. Next we turn to additive perfect price aggregation.

<u>THEOREM 2.5</u> (GORMAN (1959) and BLACKORBY *et al.* (1970)) :

Weak homothetic separability with respect to the partition *R* implies additive perfect price aggregation.

<u>THEOREM 2.6</u> (BLACKORBY *et al.* (1970)) :

If *f(.)* is weakly separable with respect to the partition *R*, additive perfect price aggregation implies weak homothetic separability.

Here also, necessary and sufficient conditions exist for additive perfect price aggregation under the presumption of weak separability of the utility (aggregator) function.

<u>THEOREM 2.7</u> (GORMAN (1971)) :

Weak separability of *f(.)* with respect to the partition *R* is both necessary and sufficient for decentralizability.

From Theorems 2.2-2.7 we may deduce that if we are ready to accept that the utility (aggregator) function is weakly separable with respect to the partition *R*, there exist necessary and sufficient conditions for (additive) perfect price aggregation, while weak separability with respect to the partition *R* is itself a necessary and sufficient condition for decentralizability.

There is, however, one remark to be made. The conditions for (additive) perfect price aggregation may turn out to be too strong for empirical purposes, and in those cases we may revert to the solution presented by BARTEN and TURNOVSKY (1966) and BARTEN (1970) in the context of differential consumer demand systems. They show, given only weak separability, that if we are prepared to work with two group price indices (defined as Divisia indices with as weights respectively average and marginal budget shares) the aggregation problem may be solved in a consistent way.

Next we apply the theory of aggregation to linkage models, where we return to our starting point, the aggregator function defined in (2.1). Because this function was assumed to have the regularity properties of Assumption 2.1, it is budgetable by Theorem 2.1. As we saw above in the discussion on the contributions of ARMINGTON (1969a) and BARTEN (1971) to import allocation models, we actually have to introduce a three-stage "budgeting" procedure in order to derive import allocation models per category of goods. In the first stage we have to assume that the aggregator function is weakly separable in a partition by which the products of each kind of good are grouped together by their categories of goods. This first-stage allocation is in the spirit of Armington. In the second stage we have to assume that each of the partial aggregator functions corresponding to each category of goods is itself weakly separable in domestic inputs and imports. This is in the spirit of Barten. The allocation process of this stage therefore determines an import quantity index μ^s per category of goods, which we will simply call μ, which is a function of the quantities of all bilateral imports of the products of that category. The weak separability in domestic inputs and imports is then necessary and sufficient to have decentralizability such that we have an import allocation model for each category of goods, which in the third stage of our three-stage optimization procedure allocates total imports of each category over the bilateral imports from the different suppliers (exporting countries).

The stated weak separability properties are therefore in themselves sufficient to guarantee the existence of the required import allocation models. Given the weak separability of the aggregator function, it depends on its functional form whether the necessary and sufficient conditions for (additive) perfect price aggregation as stated in Theorems 2.2-2.6 are valid. ARMINGTON (1969a) for instance, proposes CES functions for the partial aggregator functions of the first stage; as the CES function is (linear) homogeneous, this implies that the aggregator function is weakly homothetic separable and therefore is sufficient according to Theorem 2.5 to imply additive perfect price aggregation. The MUKERJI (1963) partial aggregator function used by BARTEN (1971) on the other hand, is not homothetic and therefore does not guarantee the same result. There is not even perfect price aggregation according to Theorem 2.4 because the partial aggregator function would then necessarily have to be of the Gorman polar form, which is not the case.

2.2.4. THE ADDING-UP CONDITION

In the previous subsection we considered the formal derivation of the import allocation model. The starting point for the import allocation model per category of goods is a partial aggregator function with as elements the bilateral imports from the trading partners of the particular category of commodities to which the partial aggregator function pertains. We will denote the partial aggregator function, or import quantity index as it is usually called, by μ, deleting therefore the subscripts of the market (importing country j) and the category of goods k. It is defined as follows

$$\mu = \mu(m_1, \ldots, m_n), \tag{2.4}$$

where $m_1, \ldots, m_n$ are the bilateral imports by country j from countries $1, \ldots, n$ (excluding j) of commodities of category k with subscripts k and j deleted.

Definition 2.5 of decentralizability gives the bilateral imports then as a function of the total imports in current prices, and the bilateral import prices. This function may be derived from classical maximization of (2.4), which then acts as a utility function, given the import budget M (total imports in current prices). In the context of producer theory, the optimization problem would be cost minimization given a certain level of the import quantity index μ defined by (2.4). In that case bilateral imports will be a function of the index μ and the bilateral import prices. In either case one would expect bilateral imports to add up to total imports in current and constant prices, because of the way they are defined in the data

(2.5) $$\Sigma_i m_i = m,$$

(2.6) $$\Sigma_i pm_i m_i = M.$$

The last condition is automatically satisfied in the case of cost minimization because there it is the constituting identity of imports in current prices, given the bilateral imports in constant prices and the bilateral import prices. For utility maximization it is the binding budget constraint and therefore also automatically satisfied.

The adding-up condition therefore is less trivially satisfied for the flows in constant prices. We will turn now to its discussion.

The equation for m_i derived from classical optimization, then, usually contains μ as an explanatory variable, but μ is not observable, unless it has a very simple form. If the partial aggregator function μ is a linear homogeneous import index, the derived demand equation will be of the form [9)]

(2.7) $$m_i = \mu\, \pi_i(pm_1, \ldots, pm_n), \qquad all\ i,$$

where $\pi_i(.)$ is a function of all bilateral import prices only for all i.

As estimation is difficult with an unobservable index such as μ, one uses (2.7) to impose (2.5) *a priori* and to eliminate μ from the estimating equation by summing both sides of (2.7) over i

$$(2.8) \qquad m = \Sigma_i \, m_i = \mu \, \Sigma_i \, \pi_i(.).$$

This formulation enables one to express μ in terms of the observable variables m, pm_1, ..., pm_n as

$$(2.9) \qquad \mu = m \, [\Sigma_i \, \pi_i(.)]^{-1} ,$$

which may then be inserted in (2.7) to obtain as nonlinear estimating equation

$$(2.10) \qquad m_i = m \, \pi_i(.) \, [\Sigma_h \, \pi_h(.)]^{-1} , \qquad \text{all } i.$$

Another solution, which might also be applied if the partial aggregator function μ is non-homothetic, would be to make use of the fact that $\pi_i(.)$ often is written in terms of the bilateral import price pm_i relative to a composite, say π, of all bilateral import prices, while the import quantity index μ may be written as M/π at the same time

$$(2.11) \qquad m_i = g_i(M/\pi, \; pm_i/\pi), \qquad \text{all } i.$$

Inserting (2.11) in (2.5) might then be used to consider π as the (implicit) price index that goes along with adding-up

$$(2.12) \qquad m = \Sigma_i \, m_i = \Sigma_i \, g_i(M/\pi, \; pm_i/\pi).$$

This type of solution to the adding-up problem was proposed by BARTEN and d'ALCANTARA (1977), but in practice only implemented by NYHUS (1978). He used an iterative estimation procedure as (2.12) implied that π was defined in terms of the parameters of the estimating equations (2.11).

After this short digression on an alternative solution to the adding-up problem, let us return to the model (2.7)/(2.10). In actual modelbuilding practice, the model will usually consist of an import equation explaining the volume of total imports per category of goods, and equations such as (2.10) or approximations to it, at least if one has as a point of departure a *linear homogeneous* (or even homothetic) import quantity index μ.

The question is how to handle the conditions of weak separability that were taken to be true in order to derive the import allocation models per category of goods. They would lead us to expect the model to consist of an equation explaining μ rather than m, as μ was assumed to appear in the (partial) aggregator function distinguished in the second stage of the three-stage procedure described above in subsection 2.2.3, and assumed to be known beforehand. After equations (2.10) have been estimated, their parameters may be used to construct the previously unknown index μ. Nothing seems to prevent the estimation of a total import equation containing this constructed μ as dependent variable, and use in the model of the original equation (2.7) instead of (2.10), except that one might be opposed to such a method because the empirical content of the import quantity index μ is less clear than that of imports in constant prices, but that seems a minor difference. But even then, it is quite simple to construct m by the identity (2.5), reducing the adding-up condition to nothing but a tautological phenomenon.

Formally, the formulation of a total import equation with m as dependent variable means that one assumes that the aggregator function has two forms : one in which it is weakly separable with respect to a partition that contains μ (which is used to derive the bilateral import demand equations), and one in which it is weakly separable with respect to a partition that contains m (which is used to incorporate the bilateral import demand equations in the framework of a model). Except for degenerate cases, these two forms will not be equal, and we must conclude that the inclusion of an import function for m is formally antagonistic to the assumption of weak separability underlying the derivation of the bilateral import demand equation.

In the rest of this study we will not be concerned with what kind of total import function per category of goods should be used in the linkage model for which the bilateral import demand equations are estimated. We have seen, however, that estimating the latter equations may in principle differ from the way in which they are finally introduced in the linkage model. As a summary we propose three solutions that in one way or another deal with the problem of adding-up.

As a first case, one might estimate (2.10), but include (2.7) in the linkage model as simulating equation, with μ calculated according to its definition (2.4) from the estimated parameters. The adding-up condition (2.5) will be automatically satisfied because it becomes the generating identity for total imports per category of goods, m.

Secondly, another possibility would be to find an approximation for μ from which it would become an observable variable, and estimate (2.7) directly using this approximation, again with (2.5) to define m.

A third option would be to derive estimating equations for m_i that are neither dependent on the import quantity index μ nor on total imports in constant prices m, but on another, observable, import quantity index, say $\bar{m}$, and again including (2.7) as simulating equation in the model with μ calculated from (2.4) with the use of the estimated parameters, and defining m through (2.5).

If these three solutions were applied correctly, the model would contain a total import equation explaining the import quantity index μ in all three cases. If one accepted that separability in both μ and m (or $\bar{m}$, for that matter) is not too conflicting, only the second possibility would still maintain an explanatory equation for μ. The two other solutions would then work with import equations for m and $\bar{m}$, respectively. Examples of all three possibilities will be given in section 5.3 in the case of a homothetic partial aggregator function μ.

Even if the index is not homothetic, or if the bilateral import demand equations are not derived from cost-minimizing conditions at all, it is still possible to apply the general idea introduced above, *viz.* the replacement of total imports m in the estimating bilateral import equations by another index, μ or $\bar{m}$, introduction of an explanatory equation for that index, and calculation of m using the identity (2.5).

Consider for instance the following bilateral import demand equation

$$(2.13) \qquad w_i \, ln \, m_i = \alpha_i + \beta_i \, ln \, m + \varepsilon_i \, ln \, pm_i - w_i \, \Sigma_h \, \varepsilon_h \, ln \, pm_h \, , \qquad \text{all } i,$$

with parameters α_i, $\beta_i > 0$, $\varepsilon_i \leqslant 0$ and known constants $w_1, \ldots, w_n$, for instance representing base year import shares. Then this equation clearly does not satisfy the adding-up condition (2.5). But, on the other hand, if we replace m by an alternative index $\bar{m}$, defined as

(2.14) $$ln\, \bar{m} = \Sigma_i\, w_i\, ln\, m_i ,$$

(which may be considered as an approximation to m, if the w_i are import shares) we obtain the model

(2.15) $$w_i\, ln\, m_i = \alpha_i + \beta_i\, ln\, \bar{m} + \varepsilon_i\, ln\, pm_i - w_i\, \Sigma_h\, \varepsilon_h\, ln\, pm_h, \qquad \text{all } i.$$

This system of equations satisfies identity (2.14) if it is estimated such that the following constraints with respect to the parameters are valid

(2.16) $$\Sigma_i\, \alpha_i = 0$$

(2.17) $$\Sigma_i\, \beta_i = 1$$

Total imports in constant prices m could, in this model, be determined by (2.5), while we should introduce an import equation with $\bar{m}$ (or $ln\, \bar{m}$) as dependent variable.

2.3. EMPIRICAL MODELS

2.3.1. THE CES MODEL

We motivated in subsection 1.4.6 our choice for estimation-consistent import allocation models. We found in the literature about 15 existing linkage models that may be classified as such, and of these about half are based on, or derived from, a CES partial aggregator function or import quantity index. These models will be treated in this subsection, and the other models in the next subsection. More specifically we will treat the CES model as developed by HICKMAN and LAU (1973), as the others may be considered to be closely related to, or copied from, their paper, which contains a detailed treatment of its derivation and estimation. That is, we do not treat the DESMOS III model (DRAMAIS (1974/1975), WAELBROECK and DRAMAIS (1974), DRAMAIS (1981)), the EPA World Economic Model (AMANO *et al.* (1980, 1981a, 1981b, 1982)), the models of HICKMAN (1973), GERACI and PREWO (1982), the Globus model (KIRKPATRICK (1983)), the Interfutures project (HALTTUNEN and WARNER (1979a, 1979b)) nor the OECD World Trade Model (SAMUELSON (1973)).

DERIVATION

The derivation of the CES model of Hickman and Lau starts off with the Armington assumption that the Allen partial Elasticities of Substitution[10] between the goods from different suppliers i on an import market j are equal and constant [11], or that the partial aggregator function μ is of the Constant-Elasticity-of-Substitution (CES) form [12]

$$(3.1) \qquad \mu = [\Sigma_i \alpha_i m_i^{-\rho}]^{-1/\rho} , \qquad \rho > -1 ,$$

$$= [\Sigma_i \alpha_i m_i^{(\sigma-1)/\sigma}]^{\sigma/(\sigma-1)} ,$$

where $\sigma = 1/(1+\rho)$ can be identified as the Allen partial Elasticity of Substitution. Furthermore Hickman and Lau set

(3.2) $\Sigma_i \alpha_i^{\sigma} = 1$.

The CES import quantity index is restrictive, as we will see, because it implies one single relative import price effect that is the same for all n bilateral import demand equations. This is at the same time one of its advantages, however, as it reduces the number of paramaters to be estimated.

The cost-minimizing quantities of attaining a given level of the quantity index μ are given by

(3.3) $m_i = \alpha_i^{\sigma} \mu (pm_i/\pi)^{-\sigma}$, all i,

where

(3.4) $\pi = [\Sigma_i \alpha_i^{\sigma} pm_i^{(1-\sigma)}]^{1/(1-\sigma)}$,

is the composite price index of imports with the additive perfect price aggregation property that

(3.5) $\pi . \mu = \Sigma_i pm_i m_i = M$.

The individual bilateral import demand functions per category of goods may therefore alternatively be written as

(3.6) $m_i = \alpha_i^{\sigma} (M/\pi)(pm_i/\pi)^{-\sigma}$, all i,

which is another variant of (2.10) with μ eliminated in favour of the composite index π, as in (2.11). Recognizing the fact that all price indices, and therefore also the linear homogeneous index π, are equal to one in the baseyear, we may identify the parameters α_i^{σ} for all i with the baseyear import shares w_i^o

(3.7) $m_i^o = M^o \alpha_i^{\sigma}$, all i,

$$(3.8) \qquad \alpha_i^{\sigma} = m_i^o/M^o = w_i^o , \qquad \text{all } i,$$

where the superscript "o" denotes the baseyear. Therefore (3.6) and (3.4) may be written as

$$(3.9) \qquad m_i = w_i^o \, (M/\pi)(pm_i/\pi)^{-\sigma} , \qquad \text{all } i,$$

$$(3.10) \qquad \pi = [\, \Sigma_i \, w_i^o \, pm_i^{(1-\sigma)} \,]^{1/(1-\sigma)} .$$

Applying the elimination method of subsection 2.2.4 to (3.3), we may introduce the volume of total imports in (3.9) as

$$(3.11) \qquad m_i = w_i^o \, m \, pm_i^{-\sigma} [\, \Sigma_h \, w_h^o \, pm_h^{-\sigma}]^{-1}$$

This expression is next linearized by Hickman and Lau around the baseyear values $m = m^o$ and $pm_i = 1$ for all i, resulting in

$$(3.12) \qquad m_i = w_i^o m - \sigma m_i^o \, (pm_i - pm),$$

where pm is the linearized version of the index π

$$(3.13) \qquad pm = \Sigma_i \, w_i^o \, pm_i .$$

The interpretation of (3.12) is as follows. If all bilateral import prices are equal, the bilateral imports in constant prices are equal to the product of the baseyear import share and total imports in constant prices. This is a result of the fact that the CES import quantity index is linear homogeneous. Next to this mechanical volume effect there is the effect of the bilateral import price relative to a weighted average of all bilateral import prices. This relative price effect is the same for all bilateral import equations (in elasticity terms) and may be interpreted as the elasticity of substitution. If we were to estimate (3.12), we would only have to estimate one coefficient for all equations, the elasticity of substitution. Although this may be an advantage from the point of view of estimation, this advantage is reached at the cost of a specification which is so simple that one may seriously wonder whether it fits economic reality. This basic simplicity is not altered by the elements that will be added to the equation in the following paragraphs, and will therefore be the subject of empirical tests in Chapter 9.

To obtain their estimation model, Hickman and Lau introduce time trends in the CES import quantity index, representing taste changes over time

$$(3.14) \qquad \mu = [\, \Sigma_i \, \alpha_i \, e^{\gamma_i t} \, m_i^{(\sigma-1)/\sigma} \,]^{\sigma/(\sigma-1)} ,$$

and furthermore they assume that the relative price term $pm_i - pm$ in (3.12) is in fact an optimal variable $pm_i^{\star} - pm^{\star}$ which should be identified through an adaptive expectations scheme with an adjustment parameter $(1-\delta)$, common for all supplying countries i

$$(3.15) \qquad (pm_{it}^{\star} - pm_t^{\star}) - (pm_{it-1}^{\star} - pm_{t-1}^{\star}) =$$

$$\beta_i + (1-\delta)\, [\, (pm_{it-1} - pm_{t-1}) - (pm_{it-1}^{\star} - pm_{t-1}^{\star})] \; + \phi_i t.$$

The constant and the trend in this equation might be justified in order to correct deviations by exporting country i from the common adaptive expectations scheme with parameter $(1-\delta)$.

The same derivation as before (including linearization), starting from (3.14) and substituting $pm_i - pm$ by its optimal value $pm_i^{\star} - pm^{\star}$, then leads, after some manipulation, to the following dynamic estimating equations [13)]

$$(3.16) \qquad m_{it} = w_i^o \, m_t + \delta \, [m_{it-1} - w_i^o \, m_{t-1}] + \sigma m_i^o (\delta r_i - \beta_i)$$

$$+ \sigma m_i^o \, [\, (1-\delta) r_i - \phi_i \,] t - \sigma (1-\delta) \, m_i^o \, [pm_{it} - pm_t] \, , \qquad \text{all } i,$$

where $r_i = \gamma_i - \Sigma_h \, w_h^o \, \gamma_h$. It is not possible to identify both trend coefficients r_i and ϕ_i, therefore one of them must arbitrarily be set equal to zero. Hickman and Lau take this to be r_i, therefore they estimate the following equations

$$(3.17)\quad m_{it} - w_i^o m_t = \delta [m_{it-1} - w_i^o m_{t-1}] - \sigma m_i^o \beta_i - \sigma m_i^o \phi_i t - \sigma(1-\delta) m_i^o [pm_{it} - pm_t], \quad \text{all } i.$$

In order for the adding-up condition (2.5) to hold, the parameters of (3.17) should satisfy the following constraints

$$(3.18)\quad \Sigma_i m_i^o \beta_i = \Sigma_i m_i^o \phi_i = 0$$

ESTIMATION

For the stochastic specification, Hickman and Lau assume that the stochastic disturbance term u_{it} is additive, such that we have

$$(3.19)\quad m_{ii} - w_i^o m_t = \delta [m_{it-1} - w_i^o m_{t-1}] - \sigma m_i^o \beta_i - \sigma m_i^o \phi_i t - \sigma(1-\delta) m_i^o [pm_{it} - pm_t] + u_{it}, \quad \text{all } i.$$

Hickman and Lau then propose three different sets of assumptions for the disturbances u_{it}

$$(3.20)\quad \begin{aligned} E(u_{it}) &= 0 && \text{all } i, t, \\ E(u_{it} u_{ht'}) &= s^2 && \text{all } h = i, t = t', \\ & 0 && \text{elsewhere,} \end{aligned}$$

$$(3.21)\quad \begin{aligned} E(u_{it}) &= 0 && \text{all } i, t, \\ E(u_{it} u_{ht'}) &= s^2 (m_i^o)^2 && \text{all } h = i, t = t', \\ &= 0 && \text{elsewhere,} \end{aligned}$$

$$(3.22)\quad \begin{aligned} E(u_{it}) &= 0 && \text{all } i, t, \\ E(u_{it} u_{ht'}) &= s^2 m_i^o && \text{all } h = i, t = t', \\ & 0 && \text{elsewhere.} \end{aligned}$$

Moreover they assume for all three specifications

(3.23) $\quad \Sigma_i u_{it} = \iota' u_t = 0$, $\qquad$ all t,

where $u_t = [u_{1t}, \ldots, u_{nt}]'$ and $\iota = [1, \ldots, 1]'$ is the n-vector of units.

Because the σ and δ coefficients appear in each equation, Hickman and Lau conclude that it is necessary to pool the equations and estimate them jointly, at the same time constraining the coefficients in order to satisfy (3.18) in view of the adding-up condition. In order to do so, let us stack the equations and write them in matrix and vector notation as

(3.24) $\quad y = X\beta + u,$

where, if there are T observations $t = 1, \ldots, T$, y is the $(nT \times 1)$ vector $y = [m_{11} - w_1^o m_1, m_{21} - w_2^o m_1, \ldots, m_{n1} - w_n^o m_1, \ldots, m_{nT} - w_n^o m_T]'$, X is the $(nT \times 2n)$ matrix

$$\begin{bmatrix}
-m_1^o & 0 & \cdots & 0 & -m_1^o.1 & 0 & \cdots & 0 & pm_{11} - pm_1 & m_{10} - w_1^o m_0 \\
0 & -m_2^o & \cdots & 0 & 0 & -m_2^o.1 & \cdots & 0 & pm_{21} - pm_1 & m_{20} - w_2^o m_0 \\
\vdots & \vdots & & \vdots & \vdots & \vdots & & \vdots & \vdots & \vdots \\
0 & 0 & \cdots & -m_{n-1}^o & 0 & 0 & \cdots & -m_{n-1}^o.1 & pm_{n-1,1} - pm_1 & m_{n-1,0} - w_{n-1}^o m_0 \\
m_1^o & m_2^o & \cdots & m_{n-1}^o & m_1^o.1 & m_2^o.1 & \cdots & m_{n-1}^o.1 & pm_{n1} - pm_1 & m_{n0} - w_n^o m_0 \\
 & & \vdots & & & & \vdots & & \vdots & \vdots \\
-m_1^o & 0 & \cdots & 0 & -m_1^o.T & 0 & \cdots & 0 & pm_{1T} - pm_T & m_{1,T-1} - w_1^o m_{T-1} \\
0 & -m_2^o & \cdots & 0 & 0 & -m_2^o.T & \cdots & 0 & pm_{2T} - pm_T & m_{2,T-1} - w_2^o m_{T-1} \\
\vdots & \vdots & & \vdots & \vdots & \vdots & & & \vdots & \vdots \\
0 & 0 & \cdots & -m_{n-1}^o & 0 & 0 & \cdots & -m_{n-1}^o.T & pm_{n-1,T} - pm_T & m_{n-1,T-1} - w_{n-1}^o m_{T-1} \\
m_1^o & m_2^o & \cdots & m_{n-1}^o & m_1^o.T & m_2^o.T & \cdots & m_{n-1}^o.T & pm_{nT} - pm_T & m_{n,T-1} - w_n^o m_{T-1}
\end{bmatrix},$$

β is the $(2n \times 1)$ vector $\beta = [\bar{\beta}_1, \ldots, \bar{\beta}_{n-1}, \bar{\phi}_1, \ldots, \bar{\phi}_{n-1}, \bar{\sigma}, \delta]'$, with $\bar{\beta}_i = \sigma\beta_i$, $\bar{\phi}_i = \sigma\phi_i$, $\bar{\sigma} = \sigma(1-\delta)$ and u is the $nT \times 1$ vector $u = [u_{11}, \ldots, u_{n1}, \ldots, u_{1T}, \ldots u_{nT}]' = [u_1' \ldots u_T']'$.

The estimates for $\bar{\beta}_n$ and $\bar{\phi}_n$ may easily be calculated from the constraint (3.18) which was used to formulate the matrix X and which is therefore automatically satisfied.

Define V as the $(nT \times nT)$ covariance matrix of the disturbance vector u of (3.24), then it may be seen, with the use of (3.20) - (3.22), to be equal to

$$(3.25) \qquad V = E(uu') = I \otimes H ,$$

where $\otimes$ is the Kronecker product, I is the $(T \times T)$ identity matrix and H is the $(n \times n)$ diagonal matrix with on the diagonal, depending on whether one assumes (3.20), (3.21) or (3.22), the elements of the n-vectors $[s^2, \ldots, s^2]'$, $[s^2(m_1^o)^2, \ldots, s^2(m_n^o)^2]'$ or $[s^2 m_1^o, \ldots, s^2 m_n^o]'$, respectively.

The Generalized Least Squares (GLS) estimator of the coefficient vector β in (3.24) is then

$$(3.26) \qquad \hat{\beta}_{GLS} = (X'V^{-1}X)^{-1} X'V^{-1}y ,$$

provided V^{-1} exists. This is however not the case, because, as may be seen with the help of (3.23), we have

$$(3.27) \qquad \iota'V = \iota' E(uu') = E(\iota'uu') = 0 ,$$

and V is therefore singular. Even worse, this result proves the contradiction of assumption (3.23) with any of the assumptions (3.20)-(3.22) made for the disturbances, unless s^2 equals zero which is a degenerate case. Therefore either (3.23) or (3.20)-(3.22) must be wrong. Because of the adding-up condition, (3.23) is actually not an assumption to be made, but a result which may be proven given the functional form of the equation, for instance by adding up the two sides of (3.19) over i and requiring that the sums be zero. Therefore assumptions (3.20)-(3.22) apparently should be modified. That is, if we maintain them, we could scale equation (3.19) by 1, $(m_{i}^{o})^2$ or m_{i}^{o} for all i respectively, and estimate the resulting equivalence of (3.24) by Ordinary Least Squares *(OLS)* without running into problems. The resulting estimator, however, would be, though unbiased, not efficient, since the implied covariance matrix behind this model is not equal to the true covariance matrix which should under all circumstances satisfy (3.27).

Whatever new (correct) assumptions we may make about the covariances, the resulting covariance matrix V will always remain singular. We will see in Chapter 4 that the standard solution to this problem is to delete one equation from the system. Suppose we delete the last, n^{th}, equation. Then (3.24) may be rewritten as

$$(3.28) \qquad \tilde{y} = \tilde{X}\beta + \tilde{u} \, ,$$

where $\tilde{y}$ is the vector y with each nth element deleted, $\tilde{X}$ is the matrix X with each nth row deleted and $\tilde{u}$ is the vector u with each nth element deleted. Let us first make the assumption for the covariances that there is no intertemporal correlation among the disturbances. Then the covariance matrix $\tilde{V}$ of $\tilde{u}$ may be written as

$$(3.29) \qquad \tilde{V} = E(\widetilde{uu'}) = I \otimes \tilde{H} \, ,$$

where $\tilde{H}$ is now an $(n-1)\text{x}(n-1)$ matrix of contemporaneous covariances, depending on the assumptions we make about them. If we do not make any further assumptions about $\tilde{H}$, it has to be estimated jointly with the coefficient vector β. It will be shown in Chapter 4 that estimation by the method of maximum likelihood gives estimators for β and V (where the latter may be calculated from the estimator for $\tilde{V}$ using (3.27)) that do not depend on the identity of the equation which is deleted.

The method of maximum likelihood is however one of the more complicated estimation methods, especially for large models, and there is no indication at all that Hickman and Lau have used it, all the more because they maintained the assumptions (3.20)-(3.22).

We must therefore assume that their estimation method rests close to the assumptions (3.20)-(3.22), but nevertheless circumvents the problem of contradiction with (3.23). One estimation method that has this property and remains relatively simple because it only requires a *GLS* estimation technique is the following.

In analogy with the method of maximum likelihood estimation, one could delete one equation of the system, say the nth. As an exception to assumptions (3.20)-(3.22), one could next assume that the contemporaneous covariances between the disturbances of this single equation and those of each of the other equations would be nonzero, and have such a value that the resulting covariance matrix V of the disturbances satisfies (3.27). This would amount to the following set of three assumptions about the disturbances.

(3.30)
$$
\begin{aligned}
E(u_{it}) &= 0 && \text{all } i,\ t,\\
E(u_{it}u_{ht'}) &= s^2 && \text{all } i = h \neq n,\ t = t',\\
&\ (n-1)s^2 && i = h = n,\ t = t',\\
&\ -s^2 && \text{all } i \neq n,\ h = n,\ t = t',\\
&\ 0 && \text{elsewhere},
\end{aligned}
$$

(3.31)
$$
\begin{aligned}
E(u_{it}) &= 0 && \text{all } i,\ t,\\
E(u_{it}u_{ht'}) &= s^2(m_i^o)^2 && \text{all } i = h \neq n,\ t = t',\\
&\ \Sigma_{k=1}^{n-1}\, s^2(m_k^o)^2 && i = h = n,\ t = t',\\
&\ -s^2(m_i^o)^2 && \text{all } i \neq n,\ h = n,\ t = t',\\
&\ 0 && \text{elsewhere},
\end{aligned}
$$

$$(3.32)\quad \begin{aligned} E(u_{it}) &= 0 && \text{all } i,\ t, \\ E(u_{it}u_{ht'}) &= s^2 m_i^o && \text{all } i = h \neq n,\ t = t', \\ &\quad \Sigma_{k=1}^{n-1} s^2\, m_k^o && i = h = n,\ t = t', \\ &\quad -s^2 m_i^o && \text{all } i \neq n,\ h = n,\ t = t', \\ &\quad 0 && \text{elsewhere.} \end{aligned}$$

The resulting contemporaneous covariance matrix H in (3.25) corresponding to any of the assumptions will consist of a bordered diagonal matrix of the form

$$(3.33)\quad H = \begin{bmatrix} h_1 & 0 & \cdots & 0 & -h_1 \\ 0 & h_2 & \cdots & 0 & -h_2 \\ \vdots & \vdots & \ddots & \vdots & \\ 0 & 0 & & h_{n-1} & -h_{n-1} \\ -h_1 & -h_2 & \cdots & -h_{n-1} & h_n \end{bmatrix}$$

where $h = [\,h_1, \ldots, h_n]'$ is any of the n-vectors $[\,s^2, \ldots, s^2, (n-1)s^2]'$, $[\,s^2(m_1^o)^2, \ldots, s^2(m_{n-1}^o)^2, \Sigma_{k=1}^{n-1} s^2(m_k^o)^2\,]'$ or $[\,s^2 m_1^o, \ldots, s^2 m_{n-1}^o, s^2\,\Sigma_{k=1}^{n-1} m_k^o]'$ respectively. It may easily be verified that the resulting covariance matrix V of (3.25) now satisfies (3.27).

The system of pooled equations with equation n deleted is now again equal to (3.28), and the corresponding covariance matrix $\tilde{V}$ of the disturbances as given in (3.29) has as matrix $\tilde{H}$ the matrix H defined in (3.33) with the last row and column deleted; it therefore has become a diagonal matrix of which all elements are known up to the scaling factor s^2. Because the covariance matrix is known, we may obtain the *GLS* estimator for β as

$$(3.34)\quad \hat{\beta}_{GLS} = (\tilde{X}'\,\tilde{V}^{-1}\,\tilde{X})^{-1}\,\tilde{X}'\,\tilde{V}^{-1}\,\tilde{y}.$$

This estimator is relatively easy to calculate and provides unbiased and efficient estimates for all parameters of the system if we use the constraint (3.18). Also it may be shown in a fashion similar to the proof of Lemma 4.3.1 of Chapter 4 that the *GLS* estimator does not depend on the identity of the equation which has been deleted. Next to these advantages there is, however, one big disadvantage, which is the asymmetric treatment of the covariances involving the disturbances of the deleted n^{th} equation. *A priori* there is no reason why these covariances should be treated differently from the other covariances.

Summarizing, we have seen that the coefficients of the CES model may be estimated in three ways. The first method would be to neglect the contradiction between (3.20)-(3.22) and (3.23), and to estimate the coefficients by *OLS* after a rescaling of the equations (3.29). This produces an unbiased estimator which is however not efficient. Secondly, we could delete one equation, leave the covariance matrix free and estimate coefficients and the covariance matrix by the method of maximum likelihood. Although computationally burdensome, this method avoids having to make assumptions on the covariance matrix, and gives estimation results which do not depend on the identity of the equation which is deleted. Thirdly, we could alter the assumptions (3.20)-(3.22) into (3.30)-(3.32) for the disturbances of one particular equation, say equation n, delete that equation and obtain a *GLS* estimate of the coefficients using a diagonal covariance matrix for the resulting model. The computational simplicity, the independence of this estimator from the identity of the deleted equation and the correct treatment of the covariance matrix (resulting in efficient estimators) have, however, as a drawback, the introduction of an arbitrary asymmetry in the treatment of the covariances of the disturbances. We have to guess which of the three methods was used by Hickman and Lau. Because they maintained the assumptions (3.20)-(3.22) on the disturbances, it seems most likely that they have used the first method, thereby using an inefficient estimator for the coefficients. In general the second method, employing maximum likelihood estimation, should however be preferred because of the advantages already enumerated above.

2.3.2. OTHER MODELS

With the CES model as estimated by Hickman and Lau we have treated the most widespread of the estimation-consistent import allocation models. In this section we treat briefly the main other existing models.

Three of these are direct applications of consumer demand systems to linkage models. The first is an application of the *Rotterdam system* by CLEMENTS AND THEIL (1978) to international linkage, while the second and third are an application of the *Linear Expenditure System* of STONE (1954) to linkage for the Interdependence model (FONTELA and LO CASCIO (1983), SALLIN-KORNBERG and FONTELA (1981), HIERONYMI (1983)), and by JOHNSON (1978). In the same category may be placed the import allocation models based on *constant value shares*, such as those tested by GANA *et al.* (1979), AMANO *et al.* (1980) and SARMA (1983), because this approach may be derived from a Cobb-Douglas partial aggregator function.

Related to the approaches using consumer demand systems is the linkage model developed by SNELLA (1979). He is one of the few authors to start from an *indirect utility function* and he thus derives the bilateral import demand functions through application of the well-known theorem of ROY (1942). His approach is also interesting because the indirect utility functions he uses are of the Gorman polar form defined in Definition 2.8 and this therefore guarantees with Theorem 2.3 perfect price aggregation if the aggregator function is strongly separable.

The approach of RESNICK and TRUMAN (1975) is a *multi-stage approach*, in which imports are first allocated between Europe and the Rest of the World. Next the imports from Europe are further allocated between those originating in the European Economic Community (EEC) as a whole and the European Free Trade Association (EFTA). Next the total imports from EEC and EFTA are each apart allocated over their member countries. Although their method is estimation-consistent, it seems to violate the separability conditions because the *GDP* deflator appears in the relative prices of all bilateral import equations, and a change in the *GDP* price index might also influence the allocation of income between domestic products and imports, thus violating the assumption of weak separability.

The last non-CES model is the linkage model of NYHUS (1978). In fact it resembles the CES model but may be considered more elaborate since the relative price effects are distinct instead of identical per equation as they are in the CES model. We have already mentioned in subsection 2.2.4 that Nyhus iterated on the composite import price index in order to meet the adding-up condition. It may be seen in Chapter 5 that his model closely resembles the model we will develop there, although he did not derive it in the context of neoclassical optimization as we do.

2.4. SUMMARY AND CONCLUDING REMARKS

In Chapter 1 we pronounced a certain preference, among possible kinds of linkage models, for estimation-consistent import allocation models. In the present chapter, the theoretical background for these models and the most important empirical models have been discussed.

The main *theoretical* aspects which were discussed concerned the consistent aggregation over commodities and the adding-up problem. The process of *aggregation* over commodities was divided into the three aspects : budgetability, decentralizability and (additive) perfect price aggregation. Necessary and sufficient conditions for the aggregation process to be consistent were presented, and turned out to imply sometimes strong restrictions on the aggregator function in terms of separability conditions. Weaker conditions were shown to be sufficient in the context of differential consumer demand systems by BARTEN (1970).

We identified as the current mainstream of *empirical* estimation-consistent import allocation models the Constant-Elasticity-of-Substitution (CES) import allocation model. We discussed the way in which this model was first specified and estimated by HICKMAN and LAU (1973). The fact that all elasticities of substitution between pairs of bilateral imports in this model are equal and constant limits its generality severely : it implies one common relative price effect for each bilateral import demand equation, for instance. Furthermore we saw that Hickman and Lau probably employed an estimation method, though simple when compared to others, with contradictory elements yielding inefficient estimators. We argued that correct estimation of the CES model under the exclusion of arbitrary assumptions would imply use of the method of maximum likelihood.

We must therefore conclude that the advantages of the CES import allocation model as estimated by Hickman and Lau were not achieved without cost. Cost in the form of a simple specification for the functional form which is possibly far from economic reality, and also cost in the form of an estimation method with contradictory elements that avoids the computationally burdensome method of maximum likelihood. The gains are however worthwile : the model may easily be applied to a large number of trade partners, and requires a relatively simple method of estimation. The challenge for any alternative model is to maintain the same gains while at the same time reducing the costs. Such an attempt will be made in Chapter 5, in particular with respect to the strong assumption of constant and equal elasticities of substitution for all pairs of trade partners. That such a model would have to be estimated by the method of maximum likelihood should not raise objections : efficient estimation of the CES import allocation model would imply the same estimation method.

FOOTNOTES TO CHAPTER 2

1) For a deepening of this view, *cfr.* BRANSON (1972).

2) The prime denotes transposition.

3) *Cfr.* BERNDT and CHRISTENSEN (1973).

4) *Cfr.* ARMINGTON (1969a).

5) A function $f(x_1, \ldots, x_n)$ is said to be homothetic if it is a monotonically increasing transformation $f\,[g(x_1, \ldots, x_n)]$ of a function $g(x_1, \ldots, x_n)$ that is homogeneous of some positive degree.

6) For a counter-argument, *cfr.* MAKS (1980, pp. 29-31).

7) This notion should not be confused with the concept of *consistent* linkage, although they are related in a certain sense.

8) *Cfr.* BLACKORBY *et al.* (1975).

9) *Cfr.* SHEPARD (1953, p. 47). The import quantity index may even be a monotonic increasing function of a linear homogeneous index. In that case μ in (2.7) would be replaced by the inverse of the monotonic transformation.

10) These will be defined in the next chapter in more detail.

11) Hickman and Lau postulate two basic assumptions for the existence of a CES quantity index : 1) an assumption of independence (or weak separability as we called it in subsection 2.2.3) between imports and domestic consumption, 2) homotheticity of the import quantity index. They claim that the CES index is the only quantity index that satisfies both these assumptions. We will see in Chapter 5 that the CRESH index we introduce there is more general and satisfies the same assumptions, however.

12) *Cfr.* ARROW *et al.* (1961).

13) *Cfr.* HICKMAN and LAU (1973, p. 358).

CHAPTER 3 - ON THE USE OF ELASTICITIES OF SUBSTITUTION

3.1. INTRODUCTION

In the framework of an import allocation model, we usually work with bilateral imports from more than two trade partners, the demand for which is derived using a partial aggregator function or import quantity index. The choice of such a function is decisive for the substitution possibilities between the products supplied by the different trade partners. The question is how one may describe the substitution possibilities between products supplied by any pair of trade partners. One would like to give physical notions such as "strong" or "weak" substitutes a quantitative analogue. One would pose a similar question regarding the substitution possibilities among production factors in producer theory and among consumer goods in consumer theory. As long as the aggregator function involved in all these cases contains only two elements, the question may be given a sufficient answer in the form of a uniquely defined concept of *elasticity of substitution* (ES) which may be shown to have an acceptable economic interpretation. This concept was originally defined as representing the elasticity of the ratio of two factors with respect to their marginal rate of substitution [1). The concept may be applied to production theory, consumer theory, linkage models and many other fields. But when the number of factors in the aggregator function becomes greater than two, there is confusion in the different notions of ES that may be employed.

The reason for this confusion is that no straightforward generalization exists of the unique two-factor ES concept to which the most important multifactor ES definitions boil down if the number of factors is limited to be equal to two.

Because the import allocation models which we will consider in principle relate to more than two trade partners, the ES concept to be used in the context of these models is therefore not determined *a priori*. In fact there are several definitions that may be used as such. In this chapter we will present the main definitions of ES that have appeared in the literature so far, and we will discuss which of these concepts is the most suitable to be used, if at all. The definitions will be imbedded into a framework that may be used to characterize ES in general, and which was first designed in a pioneering paper by MUNDLAK (1968).

In his view, different definitions of ES are the result of different "economic experiments", in the sense of different mathematical programming problems, such as constrained cost minimization, profit maximization *etc.* And it is according to the lines of these experiments that the ES should be classified and used. Whether this happens in the context of production theory, consumer demand theory or any other field to which activity analysis applies is immaterial. In this chapter we will use the context of production theory, but the applications are general and may be applied to other fields, as we will demonstrate in examples.

Basically there are five different characterizations that apply to the experiments we distinguish for ES classification.

- The *number of production factors* that are involved. As stated above, when the number is restricted to two, most concepts are equal.
- The *variables which are held constant* in the experiment. Three cases may be distinguished :
  - constant output, or constrained cost minimization (cost minimization with a given level of utility in consumer theory),
  - constant cost, or constrained output maximization (utility maximization in consumer theory),
  - constant marginal cost, or profit maximization.
- The *number of variables* involved in the experiment. Three different possibilities will be considered :
  - one-factor, one-price measures,
  - two-factor, one-price measures,
  - two-factor, two-price measures.

- The distinction between *short-run* and *long-run* experiments. It is possible that in the short run not all factors adjust to price changes, for instance if they are faced with constraints. The ES in the short run will then possibly differ from those in the long run, where all factors are allowed to respond.
- The last characterization involves the fact whether ES are *constant* or not. This is a question that has appeared several times in the literature, and it has even been the cradle of different production functions, such as the Constant ES (CES) production function of ARROW *et al.* (1961). As such it is not a characterization of an economic experiment, but rather the result of specification and estimation properties. Because of its relevance for estimation we will nevertheless take it into consideration, although in a separate treatment.

In section 3.2 we give notation and start with the uniquely defined two-factor ES and its interpretation, followed by a presentation of some commonly used ES concepts for the case of more than two factors. Section 3.3 presents the different elasticities that result from keeping different variables constant, and prepares the ground for section 3.4, in which the different ES are derived through variation of the number of variables involved in the experiments. In section 3.5 we pay attention to the question of generalization to more than two factors of the archetype two-factor ES. In section 3.6 we go briefly into the case of short-run ES, while we treat the econometrically desirable feature of constant ES in section 3.7. In section 3.8, finally, we summarize, and give concluding remarks with respect to the question of whether one should use ES at all, and if so, which concept is the most appropriate.

3.2. BASIC DEFINITIONS

3.2.1. NOTATION

We will deal with a competitive firm with a production function

(2.1) $$y = f(x_1, \ldots, x_n),$$

with inputs $x_1, \ldots, x_n$ that have given prices $p_1, \ldots, p_n$. We assume for the ease of argument that the production function is well behaved [2), and in particular that it is twice continuously differentiable with positive marginal products

(2.2) $$f_i = \frac{\partial f}{\partial x_i} > 0, \qquad i = 1, \ldots, n,$$

and second-order partial derivatives

(2.3) $$f_{ij} = \frac{\partial^2 f}{\partial x_i \, \partial x_j} = f_{ji}, \qquad i,j = 1, \ldots, n,$$

which are symmetric in view of Young's Theorem [3).

The economic experiments we consider for this firm are mathematical programming problems, be it cost minimizing at constant output, output maximizing at constant cost or profit maximizing. One of the first-order conditions for these problems will always be of the kind

(2.4) $$f_i = \lambda p_i, \qquad i = 1, \ldots, n,$$

where $\lambda \neq 0$ is the Lagrange multiplier or its reciprocal, depending on the nature of the experiment. In the case of profit maximization it is the reciprocal of the output price.

We denote the $(n+1)\times(n+1)$ bordered Hessian matrix by F

$$F = \begin{bmatrix} 0 & f_1 & \cdots & f_n \\ f_1 & f_{11} & \cdots & f_{1n} \\ \vdots & \vdots & & \vdots \\ f_n & f_{n1} & \cdots & f_{nn} \end{bmatrix}, \tag{2.5}$$

and its inverse, multiplied by λ, by K, where K is also a symmetric matrix

$$K = \begin{bmatrix} k_{00} & k_{01} & \cdots & k_{0n} \\ k_{10} & k_{11} & \cdots & k_{1n} \\ \vdots & \vdots & & \vdots \\ k_{n0} & k_{n1} & \cdots & k_{nn} \end{bmatrix} = \lambda F^{-1}. \tag{2.6}$$

The bordered Hessian matrix is nonsingular, because we assume that the second-order sufficient condition for the mathematical programming problem holds, *cfr.* TAKAYAMA (1974, pp. 123-127).

From (2.5) and (2.6) it can easily be seen that the following relationships hold [4)]

$$\Sigma_j f_j k_{ij} = 0, \qquad i = 1, \ldots, n, \tag{2.7}$$

$$\Sigma_j f_j k_{0j} = \Sigma_i f_i k_{i0} = \lambda. \tag{2.8}$$

They will be needed later.

Because the production function is assumed to behave well, a well-behaved dual cost function [5)] will exist that expresses the cost of production as a function of output y and all prices

$$c = g(y, p_1, \ldots, p_n). \tag{2.9}$$

Also for the cost function, continuous partial (positive) first-order and (symmetric) second-order derivatives exist

$$(2.10) \qquad g_i = \frac{\partial g}{\partial p_i} > 0 , \qquad i = 1, \ldots, n,$$

$$(2.11) \qquad g_{ij} = \frac{\partial^2 g}{\partial p_i \, \partial p_j} = g_{ji} , \qquad i, j = 1, \ldots, n.$$

Finally we will use in the description of the experiments a vertical bar, on the right-hand side of which we indicate the variables that are kept constant in that experiment. These may be output y, cost c, the Lagrange multiplier (or its reciprocal) λ (in the case of profit maximization), and one or more of the factor quantities or their prices. Because the prices act in general as "instruments" with respect to which we analyze elasticities, we will not always indicate that prices other than those appearing in the elasticity formulas are given and constant.

3.2.2. THE TWO-FACTOR CASE

In the two-factor case, the production function (2.1) is of the form

$$(2.12) \qquad y = f(x_1, x_2).$$

Because we assumed the production function to be well behaved, we may draw an isoquant such as in figure 2.1 which is convex to the origin.

Let us consider two points A and B along the isoquant. Taking the total differential of the production function (2.12), we obtain that along the isoquant $(dy = 0)$ the slope of the tangency line to each point of the isoquant equals

$$(2.13) \qquad -\frac{dx_2}{dx_1} = \frac{f_1}{f_2} ,$$

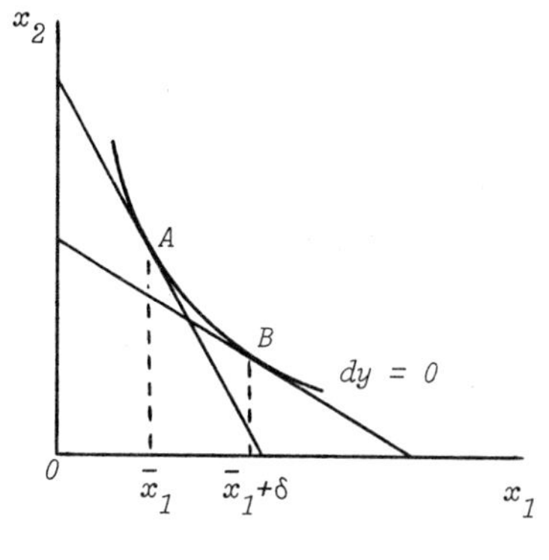

Figure 2.1 : The two-factor case

where the marginal productivities f_1 and f_2 are evaluated at the tangency points, in our case A or B. The expression (2.13) or the *marginal rate of substitution* directly translates the technical relationship (2.12) between output and production factors into a measure with which we may evaluate at each point of the isoquant the infinitesimal change in one production factor needed to maintain the same level of production upon an infinitesimal change in the other production factor. There are accordingly similar interpretations in consumer theory, regarding the substitution of consumer goods while maintaining a fixed level of utility, or for import allocation models, concerning the substitution among products supplied by different trade partners needed to keep the import quantity index constant. The actual substitution taking place between the factors x_1 and x_2 is displayed in the change of the factor ratio, which is the slope of the ray OA for point A and the slope of the ray OB for point B. If we consider figure 2.1 as a blow-up with the points A and B actually lying infinitely close to each other, the induced substitution of a change in x_1, say, from $\bar{x}_1$ to $\bar{x}_1 + \delta$ as represented in the factor ratios is therefore the change from OA to OB. This result is determined by the slope of the tangency line at point A or the marginal rate of substitution. The latter in its turn depends directly on the underlying technological structure as contained in the production function (2.12). This establishes a direct causal link between the technological structure (preference structure in consumer theory) and the implied substitution possibilities between production factors. In the form of an elasticity σ, this link may be established as the proportional change in the factor ratio x_2/x_1 with respect to a proportional change in the marginal rate of substitution f_1/f_2

$$(2.14) \qquad \sigma = \frac{dln(x_2/x_1)}{dln(f_1/f_2)} .$$

This is the form of the *elasticity of substitution* as proposed by ALLEN (1938, p. 341). Allen has furthermore shown that σ is symmetric with respect to the two factors x_1 and x_2 and positive, with two limiting cases. If x_1 and x_2 are *perfect substitutes*, constant output is maintained by changing one factor proportionately with a change in the other, and the isoquant is therefore a straight line, implying that the marginal rate of substitution is constant. This implies that the denominator of (2.14) becomes zero and therefore the ES σ tends to infinity. If x_1 and x_2 can *not be substituted* and are used in fixed proportions in the production process, an increase in only one of the production factors will not change the level of output. The isoquant therefore has a right angle at that particular point and σ will be zero. The ES therefore is bounded between zero and infinity, which values correspond exactly to the notions of non-substitutability and perfect substitutability. This confirms, at least for the two-factor case, the validity of σ as an economically meaningful concept to measure the ease with which two factors may be substituted.

An interesting illustrative case is the Constant-Elasticity-of-Substitution (CES) production function, introduced by ARROW *et al.* (1961)

$$(2.15) \qquad y = k\,[\,\alpha x_1^{-\rho} + (1-\alpha)x_2^{-\rho}\,]^{-1/\rho} .$$

The two-factor ES equals

$$(2.16) \qquad \sigma = \frac{1}{1+\rho} ,$$

and because $0 < \sigma < \infty$, the parameter $\rho \neq 0$ is restricted to $-1 < \rho < \infty$. In the limiting case $\sigma \to 0$ $(\rho \to \infty)$, the CES function reduces to the Leontief fixed input production function, and if $\sigma = 1$ $(\rho \to 0)$, we obtain the Cobb-Douglas function.

In figure 2.2 we have drawn the isoquants corresponding to different values of σ for the CES production function.

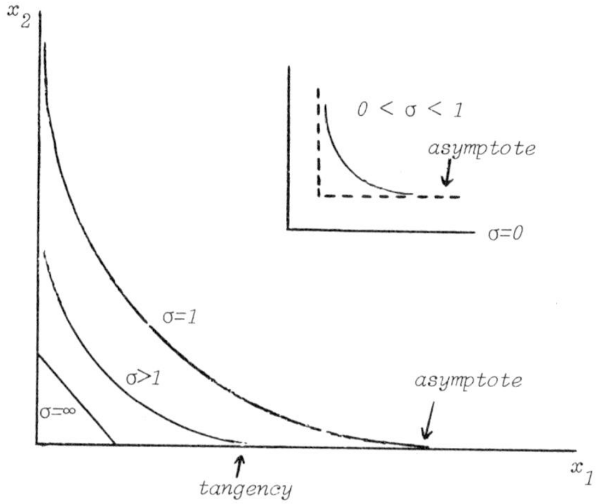

Figure 2.2 : The isoquants of the CES production function

For the Cobb-Douglas function ($\sigma = 1$) and the CES function with $0 < \sigma < 1$ the isoquant goes asymptotically to horizontal and vertical axes. If $\sigma > 1$, the isoquant is tangent to the x_1 and x_2 axis, and if $\sigma \to \infty$, the isoquant becomes a straight line. In the last case, a small shift in the marginal rate of substitution leads immediately to boundary solutions of the optimization problem to solve. The isoquant of the Leontief production function is L-shaped, and production is only possible in an efficient way along the ray through the origin and the corner of the isoquant.

3.2.3. MULTIFACTOR ELASTICITIES OF SUBSTITUTION

Perhaps the most widely used definition is that of ALLEN (1938). The partial *Allen Elasticity of Substitution* (AES) between factors i and j is defined as follows

$$(2.17) \quad A_{ij} = \frac{\Sigma_k x_k f_k}{x_i x_j} \left. \frac{F_{ij}}{|F|} \right|_y , \qquad i, j = 1, \ldots, n,$$

where F_{ij} is the co-factor of element f_{ij} in the bordered Hessian (2.5), and $|F|$ the determinant of the latter. Because of the definition of the matrix K in (2.6), we may define the AES alternatively as

$$(2.18) \quad A_{ij} = \frac{\Sigma_k x_k f_k}{x_i x_j} \left. \frac{k_{ij}}{\lambda} \right|_y , \qquad i, j = 1, \ldots, n.$$

For the definition of the AES it is assumed that cost is minimized keeping output constant, whereas all partial derivatives are evaluated at the optimal values [6)] of the factors $x_1, \ldots, x_n$.

Because we are in the framework of cost minimizing with constant output, the ratios between f_k and p_k will be equal to λ for all k from (2.4)

$$(2.19) \quad \frac{f_1}{p_1} = \ldots = \frac{f_n}{p_n} = \lambda ;$$

therefore the AES is equivalent with

$$(2.20) \quad A_{ij} = \frac{p_j}{x_i w_j} \left. k_{ij} \right|_y , \qquad i, j = 1, \ldots, n,$$

where w_j is the share of factor j in total cost in the optimum

$$(2.21) \qquad w_j = \frac{p_j\, x_j}{\Sigma_k\, p_k\, x_k}, \qquad j = 1, \ldots, n.$$

Furthermore, if the production function is homogeneous of degree one [7], we can use Euler's theorem [8] to demonstrate using (2.18) that

$$(2.22) \qquad A_{ij} = \frac{y}{x_i\, x_j} \left. \frac{k_{ij}}{\lambda} \right|_y, \qquad i, j = 1, \ldots, n.$$

The AES may also be defined in terms of the cost function. It was first shown by UZAWA (1962) that the AES can be written as [9]

$$(2.23) \qquad A_{ij} = \left. \frac{g\, g_{ij}}{g_i\, g_j} \right|_y, \qquad i, j = 1, \ldots, n.$$

Because of this important extension from duality theory, the AES is sometimes also referred to as the *Allen-Uzawa partial ES*. In the following we consider some of the properties of the AES.

First of all the AES is *symmetric*, as is clear from its definition (2.18) and the symmetry of K. We will see below that, because of this property, the AES can be considered as a "normalization" of the partial own and cross-price elasticities of demand.

Second, it is clear that the value of the AES depends on, and varies with, the *grouping of factors* that is employed. How the value varies depends on the context in which we use it. Notably in the context of import allocation models, we argued in Chapter 1 that the classification of categories of goods and the number of trade partners could be important determinants in this respect. Hypotheses concerning their influence on the equality of ES between pairs of trade partners will be tested in Chapter 9 and will shed some light on the behaviour of the AES concerning the grouping of factors.

Thirdly, there seems to be some confusion about what is the *partial* aspect of the AES. In the original contribution of ALLEN (1938, p. 504), he refers to what he calls the partial ES as :

> *"... the partial elasticity of substitution of the pair of factors ... (as against all other factors). ... it can be shown that they are related to the ordinary elasticities of substitution between two factors ... ."*

The ordinary ES he refers to is the unique two-factor ES, and therefore the AES is partial in the sense that we do not consider *all*, but only *two* factors at a time.

On the other hand, we find that MUNDLAK (1968, p. 232), when discussing partial ES in general seems to be referring to the number of prices that are changed :

> *"... one may generalize the concept of ES from partial to total, taking more price changes into account."*

Although Allen's interpretation seems more appropriate, the idea behind Mundlak's statement shows that we should be careful about which variables are involved in the definitions of ES.

A fourth property concerns conditions on the *signs* of the AES. Combine (2.19) and (2.20) to obtain

$$(2.24) \qquad w_j A_{ij} = \frac{f_j k_{ij}}{x_i \lambda}, \qquad i,j = 1, \ldots, n.$$

Summation of this expression over j and using (2.7) gives

$$(2.25) \qquad \Sigma_j w_j A_{ij} = 0 , \qquad i = 1, \ldots, n.$$

Because the second-order sufficient condition is equivalent to the condition that the principal minors of the bordered Hessian matrix F should alternate in sign [10], we obtain from (2.17) that

$$(2.26) \qquad A_{ii} < 0 \,, \qquad\qquad i = 1, \ldots, n,$$

and therefore (2.25) and (2.26) induce the following condition on the other AES

$$(2.27) \qquad \Sigma_{j\neq i}\, w_j\, A_{ij} > 0 \,, \qquad\qquad i = 1, \ldots, n.$$

The implication of (2.27) is that for $i \neq j$ the weighted sum of positive AES must exceed the absolute value of the weighted sum of negative AES, or that the weighted positive AES outweigh their negative counterparts. In particular, it is not possible that there exists a factor j for which $A_{ij} < 0$ for all $i = 1, \ldots, n$.

Finally we will consider the *interpretation* of the AES. If we extend the assumption of cost minimization at constant output by the assumption that the production function is homogeneous of degree one and that the market demand for the output of the firms is determined as a function of its product price p, equal to average cost, with elasticity η

$$(2.28) \qquad \eta = \frac{d\ln y}{d\ln p} < 0 \,,$$

then the average cost and marginal cost for the firm are both constant and equal to p [11]. It was shown by ALLEN (1938), that the (own or cross) price elasticity of the demand for factor i with respect to price j then equals

$$(2.29) \qquad \frac{\partial \ln x_i}{\partial \ln p_j} = w_j (A_{ij} + \eta), \qquad\qquad i,j = 1, \ldots, n.$$

From this expression we see that an increase in the price of factor j induces two changes. First, the product is now more expensive and this implies that it sells less, so there is a proportional decrease in the demand for all production factors. This effect is the negative term $w_j\,\eta$ in (2.29) which is negative by the law of demand. In consumption theory this effect would be the real income effect.

Secondly, factor j is now relatively more expensive than the other factors, and it is profitable to substitute other factors for it. For each factor, it depends on the sign of A_{ij} whether its demand increases or not. If $A_{ij} > 0$, Allen calls factor i *competitive* with j, we would now say that they are *substitutes*. If $A_{ij} < 0$, he calls i *complementary* to j. Upon a price increase for factor j, the demand for i will increase by $w_j A_{ij}$ if i is a substitute for j, but decrease by the same amount if they are complements. As we saw above in (2.27), on the whole the factors are more substitutable than complementary, and in particular it is not possible that a factor exists which is complementary to all others in the sense defined above.

From the interpretation of the AES in (2.29), it is clear that this concept relates the notion of substitution to prices. The direct causal link we could make in the previous section between the structure of the technology and the ease with which production factors may be substituted seems to be lost at first sight. The reason for this is that the isoquants such as the one drawn in figure 2.1 now become isoquants with not only output held constant, but also all factors other than the two displayed in the figure. But as a change in one of these two factors may induce changes in third factors, also the isoquant will move and may therefore change the result completely. This kind of analysis may for instance be used to explain the divergence between the technological or engineering *datum* of possible substitution between capital and energy and the econometric evidence in the form of AES indicating complementarity between these same two production factors [12)].

A second ES definition we turn our attention to is the *Direct Elasticity of Substitution* (DES), which, according to McFADDEN (1963), was first introduced by ALLEN and HICKS (1934). It is defined by the following expression, where partial derivatives are evaluated at the optimal values of $x_1, \ldots, x_n$

(2.30) $$D_{ij} = \frac{\dfrac{1}{x_i f_i} + \dfrac{1}{x_j f_j}}{-\dfrac{f_{ii}}{f_i^2} + 2\dfrac{f_{ij}}{f_i f_j} - \dfrac{f_{jj}}{f_j^2}} > 0 , \qquad i \neq j = 1, \ldots, n.$$

The partial DES is positive because of the strict quasi-concavity of the production function, if it is well behaved, which we assume to be the case.

Under cost minimization at constant output, the DES may be interpreted as

(2.31) $$D_{ij} = \left. \frac{\partial ln(x_i/x_j)}{\partial ln(p_j/p_i)} \right|_{y,\, x_{k\neq i,j}} , \qquad i \neq j = 1, \ldots, n,$$

the elasticity of the factor ratio with respect to its own relative price, holding constant (apart from output and other prices) all factor quantities other than i and j. This may be shown as follows. For the total differential of (2.1), put $dy = 0$ and $dx_k = 0$ for $k \neq i,j$; this gives

(2.32) $$dx_j = -\frac{f_i}{f_j}\, dx_i , \qquad i \neq j = 1, \ldots, n.$$

Similarly, the total differentials of f_i and f_j, with $dx_k = 0$ for $k \neq i,j$ and using (2.32) give

(2.33) $$df_j = (f_{ij} - \frac{f_i}{f_j} f_{jj}) dx_i , \qquad i \neq j = 1, \ldots, n,$$

(2.34) $$df_i = (f_{ii} - \frac{f_i}{f_j} f_{ij}) dx_i , \qquad i \neq j = 1, \ldots, n.$$

With (2.4), the formula for D_{ij}, (2.31), implies

$$(2.35)\qquad D_{ij} = \frac{\frac{1}{x_i}\,dx_i - \frac{1}{x_j}\,dx_j}{\frac{1}{f_j}\,df_j - \frac{1}{f_i}\,df_i}, \qquad i \neq j = 1, \ldots, n,$$

and substitution of (2.32)-(2.34) in this expression gives us the DES from (2.30).

Like the AES, the DES is *symmetric*, and it may furthermore be interpreted economically as a *short-run elasticity*, in the case that the other production factors cannot immediately adjust to factor price changes, and are fixed in the short run.

Because only two factors are allowed to change, the DES is necessarily *positive*, as stated above. This implies that we might have a situation in which the DES is positive and the AES negative for the same pair of factors. This illustrates the rather theoretical nature of the notion of DES.

Its interpretation becomes even more hampered if we consider the implications of changes in the two prices that compose the changing price ratio. Although other price ratios including one of the two changing prices then also change, we are not allowed to consider the consequences for the factor ratios corresponding to these other price ratios, since the DES for these pairs is not defined. The experiment then becomes dependent on the choice of the two factors for which we consider the DES. In the case of three factors, such as capital, labour and other inputs, it is perhaps not unreasonable that capital is fixed in the short run [13], but for other experiments similar assertions may be more difficult to defend, as in bilateral trade flow models.

Thirdly we present the definition of the *Shadow Elasticity of Substitution* (SES), introduced by McFADDEN (1963). It is defined by the following expression, where partial derivatives are evaluated at the optimal values of $y, p_1, \ldots, p_n$ [14]

$$(2.36) \qquad S_{ij} = \frac{\dfrac{-g_{ij}}{g_i^2} + 2\,\dfrac{g_{ij}}{g_i\,g_j} - \dfrac{g_{ij}}{g_i^2}}{\dfrac{1}{p_i\,g_i} + \dfrac{1}{p_j\,g_j}} > 0\,, \qquad i \neq j = 1, \ldots, n.$$

Like the DES, the SES is positive because of the concavity of the cost function that is implied by the concavity of the production function through the Shepard-Samuelson duality theorem [15].

Under cost minimization at constant output, the SES may be interpreted as

$$(2.37) \qquad S_{ij} = \left.\frac{\partial ln(x_i/x_j)}{\partial ln(p_j/p_i)}\right|_{y,c,p_{k\neq i,j}}\,, \qquad i \neq j = 1, \ldots, n,$$

the elasticity of the factor ratio with respect to its own relative price, holding constant total cost and all prices but p_i and p_j [16]. Because all other factors may adjust, it can be considered as a *long-run elasticity*. This is also the case for the AES, but the essential difference, as we will see below, is that the AES is a one-factor, one-price elasticity, whereas the SES is a two-factor, two-price measure.

Finally we give two definitions of ES that have been proposed by HANOCH (1978b). Both measures are two-factor, one-price concepts, and defined as the difference and the ratio, respectively, of two AES

$$(2.38) \qquad D_{ij}^k = A_{ik} - A_{ij}\,, \qquad i, k \neq j = 1, \ldots, n\,,$$

$$(2.39) \qquad R_{ij}^k = \frac{A_{ik}}{A_{ij}}\,, \qquad i, k \neq j = 1, \ldots, n\,.$$

Other definitions of ES applicable to production functions with more than two inputs have been proposed by authors as LAU (1978) and FRENGER (1978), but we will not consider them here.

3.3. THE NATURE OF THE EXPERIMENT

3.3.1. CONSTANT OUTPUT (CONSTRAINED COST MINIMIZATION)

The economic experiment, or mathematical programming problem, of constrained cost minimization will result in the following first-order conditions

$$f_i = \lambda\, p_i \,, \qquad i = 1, \ldots, n \,, \tag{3.1}$$

$$y - f(x_1, \ldots, x_n) = 0 \,, \tag{3.2}$$

where λ has the dimension of the inverse of the Lagrange multiplier. Taking total differentials, this system may be written in matrix notation as

$$x = Kq \,, \tag{3.3}$$

where x is the $(n+1)$x1 vector [17]

$$x = [\, -dln\, \lambda,\ dx_1,\ \ldots,\ dx_n\,]' \,, \tag{3.4}$$

K was defined in (2.6) and q is the $(n+1)$x1 vector

$$q = [\tfrac{1}{\lambda}\, dy,\ dp_1,\ \ldots,\ dp_n]' \,, \tag{3.5}$$

With the use of (3.3) we may derive the comparative statics results for a change in one of the prices or output.

First, starting from the optimum values, we keep output y constant $(dy = 0)$ and change only p_j, with all other prices unchanged. Because cost in the optimum is simply defined as

$$(3.6) \qquad c = \Sigma_k\, p_k\, x_k\,,$$

where x_k are the optimum values of factor k, we obtain for the elasticity of cost with respect to a change in p_j

$$(3.7) \qquad \left.\frac{\partial ln\ c}{\partial ln\ p_j}\right|_y = \frac{p_j\, x_j}{c} = w_j\,, \qquad j = 1, \ldots, n\,,$$

hence it equals the optimal share in total cost of factor j. Next, using (3.3) we obtain for the factor elasticity e_{ij}

$$(3.8) \qquad \left.\frac{\partial ln\ x_i}{\partial ln\ p_j}\right|_y = \frac{p_j}{x_i}\, k_{ij} = e_{ij} = A_{ij}\, w_j\,, \qquad i, j = 1, \ldots, n.$$

From this expression it is clear why the AES is sometimes called a "normalized" price elasticity :

$$(3.9) \qquad A_{ij} = \frac{e_{ij}}{w_j}\,, \qquad i, j = 1, \ldots, n\,,$$

it normalizes the factor price elasticities to be symmetric through division by the optimal value share w_j. Furthermore it shows how the factor elasticity is related to the Hessian matrix through k_{ij}.

Secondly, keeping all prices constant, we obtain from (3.3) the expression for the output elasticity e_{iy}

$$(3.10) \qquad \left.\frac{\partial ln\ x_i}{\partial ln\ y}\right|_{p_j} = e_{iy} = \frac{y}{x_i}\;\frac{k_{io}}{\lambda}\,, \qquad i, j = 1, \ldots, n.$$

3.3.2. CONSTANT COST (CONSTRAINED OUTPUT MAXIMIZATION)

The case of constrained output maximization corresponds to utility maximization subject to a budget constraint in consumer demand theory. The first-order conditions now become

$$(3.11) \qquad f_i = \lambda\, p_i\,, \qquad\qquad i = 1, \ldots, n\,,$$

$$(3.12) \qquad c - \Sigma_k\, p_k\, x_k = 0\,,$$

where λ is the Lagrange multiplier. Taking differentials we rewrite this system as follows in matrix notation

$$(3.13) \qquad x = Kr\,,$$

where x was defined in (3.4), and the $(n+1)\mathrm{x}1$ vector r equals the vector q of (3.5), except for the first element

$$(3.14) \qquad r = [\, dc - \Sigma_k\, x_k\, dp_k,\ dp_1,\ \ldots,\ dp_n]'\,.$$

Putting $dc = 0$ for constant cost we find for the partial price derivative of factor i with respect to factor j

$$(3.15) \qquad \left.\frac{\partial x_i}{\partial p_j}\right|_c = k_{ij} - x_j \left.\frac{\partial x_i}{\partial c}\right|_{p_k}$$

$$= k_{ij} - x_j\, k_{i0}\,, \qquad\qquad i, j, k = 1, \ldots, n,$$

which corresponds to the Hicks-Slutsky equation in demand theory.

Keeping all prices constant, we have for the elasticity of factor i with respect to total cost (the equivalence of income elasticity in demand theory), e_{ic},

$$(3.16) \qquad \left.\frac{\partial ln\ x_i}{\partial ln\ c}\right|_{p_k} = e_{ic} = k_{i0}\frac{c}{x_i} = \lambda\frac{c}{y}e_{iy}\ , \qquad i,\ k = 1,\ \ldots,\ n.$$

This expression may be used to derive

$$(3.17) \qquad \left.\frac{\partial ln\ x_i}{\partial ln\ p_j}\right|_{c} = e_{ij}\bigg|_{c} = e_{ij} - w_j\, e_{ic}\ , \qquad i,\ j = 1,\ \ldots,\ n.$$

Furthermore we find that the elasticity of output with respect to p_j is equal to the elasticity of production with respect to factor j, β_j, say,

$$(3.18) \qquad -\left.\frac{\partial ln\ y}{\partial ln\ p_j}\right|_{c} = \frac{p_j}{y}\lambda\, x_j = \frac{x_j}{y}f_j = \frac{\partial ln\ y}{\partial ln\ x_j} = \beta_j\ , \qquad j = 1,\ \ldots,\ n.$$

3.3.3. CONSTANT MARGINAL COST (PROFIT MAXIMIZATION)

The first-order conditions in the case of profit maximization consist of

$$(3.19) \qquad f_i = \lambda\, p_i\ , \qquad i = 1,\ \ldots,\ n\ ,$$

one of the conditions (3.2) and (3.12), and

$$(3.20) \qquad \frac{1}{\lambda} = p\ ,$$

where p is the price of output.

In (3.2) and (3.12), output y and cost c do not have to be considered as fixed in this case, they are part of the variables with respect to which the optimum is attained.

Keeping constant marginal cost amounts to $d\ln \lambda = 0$, which we are going to use in (3.3) and (3.13). From the first elements of these vector-valued equations we may derive

$$\text{(3.21)} \qquad \frac{1}{\lambda}\frac{\partial y}{\partial p_j}\bigg|_{\lambda} = \frac{\partial c}{\partial p_j}\bigg|_{\lambda} - x_j = -\frac{k_{0j}}{k_{00}}, \qquad j = 1, \ldots, n,$$

given that $k_{00} \neq 0$. But we also notice from (3.3) that

$$\text{(3.22)} \qquad k_{00} = -\frac{\partial \lambda}{\partial y}\bigg|_{p_k}, \qquad k = 1, \ldots, n.$$

Therefore $k_{00} = 0$ is equivalent to the situation in which the production function is homogeneous of degree one, which is not the case if the experiment involves profit maximization.

Next we obtain from (3.3)

$$\text{(3.23)} \qquad \frac{\partial x_i}{\partial p_j}\bigg|_{\lambda} = k_{ij} + \frac{\partial y}{\partial p_j}\bigg|_{\lambda} \frac{\partial x_i}{\partial y}\bigg|_{p_k}, \qquad i, j, k = 1, \ldots, n,$$

which can be written in elasticity form as

$$\text{(3.24)} \qquad \frac{\partial \ln x_i}{\partial \ln p_j}\bigg|_{\lambda} = e_{ij}\bigg|_{\lambda} = e_{ij} + b_j\, e_{iy}, \qquad i, j = 1, \ldots, n,$$

with b_j defined as

$$\text{(3.25)} \qquad b_j = \frac{\partial \ln y}{\partial \ln p_j}\bigg|_{\lambda}, \qquad j = 1, \ldots, n.$$

Starting from (3.12) we can calculate in a similar way

$$(3.26)\qquad \left.\frac{\partial ln\ x_i}{\partial ln\ p_j}\right|_\lambda = e_{ij}\Big|_\lambda = e_{ij}\Big|_c + a_j\, e_{ic}\,, \qquad i,j = 1, \ldots, n,$$

with a_j defined as

$$(3.27)\qquad a_j = \left.\frac{\partial ln\ c}{\partial ln\ p_j}\right|_\lambda , \qquad j = 1, \ldots, n.$$

The factor price elasticity of factor i with respect to price j under profit maximization may then be expressed in terms of that elasticity under constant output or constant cost, and the corresponding output or cost elasticities e_{iy} and e_{ic}.

Finally, using (3.16), (3.17), (3.24) and (3.26) we observe that

$$(3.28)\qquad a_j - w_j = \frac{y}{c\lambda}\, b_j = \frac{py}{c}\, b_j\,, \qquad j = 1, \ldots, n\,,$$

which links the a_j to the b_j.

3.4. A FRAMEWORK FOR ELASTICITIES

3.4.1. ONE-FACTOR, ONE-PRICE ELASTICITIES OF SUBSTITUTION (OOES)

The OOES describes the effect on a single factor of production if we change only one price and keep all other prices constant during the experiment. In fact we have already calculated all the elasticities that are involved, but we will change the notation. We will use the letters H, I and M to indicate which variables are constant during the experiment

H - constant output (demand theory : Hicks compensation)
I - constant cost (demand theory : constant Income)
M - constant marginal cost (demand theory : constant Marginal utility of income)

We will let superscripts denote prices, and subscripts denote factors. Furthermore we assume that profit maximization takes place under least cost attainment. Then we can rewrite (3.8), (3.17) and (3.26) as

$$(4.1) \qquad H_i^j = \left.\frac{dln\ x_i}{dln\ p_j}\right|_y = e_{ij} = w_j A_{ij}, \qquad i, j = 1, \ldots, n,$$

$$(4.2) \qquad I_i^j = \left.\frac{dln\ x_i}{dln\ p_j}\right|_c = \left. e_{ij}\right|_c = H_i^j - w_j e_{ic}, \qquad i,j = 1, \ldots, n,$$

$$(4.3) \qquad M_i^j = \left.\frac{dln\ x_i}{dln\ p_j}\right|_\lambda = I_i^j + a_j e_{ic}, \qquad i,j = 1, \ldots, n,$$

It is clear that the OOES framework is the one to which the partial AES belongs. Furthermore, only (4.1) measures changes along a given isoquant, the other two elasticities involve expansion effects due to a change in real costs following the price change of p_j.

3.4.2. TWO-FACTOR, ONE-PRICE ELASTICITIES OF SUBSTITUTION (TOES)

The TOES case is in fact the case in which we consider the effect on the ratio of two factors of a change in the relative price of these factors, but keeping one of the two prices constant. The general expression is

$$(4.4) \qquad (.)^j_{ir} = \frac{dln\ (x_i/x_r)}{dln\ p_j} \qquad i,j = 1, \ldots, n\ ,$$

with $(.)$ to be substituted by H, I or M. From (4.1)-(4.3) it is easy to derive

$$(4.5) \qquad H^j_{ir} = H^j_i - H^j_r = w_j(A_{ij} - A_{rj})\ , \qquad i,j,r = 1, \ldots, n,$$

$$I^j_{ir} = I^j_i - I^j_r = H^j_{ir} - w_j(e_{ic} - e_{rc})\ , \qquad i,j,r = 1, \ldots, n,$$

$$M^j_{ir} = M^j_i - M^j_r = I^j_{ir} + a_j(e_{ic} - e_{rc})\ ,$$

$$= H^j_{ir} + (a_j - w_j)(e_{ic} - e_{rc})\ , \quad i,j,r = 1, \ldots, n.$$

The three above TOES will be equal if and only if $e_{ic} = e_{rc}$ for all i, $r = 1, \ldots, n$, *e.g.* if the production function is homothetic [18] with respect to x_i and x_r. Otherwise the real-cost effects will also induce expansionary effects on the ES.

3.4.3. TWO-FACTOR, TWO-PRICE ELASTICITIES OF SUBSTITUTION (TTES)

This is the case of the usual definition of ES

$$(4.8) \qquad (.)^{js}_{ir} = \frac{dln(x_i/x_r)}{dln(p_s/p_j)} ,$$

where we will delete the superscripts if the pair js is equal to ir, which is the case with which we will start. Furthermore we will assume that both prices change, because otherwise we are in the case of TOES defined above. Taking the total differential in the numerator of (4.8) and putting the relevant partial derivatives equal to zero, the three TTES become

$$(4.9) \qquad H_{ir} = \frac{(e_{ii} - e_{ri})\ dln\ p_i + (e_{ir} - e_{rr})\ dln\ p_r}{dln\ (p_r/p_i)}$$

$$(4.10) \qquad I_{ir} = H_{ir} - \frac{(e_{ic} - e_{rc})(w_i\ dln\ p_i + w_r\ dln\ p_r)}{dln\ (p_r/p_i)}$$

$$(4.11) \qquad M_{ir} = I_{ir} + \frac{(e_{ic} - e_{rc})(a_i\ dln\ p_i + a_r\ dln\ p_r)}{dln\ (p_r/p_i)}$$

$$= H_{ir} + \frac{(e_{ic} - e_{rc})\ [\ (a_i - w_i)\ dln\ p_i + (a_r - w_r)\ dln\ p_r]}{dln\ (p_r/p_i)}$$

$$i,\ r = 1,\ \ldots,\ n$$

Like in the TOES case, the three concepts are equal if $e_{ic} = e_{rc}$ for all $i, r = 1, \ldots, n$, *e.g.* if the production function is homothetic with respect to the factors x_i and x_r. Furthermore the TTES depend on the magnitudes of $dln\ p_i$ and $dln\ p_r$. Therefore, if we consider *specific* changes in prices, we will get *specific* TTES.

One such case is the experiment in which we also keep cost fixed, apart from output. Using the fact that with (2.4) and the total differential of (2.1) we have

$$(4.12) \qquad dc = \Sigma_j\ p_j\ dx_j + \Sigma_j\ x_j\ dp_j = \frac{1}{\lambda}\ dy + \Sigma_j\ x_j\ dp_j ,$$

we obtain from imposing $dc = dy = dp_j = 0\ (j \neq i,\ r)$ the following relationship between the price changes

$$(4.13) \qquad 0 = w_i \, dln \, p_i + w_r \, dln \, p_r \qquad\qquad i, r = 1, \ldots, n.$$

Note that we obtain in this particular experiment

$$(4.14) \qquad H_{ir} \Big|_c = I_{ir} \Big|_y ,$$

because the second term in (4.10) vanishes because of (4.13). Furthermore we obtain after solving (4.13) for $dln\ p_i$ or $dln\ p_r$ from insertion in (4.9), with (3.9),

$$(4.15) \qquad H_{ir} \Big|_c = \frac{w_i \, w_r}{w_i + w_r} [- A_{ii} + 2 \, A_{ir} - A_{rr}] = S_{ir} ,$$

the SES of (2.36). The last equality follows from (2.37) because we impose $dc = dy = dp_j \ (j \neq i, r)$. Note that we only obtained the SES because we considered a specific experiment which involved a specific relationship between the price changes. Other restrictions on the price changes will induce other specific forms of the TTES.

If the pair js is not equal to ir in (4.8) we get formulas similar to (4.9)-(4.11), but with changed subscripts.

3.5. A GENERALIZATION OF THE TWO-FACTOR CASE ?

The two-factor definition of ES is in terms of fixed output y and cost minimization

(5.1) $$\sigma = \left.\frac{d\ln\,(x_1/x_2)}{d\ln\,(p_2/p_1)}\right|_y$$

Because there are in all two factors, equations (2.7) can be written as

(5.2) $$e_{11} + e_{12} = 0\,,$$
$$e_{21} + e_{22} = 0\,.$$

Substituting (5.2) in (4.9) we obtain

(5.3) $$H_{12} = e_{12} + e_{21} = A_{12}(w_1 + w_2) = A_{12} = \sigma\,.$$

Using (4.15) and (5.2) we also find that

(5.4) $$I_{12}\,\Big|_y = H_{12}\,\Big|_c = S_{12} = A_{12}\,.$$

Finally we also find that the third TTES, $M_{12}\,\Big|_y$, is equal to A_{12}. This can be established using the second formula of (4.11), (3.28) and the fact that $b_j = 0$ if y is kept constant.

(5.5) $$M_{12}\,\Big|_y = H_{12} = A_{12}\,.$$

The conclusion we can draw is that all TTES collapse into (5.1) if there are only two factors and if we keep output constant.

A question which arises is whether a natural generalization of the unique two-factor ES exists, with output assumed to be fixed. The answer is yes and no.

Yes, because H_{ir} is an unrestricted generalization of (5.1), unrestricted in the sense that (4.9) does not impose restrictions on the price changes, similar to (5.1). The SES, for instance, is not to be considered as a generalization of σ, because of the price restrictions (4.13).

But no, because H_{ir} does depend on the way in which the prices are changed, which is not the case for σ, as can be seen from (5.3).

Therefore, if a generalization of the two-factor case exists, it is H_{ir}, and certainly not the partial AES. The fundamental reason for this is the fact that the AES is based on a one-factor, one-price concept, contrary to the two-factor, two-price idea embedded in definition (5.1).

3.6. SHORT-RUN ELASTICITIES OF SUBSTITUTION

All the ES derived in section 3.4 were based on the assumption that all factor quantities can adjust freely without constraints. As we usually take it that such is the case in the long term, we may call all these measures *long-run* ES. As soon as one or more factors cannot adjust immediately, we obtain concepts that are essentially of a short-run nature (if we forget for the moment that there may exist something like the medium run). These we shall denominate therefore as *short-run ES*.

An important class of such ES is the one in which we only allow two factors to change after a change in factor prices. One member of this class is the DES defined in section 3.2. If there are more than two factors, the DES measures the substitution along an isoquant with all other inputs held constant. In terms of section 3.4, the DES is a TTES, but the concept of only two factors that may change can equally be applied to OOES and TOES.

The way to do this is to apply the formulas of section 3.4, but keeping constant all but two factors. Since these results are treated extensively by MUNDLAK (1968), we will not present them here.

One interesting conclusion of his derivations is however worthwile mentioning here : it states that a sufficient condition for the long-run and short-run H_{ir} to be equal is the weak separability of pair ir with respect to a third, composite, good, in the sense that the marginal rate of substitution between i and r is independent of the quantity of this third good.

This may be illustrated by the following example. Suppose the production function (2.1) we are considering is the two-level CES production function of SATO (1967). Partition the set of indices $N = \{1, \ldots, n\}$ into r mutually exclusive and exhaustive subjects $N_1, \ldots, N_r$. Then Sato's function is defined as

$$(6.1) \qquad y = [\Sigma_{s=1}^{r} \alpha_s z_s^{-\rho}]^{-1/\rho},$$

with $\alpha_s > 0$, $s = 1, \ldots, r$, $0 \neq \rho > -1$ and the partial aggregator function z_s defined as

$$(6.2) \qquad z_s = [\Sigma_{i \in N_s} \beta_i x_i^{-\rho_s}]^{-1/\rho_s},$$

with $\beta_i > 0$, $i = 1, \ldots, n$ and $0 \neq \rho_s > -1$, $s = 1, \ldots, r$. Next, suppose $n = 4$ and $r = 2$ with N_1 containing the production factors capital and energy and N_2 consisting of labour and other inputs, respectively. Then the DES and SES between capital and energy will be equal to each other, and similarly for labour and other inputs. This is clearly the result of the weak separability of capital and energy with respect to labour and other inputs as implied by (6.1)-(6.2).

3.7. CONSTANT ELASTICITIES OF SUBSTITUTION

Once the ES is introduced as a measure of the degree of substitutability, it is of interest to obtain empirical values for it. Given that for empirical purposes one is bound to convenient functional forms with a limited number of parameters, constancy of the ES concept one uses would be an advantage. This is the reason why several authors have been trying, given a particular ES measure, to obtain the most general functional form that keeps that particular definition of ES constant.

For the two factor case, actually, it was this way of putting matters that led ARROW *et al.* (1961) to the specification of what is now commonly known as the CES function. This is the most general functional form that has a constant ES in the two-factor case.

If there are more than two factors, the characterization depends of course on the ES concept used. Regarding the AES there are two results, both due to UZAWA (1962). The first says that the most general functional form for which the AES are *constant* and *identical*, is the multifactor CES function

$$(7.1) \qquad y = (\alpha_1 x_1^{-\rho} + \ldots + \alpha_n x_n^{-\rho})^{-1/\rho}$$

with $\rho > -1$ and $\alpha_i > 0$ for $i = 1, \ldots, n$ (and $\rho \neq 0$).

The second result says that all AES are *constant* (but not necessarily identical) if and only if there exists a partition $\{N_1, \ldots, N_K\}$ of the set $\{1, \ldots, n\}$ of n factors of production such that the AES satisfy

$$(7.2) \qquad A_{ij} = \begin{cases} 1 & \text{if } i \in N_s, \; j \in N_t, \; s \neq t \\ \sigma_k = \dfrac{1}{1+\rho_k} & \text{if } i, j \in N_k \end{cases}$$

and the production function is of the form

(7.3) $$y = \Pi_{k=1}^{K} [f^k(x^k)]^{\gamma_k} \qquad \gamma_k > 0 \; , \; \Sigma_{k=1}^{K} \gamma_k = 1 \; ,$$

where x^k is the set of factors corresponding to N_k and

(7.4) $$f^k(x^k) = [\Sigma_{i \in N_k} \alpha_i x_i^{-\rho_k}]^{-1/\rho_k}$$

with $\alpha_i > 0$, $i = 1, \ldots, n$ and $-1 < \rho_k < \infty$, $\rho_k \neq 0$, $k = 1, \ldots, K$

In the terminology of SATO (1967), this is a two-level function of which the "outer" function is a Cobb-Douglas function while the "inner" functions are CES functions. The ES between factors that belong to different partitions equals one, and between factors in the same partition they are all equal but differing per partition.

The conditions under which the DES and SES are constant have been analyzed by McFADDEN (1963). The implied functional forms are similar because of the dual nature of the DES and the SES. Essentially it concerns two-level functions of which the "outer" function is a CES function and of which the "inner" functions have the Cobb-Douglas form with the exponents equal to one. Although we do not present the rather lengthy precise definitions, it is worth noting that the implied AES within a partition equals one and is equal to one common value of ES for factors belonging to different partitions.

Constancy of the R_{ij}^k defined in (2.39) was proved by GORMAN (1965) to be equivalent to the existence of a production function $y = f(x_1, \ldots, x_n)$ that is defined implicitly as

(7.5) $$\Sigma_{i=1}^{n} D_i(y)\, x_i^{d_i(y)} \equiv 1 ,$$

where

(7.6) $$d_i(y) = 1 - \frac{1}{\theta(y) a_i} ,$$

assuming that a_i, $D_i(y)$ and $\theta(y)$ keep the production function well-behaved. The implied (non-constant) AES of this function have been calculated by HANOCH (1978b) to be equal to

(7.7) $$A_{ij} = \theta(y) \frac{a_i\, a_j}{\Sigma_{k=1}^{n} w_k\, a_k} , \qquad i \neq j = 1, \ldots, n ,$$

where

(7.8) $$w_k = \frac{p_k\, x_k}{\Sigma_h\, p_h\, x_h} ,$$

the (variable) share of costs in the optimal situation. The value of constant R_{ij}^{k} is then given by

(7.9) $$R_{ij}^{k} = a_i / a_j , \qquad i \neq j \neq k = 1, \ldots, n.$$

For obvious reasons, the model (7.5) is called the Constant Ratio of ES (CRES) model. It comprises special cases such as the CRESH function[19] of HANOCH (1971), which is homothetic, and the non-homothetic function of MUKERJI (1963).

Applying the Polar transformation (see HANOCH (1978a, p. 118)) to a somewhat less general form of (7.5) generates the cost function for which the ES defined in (2.38) are constant. The AES associated with this function equals

$$(7.10)\qquad A_{ij} = \frac{1}{a_i} + \frac{1}{a_j} - \Sigma_{k=1}^{n} w_k \frac{1}{a_k}, \qquad i \neq j = 1, \ldots, n ,$$

where w_k are optimal cost shares and a_i parameters of the cost function. The value of constant D^k_{ij} becomes

$$(7.11)\qquad D^k_{ij} = \frac{1}{a_i} + \frac{1}{a_j}, \qquad i \neq j \neq k = 1, \ldots, n.$$

The cost function associated with this model is called the Constant Difference of ES (CDE) cost function. For details we refer to HANOCH (1978b).

Although the constancy of ES is of interest for empirical purposes, we observe that the non-uniqueness of the ES concept when there are more than two production factors makes it arbitrary to look for production or cost structures that are associated with constant ES. Indeed, one might choose any suitable definition of ES which, when kept constant, would correspond to any preselected production or cost function.

And when the ES concept is unique (the two-factor case), the result is restrictive because the ES between all factor pairs is equal. The conclusion is that constancy of the ES, albeit useful for estimation, is neither of interest as a characterization, nor a desirable property of production functions.

3.8. SUMMARY AND CONCLUDING REMARKS

In this chapter we have dealt with the question of whether it is possible to describe physical substitution possibilities in a quantitative way, notably in the form of an elasticity of substitution (ES). We saw that in the case of an aggregator function with two factors there exists a unique concept of ES that provides a clear link between underlying technological structures and the implied substitution possibilities. In the framework of neoclassical optimizing behaviour, this concept may furthermore be defined in terms of relative price changes. When there are more than two factors, a natural generalization of the two-factor definition does not exist in the sense that this generalization should also be independent of the amount by which the prices change. Otherwise a generalization would be the Hicksian two-factor, two-price definition of (4.9).

The lack of a natural generalization of the two-factor concept implies the existence of several alternative ES definitions for when the aggregator function contains more than two factors. The analysis of these alternatives would be facilitated if it could start from a framework which allows one to distinguish between the different ES on the basis of different characterizations, such as the tool developed by MUNDLAK (1968). Therefore, after a presentation of the most frequently used multifactor ES, we were able to classify them according to different characteristics, such as the nature of the economic experiment (constant cost, constant output, profit maximization), the number of factors, the distinction between short run and long run and the kind of variables that are changed (prices, output). Although aggregator functions that have a constant ES for any of the multifactor definitions may be of empirical use, it was argued in section 3.7 that constancy could not be considered as a characterization of an ES.

The physical substitution possibilities as embodied in the aggregator function find a direct translation in the form of the Hessian matrix. It is therefore important that multifactor concepts of ES, in order to provide a correct link with the notion of physical substitution, can be interpreted in terms of elements of the underlying Hessian matrix. In sections 3.3 and 3.4 it was shown that this was indeed the case for concepts such as OOES, TOES and TTES. One could even go one step further and no longer look at concepts of ES, but try to deal with the elements of the Hessian matrix directly, because they are bearers of the underlying technology. The one-factor, one-price measures defined in section 3.4, although not necessarily pure measures of substitution because they are far from a generalization of the archetype two-factor ES, are the most obvious candidates in this respect, because they are directly related to the Hessian matrix. In the case of the experiment with constant output therefore (which may be identified with the derivation of the import allocation model), one would look at the own or cross-price elasticities of demand. The multifactor ES concept which comes closest to these elasticities is the AES, which can be considered as a normalization of the price elasticities rendering them symmetric.

The choice for the AES is therefore made not because it is closest to a generalization of the two-factor case, but because it is closest to the underlying technological structure.

As a final remark, it should be emphasized that we have analyzed in this chapter ES in their role as quantitative measures of physical possibilities of substitution. They may however also serve other purposes, for instance to describe second-order sufficient conditions in the context of neoclassical optimization [20)], or as characterizations for necessary and sufficient conditions for certain forms of separability of the aggregator function [21)]. We should also mention the work of *e.g.* LAU (1976) and JUNIUS (1977, pp. 25-31) who, starting from a given class of ES functions, tried to characterize the underlying technology in the form of the cost function or the production function, respectively. Their results indicate that knowledge of a set of ES functions leaves a degree of freedom in the characterization of the technology. Because a set of integrable demand functions provides a complete characterization of the technology through the cost functions, LAU (1976, p. 357) suggests that, instead of looking at the ES, one should perhaps concentrate on the reduced form demand equations and their output and price elasticities. This suggestion is close to the one we made above, although in a slightly different context.

FOOTNOTES TO CHAPTER 3

1) This definition is from ALLEN (1938, p. 341). The original definition of ES was made in the context of a linear homogeneous production function, which is a more restrictive case, *cfr.* HICKS (1932, p. 117 and 245).

2) We make this statement without stating which are the properties of the production function. We simply assume that these properties are sufficient for our purposes. Standard properties may be found in introductory texts such as TAKAYAMA (1974). For a thorough treatment, see JUNIUS (1977).

3) *Cfr.* ALLEN (1938, pp. 300-302).

4) In this chapter all summations run from 1 to n, unless otherwise indicated.

5) *Cfr., e.g.,* DIEWERT (1974).

6) We will use the expression "optimal" to indicate values that are the outcome of the optimization problem associated with (2.4).

7) A function $f(x_1, \ldots, x_n)$ is homogeneous of degree r in $x_1, \ldots, x_n$ if $f(\lambda x_i, \ldots, \lambda x_n) \equiv \lambda^r f(x_1, \ldots, x_n)$ for each real $\lambda \neq 0$.

8) Euler's theorem : suppose $f(x_1, \ldots, x_n)$ is homogeneous of degree r. Then $f_1 x_1 + \ldots + f_n x_n = r\, f(x_1, \ldots, x_n)$.

9) That is, for linear homogeneous production functions.

10) See for instance TAKAYAMA (1974, pp. 123-127).

11) This may be seen as follows. The average cost $p = c/y$ equals $\Sigma_i\, p_i\, x_i/y = (1/\lambda)\Sigma_i\, x_i\, f_i/y = 1/\lambda$ with (2.19) and Euler's Theorem. The marginal cost $\partial c/\partial y$ equals $\Sigma_i\, p_i(\partial x_i/\partial y) = (1/\lambda)\Sigma_i\, f_i\, (\partial x_i/\partial y) = (1/\lambda)$ with again (2.19) and the differential of (2.1) with respect to output y.

12) *Cfr.* BERNDT and WOOD (1977), and HOGAN (1979) for a further diagrammatic exposition.

13) Another example is from MEADE (1962, pp. 97-98), who uses a production function with three factors : machinery, labour and land, and keeps land constant.

14) These are the optimal values of the optimization of the dual problem.

15) See for instance DIEWERT (1974).

16) The proof of this assertion is exactly dual to that for the DES because of the dual nature of the two. Hence it is omitted.

17) A prime denotes transposition.

18) *Cfr.* footnote 5 of Chapter 2.

19) This function will be treated extensively in Chapter 5.

20) *Cfr.* HANOCH (1971).

21) *Cfr.* BERNDT and CHRISTENSEN (1973) or BLACKORBY *et al.* (1978, pp. 264-272).

CHAPTER 4 - MAXIMUM LIKELIHOOD ESTIMATION OF NONLINEAR MODELS WITH LINEAR CONSTRAINTS ON THE FUNCTIONAL FORM

4.1. INTRODUCTION

In several econometric applications, one encounters the problem that the functional form of the model which has to be estimated, *i.e.* the equations without the (additive) disturbance terms, should satisfy one or more homogeneous linear constraints at each point in discrete time. Examples of models in which such a situation arises are complete systems of demand equations in consumer theory and models for brand choice, traffic flows in supermarkets or consumer credit usage. The estimation-consistent import allocation models which we presented in Chapter 2 also usually fall in this category. Because of the generality of the problems that arise for the estimation of models with such constraints, we will treat them in this chapter in a general fashion such that they maintain a wide applicability.

It is possible that the constraints should apply to all functional form equations, or only to subsets, such as in the estimation of Engel curves. For such models to be true, the constraints carry over to the vector of disturbances, implying that their covariance matrix becomes singular. The singular covariance matrix impedes estimation of the model as a whole, because that requires the inverse of the covariance matrix.

We will call such models *constrained models*. Furthermore we distinguish between *linear* and *nonlinear* constrained models, depending on whether a model is linear or nonlinear in its parameters [1]. The coefficients of the linear constraints, or *weights* as we will call them, will be collected in the *matrix of weights*. If there is only one constraint, this matrix becomes a vector, and will be referred to as such.

The usual solution to the singularity problem is to delete as many equations as there are independent constraints, and to estimate only this *"lopped"* model, where one should take care to delete equations in such a way that the covariance matrix of the vector of disturbances of the remaining equations is nonsingular. If the lopped model is estimated by the method of maximum likelihood, the matter arises of whether the value of the likelihood function in its maximum and the corresponding parameter values (which may include the covariance matrix) depend on the set of equations which is deleted. Until now it has not been recognized that there may be a disparity between the conditions under which the value of the likelihood function is independent of the identity of the deleted equations and the conditions that guarantee such an independency for the maximum likelihood estimator. With the use of a nonlinear constrained model, we will make this distinction explicit in this chapter. We will allow for more than one constraint, and let the matrix of weights be time-dependent initially.

The constrained model that we have thus conceived will be sufficiently general to include as special cases the main results derived in the literature so far. These results comprise the findings of BARTEN (1969), that pertain to the linear constrained model with one constraint, although his results may be seen to be equally valid for the nonlinear constrained model with one constraint. He obtained that if the vector of weights is the vector of units, the value of the probability density function of the lopped vector of disturbances (and therefore the value of the corresponding likelihood function) does not depend on the deleted equation. Also the estimator of the parameters (including the covariance matrix) is independent of the deleted equation in that case under stepwise maximum likelihood estimation, where the covariance matrix is concentrated out.

A similar result concerning the value of the likelihood function was found by McGUIRE *et al.* (1968). Their elegant proof makes use of the properties of singular normal distributions [2)]. Furthermore, they demonstrated that generalized least squares estimation of the parameters (excluding the covariance matrix) of the lopped linear constrained model with one or more time-independent restrictions is independent of the deleted equation.

This result holds both with a known or unknown covariance matrix. In the latter case they proposed to use a two-pass generalized least squares estimator.

POWELL (1969), who proved the same result for the special case of one constraint and known covariance matrix, suggested that in the case of an unknown covariance matrix one could estimate the model parameters and the covariance matrix simultaneously, or by applying the method of ZELLNER (1962). Both methods will provide consistent estimators of the model parameters, although the asymptotic efficiency of the former method will be greater than that of the latter [3]. An obvious method to use for simultaneous estimation of the model parameters and the covariance matrix is the *maximum likelihood method*, with its desirable properties of consistency, asymptotic efficiency and asymptotically normal distribution.

Also for the purpose of the present chapter we will consider the maximum likelihood method. With the use of our general nonlinear constrained model we will analyze two different cases, corresponding to whether the covariance matrix is *homoscedastic* or *heteroscedastic*, where we assume a special form of heteroscedasticity. For each case we will look into the conditions under which the maximum likelihood estimator and the value of the likelihood function are independent of the identity of the deleted equation(s). This will be done in sections 4.3 and 4.4, after we have introduced more formal definitions for the constrained model and the lopped model in section 4.2. In the last section we summarize and give some conclusions.

4.2. CONSTRAINED MODEL AND LOPPED MODEL

The model is assumed to consist of n equations that may possibly be non-linear in their parameters. For the moment the disturbances are only assumed to be additive. We take it that this model has to be estimated for the period $t = 1, \ldots, T$. But constraints on this model will have to apply to any period outside this interval.

The functional form of the model of n equations at time period t will be written in vector notation as

$$(2.1) \qquad y_t = g(x_t, \alpha),$$

where y_t is the nx1 vector of dependent variables at time t [4)]

$$(2.2) \qquad y_t = [y_{1t}, \ldots, y_{nt}]',$$

x_t is the px1 vector of independent variables at time t

$$(2.3) \qquad x_t = [x_{1t}, \ldots, x_{pt}]',$$

α is the qx1 vector of model parameters that have to be estimated

$$(2.4) \qquad \alpha = [\alpha_1, \ldots, \alpha_q]',$$

and $g(.,.)$ is an nx1 vector-valued function.

Next, we add to this model a vector of additive disturbances u_t as follows

$$(2.5) \qquad y_t = g(x_t, \alpha) + u_t,$$

where u_t is the nx1 vector

(2.6) $u_t = [u_{1t}, \ldots, u_{nt}]'$.

We assume that the vector of disturbances has expectation zero and covariance matrix H_t [5)]

(2.7) $E[u_t] = 0$,

(2.8) $E[u_t u_t'] = H_t$.

The disturbances may therefore be contemporaneously correlated, but we will exclude for the sake of exposition correlation over time [6)]

(2.9) $E[u_t u_\tau'] = 0, \qquad all\ t \neq \tau.$

The problems with which we will be concerned in this chapter arise because it is given that the functional form (2.1) should satisfy one or more homogeneous linear constraints at each period in discrete time as follows

(2.10) $R_t' [y_t - g(x_t, \alpha)] \equiv 0$,

where R_t is the nxk matrix of *weights* that may be time-dependent initially, for instance because elements of x_t appear in R_t. We assume that the k restrictions are independent, or that the rank of R_t equals k

(2.11) $r(R_t) = k$.

The number of restrictions should furthermore satisfy

(2.12) $k < min\ \{n, q\}$,

because otherwise the model will be overrestricted (note that q may also be bounded above due to identification restrictions) [7)].

Now we have collected all elements to give the following

DEFINITION 2.1 :

A model defined by (2.2) - (2.12) will be called a *constrained model of class* $(n, \alpha, H_t; k, R_t)$. It will be called *linear* or *nonlinear* depending on whether the vector-valued function $g(x_t, \alpha)$ is linear or nonlinear in α.

The constraint (2.10) carries over to the vector of disturbances u_t. This may be seen if we premultiply (2.5) on both sides by the transposed matrix of weights R_t'

$$(2.13) \qquad R_t' \, y_t = R_t' \, g(x_t, \alpha) + R_t' \, u_t.$$

The identity (2.10) on the functional form then implies immediately for u_t

$$(2.14) \qquad R_t' \, u_t \equiv 0.$$

Combining (2.8) and (2.14) it is clear that the covariance matrix is singular, for we have

$$(2.15) \qquad R_t' \, H_t = R_t' \, E \, [u_t u_t'] = E \, [R_t' \, u_t u_t'] \equiv 0.$$

The identity (2.15) implies for the rank of H_t

$$(2.16) \qquad r(H_t) \leqslant n-k,$$

thereby imposing a maximum on its rank. It is natural to assume that this maximum is attained [8)].

For estimation purposes we will be concerned with the constrained model of which k equations are deleted. In terms of the disturbances this should happen such that the remaining $n-k$ equations have $n-k$ linear independent disturbances. Because the dependencies between the disturbances are determined by (2.14), this requirement is equivalent to the condition that the deleted disturbances can be uniquely determined from (2.14). If we order the equations such that the k deleted equations correspond to the k last equations, and if we partition the matrix R_t as

$$(2.17) \qquad R_t' = [\tilde{R}_t' \; \bar{R}_t'],$$

where $\bar{R}_t'$ has k columns, this will be the case if and only if the matrix $\bar{R}_t'$ attains maximum rank

$$(2.18) \qquad r(\bar{R}_t') = k.$$

If we partition the vector of disturbances u_t correspondingly as

$$(2.19) \qquad u_t' = [\tilde{u}_t' \; \bar{u}_t'],$$

it may be seen that (2.14) is equivalent to

$$(2.20) \qquad \tilde{R}_t' \, \tilde{u}_t \equiv -\bar{R}_t' \, \bar{u}_t,$$

from which the vector of disturbances of the deleted equations may be uniquely determined as

$$(2.21) \qquad \bar{u}_t = -(\bar{R}_t')^{-1} \, \tilde{R}_t' \, \tilde{u}_t \; ,$$

if and only if (2.18) holds.

Define the set of indices of the n equations as $N = \{1, \ldots, n\}$, and let K be any subset of k indices from this set. Then we have the following

DEFINITION 2.2 :

A (linear or nonlinear) constrained model of class $(n, \alpha, H_t; k, R_t)$ with k equations deleted according to the subset K such that (2.18) holds will be called a *(linear or nonlinear) lopped model of class* $(n, \alpha, H_t; k, R_t, K)$.

In the following two sections we will consider maximum likelihood estimation of lopped models as defined in Definition 2.2, and in particular dependency of the estimation results on K, with different hypotheses on the covariance matrix H_t.

For maximum likelihood estimation, we will assume that the vector of disturbances follows a (possibly singular) n-variate normal distribution. This assumption has to be justified given the model one actually wants to estimate in practice. For instance, if one were to estimate models in which the vector of dependent variables y_t is a vector of shares (and these are typically models that are constrained), one should actually take account of the fact that shares should lie on the unit simplex. If one specifies the disturbances (and therefore the dependent variables) to be normally distributed, there is a positive probability that the fitted share will become negative or exceed unity. It would then be appropriate to specify a distribution that takes into account these special properties of shares, such as the Dirichlet distribution, which is a generalization of the Beta distribution [9)]. The scarce empirical evidence on the significance of the error one commits by assuming a normal distribution instead of a Dirichlet distribution indicates, however, that in this particular example one cannot reject the hypothesis that the normal distribution is the true distribution [10)]. Nevertheless one should in general be careful.

4.3. A HOMOSCEDASTIC COVARIANCE MATRIX

The first case we will consider is that of a homoscedastic covariance matrix H_t

(3.1) $\qquad H_t = H \,, \qquad\qquad all\ t.$

This assumption is justified if the constrained model that we consider is specified such that we have no reason to believe that the covariances increase or decrease systematically over time. The latter depends on the scaling of the dependent variables. If, instead of over time, our sample would run over different cross-section units, differences in size might account for differences in covariance over the units, but this is not the case. The same problem might arise if, over the sample period, the dependent variables strongly increase or decrease. For the homoscedastic case we will therefore have to assume that the dependent variables have been scaled such that they fluctuate in the same range over the sample period. The Hickman-Lau model of Chapter 2 for instance [11], has a dependent variable that may change strongly over time. In that case the assumption that the covariance matrix is homoscedastic might possibly not be justified.

Because, contrary to other authors, we let the matrix R_t be time-dependent initially, the homoscedastic case immediately gives rise to a complication, which becomes clear if we combine (2.15) and (3.1) to

(3.2) $\qquad R_t' H \equiv 0 \,, \qquad\qquad all\ t.$

Unless the columns of all R_t are linear combinations of the same k base vectors of n-dimensional space, (3.2) implies that $r(H) < n-k$, contrary to the assumption previously made that all linear dependencies would be captured in the matrix of weights.

Therefore, for the case in which the covariance matrix is homoscedastic, we assume that the matrix of weights consists of columns that are in each period different linear combinations of the same vectors

$$(3.3) \qquad R_t = R\, A_t, \qquad\qquad \textit{all } t,$$

where A_t is a kxk nonsingular time-dependent matrix, and R is the nxk matrix of restrictions that are constant over time.

Finally we notice that the constrained model of class $(n, \alpha, H_t; k, R_t)$ is equal to the constrained model of class $(n, \alpha, H_t; k, R_t^\star)$, if $R_t^\star$ is obtained from postmultiplication of R_t by a nonsingular kxk matrix.

We will for our purpose define $R_t^\star$ as

$$(3.4) \qquad R_t^\star = R_t\, A_t^{-1}, \qquad\qquad \textit{all } t\,.$$

Because of assumption (3.3), we find from (3.4) for the matrix of weights

$$(3.5) \qquad R_t^\star = R, \qquad\qquad \textit{all } t.$$

In other words, we have demonstrated that the only way in which a constrained model with a homoscedastic covariance matrix remains consistent is with a matrix of weights that is basically constant over time. The starting point for our discussion in this section will therefore be the constrained model of class $(n, \alpha, H; k, R)$. We will first look into the case of one constraint, or $k=1$, because this case was most frequently analyzed in the literature. This is done in subsection 4.3.1. In the subsection thereafter we will generalize the results to the case of more than one constraint, or $k \geqslant 1$.

4.3.1. THE CASE $k=1$: ONE CONSTRAINT

We will first discuss maximum likelihood estimation of the constrained model of class $(n, \alpha, H; 1, w)$, where $w > 0$ is now the $nx1$ vector of weights[12]. The parameters to be estimated are the vector of model parameters α and the covariance matrix H. Additionally, there may also be restrictions on α and H. One such set of restrictions might be implied from the identity (2.10), that may now be written as

$$(3.6) \qquad w' [y_t - g(x_t, \alpha)] \equiv 0.$$

Because this restriction should hold for all values of y_t and x_t (also outside the sample period), it is possible that it implies restrictions on α. Take for instance the simple linear model with $p=1$ and

$$(3.7) \qquad y_t = \alpha\, m_t + u_t,$$

where $m_t = \Sigma_i\, w_i\, y_{it}$ in the data[13]. Then (3.6) implies the following restriction on the vector of parameters

$$(3.8) \qquad w'\alpha = 1.$$

Also sign restrictions on the coefficients could exist, such as negative own price elasticities in factor demand systems. We will assume that all these restrictions, that may entail both equality and inequality restrictions, may be summarized by the condition

$$(3.9) \qquad \{\alpha, H\} \in D,$$

i.e. the pair $\{\alpha, H\}$ should belong to a certain set D. D is assumed to be a non-empty compact subset of the Euclidean space $R^q x R^n$ x ... $x R^n$, which is the Cartesian product of the $n+1$ Euclidean spaces R^q, R^n, ..., R^n. This is a sufficient condition for the existence of a global maximum if the likelihood function is maximized with respect to the elements of α and H subject to (3.9), according to the Weierstrass Theorem [14].

The usual solution if the covariance matrix does not have full rank is to estimate only the $n-1$ equations of the lopped model of class $(n, \alpha, H; 1, w, K)$ where the set K contains one element. If all elements of α appear in all equations, this will directly provide an estimate for the whole vector α, otherwise the remaining elements will have to be calculated from restrictions such as (3.6), or (3.8) in the example.

Because only $(n-1)^2$ elements of H are estimated, the remaining elements corresponding to the deleted equation should always be calculated from condition (3.2), which in the present situation simplifies to

$$w'H = 0. \tag{3.10}$$

We will prove our results under the assumption that $K = \{n\}$, *i.e.* that we delete the last, n^{th} equation. Because each equation may be brought into this position, and because our results deal typically with conditions under which certain results are independent of K, or the equation which is deleted, this proves them for any equation that is deleted. Note that condition (2.18) is always met because $w > 0$.

First we introduce partitionings of the vector of disturbances u_t, the covariance matrix H and the vector of weights w [15]

$$u_t = \begin{bmatrix} \tilde{u}_t \\ \\ u_{nt} \end{bmatrix}, \tag{3.11}$$

$$H = \begin{bmatrix} \tilde{H} & \tilde{h}_n \\ \\ \tilde{h}_n' & h_{nn} \end{bmatrix}, \tag{3.12}$$

$$(3.13) \qquad w = \begin{bmatrix} \tilde{w} \\ \\ w_n \end{bmatrix} .$$

where $\tilde{u}_t$ is the $(n-1)$x1 vector of the first $n-1$ elements of u_t, $\tilde{h}_n$ is the $(n-1)$x1 vector of the first $n-1$ elements of the nth column or row of the symmetric covariance matrix H, h_{nn} is the element (n,n) of H and $\tilde{w}$ is the $(n-1)$x1 vector of the first $n-1$ elements of w.

Because we have assumed that u_t follows an n-variate normal distribution, $\tilde{u}_t$ will follow an $(n-1)$-variate normal distribution with expectation zero and covariance matrix $\tilde{H}$, as is well-known [16)]. Therefore the probability density function of the lopped vector $\tilde{u}_t$ will be equal to

$$(3.14) \qquad f(\tilde{u}_t) = (2\pi)^{-(n-1)/2} \, |\tilde{H}|^{-1/2} \, exp \, \{-\tfrac{1}{2} \, \tilde{u}_t' \, \tilde{H}^{-1} \, \tilde{u}_t\} \; ,$$

where $|\tilde{H}|$ is the determinant of $\tilde{H}$.

Because we have assumed that the disturbances are uncorrelated over time, the likelihood function for the sample is obtained as

$$(3.15) \qquad L = \prod_{t=1}^{T} f(\tilde{u}_t)$$

$$= (2\pi)^{-(n-1)T/2} \, |\tilde{H}|^{-T/2} \, exp \, \{-\tfrac{1}{2} \sum_{t=1}^{T} \tilde{u}_t' \, \tilde{H}^{-1} \, \tilde{u}_t\}$$

We then may state

<u>DEFINITION 3.1</u> :

the following mathematical programming problem will be referred to as the *maximum likelihood estimation problem of the lopped model of class* $(n, \alpha, H; 1, w, K)$:

(3.16) $\max_{\alpha, H} L$ *subject to* $\{\alpha, H\} \in D$.

Before we proceed,we first present the results on estimation of the lopped model of class $(n, \alpha, H; 1, w, K)$ that have been obtained sofar by other authors. In interpreting these results, it may be noted that the generalized least square estimator of the linear lopped model of class $(n, \alpha, H; 1, w, K)$, where H is known, is equivalent to the maximum likelihood estimator of α if H is known.

THEOREM 3.1 (BARTEN (1969)) :

The probability density function (3.14) of the lopped model of class $(n, \alpha, H; 1, w, K)$ is independent of K if $w = \iota$, where ι is the vector of units.

With the use of (3.15) this theorem implies

THEOREM 3.2 (McGUIRE *et al.* (1968), BARTEN (1969)) :

The value of the likelihood function (3.15) of the lopped model of class $(n, \alpha, H; 1, w, K)$ is independent of K if $w = \iota$.

Both these results were derived in the context of a linear constrained model, but they can be seen to be equally valid for nonlinear constrained models. Note that the condition $w = \iota$ is only a sufficient condition. We will see below that it is also a necessary condition.

Next we present two theorems on the estimators for α and H.

THEOREM 3.3 (BARTEN (1969)) :

Stepwise maximum likelihood estimation of the lopped model of class $(n, \alpha, H; 1, w, K)$ gives maximum likelihood estimators for α and H that do not depend on K if $w = \iota$.

This result was again derived for the linear constrained model, but also applies to the nonlinear model.

THEOREM 3.4 (McGUIRE *et al.* (1968), POWELL (1969)) :

Generalized least squares estimation of the linear lopped model of class $(n, \alpha, H; 1, w, K)$, with H known, gives an estimator for α that is independent of K.

The last result makes us suspect that Barten's condition $w = \iota$ is only a sufficient condition in Theorem 3.3, but not a necessary condition. The implication would be that the value of the likelihood function could depend on K, whereas the estimators for α and H would be independent of K. This is of importance for practical estimation purposes, because there one does not always need the value of the likelihood function, and independency of the deleted equation could therefore be achieved under less stringent conditions than would otherwise be required.

Before we present our theorems, we first state and prove the following

LEMMA 3.1 :

The probability density function of the lopped model of class $(n, \alpha, H; 1, w, K)$ as defined in (3.14) may be written as

$$f(\tilde{u}_t) = (2\pi)^{-(n-1)/2}\, w_n^{-1} (\Sigma_i w_i)\, |H + \iota\iota'|^{-1/2} \exp\{-\tfrac{1}{2}\, u_t'(H + \iota\iota')^{-1} u_t\}. \tag{3.17}$$

Proof :

Define the nxn symmetric matrix W as

$$W = \hat{w} - e_n w' - w' e_n \, , \tag{3.18}$$

where $\hat{w}$ is a diagonal matrix with the elements of w on the diagonal, and e_n the $nx1$ vector with unity as element n and zeroes elsewhere. Using the partitioning (3.13), this matrix may be partitioned as

$$W = \begin{bmatrix} \hat{\tilde{w}} & -\tilde{w} \\ -\tilde{w}' & -w_n \end{bmatrix} \, , \tag{3.19}$$

from which it is easy to see that the determinant of W equals

$$(3.20) \qquad |W| = -(\prod_{i=1}^{n-1} w_i)(\Sigma_i w_i)$$

Note that W is nonsingular because we required that $w > 0$. Furthermore we note that

$$(3.21) \qquad |\hat{w}| = \Pi_i w_i$$

Using (3.10) we may then derive the crucial relationship

$$(3.22) \qquad W \begin{bmatrix} \tilde{H} & 0 \\ 0 & 1 \end{bmatrix} W = \hat{w}(H+\iota\iota')\hat{w} \; ,$$

which gives, with (3.20) and (3.21), the determinant of $\tilde{H}$ as

$$(3.23) \qquad |\tilde{H}| = w_n^2 \; (\Sigma_i w_i)^{-2} \; |H+\iota\iota'| .$$

Note that $(H+\iota\iota')$ is nonsingular, because the left-hand side of (3.22) and $\hat{w}$ are nonsingular by assumption.

Furthermore the condition $w'u_t \equiv 0$ implies

$$(3.24) \qquad W \begin{bmatrix} \tilde{u}_t \\ 0 \end{bmatrix} = \hat{w}_t u_t$$

This equation, together with (3.22), gives for the quadratic form that appears in the exponential power in the probability density function

$$(3.25) \qquad \tilde{u}_t' \tilde{H}^{-1} \tilde{u}_t = [\tilde{u}_t' \ 0] \begin{bmatrix} \tilde{H}^{-1} & 0 \\ 0 & 1 \end{bmatrix} \begin{bmatrix} \tilde{u}_t \\ 0 \end{bmatrix}$$

$$= [\tilde{u}_t' \ 0] \begin{bmatrix} \tilde{H} & 0 \\ 0 & 1 \end{bmatrix}^{-1} \begin{bmatrix} \tilde{u}_t \\ 0 \end{bmatrix}$$

$$= [\tilde{u}_t' \ 0] WW^{-1} \begin{bmatrix} \tilde{H} & 0 \\ 0 & 1 \end{bmatrix}^{-1} W^{-1}W \begin{bmatrix} \tilde{u}_t \\ 0 \end{bmatrix}$$

$$= u_t' (H+\iota\iota')^{-1} u_t$$

Insertion of (3.23) and (3.25) in (3.14) gives (3.17)

Q.E.D.

With the use of this Lemma, we may prove the following

THEOREM 3.5 :

The value of the probability density function of the lopped model of class $(n, \alpha, H; 1, w, K)$, as defined in (3.14), is independent of K if and only if [17] $w = \iota$.

Proof :

(⇒) By Lemma 3.1, the probability density function of (3.14) may be written as in (3.17). It can easily be verified that if we delete an equation other than equation n, say equation $m < n$, the expression w_n^{-1} in (3.17) changes into w_m^{-1}. Therefore, if (3.17) does not depend on K, this implies that all w_i should be equal. Applying the arbitrary normalization $w'\iota = n$, this implies $w = \iota$.

($\Leftarrow$) Trivial, with Lemma 3.1.

Q.E.D.

This theorem therefore shows that Barten's condition of Theorem 3.1 is not only sufficient, but also necessary for the probability density function of the lopped model of class $(n, \alpha, H; 1, w, K)$ to be independent of K. A similar observation regarding Theorem 3.2 may be made if we consider the following

COROLLARY 3.1 :

The value of the likelihood function (3.15) of the lopped model of class $(n, \alpha, H; 1, w, K)$ is independent of K if and only if $w = \iota$.

Proof :

As for Theorem 3.5.

Now that we have looked at the conditions under which the values of the probability density function and the likelihood function are independent of K, we turn to the conditions for independency of the maximum likelihood estimator, in particular to see whether our conjecture that the condition $w = \iota$ is too stringent turns out to be true.

THEOREM 3.6 :

The solution of the maximum likelihood estimation problem for the lopped model of class $(n, \alpha, H; 1, w, K)$ as defined in Definition 3.1, *i.e.* the maximum likelihood estimator for α and H, does not depend on K.

Proof :

With (3.15) and (3.17) the likelihood function may be written as

$$(3.26) \qquad L = (2\pi)^{-(n-1)T/2}\, w_n^{-T} (\Sigma_i w_i)^T |H+\iota\iota'|^{-T/2} \exp\{-\tfrac{1}{2} \sum_{t=1}^{T} u_t'(H+\iota\iota')^{-1} u_t\}.$$

Maximization of this expression with respect to α and H subject to (3.9) is equivalent to

$$(3.27) \qquad \underset{\alpha, H}{Max}\ L^{\star} = |H+\iota\iota'|^{-T/2} \exp\{-\tfrac{1}{2} \sum_{t=1}^{T} u_t'(H+\iota\iota')^{-1} u_t\}$$

subject to $\{\alpha, H\} \in D$.

Because $L^{\star}$ is continous and because D is nonempty and compact, this mathematical programming problem has a global solution for α and H. Because $L^{\star}$ and D do not depend on K, the solution will also be independent of K (although the value of L in the optimum may depend on it).

Q.E.D.

Theorems 3.5 and 3.6 and Corollary 3.1 show that for the lopped model of class $(n, \alpha, H; 1, w, K)$ it is possible that the maximum likelihood estimator does not depend on the deleted equation, while the value of the probability density function or, which is equivalent in this case, the value of the likelihood function may. For estimation problems in which the value of the likelihood function is only a byproduct which is not needed for other purposes such as hypothesis testing, we have therefore weakened the conditions under which the estimation results are independent of the deleted equation. The results hold for a broad class of (linear and nonlinear) constrained models with one constraint, including models with equality or inequality restrictions on the model parameters and/or the covariance matrix.

In the next subsection, we will generalize the results to similar models with more than one constraint, *i.e.* lopped models of class $(n, \alpha, H; k, R, K)$ with $k \geqslant 1$.

4.3.2. THE CASE $k \geqslant 1$: MORE THAN ONE CONSTRAINT

Generalization of the results of the previous subsection to the case of k constraints seems relatively straightforward intuitively. Nevertheless, the only authors that have, as far as we know, published results in this field are McGUIRE *et al.* (1968). They provided the following

THEOREM 3.7 (McGUIRE *et al.* (1968)) :

Generalized least squares estimation of the linear lopped model of class $(n, \alpha, H; k, R, K)$, with H known, gives an estimator for α that is independent of K.

Let us consider the lopped model of class $(n, \alpha, H; k, R, K)$. The restrictions on this model are now, from (2.10)

$$(3.28) \qquad R' \, [y_t - g(x_t, \alpha)] \equiv 0 ,$$

implying for the covariance matrix H

$$(3.29) \qquad R'H = 0.$$

As for the case $k=1$, we collect all equality and inequality restrictions on α and H in the condition

$$(3.30) \qquad \{\alpha, H\} \in D ,$$

with D defined as in (3.9).

The vector of disturbances u_t, the covariance matrix H and the matrix of weights are now partitioned as

$$(3.31) \qquad u_t = \begin{bmatrix} \tilde{u}_t \\ \bar{u}_t \end{bmatrix}$$

(3.32) $$H = \begin{bmatrix} \tilde{H} & \bar{H} \\ \bar{H}' & \bar{H}_k \end{bmatrix}$$

(3.33) $$R = \begin{bmatrix} \tilde{R} \\ \bar{R} \end{bmatrix}$$

where $\tilde{u}_t$ is the $(n-k)$x1 vector of the first $n-k$ elements of u_t, $\bar{u}_t$ the kx1 vector of the last k elements of u_t, $\tilde{H}$ the $(n-k)$x$(n-k)$ matrix in the upper left corner of H, $\bar{H}$ the $(n-k)$xk rectangular matrix in the upper right corner of H, $\bar{H}_k$ the kxk matrix in the lower right corner of H and R is partitioned according to (2.17) with $r(\bar{R}) = k$.

The lopped vector of disturbances $\tilde{u}_t$ will follow an $(n-k)$-variate normal distribution with expectation zero, covariance matrix $\tilde{H}$ and probability density function [18)]

(3.34) $$f(\tilde{u}_t) = (2\pi)^{-(n-k)/2}|\tilde{H}|^{-1/2} \; exp \; \{-\tfrac{1}{2}\tilde{u}_t' \tilde{H}^{-1} \tilde{u}_t\} \; .$$

Because the disturbances are assumed to be uncorrelated over time, the likelihood function for the sample is obtained as

(3.35) $$L = \prod_{t=1}^{T} f(\tilde{u}_t)$$

$$= (2\pi)^{-(n-k)T/2}|\tilde{H}|^{-T/2} \; exp \; \{-\tfrac{1}{2}\sum_{t=1}^{T} \tilde{u}_t' \tilde{H}^{-1} \tilde{u}_t\}.$$

The maximum likelihood estimation problem for the lopped model of class $(n, \alpha, H; k, R, K)$ is the same as that of Definition 3.1.

The generalization of Lemma 3.1 may now be stated.

LEMMA 3.2 :

The probability density function (3.34) of the lopped model of class $(n, \alpha, H; k, R, K)$ may be written as

$$f(\tilde{u}_t) = (2\pi)^{-(n-k)/2} |\bar{R}|^{-1} |R'R| \, |H+RR'|^{-1/2} \, exp \, \{-\tfrac{1}{2} u_t'(H+RR')^{-1} u_t\}. \tag{3.36}$$

Proof :

Define the nxn symmetric matrix V as

$$V = \begin{bmatrix} I_{n-k} & -\tilde{R} \\ -\tilde{R}' & -\bar{R}'\bar{R} \end{bmatrix} , \tag{3.37}$$

where I_{n-k} is the $(n-k)$x$(n-k)$ identity matrix.

The determinant of V may be seen to be equal to

$$|V| = -|R'R|. \tag{3.38}$$

Because $r(R) = k$, this implies that V is nonsingular. With the use of (3.29), (3.32) and (3.33) we may now derive

$$V \begin{bmatrix} \tilde{H} & 0 \\ 0 & I_k \end{bmatrix} V = F'(H+RR')F , \tag{3.39}$$

where the nxn nonsingular matrix F is defined by

$$F = \begin{bmatrix} I_{n-k} & 0 \\ 0 & \bar{R} \end{bmatrix} . \tag{3.40}$$

The determinant of $\tilde{H}$ therefore equals

$$(3.41) \qquad |\tilde{H}| = |\bar{R}|^2 |R'R|^{-2} |H+RR'| \ .$$

Note that $(H+RR')$ is nonsingular because V, F and $\tilde{H}$ are nonsingular matrices.

From the condition $R'u_t \equiv 0$ we obtain the following result

$$(3.42) \qquad V \begin{bmatrix} \tilde{u}_t \\ 0 \end{bmatrix} = F'u_t \ .$$

Use (3.39) and (3.42) to rewrite the quadratic form that appears in (3.34) as

$$(3.43) \qquad \tilde{u}_t' \tilde{H}^{-1} \tilde{u}_t = [\tilde{u}_t' \ \ 0] \begin{bmatrix} \tilde{H}^{-1} & 0 \\ 0 & I_k \end{bmatrix} \begin{bmatrix} \tilde{u}_t \\ 0 \end{bmatrix}$$

$$= [\tilde{u}_t' \ \ 0] \ VV^{-1} \begin{bmatrix} \tilde{H} & 0 \\ 0 & I_k \end{bmatrix}^{-1} V^{-1}V \begin{bmatrix} \tilde{u}_t \\ 0 \end{bmatrix}$$

$$= u_t' \ (H+RR')^{-1} \ u_t.$$

Substitution of (3.41) and (3.43) in (3.34) gives (3.36).

Q.E.D.

Combination of Lemmas 3.1 and 3.2 gives the following result on quadratic forms as a byproduct.

COROLLARY 3.2

Let H be an nxn symmetric matrix of rank $n-1$ and w an $nx1$ positive vector such that $w'H = 0$; then

$$(3.44) \qquad u'(H+\iota\iota')^{-1}u = u'(H+ww')^{-1}u$$

for each $nx1$ vector u such that $w'u = 0$.

Proof :

Combine Lemma 3.1 with Lemma 3.2 for $k=1$ and $R=w$.

With the use of Lemma 3.2 we can establish the following result for lopped models with more than one constraint and a homoscedastic covariance matrix.

THEOREM 3.8

The value of the probability density function (3.34) of the lopped model of class $(n, \alpha, H; k, R, K)$ is independent of K if and only if $|\bar{R}|$ is the same for all feasible K, *i.e.* K for which $|\bar{R}| \neq 0$.

Proof :

Trivial with Lemma 3.2. $|\bar{R}|$ is the only expression in (3.36) that depends on K.

The generalization of Corollary 3.1 is now straightforward.

COROLLARY 3.3 :

The value of the likelihood function (3.35) of the lopped model of class $(n, \alpha, H; k, R, K)$ is independent of K if and only if $|\bar{R}|$ is the same for all feasible K, *i.e.* K for which $|\bar{R}| \neq 0$.

Proof :

As for Theorem 3.8, but with (3.36) substituted in (3.35).

Finally we turn to the conditions under which the maximum likelihood estimator is independent of the deleted equations. The generalization of Theorem 3.6 is

THEOREM 3.9 :

The solution of the maximum likelihood estimation problem for the lopped model of class $(n, \alpha, H; k, R, K)$, *i.e.* the maximum likelihood estimator for α and H, does not depend on K.

Proof :

With (3.35) and (3.36) the likelihood function may be written as

$$(3.45) \qquad L = (2\pi)^{-(n-k)T/2}|\bar{R}|^{-T}|R'R|^{T}|H+RR'|^{-T/2} \exp\{-\frac{1}{2}\sum_{t=1}^{T} u_t'(H+RR')^{-1}u_t\}$$

Maximization of this expression with respect to α and H subject to (3.30) is equivalent to

$$(3.46) \qquad \underset{\alpha,H}{Max}\ L^{\star} = |H+RR'|^{-T/2} \exp\{-\frac{1}{2}\sum_{t=1}^{T} u_t'(H+RR')^{-1}\ u_t\}$$

subject to $\{\alpha, H\} \in D$.

Because $L^{\star}$ is continuous and D is nonempty and compact, the mathematical programming problem has a global solution for α and H. Because $L^{\star}$ and D are independent of K, the solution of (3.46) will also be independent of K.

Q.E.D.

As could be expected, we have also for lopped models with more than one constraint a disparity concerning dependency on the set of deleted equations between the probability density function (or the likelihood function) and the maximum likelihood estimators. Again the conditions for independency of the latter are weaker than those for independency of the former, which may be useful should one be interested in the estimators of a and H, and not in the value of the likelihood function *per se*.

4.4. A SPECIAL CASE WITH A HETEROSCEDASTIC COVARIANCE MATRIX

In a number of consumer demand models, the dependent variable in each equation consists of the share in total expenditure of the good in question, multiplied by a logarithmic growth rate, of the corresponding quantity or other variables [19]. In those cases, the covariance matrix is assumed to be constant over time. But one might also divide each equation on both sides by the - time-dependent - share in question, and assume that the covariance matrix of the disturbances (that have now been divided by the shares) is heteroscedastic. More precisely, one would then assume that the covariance between two disturbances i and j would be inversely proportional to the product of the expenditure shares of good i and good j.

Conversely, one might have a model for which one suspects heteroscedasticity, and multiply each equation by a variable in the hope that the resulting covariance matrix will be homoscedastic.

Of course, if one has a model of which one assumes that the covariance matrix is heteroscedastic, without any idea about the form or structure of the covariance matrix, it is a vain hope ever to obtain asymptotically consistent estimates for this matrix.

That is the reason why in this section we will assume that the covariance matrix is of a *specific* nature, where the above examples serve as inspiration for the specification that we will use. Because we analyze this case in the framework of constrained models of class $(n, \alpha, H_t; k, R_t)$, the specification of the covariance matrix will have to be chosen in conjunction with a specification for the matrix of weights R_t.

In particular, we will assume that R_t is of the following form

$$R_t = B_t R , \qquad \text{all } t, \tag{4.1}$$

where B_t is an nxn nonsingular time-dependent matrix, and R is an nxk matrix of k constraints which are constant over time and assumed to be independent. Contrary to the previous section, this leaves the matrix of weights dependent on time, however.

The specification of the covariance matrix of the constrained model of class $(n, \alpha, H_t; k, B_tR)$ that we assume to prevail is the following

$$(4.2) \qquad H_t = (B_t')^{-1} H\, B_t^{-1} \ .$$

This model, the constrained model of class $(n, \alpha, (B_t')^{-1}H\, B_t^{-1}; k, B_tR)$ is still very general.

For instance, if B_t is a diagonal matrix, with on the diagonal expenditure shares, $k=1$ and $R=\iota$, we are back to the model of our first example, or to the case of complete systems of demand equations with covariances that are inversely proportional to the product of the corresponding expenditure shares in general.
In accordance with section 4.3 we will assume that H_t has $r(H_t) \geqslant n-k$, a property that carries over to H as B_t is nonsingular.

If we consider maximum likelihood estimation of the lopped model of class $(n, \alpha, (B_t')^{-1}H\, B_t^{-1}; k, B_tR, K)$, we run against the same problems regarding independency with respect to K, or the deleted equations, of the likelihood function and the maximum likelihood estimator that occupied us in the previous section. Because of the special form of R_t and H_t, we will see that these questions may all be answered using the theorems that were proved in the previous section.

Premultiply the model (2.5) first by the matrix B_t' on both sides. This gives

$$(4.3) \qquad B_t' y_t = B_t' g(x_t, \alpha) + B_t' u_t$$

This model is equivalent to the following model

$$(4.4) \qquad z_t = h(x_t, \alpha, B_t) + v_t,$$

where we have introduced the following transformations

(4.5) $z_t = B'_t \, y_t$,

(4.6) $h(x_t, \alpha, B_t) = B'_t \, g(x_t, \alpha)$,

(4.7) $v_t = B'_t \, u_t$.

Using these transformations, the constraint (2.10) gets the following form

(4.8) $R' \, [z_t - h(x_t, \alpha, B_t)] \equiv 0.$

The new vector of disturbances has expectation

(4.9)
$$E\,[v_t] = E\,[B'_t \, u_t\,]$$
$$= B'_t \, E\,[u_t\,]$$
$$= 0\ ,$$

and covariance matrix

(4.10)
$$E\,[v_t v'_t] = E\,[B'_t \, u_t \, u'_t \, B_t\,]$$
$$= B'_t \, E\,[u_t \, u'_t] \, B_t$$
$$= H.$$

The constraint (4.8) implies for the disturbances v_t

(4.11) $R'v_t \equiv 0,$ $\qquad$ *all t*,

so that we find that the covariance matrix H of v_t is singular and even decreases k in rank from

(4.12) $\quad R'H = 0.$

Because $r(H) \geqslant n-k$, this implies that H has rank $n-k$. Finally we find that the disturbances v_t are uncorrelated over time, with the use of (2.9), from

$$\begin{aligned}(4.13) \qquad E\,[v_t\, v_\tau'] &= E\,[B_t'\, v_t\, v_\tau'\, B_t\,] \\ &= B_t'\, E\,[u_t\, u_\tau'\,]\, B_t \\ &= 0 \qquad\qquad\qquad all\ t \neq \tau\end{aligned}$$

This completes the list of properties of model (4.4), which by Definition 2.1 may now be identified as a constrained model of class $(n, \alpha, H; k, R)$. The properties of this model with respect to maximum likelihood estimation were already derived in the previous section, and all apply to this model. In fact, we have proved the following

THEOREM 4.1 :

The constrained model of class $(n, \alpha, (B_t')^{-1}\ H\ B_t^{-1};\ k,\ B_tR)$ as defined above is equivalent to a constrained model of class $(n, \alpha, H; k, R)$.

This completes our discussion of a special constrained model with heteroscedastic covariance matrix. The model that was presented is fairly general, and may for instance be applied to complete systems of demand equations. We may have left other cases of heteroscedasticity out of the discussion, but we feel that with this special model we have captured the most important ones. After all, we can only say something about constrained models with heteroscedastic covariance matrices if we know something about the form or structure of these matrices. And specifying a rather general form should in that case be preferred to leaving the problem completely aside.

4.5. SUMMARY AND CONCLUSIONS

In this chapter we have analyzed *constrained models*. These are models, possibly nonlinear in their parameters, of which the functional form should satisfy one or more independent homogenous linear constraints by assumption. That is, premultiplication of the difference between left-hand side and right-hand side of the functional form by a *matrix of weights* should be identical to zero. The matrix of weights may in principle vary over time. The constraints render the covariance matrix of the contemporaneous disturbances singular. If the vector of these disturbances is assumed to follow a multivariate normal distribution of the same order as there are equations, its probability density function will no longer be defined. The solution to this problem is to delete as many equations from the constrained model as there are independent constraints. This should happen such that the covariance matrix of the remaining vector of disturbances is no longer singular. The resulting model was called a *lopped model*.

In general one has to make a choice as to which equations to delete in order to obtain a lopped model from a constrained model. The main part of the chapter was devoted to an analysis of the effects of this choice on maximum likelihood estimation of the lopped model.

In general, maximum likelihood estimation entails maximization of a likelihood function with respect to functional form parameters and elements of the covariance matrix (assuming this matrix is unknown), possibly subject to restrictions on the two. It is possible that both the likelihood function and the maximum likelihood estimator of the parameters of the lopped model may depend on the deleted equations. We argued that we should analyze *separately* the conditions under which each of the two is independent of the deleted equations. This was done for the lopped model with *homoscedastic* covariance matrix, and for a special lopped model with *heteroscedastic* covariance matrix.

It was found that the lopped model with *homoscedastic* covariance matrix only remained consistent if the matrix of weights, which initally was allowed to vary over time, had a special form which makes it basically constant. This form also proved to be a sufficient condition for the maximum likelihood estimator of the corresponding lopped model to be independent of the deleted equations. The necessary and sufficient condition under which this property holds for the value of the likelihood function, however, was shown to be *more restrictive*. These two results constitute the argument that the value of the likelihood function corresponding to this lopped model may depend on which equations are deleted, while the maximum likelihood estimator may not.

Maximum likelihood estimation of a model with a heteroscedastic covariance matrix without any further qualification on this matrix is impossible. That is why we only analyzed a special lopped model with a specific form of *heteroscedasticity*. This model is, however, not so specific that it does not include, for instance, complete systems of demand equations with a covariance matrix of which the elements vary over time with the value of the expenditure shares. It was shown that this model could be transformed into a lopped model with homoscedastic covariance matrix. As a consequence, all theorems that were proved for the latter also apply to the former.

The main *conclusions* of this chapter are twofold, and follow the homoscedastic and heteroscedastic cases.

For the constrained model with homoscedastic covariance matrix, we may conclude that if one is only interested in maximum likelihood estimation of this model as such, that is, the resulting maximum likelihood estimator, and not in any further use of the value of the likelihood function (such as for purposes of statistical inference), independency with respect to the deleted equations of the lopped model may be ascertained under weaker conditions than if this were not the case. This conclusion was reached with a constrained model encompassing the results of McGUIRE *et al.* (1968), BARTEN (1969) and POWELL (1969).

The second conclusion may be reached with the results obtained for the special lopped model with heteroscedasticity that was analyzed in the previous section. For it may be seen that the basic virtue of this model is that it allows us to work with a matrix of weights that may be time-dependent, contrary to the constrained model with homoscedastic covariance matrix that forces this matrix to be essentially constant. It is, as it were, a reverse conclusion : given a constrained model with time dependent weights, it tells which form we should assume for the covariance matrix such that the resulting model may be analyzed in terms of dependency with respect to deleted equations. Whether this form of the covariance matrix is realistic is up to the researcher.

FOOTNOTES TO CHAPTER 4

1) Models that are nonlinear in the independent variables but linear in the parameters can be made linear in these variables through application of a suitable transformation.

2) *Cfr.* ANDERSON (1958, pp. 25-26) and CRAMER (1946, p. 312).

3) *Cfr. e.g.* MADDALA (1977, p. 466).

4) A prime denotes transposition.

5) Everywhere we will assume that the null vector 0 is properly dimensioned.

6) For a special case in which this restriction is relaxed, see POWELL (1969).

7) The number of restrictions k has to be smaller than the number of coefficients q because the restrictions on the functional form may imply restrictions on the coefficients. For an example in the linear case, see McGUIRE *et al.* (1968).

8) A rank lower than $n-k$ would imply the existence of eigenvectors, independent of the columns of R_t, with eigenvalue zero, which would also act as restrictions. We therefore take it that R_t is exhaustive in that respect.

9) *Cfr.* WILKS (1962, pp. 177-182).

10) *Cfr.* WOODLAND (1979).

11) *Cfr.* equation (2.3.16).

12) We assume that $w_i \neq 0$ for all i, because equations with $w_i = 0$ may be left out of the system. Additionally we assume $w_i > 0$ through an appropriate definition of the elements of y_t and $g(x_t, \alpha)$.

13) Throughout this chapter, all summations or multiplications will run from 1 to n, unless otherwise indicated.

14) *Cfr.* TAKAYAMA (1974, p. 29).

15) We will, in general, denote by a tilde " ~ " elements of vectors or matrices corresponding to equations that are not deleted, and if necessary, elements corresponding to equations that are deleted by a bar " - ".

16) *Cfr. e.g.* ANDERSON (1958, p. 26).

17) We have applied the normalization $w'\iota = n$. Otherwise the condition would be that all elements of w should be equal.

18) *Cfr. e.g.* ANDERSON (1958, p. 26).

19) Examples are the Rotterdam model, cfr. THEIL (1965, 1975/1976) and BARTEN (1966, 1967, 1968, 1969), the CBS model of KELLER and VAN DRIEL (1981) and the Almost Ideal Demand System of DEATON and MUELLBAUER (1980). The dependent variable of the last model in infinitesimal changes is dw_i, with w_i the budget share for category of goods i. This may be seen to be equivalent to $w_i d\ ln\ w_i$, which is of the form described in the text.

CHAPTER 5 - A MODEL WITH PAIRWISE DIFFERING ELASTICITIES OF SUBSTITUTION

5.1. INTRODUCTION

After the theoretical chapters on the use of elasticities of substitution and on maximum likelihood estimation of nonlinear models with linear constraints on the functional form, the following chapters will be devoted to specification, estimation and testing around actual estimation-consistent import allocation models. We already argued in Chapter 2 that the widespread CES import allocation model could need improvement because it contained only one single relative price effect for all bilateral import demand equations. In terms of elasticities of substitution (ES), the ES are all equal and constant in this model. At the same time it was brought forward, however, that such an alternative model would only be feasible if it could be estimated with approximately the same ease as the CES model, and if it could be applied to a relatively large linkage model, *i.e.* a model with a large number of trade partners. Concerning estimation of the CES model, we saw that the method which was the least arbitrary in a number of respects would be the method of maximum likelihood. It would therefore not be an objection if our alternative model would have to be estimated by this method as well. Because we are dealing with estimation-consistent import allocation models which should satisfy linear constraints on the functional form, the theory developed in the previous chapter therefore is of direct use for the maximum likelihood estimation of these models.

Next to developing a viable alternative for the CES import allocation model, we also argued that the hypothesis of weak separability between imports and domestic products should be tested. Both for the alternative import allocation model and the testing of the weak separability hypothesis we will develop a model that starts off from the same (partial) aggregator function. Instead of one single relative price effect such as in the CES model, this alternative results in n^2 different price effects, derived from n parameters so that they are not independent. The aggregator function generates therefore pairwise different ES. In fact, the index is homothetic and has the property that the ratios of any pair of partial Allen Elasticities of Substitution (AES) are constant. For these properties, this aggregator function was named CRESH (Constant Ratios of Elasticities of Substitution Homogeneous/Homothetic) by its author HANOCH (1971). This aggregator function, which contains the CES function as a special case, has already appeared in Chapter 3 in section 3.7 on constant elasticities of substitution, where it was mentioned as a special case of a general class of functions for which the ratios of ES were constant (but which were not necessarily homogeneous or homothetic). Starting from this CRESH aggregator function, we take the Constant-Returns-to-Scale (CRS) form, which makes the function homogeneous of degree one.

In section 5.2 we account for and introduce the CRESH function as an import quantity index for the imports of a particular country for a particular category of goods. In the different subsections we analyze the first-order and second-order conditions for a regular minimum of the Lagrange function if we minimize import costs subject to the definition of the import quantity index, whose level is assumed to be given. We also derive the different elasticities of substitution that were given in section 3.2, among which the AES.

In section 5.3 we present three different approximations to the bilateral import demand equations that are derived from the cost minimization problem of section 5.2, and we introduce furthermore dynamic elements that make the specifications more suitable for testing against the CES model and more realistic in general. The reason why we derive *three* approximations is twofold. In the first place, the three approximations correspond to the three different alternative solutions for the adding-up problem in the case of homothetic (partial) aggregator functions that were presented in subsection 2.2.4. They therefore serve as examples for each of the three solutions, which were presented in a rather abstract way. Secondly, the three approximations correspond to the different functional forms that were discussed in the light of the functional form debate presented in sub-section 1.3.2. They represent import allocation models which are linear, loglinear and in logarithmic differences respectively, and may therefore be compared with respect to their empirical performance. The outcome of a comparison could perhaps give an indication of the empirical merits of the different functional forms on the basis of the same dataset.

In order to test the assumption of weak separability, we re-interpret the import allocation models derived in section 5.3 as total allocation models. Total expenditure is then allocated between domestic products and imported products. The resulting specification allows one to test for the assumption of weak separability between imports and domestic products, which is the root of the import allocation models so frequently used in empirical work. The total allocation model is presented in section 5.4.

The three approximations derived in section 5.3 are approximations for the same bilateral import demand equations. The last section therefore contains a general specification that captures in one stroke all the models that are derived from the approximations, by way of summary. Additionally, we will make some concluding remarks.

5.2. THE CRESH MODEL WITH CONSTANT RETURNS TO SCALE

5.2.1. THE CHOICE FOR THE CRESH FUNCTION

We will derive from the CRESH function that is to be presented in this section two types of models : import allocation models and total allocation models, both defined in subsection 1.4.2. In the case of the CRESH model as import allocation model, it will be used to be tested against the CES import allocation model first presented in subsection 2.3.1. In the case of the total allocation model it will be used to impose restrictions of weak separability between imports and domestic products such that the hypothesis of weak separability may be tested. In both cases, the model derived from the CRESH aggregator function is assumed to be the general "true" model of which special cases will be tested as nested hypotheses. This choice of a true model asks for explanation, apart from the question of whether it is legitimate to suppose that it is the *true* model. The latter will be assumed to be the case as *maintained hypothesis*, and we therefore abstract from the problems concerning the validity of the test results *etc.* if this maintained hypothesis were to prove false.

The choice for the CRESH function, then, has been guided by three principles. First, the resulting import allocation model should have a certain *generality* in the price effects and be *estimable* for importing countries facing a relatively large number of trade partners. The demand for generality joins the conclusions of the discussion on functional forms in subsection 1.3.2, while feasibility of estimation is a *conditio sine qua non* for any import allocation or total allocation model to be estimated empirically. Secondly, we require the function to contain the *CES function* as a special case. This demand arises from the wish to test the CES import allocation model in a nested hypothesis against a more general model.

We take the CES model because it is the most widespread of empirically estimated estimation-consistent import allocation models and because it is clearly a simple model and, as such, an exponent of a class of models which are empirically feasible and of which one may ask whether they are not too simple to describe economic reality. In other words : a test of the CES model versus a more general model is a *pars pro toto* for the answer to the question whether the need for more general functional forms is indeed justified. Thirdly the function should be capable of testing the hypothesis of weak separability between domestic products and imports. That is, it should be able to represent the weak separability as a special case of a general total allocation model.

The possible candidates for a function that satisfies these three principles fall into two broad categories : one is the group of models that may be characterized as second-order approximations to a general aggregator function (or flexible functional forms) and the other is the group of models derived from a specific aggregator function. Because the flexible functional forms are second-order approximations to a general aggregator function, they also may be constrained to be such an approximation of the CES function, which therefore implies that they contain the CES model (in approximation) as a special case. They also should be considered very general models because of the way in which they are defined. There are however two disadvantages of flexible functional forms which make them unsuitable for our purposes. The first is that the number of parameters increases quadratically with the number of trade partners that are considered per import market. Given the present state of the length of available time series, this makes it impossible to estimate them for a relatively large number of trade partners. The second disadvantage, which will be discussed more extensively in section 5.4, is the fact that when weak separability is imposed on flexible functional forms, most of them may no longer be considered as second-order approximations of weakly separable aggregator functions. In fact, a test of weak separability on most of the flexible functional forms actually turns into a test for strong or homothetic separability. This impropriety of flexible functional forms leaves us models derived from specific aggregator functions. Two such classes of models have been defined by HANOCH (1975). If an aggregator function in any of the two classes contains n factors, the resulting demand equations will have less than $3n$ parameters. Both classes may be considered as generalizations of the homogeneous n-factor CES model of equation (3.7.1) and are therefore already suitable from the point of view that the CES model should be contained as a special case. Furthermore their estimation remains feasible for a large number of trade partners because the number of parameters increases only proportionately with the number of trade partners. Both classes are derived through assumptions of separability on the aggregator function.

The first class, the class of *implicit additive* models, is derived from the assumption that the aggregator function is implicitly additive, *i.e.* that the indifference or isoquant surfaces are strongly or additively separable such as defined in Definition 2.2.2, while the explicit function itself need not be additive. The second class, that of *explicit additive* models, is derived from an explicit additive aggregator function, *i.e.* one which is strongly or additively separable, also as an explicit function. The second class, however, is much more restrictive than the first, because of the existence of multiplicative or additive relationships between each substitution effect and its related income or expansion effect[1]. Members of the second class are aggregator functions such as the Cobb-Douglas function, the CES function or the function of MUKERJI (1963). The first class, although a generalization of the homogeneous CES function, allows for non-homotheticity as well as for non-constancy of the Allen Elasticities of Substitution (AES), the latter being determined from n "substitution functions". They therefore have the characteristic that n^2 different AES are generated from n substitution functions. Imposing the natural specialization of constancy on the n substitution functions, the class of implicit additive models reduces to the class of CRES (Constant Ratio of (Allen) Elasticity of Substitution) models, first introduced by GORMAN (1965). Imposing linear homogeneity then results in the Constant-Returns-to-Scale version of the CRESH model that will be developed further in this section. The imposition of linear homogeneity is done in view of the treatment of the adding-up problem in subsection 2.2.4. and the resulting possible alternatives for estimation-consistent models. It should be admitted that similar properties also could have been obtained with a version of the CRESH model that would have been homogeneous of a degree other than one or even homothetic. Because the model is mainly applied to import allocation models, we did not think a maintained hypothesis of a linear homogeneous import quantity index unrealistic, however.

5.2.2. DEFINITION

For our purposes, the CRESH function will in a first instance be applied to an import allocation model, and will therefore serve to define an import quantity index μ whose value is assumed to have been defined in a previous step in a way as described in subsection 2.2.3.

It therefore is the partial aggregator function that is the point of departure for the last stage of the three-stage procedure described in that subsection. In a first stage, there has been an allocation among different categories of goods k, including per category products of both domestic and foreign origin. In a second stage, there has been an allocation per category between domestic and imported products, and in the third and last stage imports per category are allocated over the different countries supplying import market j. The dimension of the import quantity index should therefore include subscripts k and j for the category of goods and the importing country, respectively. Throughout the chapter, these indices are, however, suppressed completely for the category of goods and, as far as possible, for the importing country.

The bilateral import prices pm_i $(i = 1, \ldots, n)$, which are assumed to be equal to one in the baseyear, are exogenous for the problem that is faced by the importer (or importing country) j, *viz.*, cost minimization subject to a technical relationship between μ and m_i for all $i \neq j$.

This relationship will be a special case of the CRESH function of HANOCH (1971), which is defined as [2)]

$$(2.1) \qquad F(\mu, m_1, \ldots, m_n) = \Sigma_i\ \delta_i (\frac{m_i}{h(\mu)})^{-\rho_i} - 1 \equiv 0,$$

for $m_i > 0$, $0 \leqslant \mu \leqslant \bar{\mu} \leqslant \infty$, where $h(\mu)$ should be continuously differentiable with $h(0) = 0$, $h(\bar{\mu}) = \infty$ and $h'(\mu) > 0$ ($\bar{\mu}$ denotes the maximum of the import quantity index). Also $F(0, 0, \ldots, 0) = 0$. The relationship yields a unique, continuously differentiable import quantity index $\mu = f(m_1, \ldots, m_n)$ through the implicit function theorem if and only if $max_i\ \delta_i > 0$ and $\{\delta_i \rho_i\}$ are of the same sign for all i [3)]. We will therefore assume that the parameters satisfy these restrictions.

We will work with the form of (2.1) which exhibits Constant Returns to Scale (CRS), *i.e.* when $h(\mu) = \mu$, and we will furthermore include a trend term, as follows

$$(2.2) \qquad F(\mu, m_1, \ldots, m_n, t) = \Sigma_i\ \delta_i\ e^{\gamma_i t} (\frac{m_i}{\mu})^{-\rho_i} - 1 \equiv 0.$$

The trend coefficient γ_i is assumed to represent shifts over time in the import quantity index due to non-price factors, while t is defined such that $t=0$ in the baseyear.

The conditions for (2.1) also apply to the CRS case defined in (2.2). The CRS property, or linear homogeneity of the index μ in the bilateral imports $m_1, \ldots, m_n$ is easily verified, because m_i is divided by μ in the implicit definition of μ.

Minimizing import cost $\Sigma_i\ pm_i\ m_i$ subject to (2.2) with respect to m_i for all i is equivalent to minimization of the Lagrangean

$$(2.3) \qquad L = \Sigma_i\ pm_i\ m_i + \lambda\ [\ \Sigma_i\ \delta_i\ e^{\gamma_i t} (\frac{m_i}{\mu})^{-\rho_i} - 1\ ],$$

with respect to $m_1, \ldots, m_n$ and the Lagrange multiplier λ.

We first analyze the first-order conditions for a solution of this minimization problem.

5.2.3. FIRST-ORDER CONDITIONS

The first-order conditions for minimization of (2.3) are

$$(2.4) \qquad \frac{\partial L}{\partial m_i} = pm_i - \lambda\delta_i\,\rho_i\, e^{\gamma_i t} \left(\frac{m_i}{\mu}\right)^{-\rho_i} \frac{1}{m_i} = 0 \qquad i = 1, \ldots, n,$$

$$(2.5) \qquad \frac{\partial L}{\partial \lambda} = \Sigma_i\, \delta_i\, e^{\gamma_i t} \left(\frac{m_i}{\mu}\right)^{-\rho_i} - 1 \equiv 0.$$

From condition (2.4) we find again that $\{\delta_i\, \rho_i\}$ should have the same sign for all i, and more specifically, this should be the sign of λ, because $\{\lambda\, \delta_i\, \rho_i\}$ should be positive for all i. If this were not the case, there would be no solution to (2.4) - (2.5). The system (2.4) - (2.5) has to be solved for all m_i and the Lagrange multiplier λ in terms of all the prices pm_i, t and μ. Because μ is a homothetic (and even linear homogenous) quantity index, we know from (2.2.7) that the elasticity of m_i with respect to μ in the cost-minimizing optimum should be equal to one. This implies that the solution to (2.4) - (2.5) for the absolute value of the Lagrange multplier λ, in terms of the predetermined variables only, should be of the form

$$(2.6) \qquad |\lambda| = \mu\, P(pm_1, \ldots, pm_n, t)$$

where $P(.)$ is a real positive function of the prices pm_i and time t. This may be seen as follows. Solve (2.4) for m_i. Requiring $\partial ln\, m_i/\partial ln\, \mu = 1$ implies then $\partial ln|\lambda|/\partial ln\, \mu = 1$. Because $|\lambda|$ is a function of all pm_i, μ and t, integrating back gives (2.6).

The solution for m_i therefore becomes

$$(2.7) \qquad m_i = \mu \, [\, |\delta_i \, \rho_i| \, e^{\gamma_i t} \, (\frac{pm_i}{P})^{-1} \,]^{a_i}, \qquad i = 1, \ldots, n,$$

where $a_i = 1/(1+\rho_i)$, and P still has to be determined. The a_i correspond to the substitution functions mentioned in subsection 5.2.1 and are indeed constant as they should be.

The import quantity index μ being defined implicitly, the solution for P also takes an implicit form. Consider the variable $\pi > 0$, defined implicitly by

$$(2.8) \qquad G(\pi, pm_1, \ldots, pm_n, t) = \Sigma_i \, \delta_i \, [\, |\delta_i \, \rho_i|^{-\rho_i} \, e^{\gamma_i t} \, (\frac{pm_i}{\pi})^{\rho_i} \,]^{a_i} - 1 \equiv 0,$$

and substitute π for P in (2.6) - (2.7). This gives

$$(2.9) \qquad |\lambda| = \mu \, \pi,$$

$$(2.10) \qquad m_i = \mu \, [\, |\delta_i \, \rho_i| e^{\gamma_i t} \, (\frac{pm_i}{\pi})^{-1} \,]^{a_i}, \qquad i = 1, \ldots, n.$$

It can be verified that (2.9) - (2.10) represents the solution for $|\lambda|$ and all m_i that satisfies the first-order conditions (2.4) - (2.5), given that π is defined as in (2.8). In fact, the solution for P was derived by substituting (2.6) - (2.7) in (2.4) - (2.5).

Next we eliminate μ, which is unobservable, from (2.10) in analogy to (2.2.8) - (2.2.10). Take the summation over i of both sides of (2.10). Remembering that m is the sum of all bilateral imports of country j in constant prices, we obtain

$$(2.11) \qquad m = \Sigma_i \, m_i = \mu \Sigma_i \, [\, |\delta_i \, \rho_i| \, e^{\gamma_i t} \, (\frac{pm_i}{\pi})^{-1} \,]^{a_i},$$

and therefore we can express μ as a function of the observable m (and time t and all prices pm_i). The solution for m_i as a function of m, time t and all prices pm_i then becomes

$$(2.12) \qquad m_i = m\, [\, |\delta_i\, \rho_i\,| e^{\gamma_i i} (\frac{pm_i}{\pi})^{-1}\,]^{a_i} \; \{\Sigma_\kappa\, [\, |\delta_\kappa\, \rho_k|\, e^{\gamma_k t} (\frac{pm_k}{\pi})^{-1}\,]^{a_k}\}^{-1}$$

$$i = 1, \ldots, n.$$

This form corresponds to (2.2.10) of subsection 2.2.4.

<u>The composite index π</u>

The existence of π as a continuously differentiable function of t and all prices pm_i is guaranteed by the implicit function theorem if $\partial G/\partial\pi \neq 0$ at all points for which we define (2.8), *viz.* for real positive pm_i $(i = 1, \ldots, n)$ and t a natural number.

The partial derivative of G with respect to π equals

$$(2.13) \qquad \frac{\partial G}{\partial \pi} = -\Sigma_i\, \delta_i\, \rho_i\, a_i\, [\, |\delta_i\, \rho_i|^{-\rho_i}\, e^{\gamma_i t} (\frac{pm_i}{\pi})\,]^{\rho_i a_i}\, \pi^{-1}.$$

Because $\{\delta_i\, \rho_i\}$ have the same sign for all i, this expression equals zero if and only if some a_i are positive and some a_i are negative. We will see below in subsection 5.2.5. that the second-order conditions rule out the possibility that more than one a_i is negative. If only one a_i is negative, say a_1, the condition $\partial G/\partial\pi \neq 0$ becomes equivalent to

$$(2.14) \qquad [\, |\delta_1\, \rho_1| e^{-\gamma_1 t/\rho_1} (\frac{pm_1}{\pi})^{-1}\,]^{a_1}$$

$$\neq \{\Sigma_{i=2}^{n} \frac{\delta_i\, \rho_i\, a_i}{\delta_1\, \rho_1 |a_1|}\, [\, |\delta_i\, \rho_i|^{-\rho_i}\, e^{\gamma_i t} (\frac{pm_i}{\pi})\,]^{\rho_i a_i}\}^{-1/\rho_1}$$

As we will see below in equation (2.40), this condition is met if the second-order conditions are satisfied.

It would be attractive to interpret π as a *price index,* because then m_i becomes a function of the relative price pm_i/π, which gives it a clear-cut interpretation. One property of the price indices that we use is that they are equal to one in the baseyear, where also $t=0$. From the definition of π in (2.8) it may be seen that this requirement imposes the following constraint, or "normalization" on the parameters of the import quantity index

$$(2.15) \qquad \Sigma_i \, \delta_i |\delta_i \, \rho_i|^{-\rho_i \, a_i} = 1.$$

If we define the real scalar B as

$$(2.16) \qquad B = \Sigma_i \, \delta_i |\delta_i \, \rho_i|^{-\rho_i \, a_i},$$

the normalization (2.15) may be accomplished if we define a new parameter d_i as

$$(2.17) \qquad d_i = sgn(B)\beta^{-\rho_i} \, \delta_i \qquad\qquad i = 1, \ldots, n$$

where $sgn(B)$ denotes the sign of B and the real scalar $\beta > 0$ is defined implicitly by

$$(2.18) \qquad \Sigma_i \, \delta_i \, \beta^{-\rho_i \, a_i} |\delta_i \, \rho_i|^{-\rho_i \, a_i} = 1.$$

It may be seen that the conditions under which the implicit function theorem holds for β in this case are equivalent to (2.14) with $t=0$, $\pi=1$ and $pm_i = 1$ for all i, *i.e.* at their base year values.

Solving δ_i from (2.17) and substitution in the definition of the import quantity index (2.2) gives

$$(2.19) \qquad F(\mu, m_1, \ldots, m_n, t) = sgn(B)\Sigma_i\, d_i\, e^{\gamma_i t} \left(\frac{m_i}{\beta\mu}\right)^{-\rho_i} - 1 \equiv 0.$$

This definition is virtually equivalent to (2.2) if we interpret δ_i as $sgn(B)d_i$ and if we interpret μ as $\beta\mu$, but now with the additional restriction

$$(2.20) \qquad sgn(B)\Sigma_i\, d_i |d_i\, \rho_i|^{-\rho_i a_i} = 1.$$

Interpretation of π as a composite price index has one drawback, however. This may be seen if we look at the partial derivative of π with respect to each price pm_i, which may be obtained by taking the total differential of (2.8). The result is

$$(2.21) \qquad \frac{\partial\pi}{\partial pm_i} = \frac{\pi}{pm_i} \frac{\delta_i\, \rho_i\, a_i\, [\,|\delta_i\, \rho_i|^{-\rho_i} e^{\gamma_i t} (\frac{pm_i}{\pi})^{\rho_i}]^{a_i}}{\Sigma_k\, \delta_k\, \rho_k\, a_k\, [\,|\delta_k\, \rho_k|^{-\rho_k} e^{\gamma_k t} (\frac{pm_k}{\pi})^{\rho_k}]^{a_k}}, \; i = 1, \ldots, n.$$

If we are in the situation that one of the a_i is negative, and the others are positive, we find as a result that the partial derivative of π with respect to that price is of opposite sign compared to all other partial derivatives. We would then be saddled with a price index that possibly decreases upon an increase in one of its constituent prices, which is not a desirable property of price indices. It concerns however an exceptional situation, in the normal case all a_i are positive and the abnormal behaviour is absent.

5.2.4. ELASTICITIES OF SUBSTITUTION

In this subsection we will derive all the elasticities of substitution (ES) that were presented in subsection 3.2.3. of Chapter 3. These ES correspond to the derived bilateral import demand equations (2.10). We find that if the ES are assumed to be equal between all pairs of partners on the same import market (importing country), which is the CES case, the notions of Allen partial Elasticity of Substitution (AES), Direct Elasticity of Substitution (DES) and Shadow Elasticity of Substitution (SES) are one and the same [4)]. Therefore, if we test the CES model against our model (which is an implicit test of the hypothesis that all ES are equal versus the alternative that they are not equal), this test will be the same irrespective of the kind of ES we analyze. We therefore do not have to make a choice between the multifactor ES, for this purpose at least.

We start with the AES. We already argued in section 3.8 that if one needed a measure of ES, the AES would probably be the most appropriate because it is the closest to the elements of the Hessian matrix, apart from the own and cross-price elasticities. We saw, however, that the AES could be considered as a normalization of the latter, a normalization which makes them symmetric. To this advantage is added the use that we can make of the AES in analyzing the second-order conditions for minimization of the Lagrangean (2.3), because this analysis may be performed in terms of the matrix of AES. This will be done in subsection 5.2.5.

In order to derive the AES, we first calculate the own and cross-price elasticities of the demand for bilateral imports m_i from (2.10) and (2.21).

$$(2.22)\qquad e_{ii} = \frac{\partial ln\ m_i}{\partial ln\ pm_i} = \frac{w_i\ a_i^2}{a} - a_i\ , \qquad i = 1, \ldots, n,$$

$$(2.23)\qquad e_{ik} = \frac{\partial ln\ m_i}{\partial ln\ pm_k} = \frac{w_k\ a_i\ a_k}{a}\ , \qquad i \neq k = 1, \ldots, n,$$

where $w_i = pm_i\, m_i \,/\, \Sigma_k\, pm_k\, m_k$, the value share of imports from partner i in total cost at the cost-minimizing optimum, and $a = \Sigma_k\, w_k\, a_k$, a weighted average of the a_i over i, with the optimal value shares as weights.

As we demonstrated in equation (3.3.9), the AES may be obtained through division of the price elasticities by the optimal value share in total costs corresponding to the changing price.

For the pairwise AES this results in

$$(2.24) \qquad A_{ik} = \frac{a_i\, a_k}{a}, \qquad\qquad i \neq k = 1, \ldots, n,$$

which corresponds to the result that was already given in equation (3.7.7) with $\theta(y) = 1$.

For the "own" AES we obtain in a similar way

$$(2.25) \qquad A_{ii} = \frac{a_i^2}{a} - \frac{a_i}{w_i}, \qquad\qquad i = 1, \ldots, n.$$

The DES was defined in equation (3.2.30). The partial derivatives needed in this definition, which should be evaluated at the cost-minimizing optimum, may be derived by taking the total differential of (2.2) and use of (2.10). The results are

$$(2.26) \qquad f_i = \frac{\partial \mu}{\partial m_i} = \frac{\mu}{m_i}\, w_i, \qquad\qquad i = 1, \ldots, n,$$

$$(2.27) \qquad f_{ik} = \frac{\partial f_i}{\partial m_k} = \frac{f_i\, f_k}{\mu} \{\frac{1}{a_i} + \frac{1}{a_k} - \Sigma_h\, w_h/a_h\}, \qquad i \neq k = 1, \ldots, n,$$

$$(2.28) \qquad f_{ii} = \frac{\partial f_i}{\partial m_i} = \frac{f_i^2}{\mu} \{- \frac{1}{w_i\, a_i} + \frac{2}{a_i} - \Sigma_h\, w_h/a_h\} \qquad\qquad i = 1, \ldots, n,$$

where all m_i, w_i and f_i are evaluated in the optimum. Substitution of (2.26) - (2.28) gives the following simple form for the DES

$$(2.29) \qquad D_{ik} = \frac{a_i \, a_k}{(w_i \, a_i + w_k \, a_k)/(w_i + w_k)} \qquad i \neq k = 1, \ldots, n,$$

which resembles the AES, albeit that the denominator is now only a weighted average of a_i and a_k.

Finally we come to the SES, which was defined in terms of the AES in (3.4.15), and may therefore be calculated upon substitution of (2.24) and (2.25) in this formula. The result is

$$(2.30) \qquad S_{ik} = \frac{w_i \, w_k}{(w_i + w_k)} \{\frac{a_i}{w_i} + \frac{a_k}{w_k} - \frac{1}{a} (a_i - a_k)^2\}, \qquad i \neq k = 1, \ldots, n ,$$

where again the value shares in total cost should be taken at the cost-minimizing optimum.

From (2.24), (2.29) and (2.30) we find that if any of these ES have to be equal for all pairs of partners i and k, this is happening if and only if $a_i = a_k$ for all $i \neq k$, say equal to σ, and that then

$$(2.31) \qquad A_{ik} = D_{ik} = S_{ik} = \sigma , \qquad i \neq k = 1, \ldots, n.$$

The immediate implication of (2.31) is clear : estimation of our model under the assumption that all ES are pairwise equal on the same import market does not require that we specify for which ES they should be equal, because in that case all three concepts are identical. We may therefore test in a very general way the hypotheses on ES that were put forward in Chapter 1.

The CRES property becomes clear if we see that the R^k_{ih} from (3.2.39) equals a_k/a_h, which is constant.

5.2.5. SECOND-ORDER CONDITIONS

It is well known that the second-order conditions imply that the nxn matrix S with element (i, k) equal to $\partial m_i/\partial pm_k$ should be negative semi-definite [5], and because of the definition of the AES this result carries over to the nxn matrix A with element (i, k) equal to A_{ik}.

Negative semi-definiteness of A is equivalent to the requirement [6]

$$(2.32) \qquad (-1)^m |A_m| \geqslant 0 \,, \qquad\qquad m = 1, \ldots, n \,,$$

where $|A_m|$ is any principal minor determinant of order m of A. Because we know from (3.2.25) that $|A| = 0$ and therefore all $|A_n| = 0$, condition (2.32) only has to be verified for $m = 1, \ldots, n-1$.

From definitions (2.24) and (2.25) we can calculate

$$(2.33) \qquad (-1)^m |A_m| = (\Pi_{i=1}^m \frac{a_i}{w_i})(1 - \Sigma_{i=1}^m \frac{w_i\, a_i}{a}), \qquad m = 1, \ldots, n,$$

so that condition (2.32) is equivalent to

$$(2.34) \qquad (\Pi_{i=1}^m a_i)(1 - \Sigma_{i=1}^m \frac{w_i\, a_i}{a}) \geqslant 0, \qquad\qquad m = 1, \ldots, n.$$

Instead of (2.34), HANOCH (1971, p. 699) supposes that (2.32) is equivalent to

$$(2.35) \qquad (\Pi_{i=1}^m a_i)(\Sigma_{i=1}^m w_i\, a_i) > 0 \,, \qquad\qquad m = 1, \ldots, n.$$

Numerous counterexamples show, however, that (2.35) is in contradiction [7] with requiring (2.33) to be positive for $m = 1, \ldots, n-1$. Take for example

$m = 1$, $n = 2$, $w_1 = w_2 = .5$, $a_1 = -1$ and $a_2 = 3$. Expression (2.33) then equals -3, while the left-hand side of (2.35) is equal to .5, which is a contradiction.

The condition (2.34) excludes the possibility that more than one a_i is negative. This may be shown as follows.

Suppose $a_i < 0$ for $i = 1, \ldots, k$ with $2 \leqslant k \leqslant n$ and $a_i > 0$ for $i = k+1, \ldots, n$. Suppose furthermore that (2.34) holds. Then there are two possibilities (if we exclude $a = 0$) : either $a > 0$ or $a < 0$. Suppose $a > 0$ and take $m = 1$. Condition (2.34) then implies $\Sigma_{i=2}^{n} w_i a_i \leqslant 0$. Because $w_1 a_1 < 0$, this implies $a < 0$. Contradiction. Next suppose $a < 0$ and take $m = 1$. Applying a similar reasoning as above, this implies $\Sigma_{i=2}^{n} w_i a_i \geqslant 0$. Next take $m = 2$. Then (2.34) implies $\Sigma_{i=3}^{n} w_i a_i \leqslant 0$ from which it follows with $w_2 a_2 < 0$ that $\Sigma_{i=2}^{n} w_i a_i < 0$. Contradiction.

Next we consider the possiblity that one a_i is negative while all others are positive. HANOCH (1971, p. 700) showed that a sufficient condition for (2.34) to hold in that case would be $a < 0$, but on the basis of (2.35), which is not correct. We will therefore reconsider the case, but on the basis of (2.34).

If $n = 2$, it can easily be verified that (2.34) holds if and only if $a < 0$, or (if we take $a_1 < 0$)

$$(2.36) \qquad - w_1 a_1 > w_2 a_2 > 0 \, ,$$

which, using the first-order condition (2.4), is equivalent to

$$(2.37) \qquad -1 < \frac{\delta_2 \, \rho_2 \, a_2 \, e^{\gamma_2 t} \left(\frac{m_2}{\mu}\right)^{-\rho_2}}{\delta_1 \, \rho_1 \, a_1 \, e^{\gamma_1 t} \left(\frac{m_1}{\mu}\right)^{-\rho_1}} < 0 \, ,$$

or, if we solve for (m_1/μ)

$$(2.38)\qquad \frac{m_1}{\mu} > \left[\frac{\delta_2\,\rho_2\,a_2\,e^{\gamma_2 t}}{\delta_1\,\rho_1|a_1|e^{\gamma_1 t}}\left(\frac{m_2}{\mu}\right)^{-\rho_2}\right]^{-1/\rho_1} .$$

Let us next consider the case when $n > 2$. Suppose, without loss of generality, that $a_2 < 0$ and $a_i > 0$ for all $i \neq 2$. For $m = 1$, (2.34) holds if and only if $\Sigma_{i=2}^{n} w_i\, a_i/a > 0$. For $m = 2$, the necessary and sufficient condition is $\Sigma_{i=3}^{n} w_i\, a_i/a < 0$. Because $\Sigma_{i=3}^{n} w_i\, a_i > 0$ by assumption, this is equivalent to $a < 0$. By induction we find that $a < 0$ is a sufficient condition for (2.34) to hold. It is not a necessary condition, as can be seen from the case $m = 1$.

If we put next for the sake of exposition the negative a_i in the first position, $a_1 < 0$ and $a_i > 0$ for all $i > 1$, the sufficient condition $a < 0$ for quasi-concavity of $\mu = f(m_1, \ldots, m_n, t)$ becomes

$$(2.39)\qquad \frac{m_1}{\mu} > \left[\Sigma_{i=2}^{n}\frac{\delta_i\,\rho_i\,a_i\,e^{\gamma_i t}}{\delta_1\,\rho_1|a_1|e^{\gamma_1 t}}\left(\frac{m_i}{\mu}\right)^{-\rho_i}\right]^{-1/\rho_1} ,$$

or, using (2.10)

$$(2.40)\qquad \left[\,|\delta_1\,\rho_1|e^{-\gamma_1 t/\rho_1}\left(\frac{pm_1}{\pi}\right)^{-1}\right]^{a_1}$$

$$> \left\{\Sigma_{i=2}^{n}\frac{\delta_i\,\rho_i\,a_i}{\delta_1\,\rho_1|a_1|}\left[\,|\delta_i\,\rho_i|^{-\rho_i}\,e^{\gamma_i t}\left(\frac{pm_i}{\pi}\right)\right]^{\rho_i a_i}\right\}^{-1/\rho_1} ,$$

which is sufficient for the condition (2.14), which implies the existence of the implicit price index π, to hold.

As long as (2.39) holds, we observe that bilateral imports, m_1 are a substitute for all other bilateral imports because $A_{1k} > 0$ for all $k > 1$. All these other bilateral imports, on the other hand, form a group of complements because $A_{hk} < 0$ for all $1 \neq h \neq k > 1$.

Finally, if all $a_i > 0$, it can easily be verified that (2.34) always holds. In that case all bilateral imports are substitutes because all $A_{ik} > 0$ for $i \neq k$.

Summarizing, we see that the existence of a cost-minimizing optimum for the CRS form of the CRESH model implies that all bilateral imports are supposed to be substitutes in the sense of the AES, or that bilateral imports from one partner act as a substitute for all others, which themselves form a group of complements in that case. The latter is only allowed for a partner with a relatively large import share, as may be observed from the condition (2.39). Such a case may be imagined if there is a small country whose imports are mainly supplied by one big trading partner, such as the case of Ireland and the United Kingdom, Austria and the Federal Republic of Germany etc.

If we take it that the situation generally prevails where all bilateral imports are substitutes, one may ask whether this is not too restrictive.

First of all, in view of testing the hypotheses on the CES model as formulated in Chapter 1, this is not so. We are perfectly able to test the influences of the goods classification and the number of trading partners on the outcome of a test of the CES model versus our model, because the CES model is a special case of our model if all a_i are equal for all i (with the additional advantage that we do not have to make a distinction as to whether we make this hypothesis for the AES, DES, or SES).

Secondly, we know already from subsection 3.2.3. that the weighted positive AES are more numerous than their negative counterparts, *i.e.* there already exists a tendency towards substitutability prevailing over complementarity according to the AES definition.

Finally, the fact that generally the AES of our model are positive is in a sense the price we have to pay for a model with relatively few parameters but which is still so general that for instance all bilateral import prices appear - albeit in a structured way - in each bilateral import demand equation as we will see below. If we were to work with a still more general model, this would certainly be at the expense of an increase in the number of parameters to be estimated [8).

5.3. THREE APPROXIMATIONS

The bilateral import demand equations derived in (2.12) are highly nonlinear and contain the implicitly defined composite price index π. Direct estimation of these equations therefore seems impossible. In this section we present therefore three approximations to (2.12) that reduce the nonlinearities and at the same time eliminate the unobservable index π. The three approximations correspond to the three solutions of the adding-up problem presented in subsection 2.2.4. Furthermore, because it concerns approximations which are linear, loglinear and in logarithmic differences, respectively, we obtain the three kinds of functional forms which are commonly proposed in international trade linkage models. We discussed their advantages and disadvantages in subsection 1.3.2. Because we dispose of the three kinds of functional forms relating to the same model, we may use them in the empirical part of this study to see whether any of the three specifications has to be preferred from an empirical point of view.

5.3.1. A LINEARIZATION IN LEVELS

For the linearization in levels, we start with the expression for bilateral imports m_i which was derived in (2.12), and which is reproduced here for convenience.

$$(3.1) \qquad m_i = m\,[\,|\delta_i \rho_i|\,e^{\gamma_i t}\,(\frac{pm_i}{\pi})^{-1}\,]^{a_i}\,\{\Sigma_k[\,|\delta_k \rho_k|\,e^{\gamma_k t}\,(\frac{pm_k}{\pi})^{-1}\,]^{a_k}\}^{-1}, \qquad i = 1, \ldots, n.$$

If all a_i are equal, say to σ, we have the case where all ES are equal, which is the CES form

$$(3.2) \qquad m_i = m\, \delta_i^{\sigma} e^{\sigma \gamma_i t} pm_i^{-\sigma} \{\Sigma_k [\delta_k e^{\gamma_k t} pm_k^{-1}]^{\sigma -1}\}, \qquad i = 1, \ldots, n,$$

where σ is now the unique ES, equal to AES, DES and SES.

The determination of the distribution parameters

HICKMAN and LAU (1973) imposed the normalization (2.3.2) on (3.2)

$$(3.3) \qquad \Sigma_i \delta_i^{\sigma} = 1 ,$$

so that for the baseyear (in which all bilateral prices are equal to one, and $t = 0$) we obtain from (3.2)

$$(3.4) \qquad w_i^o = m_i^o/m^o = \delta_i^{\sigma} , \qquad i = 1, \ldots, n,$$

where the superscript "o" denotes baseyear values. Given an estimated value for σ, this expression makes it possible to calculate the distribution parameters δ_i.

For our model we obtain a similar result. Expression (3.1), when evaluated at baseyear values, gives us

$$(3.5) \qquad w_i^o = m_i^o/m^o = |\delta_i \rho_i|^{a_i} [\Sigma_k |\delta_k \rho_k|^{a_k}]^{-1} , \qquad i = 1, \ldots, n.$$

Given estimates for ρ_i (or a_i) for all i and the normalization (2.15), we are able to calculate the distribution parameters δ_i, although this is not as easy as for the CES case.

First observe, with $\rho_k a_k = 1 - a_k$, that (2.15) is equivalent to

$$(3.6) \qquad \Sigma_k \, sgn(\delta_k) \, |\delta_k|^{a_k} \, |\rho_k|^{a_k - 1} = 1.$$

Multiplying both sides of (3.5) by $sgn(\delta_i)/|\rho_i|$ and summing over i, the denominator on the right-hand side of (3.5) may, with (3.6), be seen to be equal to

$$(3.7) \qquad \Sigma_k \, |\delta_k \rho_k|^{a_k} = [\, \Sigma_k \, sgn(\delta_k) \, w_k^o / |\rho_k|]^{-1} .$$

Because $\{\delta_i \rho_i\}$ are of the same sign for all i, this results in

$$(3.8) \qquad \Sigma_k \, |\delta_k \rho_k|^{a_k} = |\Sigma_k \, w_k^o / \rho_k|^{-1}.$$

This gives as a solution for δ_i from (3.5) and (3.8)

$$(3.9) \qquad \delta_i = sgn(\delta_i \, \rho_i) \, [w_i^o |\Sigma_k \, w_k^o / \rho_k|^{-1}]^{1/a_i} \, \rho_i^{-1} , \qquad i = 1, \ldots, n,$$

where $sgn(\delta_i \rho_i)$, which is the same for all i, has to be determined empirically upon insertion of (3.9) in (2.15). This way of calculating the distribution parameters δ_i may be applied to any of the three approximations.

The linearization in levels

A first-order Taylor expansion of (3.1) around the baseyear values $m = m^o$, $t = 0$ and $pm_i = 1$ for all i results, with the use of (2.21), in

$$(3.10) \qquad m_i = w_i^o m + m_i^o c_i \, t - m_i^o a_i \, [pm_i - \Sigma_k \frac{w_k^o \, a_k}{a^o} \, pm_k] , \quad i = 1, \ldots, n,$$

where the trend coefficient c_i equals

$$(3.11) \qquad c_i = a_i \, [\gamma_i + \Sigma_k \frac{w_k^o \, a_k}{a^o} (\gamma_k/\rho_k)] - \Sigma_k \, w_k^o(\gamma_k/\rho_k) \, , \qquad i = 1, \ldots, n \, ,$$

and a^o is a weighted average of the a_i

$$(3.12) \qquad a^o = \Sigma_k \, w_k^o \, a_k \, ,$$

with the baseyear bilateral import shares as weights. Note that $\Sigma_i \, w_i^o \, c_i = 0$ using the definition of $a_i = 1/(1+\rho_i)$.

If we define A_{ik}^o for all i and k to be the baseyear values of the AES defined in (2.24) and (2.25), we may rewrite (3.10) as

$$(3.13) \qquad m_i = w_i^o \, m + m_i^o \, c_i \, t - m_i^o \;\; \Sigma_k \, w_k^o \, A_{ik}^o \;\; pm_k \, , \qquad i = 1, \ldots, n,$$

which clearly demonstrates the role of the AES.

Because the AES are equal to the own and cross-price elasticities of demand, divided by the share of the price that is changed, an alternative way of writing (3.10) would be in terms of the price elasticities in the baseyear e_{ik}^o $(= w_k^o \, A_{ik}^o)$ as follows

$$(3.14) \qquad m_i = w_i^o \, m + m_i^o \, c_i \, t + m_i^o \;\; \Sigma_k \, e_{ik}^o \, pm_k \, , \qquad i = 1, \ldots, n$$

As we saw in subsection 3.3.1, this concept is very close to the elements of the Hessian matrix corresponding to the import quantity index μ, *cfr.* equation (3.3.8).

It would be attractive to estimate the AES or price elasticities directly from (3.13) or (3.14). But as there are n equations, which moreover form a constrained model so that we would have to delete one equation [9], we would have $n(n-1)$ freely estimated price coefficients, while we only need n coefficients (the a_i), and we must conclude that such a system would be over-identified. Even if we imposed constraints from demand theory such as homogeneity and symmetry, the system remains over-identified because of the implicit additivity of the import quantity index.

Furthermore, given estimates for the c_i and the a_i, it is clear that the parameters for shifts in the import quantity index over time, the γ_i, are underidentified, because the c_i should obey the linear restrictions $\Sigma_i m_i^o c_i = 0$. We would only get as far as calculating the ratios between the different γ_i.

We may write (3.10) alternatively as

$$(3.15) \qquad m_i = w_i^o m + m_i^o c_i t - m_i^o a_i [pm_i - \Sigma_k w_k^o pm_k],$$
$$+ m_i^o a_i \Sigma_k w_k^o \frac{a_k - a^o}{a^o} pm_k , \qquad i = 1, \dots, n,$$

from which it is clear that the last term on the right-hand side is the deviation from the linearized CES case [10], because then all a_i are equal, say to σ, and we have the formulation of HICKMAN and LAU (1973, p. 354)

$$(3.16) \qquad m_i = w_i^o m + m_i^o \sigma r_i t - m_i^o \sigma [pm_i - \Sigma_k w_k^o pm_k] \qquad i = 1, \dots, n,$$

with $r_i = \gamma_i - \Sigma_k w_k^o \gamma_k$ for all i.

The total export equation

We may also derive a total export equation from (3.10). If we disregard cif-fob differences, this equation can be calculated by introducing the subscript j for the importing country and summing both sides of (3.10) over j.

$$(3.17) \qquad x_i = \Sigma_j m_{ij} = \Sigma_j w_{ij}^o m_j + x_i^o c_i^\star t - x_i^o a_i^\star (px_i - pw_i) ,$$

where x_i are exports of country/zone i in constant prices [11], the time trend coefficient is an average over the c_{ij}

(3.18) $$c_i^{\star} = \Sigma_j \, v_{ij}^o \, c_{ij} \, ,$$

with as weights the share of exports from i to j in total exports of i in the baseyear

(3.19) $$v_{ij}^o = m_{ij}^o / x_i^o \, , \qquad j = 1, \ldots, n \, ,$$

while $a_i^{\star}$ is an average over importers j of the a_{ij} defined as

(3.20) $$a_i^{\star} = \Sigma_j \, v_{ij}^o \, a_{ij} .$$

The "relative price" that appears in the total export equation consists of an export price px_i defined as a weighted average of the bilateral import prices as follows

(3.21) $$px_i = \Sigma_j \, \frac{v_{ij}^o \, a_{ij}}{a_i^{\star}} \, pm_{ij} \, ,$$

and a competitors' price pw_i which is a double-weighted average of the bilateral import prices of the trading partners of exporter i with weights specific both to the exporting country i and the importers j

(3.22) $$pw_i = \Sigma_j \, \frac{v_{ij}^o \, a_{ij}}{a_i^{\star}} \; \Sigma_k \, \frac{w_{kj}^o \, a_{kj}}{a_j^o} \; pm_{kj} \, .$$

Adding-up

If we make a summation of both sides of (3.10) over i, we find that bilateral flows in constant prices m_i add up to total imports in constant prices m, as could be expected of a linearization in levels of a system of equations that already satisfied the adding-up criterion. If such a system is to be estimated, the linear restriction $\Sigma_i\, w_i^o\, c_i = 0$ (or $\Sigma_i\, m_i^o\, c_i = 0$) should be imposed on the coefficients c_i. Also for (3.13) and (3.14), which are nothing but rewritings of (3.10), we find with $\Sigma_i\, w_i^o\, A_{ik}^o = 0$ and $\Sigma_i\, w_i^o\, e_{ik}^o = 0$ that

$$(3.23) \qquad \Sigma_i\, m_i = m.$$

Still disregarding the cif-fob differences we also find that world imports will add up to world exports because of the way in which total exports x_i in constant prices were defined in (3.17)

$$(3.24) \qquad \Sigma_i\, x_i = \Sigma_i\, \Sigma_j\, m_{ij} = \Sigma_j\, \Sigma_i\, m_{ij} = \Sigma_j\, m_j.$$

Dynamics

Next we will introduce dynamic elements in (3.10) by assuming that the bilateral import prices pm_{it} which appear in that equation are not the observed prices, but an infinitely distributed lag pm_{it}^e of the observed prices as follows

$$(3.25) \qquad pm_{it}^e = \Sigma_{k=0}^{\infty}\, (1 - \lambda)\, \lambda^k\, B^k\, pm_{it}\,, \qquad\qquad i = 1, \ldots, n,$$

with $0 \leqslant \lambda < 1$ and B the lag operator $B^k x_t = x_{t-k}$. This price pm_{it}^e may alternatively be obtained as the expectation of a function $h_i(\tau) = B^{\tau}\, pm_{it}$, $\tau = 0,1,2, \ldots, i = 1, \ldots, n$ of a random variable τ, where τ is assumed to follow the geometric discribution with the following probability density function

$$(3.26) \qquad f_{\tau}(z) = \begin{cases} (1 - \lambda)\, \lambda^z & \text{for } z = 0,1,2, \ldots, \\ 0 & \text{otherwise,} \end{cases}$$

with the same parameter λ as in (3.25) [12).

The expectation pm^e_{it} of $h_i(\tau)$ is then obtained as

$$(3.27) \quad pm^e_{it} = \Sigma^{\infty}_{k=0} \quad f_{\tau}(k)\ h_i(k)$$

$$= \Sigma^{\infty}_{k=0}\ (1 - \lambda)\ \lambda^k\ B^k\ pm_{it}$$

$$= (1 - \lambda)(1 - \lambda\ B)^{-1}\ pm_{it}\ , \qquad i = 1, \ldots, n,$$

where $(1 - \lambda\ B)^{-1} = \Sigma^{\infty}_{k=0}\ \lambda^k\ B^k$ from the algebra of lag operators [13]. This expression is equal to (3.25).

This way of deriving the price pm^e_{it} provides an interpretation for pm^e_{it} as being the expectation of a random drawing of the set of present and past bilateral import prices $\{pm_{it}, pm_{it-1}, pm_{it-2}, \ldots\}$, with the recent prices having a higher probability to be drawn than older prices. This represents the case in which our fictive importer does not have perfect information at his disposal and is assumed to observe prices in function of the real prices, where recent prices have a higher weight. Note that we assume that the probabilities are equal for each trading partner i. This is reasonable if we assume that the importer's information is spread evenly over all prices pm_{it} : he knows as much of the bilateral import price for partner i as for partner k for all i and k. The main advantage of this assumption lies in the fact that it still assures the adding-up of the m_{it} with respect to total imports m_t. This may be seen if we replace the pm_{it} in (3.10) by the infinitely distributed lag (3.25) or the price expectation of (3.27), and make the Koyck transformation [14]

$$(3.28) \quad m_{it} = w^o_i\ m_{it} + \lambda(m_i - w^o_i\ m)_{t-1} + m^o_i\ c_i(1 - \lambda)t + m^o_i\ c_i\ \lambda$$

$$- m^o_i\ a_i(1 - \lambda)\ [pm_{it} - \Sigma_k \frac{w^o_k\ a_k}{a^o}\ pm_{kt}]$$

It can easily be verified that $\Sigma_i\, m_{it} = m_t$, despite the introduction of dynamics.

There are other ways of introducing dynamics in (3.10), for instance to assume a partial adjustment process whereby bilateral imports adjust partially to an optimal value described by the right-hand side of (3.10), or to assume that bilateral imports follow an error correction mechanism with respect to the same optimal value [15]. But, even if we assume that the adjustment parameter or the error correction parameters are equal for all partners i, it is much more difficult to maintain adding-up with respect to total imports of the resulting dynamic equations.

Estimating equation

In order to derive an estimating equation from (3.28), we force the coefficient of $w_i^o\, m_t$ to be equal to one by bringing it to the left-hand side, while we divide the whole equation by m_i^o such that the left-hand side may be interpreted in terms of differences of growth rates of bilateral imports and total imports with respect to the baseyear

$$\text{(3.29)} \qquad \frac{m_{it} - w_i^o\, m_t}{m_i^o} = \lambda\, \frac{(m_i - w_i^o\, m)_{t-1}}{m_i^o} + c_i(1 - \lambda)t + c_i\, \lambda$$

$$- a_i(1 - \lambda)\, [pm_{it} - \Sigma_k\, \frac{w_k^o\, a_k}{a^o}\, pm_{kt}]\, .$$

5.3.2. A LOGLINEAR APPROXIMATION

Derivation

For a loglinear approximation to (2.10), we first rewrite it in terms of logarithms as

$$\ln m_i = \ln \mu + a_i \,[\,\ln|\delta_i \rho_i| + \gamma_i t - (\ln pm_i - \ln \pi)], \quad i = 1, \ldots, n, \tag{3.30}$$

where the logarithmic price index $\ln \pi$ is defined implicitly in terms of the $\ln pm_i$ as follows

$$\Sigma_i \, \delta_i \, \exp \{a_i \,[- \rho_i \ln|\delta_i \rho_i| + \gamma_i t + \rho_i(\ln pm_i - \ln \pi)]\} - 1 = 0 \tag{3.31}$$

Because $\ln \mu$ is an unobservable variable, we want to substitute it with an observable variable for purposes of estimation. In the linear case, the obvious candidate to replace μ was total imports in constant prices $m = \Sigma_i m_i$, but in the loglinear case replacement of $\ln \mu$ by $\ln m$, which could be effectuated by writing (2.12) in terms of logarithms, guarantees no longer that the adding-up condition $\Sigma_i m_i = m$ will be satisfied exactly [16].

In subsection 2.2.4. we argued that the inclusion in a model of bilateral import equations which are a function of total imports m, and a function that explains m (instead of the import quantity index μ), is as arbitrary as writing the bilateral import equations as a function of another index, say $\bar{m}$, instead of m, and to include a separate equation explaining $\bar{m}$ instead of m, while the latter could then be calculated through the identity $m = \Sigma_i m_i$, in this way automatically satisfying the adding-up condition. For the loglinear approximation we will opt for this alternative, and we therefore assume that for the bilateral import demand equations the following import quantity index $\bar{m}$ is given

(3.32) $\bar{m} = \Pi_i \, m_i^{w_i^o}$

which is a weighted geometric mean of the bilateral imports, with as weights the baseyear value shares. In logarithms this index equals

(3.33) $ln\, \bar{m} = \Sigma_i \, w_i^o \, ln\, m_i.$

We are now going to eliminate $ln\, \mu$ from (3.30). Premultiplication of both sides of (3.30) by w_i^o and summation over i gives, with (3.33),

(3.34) $ln\, \mu = ln\, \bar{m} - \Sigma_i \, w_i^o \, a_i \, [\, ln|\delta_i \rho_i| + \gamma_i t - (ln\, pm_i - ln\, \pi)],$

which may next be substituted in (3.30) to replace $ln\, \mu$ by $ln\, \bar{m}$. The result may be written as

(3.35) $ln\, m_i = ln\, \bar{m} + ln\, \eta_i + \bar{c}_i t - a_i \, (ln\, pm_i - ln\, \pi)$

$+ \Sigma_k \, w_k^o \, a_k \, (ln\, pm_k - ln\, \pi)\,, \qquad i = 1, \ldots, n$

where $\bar{c}_i = a_i \gamma_i - \Sigma_i \, w_i^o \, a_i \gamma_i$ and $ln\, \eta_i$ equals

(3.36) $ln\, \eta_i = a_i \, ln\, |\delta_i \rho_i| - \Sigma_k \, w_k^o \, a_k \, ln|\delta_k \rho_k|,$

$i = 1, \ldots, n$

Define the "share" $\bar{w}_i$ by

(3.37) $\bar{w}_i = m_i / \bar{m}\,, \qquad i = 1, \ldots, n,$

then we observe that in the baseyear (3.35) reduces to

(3.38) $ln\, m_i^o = ln\, \bar{m}^o + ln\, \eta_i\,, \qquad i = 1, \ldots, n,$

such that η_i may be identified with the baseyear value of the share defined in (3.37)

$$(3.39) \qquad \eta_i = \bar{w}_i^o , \qquad\qquad i = 1, \ldots, n.$$

Using (2.21) we may now calculate a first-order Taylor expansion in logarithms of (3.35) around the baseyear values $ln\ \bar{m} = ln\ \bar{m}^o$, $t = 0$ and $ln\ pm_i = 0$ for all i. This gives

$$(3.40) \qquad ln\ m_i = ln\ (\bar{w}_i^o\ \bar{m}) + c_i t - a_i\ [\ ln\ pm_i - \Sigma_k \frac{w_k^o\ a_k}{a^o}\ ln\ pm_k] \qquad i = 1, \ldots, n,$$

where the trend parameter c_i was already defined in (3.11). Therefore it should satisfy

$$(3.41) \qquad \Sigma_k\ w_i^o\ c_i = 0$$

Similarities with linear case

Model (3.40) has a number of similarities with the linear case of the previous section.

First, we may rewrite (3.40) in terms of the baseyear AES, A_{ik}^o, as

$$(3.42) \qquad ln\ m_i = ln(\bar{w}_i^o\ \bar{m}) + c_i t + \Sigma_k\ w_k^o\ A_{ik}^o\ ln\ pm_k\ , \quad i = 1, \ldots, n,$$

or directly in terms of the own and cross-price elasticities in the baseyear, e_{ik}^o,

$$(3.43) \qquad ln\ m_i = ln(\bar{w}_i^o\ \bar{m}) + c_i t + \Sigma_k\ e_{ik}^o\ ln\ pm_k\ , \qquad i = 1, \ldots, n,$$

As before, the AES or price elasticities in the baseyear cannot be estimated directly because they are overidentified.

Secondly, given estimates for c_i and a_i for all i, the trend parameters γ_i are again under-identified because the estimated c_i should obey the linear restriction (3.41).

Thirdly, if all a_i are equal, say to σ, which is the CES case, the model reduces to

$$(3.44) \qquad ln\ m_i = ln(\bar{w}_i^o\ \bar{m}) + \sigma\ r_i t - \sigma\ [\ ln\ pm_i - \Sigma_k\ w_k^o\ ln\ pm_k\ ], \qquad i = 1, \ldots, n,$$

where the r_i were defined below (3.16). The CES model is clearly nested in our model and may therefore be tested with a nested hypothesis against our model.

Fourthly, introducing a subscript j for the importing country, we may derive a total export equation for exporter i. The dependent variable in this equation will however not be the logarithm of exports in constant prices x_i, but the logarithm of an export quantity index $\bar{x}_i$, defined in analogy to (3.32) as

$$(3.45) \qquad \bar{x}_i = \Pi_j\ m_j^{v_{ij}^o},$$

a weighted geometric average of the bilateral exports of country i (which are equal to the bilateral imports because we disregard cif-fob differences), with as weights the baseyear export shares v_{ij}^o defined in (3.19).

Multiplying both sides of (3.40) by v_{ij}^o and summing over j we obtain as a total export equation for $\bar{x}_i$

$$(3.46) \qquad ln\ \bar{x}_i = \Sigma_j\ ln\ (\bar{w}_{ij}^o\ \bar{m}_j) + c_i^{\star} t - a_i^{\star}\ (ln\ \overline{px}_i - ln\ \overline{pw}_i),$$

where the time trend coefficient is a weighted average of the c_{ij} defined, as in (3.18), as

$$(3.47) \qquad c_i^\star = \Sigma_j \, v_{ij}^o \, c_{ij} \, ,$$

and $a_i^\star$ was already defined in (3.20). The relative price component consists of an export price $\overline{px}_i$ defined as a weighted geometric average of the pm_{ij} as

$$(3.48) \qquad ln \; \overline{px}_i = \Sigma_j \frac{v_{ij}^o \, a_{ij}}{a_i^\star} \, ln \; pm_{ij} \, ,$$

and a competitors' price index $\overline{pw}_i$ which is a double-weighted geometric average of all pm_{ij} defined as

$$(3.49) \qquad ln \; \overline{pw}_i = \Sigma_j \frac{v_{ij}^o \, a_{ij}}{a_i^\star} \; \Sigma_k \frac{w_{kj}^o \, a_{kj}}{a_j^o} \, ln \; pm_{kj} .$$

Fifthly we may introduce dynamic elements in (3.40) by making the assumption that each logarithmic price $ln \; pm_{it}$ is in fact an infinitely distributed lag of the observed logarithmic prices as in (3.25). Similarly to (3.28)-(3.29) this results in the following dynamic loglinear import flow equation

$$(3.50) \qquad ln \left(\frac{m_{it}}{\bar{w}_i^o \; \bar{m}_t}\right) = \lambda \; ln \left(\frac{m_i}{\bar{w}_i^o \; m}\right)_{t-1} + c_i(1 - \lambda)t + c_i \, \lambda$$

$$- \; a_i(1 - \lambda) \left[ln \; pm_{it} - \Sigma_k \frac{w_k^o \, a_k}{a^o} \, ln \; pm_{kt} \right] ,$$

It is a simple matter to verify that (3.50) still satisfies the adding-up condition with respect to $ln \; \bar{m}_t$ if we multiply the equation by w_i^o and add up over i

$$(3.51) \qquad \Sigma_i\, w_i^o\, ln\, (\frac{m_{it}}{\bar{w}_i^o\, \bar{m}_t}) \equiv 0\ ,$$

given that (3.41) holds.

5.3.3. A DIFFERENTIAL APPROXIMATION

Derivation

We suggested in subsection 2.2.4 three possibilities to maintain the adding-up criterion and to deal at the same time with the fact that the import quantity index μ is not observable. Two of them were used in the two previous subsections, and in this subsection we will provide an example of the last possibility, *i.e.* to find an observable approximation for μ.

Instead of linearizing around a baseyear value, as we did in the two previous subsections, we now derive a specification through application of a *differential approach* to the first-order conditions that were given in subsection 4.2.3, and next we give a suitable parametrization.

From the first-order conditions (2.4) we find that

$$(3.52) \qquad |\delta_i \rho_i|\, e^{\gamma_i t}\, (\frac{m_i}{\mu})^{-\rho_i} = \frac{pm_i\, m_i}{|\lambda|}\ , \qquad\qquad i = 1, \ldots, n.$$

If we take the total differential of (2.5) with respect to μ, t, and all m_i, we obtain, with (3.52),

$$(3.53) \qquad dln\ \mu = \Sigma_i\, w_i\, dln\ m_i - \Sigma_i\, w_i (\gamma_i/\rho_i)\ dt\ ,$$

where it should be remembered that w_i is the cost-minimizing value share of imports from partner i in total import cost of importer j.

The total differential of (2.4) and definition (3.53) of the import quantity index μ result in

$$(3.54) \qquad dln\, m_i = dln\, \tilde{m} + \tilde{c}_i dt - a_i [dln\, pm_i - \Sigma_k \frac{w_k\, a_k}{a}\, dln\, pm_k]\ , \qquad i = 1, \ldots, n,$$

where the import quantity index $\tilde{m}$ is defined as

$$(3.55) \qquad dln\, \tilde{m} = \Sigma_i\, w_i\, dln\, m_i\ ,$$

and the trend parameter $\tilde{c}_i$ as

$$(3.56) \qquad \tilde{c}_i = a_i\, [\gamma_i + \Sigma_k \frac{w_k \gamma_k (a_k/\rho_k)}{a}] - \Sigma_k\, w_k\, (\gamma_k/\rho_k)\ , \qquad i = 1, \ldots, n,$$

which should satisfy $\Sigma_i\, w_i\, \tilde{c}_i = 0$, while a is a weighted average of the a_i with as weights the optimal value shares w_i

$$(3.57) \qquad a = \Sigma_i\, w_i\, a_i.$$

Note that we may write (3.54) both in terms of the AES A_{ik} and own and cross-price elasticities e_{ik} as

$$(3.58) \qquad dln\, m_i = dln\, \tilde{m} + \tilde{c}_i\, dt + \Sigma_k\, w_k\, A_{ik}\, dln\, pm_k\ , \qquad i = 1, \ldots, n,$$

or

$$(3.59) \qquad dln\, m_i = dln\, \tilde{m} + \tilde{c}_i\, dt + \Sigma_k\, e_{ik}\, dln\, pm_k\ , \qquad i = 1, \ldots, n.$$

Discrete approximation

We can relate (3.54), which is written in continuous time, to observable quantities if we make the following discrete approximations to the logarithmic differences (where Δ is the difference operator $\Delta x_t = x_t - x_{t-1}$).

$$(3.60) \qquad d\ln m_i = \Delta \ln m_{it} , \qquad i = 1, \ldots, n,$$

$$(3.61) \qquad d\ln pm_i = \Delta \ln pm_{it} , \qquad i = 1, \ldots, n,$$

$$(3.62) \qquad dt = 1 .$$

It remains then to specify a discrete approximation for the cost-minimizing value shares w_i. Following well-known studies in differential consumer demand systems [17)], we might specify w_i to be equal to the average of the value shares of periods t and $t-1$

$$(3.63) \qquad w_i = \tilde{w}_{it}$$

$$= (w_{it} + w_{i,t-1})/2 \qquad i = 1, \ldots, n.$$

This results in the following model

$$(3.64) \qquad \Delta \ln m_{it} = \Delta \ln \tilde{m}_t + \tilde{c}_{it} - a_i \left[\Delta \ln pm_{it} - \Sigma_k \frac{\tilde{w}_{kt}\, a_k}{\Sigma_h \tilde{w}_{ht} a_h} \Delta \ln pm_{kt}\right],$$

$$i = 1, \ldots, n,$$

with $\Delta \ln \tilde{m}_t$ defined as the observable variable [18)]

$$(3.65) \qquad \Delta \ln \tilde{m}_t = \Sigma_i \tilde{w}_{it} \Delta \ln m_{it} ,$$

while the coefficient c_{it} is now time dependent, and defined as

$$(3.66)\qquad \tilde{c}_{it} = a_i \left[\gamma_i + \Sigma_k \frac{\tilde{w}_{kt}\, \gamma_k (a_k/\rho_k)}{\Sigma_h \tilde{w}_{ht}\, a_h} \right] - \Sigma_k\, \tilde{w}_{kt}\, (\gamma_k/\rho_k)$$

$$i = 1, \ldots, n.$$

Stochastic specification and consequences

Model (3.64) may seem normal at first sight, but once we transform it into a stochastic specification, difficulties appear on the horizon. To see this, first, write (3.64) in vector notation as

$$(3.67)\qquad y_t = f(x_t, \alpha)$$

where y_t is the nx1 vector with element i equal to $\Delta ln\ m_{it}$, and $f(.)$ is an n-vector valued function of the vectors x_t and α defined by the right-hand side of (3.64). The $(2n+1)$x1 vector x_t is defined as

$$(3.68)\qquad x_t = [\, \Delta ln\ \tilde{m}_t,\ \Delta ln\ pm_{1t}\ , \ldots, \Delta ln\ pm_{nt}, \tilde{w}_{1t}\ , \ldots, \tilde{w}_{nt}]'$$

while the $2n$x1 vector α of parameters equals

$$(3.69)\qquad \alpha = [\, a_1, \ldots, a_n, \gamma_1\ , \ldots, \gamma_n]' .$$

Suppose then that (3.67) has an nx1 vector of additive disturbances $u_t = [\, u_{1t}, \ldots, u_{nt}]'$, which follows a - possibly singular - n-variate normal distribution with expectation zero

$$(3.70)\qquad E\,[u_t] = 0\ ,$$

and contemporaneous n x n covariance matrix H_t

(3.71) $E\,[u_t\, u_t'] = H_t$,

while the disturbances are uncorrelated over time

(3.72) $E\,[u_t\, u_\tau'] = 0$ for all $t \neq \tau$.

The stochastic specification of (3.67) then becomes

(3.73) $y_t = f(x_t, \alpha) + u_t$.

From the definition of (3.64) it is then clear that (3.67) should satisfy

(3.74) $\tilde{w}_t'\,[y_t - f(x_t, \alpha)] \equiv 0$,

where $\tilde{w}_t$ is the nx1 vector of shares

(3.75) $\tilde{w}_t = [\tilde{w}_{1t}, \ldots, \tilde{w}_{nt}]'$.

This implies from (3.73) for the disturbances

(3.76) $\tilde{w}_t'\, u_t \equiv 0$,

and therefore the covariance matrix is singular from

(3.77) $\tilde{w}_t'\, H_t \equiv 0$.

Because $r(\tilde{w}_t) = 1$, we may now identify (3.67) according to Definition 4.2.1 as a *nonlinear constrained model of class* $(n, \alpha, H_t;\ 1, \tilde{w}_t)$.

Let us, as in Chapter 4, distinguish two possibilities for the form of the covariance matrix H_t. One in which it is assumed to be homoscedastic $(H_t = H)$, and one in which it takes the special shape of heteroscedasticity defined in (4.4.2).

We know from equation (4.3.3) that if the disturbances u_t are *homoscedastic* and H_t is thus equal to the n x n matrix H, the vector $\tilde{w}_t$ of weights must be of the form

$$(3.78) \qquad \tilde{w}_t = w\, A_t \ ,$$

where w is an nx1 vector of weights that have to be constant over time, while the scalar A_t may be time dependent (but may for convenience also be put equal to one). The conclusion is that estimation of (3.64) under the assumption of a homoscedastic covariance is not feasible, unless we define the weights $\tilde{w}_{it}$ to be constant over time. For instance, if we let the $\tilde{w}_{it}$ be equal to the baseyear shares w_i^o, we obtain the model

$$(3.79) \qquad \Delta ln\ m_{it} = \Delta ln\ \tilde{m}_t^o + c_i - a_i \ [\Delta ln\ pm_{it} - \Sigma_k \frac{w_k^o\, a_k}{a^o} \Delta ln\ pm_{kt}] ,$$

$$i = 1, \ldots, n \ ,$$

where $\Delta ln\ \tilde{m}_t^o$ is defined as

$$(3.80) \qquad \Delta ln\ \tilde{m}_t^o = \Sigma_i\ w_i^o\ \Delta ln\ m_{it} \ ,$$

The model is now a constrained model of class $(n, \alpha, H; 1, w^o)$, where w^o is the nx1 vector of baseyear shares $w^o = [w_1^o, \ldots, w_n^o]'$, and the γ_i in the vector of parameters α should be replaced by the c_i. According to Theorem 4.3.6 and Corollary 4.3.1, estimation of the lopped model (3.79) of class $(n, \alpha, H; 1, w^o, \{n\})$ with the method of maximum likelihood will provide maximum likelihood estimators for α and H that are independent of the deleted, n^{th}, equation (or any other deleted equation), although the value of the likelihood function will depend on that equation.

Next we consider the case in which H_t is assumed to be *heteroscedastic* of the special form given by (4.4.2),

(3.81) $H_t = \tilde{\tilde{w}}_t^{-1} \, H \, \tilde{\tilde{w}}_t^{-1}$,

where $\tilde{\tilde{w}}_t$ is the diagonal matrix with the elements of $\tilde{w}_t$ on the main diagonal, and H an nxn constant matrix. In terms of (4.4.1) we therefore assume $B_t = \tilde{\tilde{w}}_t$ and $R = \iota$.

Then we know from Theorem 4.4.1 that the model (3.67) of class $(n, \alpha, \tilde{\tilde{w}}_t^{-1}, H \tilde{\tilde{w}}_t^{-1}; 1, \tilde{\tilde{w}}_t \iota)$ is equivalent to a constrained model of class $(n, \alpha, H; 1, \iota)$. According to Theorem 4.3.6 and Corollary 4.3.1, maximum likelihood estimation of the lopped form of class $(n, \alpha, H; 1, \iota, \{n\})$ of the latter model will give maximum likelihood estimators for α and H independent of the deleted, n^{th}, equation (or any other deleted equation), while also the value of the likelihood function will be independent of the deleted equation. This model may be obtained from premultiplication on both sides of (3.67) by $\tilde{\tilde{w}}_t$, or, which is equivalent, multiplication on both sides of (3.64) by $\tilde{w}_{it}$. The resulting equation is

(3.82)
$$\tilde{w}_{it} \, \Delta ln \, m_{it} = \tilde{w}_{it} \, \Delta ln \, \tilde{m}_t + \tilde{w}_{it} \, \tilde{c}_{it}$$
$$- a_i \, \tilde{w}_{it} \, [\Delta ln \, pm_{it} - \Sigma_k \frac{\tilde{w}_{kt} \, a_k}{\Sigma_h \, \tilde{w}_{ht} \, a_h} \Delta ln \, pm_{kt}]$$
$$i = 1, \ldots, n$$

Estimation of this equation should be done directly on the shift parameters γ_i that are contained in the time-dependent coefficient c_{it}. Like the a_i, they are all identified, contrary to estimation of (3.79), where one can only estimate the c_i subject to the linear restriction (3.41). If the γ_i are estimated directly, the constraint $\Sigma_i \, \tilde{w}_{it} \, \tilde{c}_{it} = 0$ will be satisfied automatically.

Properties

By putting all a_i equal to, say, σ, we obtain the CES forms of (3.79) and (3.82)

$$(3.83)\qquad \Delta ln\ m_{it} = \Delta ln\ \tilde{m}_t^o + \sigma\ r_i - \sigma[\Delta ln\ pm_{it} - \Sigma_k\ w_k^o\ \Delta ln\ pm_{kt}],$$

$$i = 1, \ldots, n,$$

$$(3.84)\qquad \tilde{w}_{it}\ \Delta ln\ m_{it} = \tilde{w}_{it}\ \Delta ln\ \tilde{m}_t + \tilde{w}_{it}\ \sigma\ \tilde{r}_{it}$$

$$- \sigma\ \tilde{w}_{it}\ [\Delta ln\ pm_{it} - \Sigma_k\ \tilde{w}_{kt}\ \Delta ln\ pm_{kt}],$$

$$i = 1, \ldots, n,$$

where r_i was defined below (3.16) and $\tilde{r}_{it}$ is its time-dependent form

$$(3.85)\qquad \tilde{r}_{it} = \gamma_i - \Sigma_k\ \tilde{w}_{kt}\ \gamma_k, \qquad i = 1, \ldots, n.$$

To derive the total export equations for the two models, we have to define the export quantity indices whose logarithmic growth rates will be the dependent variables of the aggregate equations. Introducing a subscript j for the importing country, their definitions are similar to those of $\tilde{m}_t^o$ and $\tilde{m}_t$, respectively,

$$(3.86)\qquad \Delta ln\ \tilde{x}_{it}^o = \Sigma_j\ v_{ij}^o\ \Delta ln\ m_{ijt}$$

$$(3.87)\qquad \Delta ln\ \tilde{x}_{it} = \Sigma_j\ \tilde{v}_{ijt}\ \Delta ln\ m_{ijt},$$

with export shares v_{ij}^o defined in (3.19) and $\tilde{v}_{ijt}$ defined as

$$(3.88)\qquad \tilde{v}_{ijt} = (v_{ijt} + v_{ijt-1})/2 \qquad\qquad j = 1, \ldots, n.$$

where, disregarding cif-fob differences,

$$(3.89)\qquad v_{ijt} = pm_{ijt}\, m_{ijt} / \Sigma_k\, pm_{ikt}\, m_{ikt}, \quad j = 1, \ldots, n.$$

The total export equation - in logarithmic differences - is then derived for (3.79) through premultiplication of both sides by v^o_{ij} and adding over j, which gives

$$(3.90)\qquad \Delta ln\, \tilde{x}^o_{it} = \Sigma_j\, v^o_{ij}\, \Delta ln\, \tilde{m}^o_{jt} + \overset{\star}{c}_i - \overset{\star}{a}_i\, [\, \Delta ln\, \tilde{px}^o_{it} - \Delta ln\, \tilde{pw}^o_{it}],$$

where $\overset{\star}{c}_i$ was defined in (3.18), $\overset{\star}{a}_i$ in (3.20), and the relative price is composed of the logarithmic growth rates of the following export price index $\tilde{px}^o_{it}$ and competitors' price index $\tilde{pw}^o_{it}$

$$(3.91)\qquad \Delta ln\, \tilde{px}^o_{it} = \Sigma_j\, \frac{v^o_{ij}\, a_{ij}}{\overset{\star}{a}_i}\, \Delta ln\, pm_{ijt},$$

$$(3.92)\qquad \Delta ln\, \tilde{pw}^o_{it} = \Sigma_j\, \frac{v^o_{ij}\, a_{ij}}{\overset{\star}{a}_i}\, \Sigma_k\, \frac{w^o_{kj}\, a_{kj}}{a^o_j}\, \Delta ln\, pm_{kjt}.$$

For (3.82) the total export equation may be derived through premultiplication by $(\tilde{v}_{ijt}/\tilde{w}_{ijt})$ and adding up over the j. The result is

$$(3.93)\qquad \Delta ln\, \tilde{x}_{it} = \Sigma_j\, \tilde{v}_{ijt}\, \Delta ln\, \tilde{m}_{jt} + \tilde{\overset{\star}{c}}_{it} - \overset{\star}{a}_{it}\, [\Delta ln\, \tilde{px}_{it} - \Delta ln\, \tilde{pw}_{it}]$$

with $\tilde{\overset{\star}{c}}_{it}$ defined as

$$(3.94)\qquad \tilde{\overset{\star}{c}}_{it} = \Sigma_j\, \tilde{v}_{ijt}\, \tilde{c}_{ijt},$$

and a relative price elasticity $\overset{\star}{a}_{it}$ which is now time dependent

$$(3.95) \qquad a^{\star}_{it} = \Sigma_j \, \tilde{v}_{ijt} \, a_{ij}$$

The export price index $\widetilde{px}_{it}$ and the competitors' price index $\widetilde{pw}_{it}$ are defined in logarithmic growth rates as

$$(3.96) \qquad \Delta ln \, \widetilde{px}_{it} = \Sigma_j \frac{\tilde{v}_{ijt} \, a_{ij}}{a^{\star}_{it}} \Delta ln \, pm_{ijt}$$

$$(3.97) \qquad \Delta ln \, \widetilde{pw}_{it} = \Sigma_j \frac{\tilde{v}_{ijt} \, a_{ij}}{a^{\star}_{it}} \Sigma_k \frac{\tilde{w}_{kjt} \, a_{kj}}{\Sigma_h \, \tilde{w}_{hjt} \, a_{hj}} \Delta ln \, pm_{kjt}$$

Both models (3.79) and (3.82) are already of a dynamic nature because they are defined in logarithmic differences. To complete the analogy with the previous two approximations in levels and logarithms, we will however also for these two models assume that the logarithmic price changes $\Delta ln \, pm_{ijt}$ are to be interpreted as infinitely distributed lags as (3.25) in the observed logarithmic price changes.

After application of the Koyck transformation, this results in the following two models

$$(3.98) \qquad \Delta ln \, (m_{it}/\tilde{m}^o_t) = \lambda \, \Delta ln \, (m_i/\tilde{m}^o)_{t-1} + c_i(1 - \lambda)$$

$$- a_i(1 - \lambda)[\Delta ln \, pm_{it} - \Sigma_k \frac{w^o_k \, a_k}{a^o} \Delta ln \, pm_{kt}]$$

$$i = 1, \ldots, n ,$$

$$(3.99) \quad w_{it}\ \Delta ln\ (m_{it}/\tilde{m}_t) = \lambda\ \tilde{w}_{it-1}\ \Delta ln\ (m_i/\tilde{m})_{t-1}$$

$$+ \tilde{w}_{it}\ \tilde{c}_{it} - \lambda\ \tilde{w}_{it-1}\ \tilde{c}_{it-1}$$

$$- a_i(1-\lambda)\tilde{w}_{it}\ [\Delta ln\ pm_{it} - \Sigma_k \frac{\tilde{w}_{kt}\ a_k}{\Sigma_h\ \tilde{w}_{ht}\ a_h}\ \Delta ln\ pm_{kjt}]$$

$$i = 1, \ldots, n.$$

It can easily be verified that the two models satisfy the following adding-up conditions

$$(3.100) \quad \Sigma_i\ w_i^o\ \Delta ln\ (m_{it}/\tilde{m}_t^o) \equiv 0\ ,$$

$$\Sigma_i\ \tilde{w}_{it}\ \Delta ln\ (m_{it}/\tilde{m}_t) \equiv 0.$$

5.4. AN INTERPRETATION AS TOTAL ALLOCATION MODEL

Up to now, the present chapter has only elaborated on the derivation of estimable *import allocation models*. A common feature of the models derived in the previous section is that they allow one to test the CES model as a nested hypothesis, with the additional advantage that it is not required for testing to specify in which kind of elasticity of substitution one is interested.

But this is only one of the hypotheses we put forward in Chapter 1 to be tested. The other is the separability assumption underlying the import allocation model. Indeed, the original contribution of ARMINGTON (1969a) was in terms of total allocation, as defined in subsection 1.4.2. and therefore the import allocation model is valid only conditional upon the separability of the (branchwise or national) aggregator function - pertaining to products both from domestic and foreign origin - in one part containing only bilateral imports, and one part containing products from domestic origin. Because our interest is in bilateral imports, we will not decompose the products of domestic origin and assume that they may be represented by an observable aggregate y with corresponding price index py.

The starting-point of the analysis then becomes an aggregator function u, defined (possibly) implicitly as

$$(4.1) \qquad H(u, y, m_1, \ldots, m_n) \equiv 0$$

where a functional form for H has to be chosen.

Let the total expenditure on domestic and foreign products be denoted by z and Z in constant and current prices respectively. Then the following equivalents of (2.2.5) and (2.2.6) act as adding-up conditions

(4.2) $$y + \Sigma_i\, m_i = z$$

(4.3) $$py\, y + \Sigma_i\, pm_i\, m_i = Z.$$

The aggregator function is weakly separable in the domestic aggregate y on the one hand, and bilateral imports $m_1, \ldots, m_n$, on the other hand, if and only if

(4.4) $$\frac{\partial}{\partial y}\left(\frac{\partial u/\partial m_i}{\partial u/\partial m_k}\right) = 0 \qquad i \neq k = 1, \ldots, n$$

The general way to test the separability hypothesis associated with (4.4) is to specify a functional form for the aggregator function u which is general enough to contain as a nested case the structural hypothesis of separability between bilateral imports and the domestic aggregate y.

The functional form to be chosen for the aggregator function u may either be a flexible functional form [19)] or a specific aggregator function (provided that weak separability is a nested case). In empirical work, notably in production theory, flexible functional forms have been used frequently to test separability hypotheses [20)]. It was shown rigorously by BLACKORBY *et al.* (1978, Ch. 8), however, that the most commonly used flexible functional forms all suffer from the so-called *separability-inflexibility;* that is, when weak separability is imposed on them, they are no longer approximations to any arbitrary well-behaved twice differentiable (utility) function. More particularly, they are then no longer approximations of *weakly* separable aggregator functions. Only functions with stronger notions of separability, such as strong separability or homothetic separability, can then be approximated. This conclusion prohibits the use of flexible functional forms to test the hypothesis of weak separability.

Therefore we are bound to a specific functional form that is general enough to contain the structured hypothesis of weak separability in it as a nested case. We will choose for this specific form the form of the import quantity index analyzed in the preceding sections, *i.e.* the CRESH function with constant returns to scale. The first reason for this choice is that this function satisfies the requirement that it should have nested in itself the case of weak separability. The second reason is that the restrictions that are implied for the parameters by weak separability are very simple, and therefore easy to implement in empirical estimation and hypothesis-testing.

Similarly to section 5.3, we may then write the aggregator function u implicitly as

$$(4.5) \qquad H(u,y,m_1, \ldots, m_n) = \delta_y e^{\gamma_y t} \left(\frac{y}{u}\right)^{-\rho_y} + \Sigma_i \, \delta_i \, e^{\gamma_i t} \left(\frac{m_i}{u}\right)^{-\rho_i} - 1 \equiv 0$$

to which, *mutatis mutandis*, the same conditions as to (2.2) should apply.

The partial derivative of u with respect to imports from any trading partner i, m_i, then results upon total differentiation of (4.5) as

$$(4.6) \qquad \frac{\partial u}{\partial m_i} = \delta_i \, \rho_i \, e^{\gamma_i t} \left(\frac{m_i}{u}\right)^{-(1+\rho_i)} \left[\delta_y \rho_y e^{\gamma_y t} \left(\frac{y}{u}\right)^{-\rho_y} + \Sigma_i \delta_i \rho_i e^{\gamma_i t} \left(\frac{m_i}{u}\right)^{-\rho_i} \right]^{-1}$$

$$i = 1, \ldots, n.$$

As an implication, the marginal rate of substitution between imports from partner i and partner k becomes

$$(4.7) \qquad \frac{\partial u/\partial m_i}{\partial u/\partial m_k} = \frac{\delta_i \, \rho_i}{\delta_k \, \rho_k} \, e^{(\gamma_i - \gamma_k)t} \, \frac{m_i^{-(1+\rho_i)}}{m_k^{-(1+\rho_k)}} \, u^{-(\rho_i - \rho_k)}$$

$$i \neq k = 1, \ldots, n$$

For the weak separability condition (4.4) it is of importance that in (4.7) only u depends on the domestic aggregate y. It is an easy matter to verify that (4.4) therefore is true if and only if

(4.8) $\rho_i = \rho_k$ $\qquad i \neq k = 1, \ldots, n,$

or if all ρ_i are equal for the same importer j [21)]. Therefore, under weak separability, the total allocation model only has two rho parameters left, ρ_y and ρ $(= \rho_1 = \ldots = \rho_n)$, say.

Because the derived demand equations for the total allocation model are, *mutatis mutandis*, equal to those previously derived for the import allocation model (only the domestic aggregate y has to be included as an additional factor), we will not repeat them here.

Although for the import allocation model the alternative specification is under the hypothesis of pairwise equality of elasticities of substitution and for the total allocation model this specification corresponds to imposition of weak separability, both alternatives amount to almost the same restrictions on the parameters.

Additionally, we note that the assumption made by ARMINGTON (1969a) of pairwise equality of elasticities of substitution between both bilateral imports and domestically produced goods can also be tested as for the import allocation models through the imposition of the following restrictions on the parameters

(4.9) $\rho_y = \rho_1 = \ldots = \rho_n.$

This is of course equivalent to $a_y = a_1 = \ldots = a_n$.

In the following chapters this line of testing will not be pursued, as we are primarily interested in the weak separability hypothesis and the testing of the CES *import* allocation model against our more general model.

The model proposed in this section, the total allocation model, should be considered independently of the import allocation model of the previous sections, albeit they have the same functional form. In particular it is not the case, if we impose weak separability in the partitioning $\{y\}$, $\{m_1, \ldots, m_n\}$ on the total allocation model, that the functional form used for the import allocation model may be deduced from it.

5.5. SUMMARY AND CONCLUSIONS

The purpose of this chapter has been to derive import allocation and total allocation models from an aggregator function that would satisfy the following criteria : 1) the models should be sufficiently general in their price effects and at the same time remain feasible for the estimation of relatively large models, 2) they should contain the CES model, the most widespread of empirically implemented estimation-consistent import allocation models as a special case, 3) the model should be capable, as a total allocation model, to test the hypothesis of weak separability between domestic products and imports. We argued subsequently that a (partial) aggregator function of the CRESH form with constant returns to scale would meet these criteria. The derived demand equations from this function being highly nonlinear and containing unobservable variables, we next proposed three approximations of these demand equations. These three approximations corresponded to the three solutions to the adding-up problem proposed in Chapter 2, and also to the different functional forms proposed for international trade models, as they are linear, loglinear and in logarithmic differences, respectively.

By way of summary, we will present one single specification that captures all three approximations [22], which we condense in their dynamic forms (3.29), (3.50), (3.98) and (3.99) as

$$(5.1) \qquad s_{it} = \lambda\, s_{it-1} + \beta_{it}\, T_t - \lambda\, \beta_{it-1}\, T_{t-1}$$

$$- a_i(1-\lambda)\, [p^i_{it} - \Sigma_k \frac{\omega_{kt}\, a_k}{\Sigma_h\, \omega_{ht}\, a_h}\, p^i_{kt}] \qquad i = 1, \ldots, n$$

The correspondences between the original equations (to which we refer for the symbols) and (5.1) are as follows

Model I : linearization in levels (3.29)

(5.2) $$s_{it} = \frac{m_{it} - w_i^o m_t}{m_i^o}$$

(5.3) $$\beta_{it} = a_i \left[\gamma_i + \Sigma_k \frac{w_k^o a_k}{\Sigma_h w_h^o a_h} (\gamma_k/\rho_k) \right] - \Sigma_k w_k^o (\gamma_k/\rho_k)$$

(5.4) $$T_t = t$$

(5.5) $$\omega_{it} = w_i^o$$

(5.6) $$p_{kt}^i = pm_{kt}$$

Model II : loglinear approximation (3.50)

(5.7) $$s_{it} = ln \left(\frac{m_{it}}{\bar{w}_i^o \bar{m}_t} \right)$$

(5.8) $$\beta_{it} = a_i \left[\gamma_i + \Sigma_k \frac{w_k^o a_k}{\Sigma_h w_h^o a_h} (\gamma_k/\rho_k) \right] - \Sigma_k w_k^o (\gamma_k/\rho_k)$$

(5.9) $$T_t = t$$

(5.10) $$\omega_{it} = w_i^o$$

(5.11) $p^{i}_{kt} = ln\ pm_{kt}$

<u>Model III</u> : <u>differential approximation with constant shares (3.98)</u>

(5.12) $s_{it} = \Delta ln\ (\frac{m_{it}}{\tilde{m}^{o}_{t}})$

(5.13) $\beta_{it} = a_{i}\ [\gamma_{i} + \Sigma_{k} \frac{w^{o}_{k}\ a_{k}}{\Sigma_{h}\ w^{o}_{h}\ a_{h}} (\gamma_{k}/\rho_{k})] - \Sigma_{k}\ w^{o}_{k}\ (\gamma_{k}/\rho_{k})$

(5.14) $T_{t} = 1$

(5.15) $\omega_{it} = w^{o}_{i}$

(5.16) $p^{i}_{kt} = \Delta ln\ pm_{kt}$

<u>Model IV</u> : <u>differential approximation with heteroscedasticity (3.99)</u>

(5.17) $s_{it} = \tilde{w}_{it}\ \Delta ln\ (\frac{m_{it}}{\tilde{m}_{t}})$

(5.18) $\beta_{it} = \tilde{w}_{it}\ \{a_{i}\ [\gamma_{i} + \Sigma_{k} \frac{\tilde{w}_{kt}\ a_{k}}{\Sigma_{h}\ \tilde{w}_{ht}\ a_{h}} (\gamma_{k}/\rho_{k})] - \Sigma_{k}\ \tilde{w}_{kt}\ (\gamma_{k}/\rho_{k})\}$

(5.19) $T_{t} = 1$

(5.20) $\omega_{it} = \tilde{w}_{it}$

(5.21) $p^{i}_{kt} = \tilde{w}_{it} \quad \Delta ln\ pm_{kt}$

Models I-III satisfy the following adding-up condition

(5.22) $\Sigma_i\ w^o_i\ s_{it} = 0$,

whereas Model IV meets the condition

(5.23) $\Sigma_i\ s_{it} = 0.$

The condensed model may be interpreted, as for the individual models, in terms of own and cross-price elasticities and AES. We also use it to define a total dynamic export equation for the total exports of partner i after the introduction of a subscript j for the importing country as

(5.24) $$x^{\star}_{it} = \Sigma_j\ v^{\star}_{ijt}\ \lambda_j\ s_{ijt-1} + (\Sigma_j\ v^{\star}_{ijt}\ \lambda_j\ \beta_{ijt})T_t - (\Sigma_j\ v^{\star}_{ijt}\ \lambda_j\ \beta_{ijt-1})T_{t-1} - \alpha^{\star}_{it}(1-\lambda^{\star}_{it})\ [px^{\star}_{it} - pw^{\star}_{it}]$$

where, using previously defined symbols,

(5.25) $x^{\star}_{it} = \Sigma_j\ v^{\star}_{ijt}\ s_{ijt}$

(5.26) $$v^{\star}_{ijt} = v^{o}_{ij} \qquad \text{for Models I-III}$$

$$= \tilde{v}_{ijt}/\tilde{\omega}_{ijt} \qquad \text{for Model IV}$$

(5.27) $$\alpha^{\star}_{it} = \Sigma_j\, v^{o}_{ij}\, a_{ij} \qquad \text{for Models I-III}$$

$$= \Sigma_j\, \tilde{v}_{ijt}\, a_{ij} \qquad \text{for Model IV}$$

(5.28) $$\lambda^{\star}_{it} = \Sigma_j\, v^{o}_{ij}\, \frac{a_{ij}}{\alpha^{\star}_{it}}\, \lambda_j \qquad \text{for Models I-III}$$

$$= \Sigma_j\, \tilde{v}_{ijt}\, \frac{a_{ij}}{\alpha^{\star}_{it}}\, \lambda_j \qquad \text{for Model IV}$$

(5.29) $$px^{\star}_{it} = \Sigma_j\, v^{\star}_{ijt}\, \frac{a_{ij}}{\alpha^{\star}_{it}}\, \frac{1-\lambda_j}{1-\lambda^{\star}_{it}}\, p^{i}_{ijt}$$

(5.30) $$pw^{\star}_{it} = \Sigma_j\, v^{\star}_{ijt}\, \frac{a_{ij}}{\alpha^{\star}_{it}}\, \frac{1-\lambda_j}{1-\lambda^{\star}_{it}}\, \Sigma_k\, \frac{\omega_{kjt}\, a_{kj}}{\Sigma_h\, \omega_{hjt}\, a_{hj}}\, p^{i}_{kjt}.$$

The coefficient $\alpha^{\star}_{it}$ of this condensed total export equation may be interpreted as its long-run relative price coefficient with respect to the export price $px^{\star}_{it}$ relative to a competitors' price $pw^{\star}_{it}$. Its short-run value equals $\alpha^{\star}_{it}(1 - \lambda^{\star}_{it})$.

The import allocation models that are summarized in (5.1) only serve to test against the CES model, which is nested in them. They are neither capable of testing the hypothesis that the elasticities of substitution are equal not only between bilateral imports, but also between domestically produced products and bilateral imports, nor are they suited for testing the hypothesis of weak separability between domestic products and imports. As the hypothesis of weak separability cannot be tested using most of the so-called flexible functional forms for the aggregator function, a specific function is needed. The interpretation of the import allocation models derived in this chapter as total allocation models provides us with such a function, and the resulting derived demand equations are apt for testing the required hypotheses.

The *conclusions* of this chapter pertain to the suitability of the four models developed here for the purposes of this study. First, they permit estimation of import allocation or total allocation models with and without pairwise differing elasticities of substitution. Secondly, they have the property that pairwise equality of AES, DES or SES all amount to the same (CES) specification, such that *a fortiori* one does not need to specify which elasticity of substitution is being taken into consideration. This circumvents the difficulty of making a choice between elasticities of substitution. Thirdly, they permit estimation with and without the assumption of weak separability between domestically produced goods and imports.

These three properties make the four models suitable for testing the hypotheses of Chapter 1 through empirical estimation. The exact formulation of the hypotheses, the estimation and the testing of the hypotheses are the subjects of the next chapters.

FOOTNOTES TO CHAPTER 5

1) *Cfr.* HANOCH (1975, p. 396).

2) Throughout this chapter, summations and multiplications run from *1* to n. For the sake of exposition it is assumed that $j > n$.

3) *Cfr.* HANOCH (1971, p. 697), also for the case $\rho_i = 0$ for some i.

4) The ES D^k_{ih} and R^k_{ih} as defined in (3.2.38) and (3.2.39), being a difference and a ratio of AES, respectively, will equal *0* and *1* in that case.

5) *Cfr. e.g.* TAKAYAMA (1974, pp. 154-160).

6) *Cfr. e.g.* TAKAYAMA (1974, p. 119).

7) If the second term of (2.35) were to equal $\Sigma^n_{i=m+1}\ w_i\ a_i$, the expression would be correct.

8) Examples of such models are the Rotterdam model, the CBS model and the Almost Ideal Demand System cited in footnote 19 of Chapter 4.

9) This is shown below.

10) The c_i parameters should also be decomposed to show the deviation from the CES case, but this is neglected for convenience.

11) For the sake of exposition we assume for the derivation of export equations like these that $i > n$, just as we assumed $j > n$ for the import equations.

12) The parameter λ should not be confused with the Lagrange multiplier.

13) *Cfr. e.g.* DHRYMES (1971, Ch. 2).

14) *Cfr.* KOYCK (1954).

15) The error correction mechanism contains the partial adjustment process as a special case, *Cfr.* DAVIDSON *et al.* (1978).

16) It may be seen that in that case, after linearizing in the logarithmic variables, we would obtain the condition $\Sigma_i (m_i/m^o_i)^{w^o_i} = m/m^o$. A first-order Taylor approximation of the left-hand side around $(m_i/m^o_i) = 1$ does satisfy this condition, however.

17) *Cfr.* BARTEN (1969) or KELLER and VAN DRIEL (1981).

18) Strictly speaking, this is not the observable approximation to μ, because that should have the form (3.53). We neglect the second term, which will be close to zero, being a weighted average of the trend parameters γ_i.

19) A *flexible* functional form is a functional form that contains exactly the number of parameters whose values can be chosen to make the values of its first- and second-order derivatives (and the function value itself) equal to the first- and second-order derivatives (and the level) of any arbitrary well-behaved twice differentiable (aggregator) function at any point of approximation in the domain. *Cfr.* DIEWERT (1973).

20) One of the most well-known flexible functional forms is the so-called translog model of CHRISTENSEN *et al.* (1973, 1975), see also the other references cited in BLACKORBY *et al.* (1978, Ch. 8).

21) This may also be obtained using the result of BERNDT and CHRISTENSEN (1973) that u is weakly separable in the partitioning $\{y\}$, $\{m_1, \ldots, m_n\}$ if and only if $A_{iy} = A_{ky}$ for all $i \neq k$, where A_{iy} is the AES between imports from partner i and the domestic aggregate. The AES equals $a_i\, a_y \,/\, [w_y\, a_y + \Sigma_i\, w_i\, a_i]$, where $a_i = 1/(1+\rho_i)$ as before, $a_y = 1/(1+\rho_y)$, and w_y and all w_i are the shares of the domestic aggregate and all bilateral imports in total costs in the optimum.

22) The third approximation consists of two different equations because of its stochastic properties. Therefore there are four models to be captured in the specification.

CHAPTER 6 - ECONOMETRIC SPECIFICATION

6.1. INTRODUCTION

In this chapter we present the econometric specification of the general functional form presented in section 5.5 of the previous chapter. As a first step towards estimation, we further simplify this specification in order to deal with the fact that it is nonlinear in its parameters. Next we introduce stochastic elements such that the resulting models may be identified with the constrained models first presented in Chapter 4. In the sections following the stochastic specification we develop the econometric specification and estimation methods to be used for *four* different forms of the general specification. These four forms correspond to the cases where we do, or do not, introduce dynamics and/or trends in the equations. Notably in section 6.4 a stepwise estimation procedure is proposed starting from three possibly differing specifications for the covariance matrix of the residuals. This estimation procedure may be used for all four different forms of the model, either directly or slightly modified. In the last section we summarize and draw some conclusions.

6.2. A FURTHER SIMPLIFICATION

The general formulation (5.5.1) of the four models that were derived in the previous chapter has the disadvantage that it is still highly nonlinear in the a_i coefficients that appear in the βs and the "relative price term". If the number of partners that are distinguished is small, this might perhaps be of minor importance during estimation. But if this number increases, the nonlinearities also become more numerous and they will render estimation more and more difficult.

This is why, for purposes of actual estimation, we seek to further simplify the estimating equations, which are themselves approximations of the original demand equations that were derived in section 5.2 as (5.2.10). This may be accomplished if we take a first-order Taylor expansion of (5.5.1) in the a_i parameters around an arbitrary value a, which may be taken as a weighted average of the a_i for instance. It will be remembered that the a_i coefficients are of importance for the calculation of price and substitution elasticities as in formulas (5.2.22) - (5.2.25). The value of a may for instance be interpreted as an average Allen partial elasticity of substitution. The resulting equation is

$$(2.1) \qquad s_{it} = \lambda s_{it-1} + b_{it}\, T_t - \lambda\, b_{it-1}\, T_{t-1} - a_i(1-\lambda)\, [p^i_{it} - \Sigma_h\, \omega_{ht}\, p^i_{ht}]$$

$$+ (1-\lambda)\, \Sigma_h\, \omega_{ht}\, a_h\, [p^i_{ht} - \Sigma_l\, \omega_{lt}\, p^i_{lt}]$$

$$i = 1, \ldots, n,$$

where the same notation as for (5.5.1) has been maintained, except for the introduction of the trend coefficient b_{it}, which equals for model IV

$$(2.2)\qquad b_{it} = \tilde{w}_{it} \{a_i\gamma_i - \Sigma_h \tilde{w}_{ht}\, a_h\, \gamma_h + \frac{a}{1-a} [a_i - \Sigma_h \tilde{w}_{ht}\, a_h] \Sigma_h \tilde{w}_{ht}\, \gamma_h\} \qquad i = 1, \ldots, n.$$

For models I-III the weights ω_{ht} are constant (w_h^o), which transforms the approximations to b_{it} in constants b_i (provided that a does not depend on time), that are equal to

$$(2.3)\qquad b_i = a_i\, \gamma_i - \Sigma_h\, w_h^o\, a_h\, \gamma_h + \frac{a}{1-a} [a_i - \Sigma_h\, w_h^o\, a_h]\; \Sigma_h\, w_h^o\, \gamma_h\, , \qquad i = 1, \ldots, n.$$

Only $n-1$ of the b_i may be chosen independently, because they should satisfy the following constraint

$$(2.4)\qquad \Sigma_i\, w_i^o\, b_i = 0.$$

As noted before at the derivation of the individual models, only $n-1$ of the γ_i parameters can be determined from (2.3) if the value of the b_i parameters are given.

Because the γ_i are parameters that represent shifts in imports by country j from supplying country i, we know however that a shift away from imports of one particular trading partner should be reflected in a shift in favour of another partner, given the allocative nature of our import allocation model. On average, the changes in the shifts should therefore cancel each other out. We formalize this through the requirement that a weighted average of the γ_i should equal zero, where we take as weights the baseyear import shares w_i^o. This results in the following condition

$$(2.5)\qquad \Sigma_i\, w_i^o\, \gamma_i = 0.$$

Together with estimates for the b_i parameters, whose definition now becomes

$$(2.6) \qquad b_i = a_i \gamma_i - \Sigma_h w_h^o a_h \gamma_h, \qquad i = 1, \ldots, n,$$

condition (2.5) makes it possible to determine the trend parameters γ_i for $i = 1, \ldots, n$.

For model IV, the weights appearing in (2.2) depend on time, and we should introduce its righthand side in the estimating equation (2.1), and estimate the γ_i parameters directly. The resulting expression is rather burdensome and contains nonlinear combinations of the a_i and γ_i parameters. Furthermore we would need to specify further the a parameter. However, we may translate the requirement that the trend parameters should on average equal zero into the following assumption

$$(2.7) \qquad \Sigma_i \tilde{w}_{it} \gamma_i \approx 0, \qquad all\ t\ .$$

Although this expression is not compatible with the fact that the γ_i are constant, we may assume that deviations from it are transferred to the residual of the equation and that it therefore holds approximately.

The expression for b_{it} reduces then to

$$(2.8) \qquad b_{it} = \tilde{w}_{it} (a_i \gamma_i - \Sigma_h \tilde{w}_{ht} a_h \gamma_h), \qquad i = 1, \ldots, n\ ,$$

and we may eliminate the nonlinearities through the transformation

$$(2.9) \qquad g_i = a_i \gamma_i - a_k \gamma_k \qquad i = 1, \ldots, n\ , \quad i \neq k\ ,$$

where the g_i should be estimated for all $i \neq k$.

The knowledge that the trend parameters γ_i should on average equal zero therefore serves two purposes. For models I-III it solves the problem of the unknown γ_i parameter and for model IV it reduces the nonlinearity.

6.3. STOCHASTIC SPECIFICATION

For the sake of generality we maintain the general specification (2.1), but the b_{it} should now be interpreted as (2.6) for models I-III and as (2.8) for model IV. We then assume that (2.1) actually describes a relationship of a stochastic nature with additive disturbances u_{it}

$$(3.1) \qquad s_{it} = \lambda\, s_{it-1} + b_{it}\, T_t - \lambda\, b_{it-1}\, T_{t-1} - a_i(1-\lambda)\, [p^i_{it} - \Sigma_h\, \omega_{ht}\, p^i_{ht}]$$

$$+ (1-\lambda)\Sigma_h\, \omega_{ht}\, a_h\, [p^i_{ht} - \Sigma_l\, \omega_{lt}\, p^i_{lt}\,] + u_{it}$$

$$i = 1, \ldots, n.$$

We may write (3.1) concisely in vector notation as

$$(3.2) \qquad y_t = f(x_t,\, \alpha) + u_t,$$

where y_t is the nx1 vector of dependent variables $[s_{1t}, \ldots, s_{nt}]'$, $f(.)$ is an n vector-valued function of the vector x_t of predetermined variables and the $(2n+1)$ x 1 parameter vector $\alpha = [a_1, \ldots, a_n, \gamma_1, \ldots, \gamma_n, \lambda]'$, and u_t is the nx1 vector of disturbances $[u_{1t}, \ldots, u_{nt}]'$. We leave the vector x_t unspecified because its elements vary per model. In general it contains the lagged dependent variables s_{it-1}, the trend variables T_t and T_{t-1}, weights ω_{it} and (transformations and/or lagged values of) the bilateral prices pm_{it}.

We assume that the vector of disturbances follows an n-variate distribution with expectation zero

$$(3.3) \qquad E(u_t) = 0\ ,$$

and an nxn contemporaneous covariance matrix H that is constant over time

$$(3.4) \qquad E\,[u_t u_t'] = H.$$

The assumption that the covariance matrix of contemporaneous disturbances is constant over time or homoscedastic is justified because for all four models the dependent variables s_{it} have been defined such that we do not expect their order of magnitude to change over the sample period.

Furthermore, the equations have a dynamic formulation through the inclusion of a distributed lag in the prices with lag parameter λ. If the residuals of the equation before the Koyck-transformation follow a first-order autocorrelation scheme with the same parameter λ, this autocorrelation is removed through the Koyck transformation. We assume indeed that this autocorrelation is present, or that the transformation is at least sufficient to reduce the autocorrelation to such an extent that we may ignore it and are allowed to make the following assumption concerning the covariances among disturbances of different points in time

$$(3.5) \qquad E\,[u_t u_\tau'] = 0, \qquad\qquad all\ t \neq \tau.$$

We know from (5.5.22) - (5.5.23) that constraints exist on the functional form of (3.2). For models I-III the constraint is written in vector notation as

$$(3.6) \qquad w'\,[y_t - f(x_t, \alpha)] \equiv 0,$$

where w is the nx1 vector of baseyear import shares $[w_1^o, \ldots, w_n^o]'$. For model IV, the vector of weights is the nx1 vector of units $\iota = [1, \ldots, 1]'$

$$(3.7) \qquad \iota'\,[y_t - f(x_t, \alpha)] \equiv 0.$$

Because of the assumptions on the vector of disturbances u_t and the constraints (3.6) - (3.7), we know from Definition 4.3.1 that models I-III are all constrained models of class $(n, \alpha, H; 1, w)$, while model IV is of class $(n, \alpha, H; 1, \iota)$. It should however be remembered that this last model was originally formulated as a constrained model with time-dependent covariance matrix and vector of weights. With the techniques used for the proof of Theorem 4.4.1 it was transformed, in subsection 5.3.3, into its present state with constant covariance matrix and vector of weights.

As a next step towards estimation we have to specify the distribution that is followed by the vector of disturbances u_t. A natural assumption would be that they follow an n-variate normal distribution, which would be singular because we are considering constrained models. We noted before, in section 4.2, that this assumption may cause problems.

In particular, if the (fitted) dependent variables should lie within a given interval (such as the unit simplex for shares), an unconstrained normal distribution would assign a positive probability to values that exceed the bounds of the interval.

For the present four models, however, the dependent variables s_{it} are all defined such that they may be interpreted as (weighted) differences in growth rates, and therefore we avoid the interval-problem.

Because the four models all have *one* constraint, the lopped models are obtained by deleting *one* equation. We know from Theorem 4.3.6 that the maximum likelihood estimators for the parameter vector α and the covariance matrix H will not depend upon which equation is deleted. Corollary 4.3.1 tells us, however, that the value of the likelihood function of the lopped forms of models I-III will vary with the equation that is deleted because the vector of weights w does not equal the vector of units ι. The latter is the vector of weights of model IV, and therefore the value of its likelihood function will not depend on the index of the deleted equation.

In the following four subsections we will look at the estimating equations for (3.2) that result under different assumptions regarding the presence (or not) of trend parameters or lagged values. The absence of trend effects is represented by setting all parameters γ_i, and *a fortiori* b_{it}, equal to zero

$$\text{(3.8)} \qquad \gamma_i = b_{it} = 0 , \qquad\qquad i = 1, \ldots, n.$$

Dynamics may be excluded by putting the parameter λ of the infinitely distributed lag (5.3.25) equal to zero

$$(3.9) \qquad \lambda = 0 \ .$$

This case corresponds to the situation in which our fictive importer is fully informed about bilateral import prices, and does not need to take past (changes in) prices into consideration to form an idea of the price developments.

It may be argued that in some cases either the presence of trends, or dynamics, or both are not reasonable assumptions for a particular import allocation model. For instance, the importing country may be a member of a customs union, and the explicitly distinguished partner countries might be the other members of the customs union with the rest of the world treated as a residual. If the integration within the customs union has been completed before the start of the sample period, then, other things being equal over this period, there are no *a priori* reasons to assume trendlike changes with respect to the allocation of total imports. One might also argue that because the explanatory prices in models III-IV are expressed as logarithmic growth rates, the allocation model is already sufficiently dynamic, and that the additional expectations interpretation of the logarithmic changes in the bilateral import prices would therefore be superfluous.

For the time being we keep an open mind with respect to these considerations, and we therefore analyze the model (3.1) under all four possible combinations regarding presence or absence of trends and dynamics.

6.4. STATIC MODEL WITHOUT TIME TREND

Applying (3.8) and (3.9) to (3.1) the static model without trend may be written in vector and matrix notation as

$$(4.1) \qquad y_i = Z_i\ \alpha + u_i, \qquad\qquad i = 1, \ldots, n,$$

where y_i is the Tx1 vector $[s_{i1}, \ldots, s_{iT}]'$ of T observations on the dependent variable; Z_i is the Txn matrix of predetermined variables with element (t,h) equal to

$$(4.2) \qquad (\omega_{ht} - \delta_{ih})\ [p^i_{ht} - \Sigma_l\ \omega_{lt}\ p^i_{lt}]\ ,$$

where δ_{ih} is the Kronecker delta; α is the nx1 parameter vector $[a_1, \ldots, a_n]$ and u_i is the Tx1 vector of disturbances $[u_{i1}, \ldots, u_{iT}]'$.

The parameter vector α is common to all n equations, therefore we "stack" them in the following manner

$$(4.3) \qquad y = Z\ \alpha + u$$

where the nTx1 vector y equals $[y_1', \ldots\ y_n']'$, the nTxn matrix Z equals $[Z_1', \ldots\ Z_n']'$, while the nTx1 vector of disturbances u is defined by $[u_1', \ldots\ u_n']'$. With (3.3) - (3.5), the nTxnT covariance matrix Ω of the normally distributed vector of disturbances n may be seen to be equal to

$$(4.4) \qquad E\ [uu'] = \Omega = H \otimes I_T$$

the Kronecker product of the nxn covariance matrix H and the TxT identity matrix I_T.

With (4.4), model (4.3), which was derived from a constrained model, is itself a *linear* constrained model of class $(nT, \alpha, \Omega; T, R)$ with a TxnT matrix R as matrix of weights. For model I-III the latter is equal to

(4.5) $$R = w' \otimes I_T,$$

while for model IV it takes the form

(4.6) $$R = \iota' \otimes I_T.$$

To obtain the lopped form of (4.3), we have to delete T equations. It was shown in section 4.2 that the T columns of R corresponding to the deleted equations should form a *nonsingular* matrix $\bar{R}$. It can easily be verified that this condition is met if we delete the ith T equations $(i = 1, \ldots, n)$. This could of course be predicted, because we know already that one equation should bedeleted, and that corresponds exactly to disregarding the ith T equations, given the formulation of (4.3). Additionally we note howevern that this is only a *sufficient* condition. The *necessary and sufficient* condition, if we number the equations from 1 to nT, is that the indices for the T deleted equations are all different, *modulo* T [1].

If we delete the ith T equations, the determinant of $\bar{R}$ will be equal to $(w_i^o)^T$ for models I-III, and equal to 1 for model IV. The value of the likelihood function for models I-III will therefore depend on the index of the deleted equation according to corollary 4.3.3. This could have been avoided if we would have chosen the indices of the T deleted equations such that, first, they are pairwise different *modulo* T and second, there is one index belonging to each of the n sets of T equations. For example, the set of indices $\{1, (T+1)+1, 2(T+1)+1, \ldots, (n-1)(T+1)+1\}$ meets this criterion. For practical estimation, this way of proceeding is too complicated, however, and we will assume that the ith T equations are deleted, thereby entering the obligation, in view of hypothesis testing, to delete each time the same T equations. For convenience we will henceforth assume that it concerns the *last* T equations, or that the deleted equations have been given the index $i = n$ in (4.1).

The resulting model may be written as

(4.7) $$\tilde{y} = \tilde{Z}\alpha + \tilde{u},$$

where the tilde "~" denotes that the last T elements of the vectors $\tilde{y}$ and $\tilde{u}$, and the last T rows of the matrix Z have been deleted. The covariance matrix of the lopped vector of disturbances equals

$$(4.8) \qquad E\,[\tilde{u}\,\tilde{u}'\,] = \tilde{\Omega} = \tilde{H} \otimes I_T \,,$$

where the tilde indicates that the last T rows and columns of Ω , and the last row and column of H have been deleted.

The assumption of normality of the disturbances implies the following likelihood function for the sample

$$(4.9) \qquad L = (2\pi)^{-(n-1)T/2}\, |\tilde{\Omega}|^{-1/2}\, exp\, \{-\tfrac{1}{2}\,\tilde{u}'\,\tilde{\Omega}^{-1}\,\tilde{u}\}$$

Given the definitions of the covariance matrix $\tilde{\Omega}$, in (4.8), and the lopped vector of disturbances $\tilde{u}$, in (4.7), this is equivalent to

$$(4.10) \qquad L = (2\pi)^{-(n-1)T/2}\, |\tilde{H}|^{-T/2}\, exp\, \{-\tfrac{1}{2}\,(\tilde{y} - \tilde{Z}\,\alpha)'(\tilde{H}^{-1} \otimes I_T)(\tilde{y} - \tilde{Z}\,\alpha)\}$$

The likelihood function should be maximized with respect to the elements of α and H, subject to

$$(4.11) \qquad \alpha_i \geqslant 0 \,, \qquad\qquad i = 1, \ldots, n \,,$$

and

$$(4.12) \qquad w'H = 0 \,,$$

for models I-III and

$$(4.13) \qquad \iota\,'H = 0 \,,$$

for model IV. Condition (4.11) could be weakened to allow the possibility of one negative a_i, but the corresponding second-order condition (5.2.40) that should subsequently be fulfilled makes the maximum likelihood estimation problem unduly complicated [2).

The maximum likelihood estimators for α and H follow from the following set of equations, together with (4.11) and (4.12) or (4.13), if we put the derivatives of (the logarithm of) (4.10) with respect to the elements of α and $\tilde{H}$ equal to zero

$$(4.14) \qquad \alpha = [\tilde{Z}'(\tilde{H}^{-1} \otimes I_T)\tilde{Z}]^{-1}\tilde{Z}'(\tilde{H}^{-1} \otimes I_T)\tilde{y}$$

$$(4.15) \qquad h_{ik} = \frac{1}{T}(y_i - Z_i\,\alpha)'(y_k - Z_k\,\alpha)$$

where h_{ik} is element (i,k) of the matrix H.

If $\tilde{H}$ and therefore H, were known, (4.14) would simply be the Generalized Least Squares estimator of α. This is, in general, however not the case. Therefore an iterative procedure to obtain maximum likelihood estimates both for α and H would be the following [3)]

Step 1 : Find an initial value for $\tilde{H}$, that has the same properties as $\tilde{H}$ (symmetric, nonsingular).

Step 2 : Estimate α from (4.14), using the initial value of $\tilde{H}$.

Step 3 : Calculate an estimate for $\tilde{H}$ from (4.15), using the value of α obtained in step 2.

Step 4 : Go to step 2, using the value for $\tilde{H}$ calculated in step 3. If α and $\tilde{H}$ do not change any more, the method has converged.

Several starting values for $\tilde{H}$ might be considered. Use the nx1 vector r to denote the vector of weights. For models I-III, $r = w$, and for model IV, $r = \iota$. Similarly $\tilde{r}$ is the vector r with the last element deleted. Then the following three possibilities will be analyzed

$$(4.16) \qquad \tilde{H} = \sigma^2\,\hat{\tilde{r}}^{-1}$$

$$(4.17) \qquad \tilde{H} = \sigma^2\,\hat{\tilde{r}}^{-1}\,[I_{n-1} - \frac{1}{n}\iota\iota']\,\hat{\tilde{r}}^{-1},$$

$$(4.18) \qquad \tilde{H} = \sigma^2\,\hat{\tilde{r}}^{-1}\,[\hat{\tilde{w}} - \tilde{w}\,\tilde{w}']\,\hat{\tilde{r}}^{-1}.$$

With (4.12), these three possibilities imply for the complete matrix H of models I-III,

$$(4.19) \qquad H = \sigma^2 \left[\hat{w}^{-1} - \frac{1}{w_n^o} e_n \iota' - \frac{1}{w_n^o} \iota e_n' + \frac{1}{(w_n^o)^2} e_n e_n' \right],$$

$$(4.20) \qquad H = \sigma^2 \hat{w}^{-1} \left[I - \frac{1}{n} \iota \iota' \right] \hat{w}^{-1},$$

$$(4.21) \qquad H = \sigma^2 \hat{w}^{-1} \left[\hat{w} - w w' \right] \hat{w}^{-1},$$

$$= \sigma^2 \left[\hat{w}^{-1} - \iota \iota' \right],$$

while for model IV they amount to

$$(4.22) \qquad H = \sigma^2 \left[I - e_n \iota' - \iota e_n' + n e_n e_n' \right]$$

$$(4.23) \qquad H = \sigma^2 \left[I - \frac{1}{n} \iota \iota' \right],$$

$$(4.24) \qquad H = \sigma^2 \left[\hat{w} - w w' \right];$$

The nx1 vector e_i has element i equal to one and zeroes elsewhere.

The first possibility, (4.16), is tantamount to a diagonal covariance matrix for the first $n-1$ equations, relegating nonzero covariances to the interactions involving the last equation. The interpretation of this "asymmetric" covariance structure could be that the import allocation between the first $n-1$ partners takes place completely independently, whereas the last partner acts as a "lender of last resort" or residual. A random shock in the bilateral imports from one of the first $n-1$ partners will only affect the bilateral imports from the last partner. This specification of the covariance matrix corresponds to one of the possibilities for the specification of the covariance matrix that was already mentioned in subsection 2.3.1 with respect to estimation of the CES model. It was already argued there that the disadvantage of using such a covariance matrix as the *true* covariance matrix was the asymmetric treatment given to the last partner. It should be remembered however that we are here only talking about a *starting* value for the covariance matrix.

The second possibility is a generalization, towards a vector of weights with unequal elements, of a covariance matrix that has been proposed as a "symmetric" alternative to (4.22), which indeed is not very realistic in the absence of prior information [4]. Although its form is simple, it has at least the advantage that all covariances are treated in a symmetric way.

In the context of the Rotterdam model, a theoretical structure for the form of the covariance matrix similar to the third possibility (4.24) was derived by BARTEN (1968), with a vector of marginal budgetshares (assumed to be constant over time) instead of the vector of baseyear shares ω used here. However, if the elasticity of bilateral imports with respect to the import quantity index μ is equal to one, the marginal shares will be equal to the average shares, and this corresponds exactly to our model. Therefore, if we make the assumption, in the spirit of Barten, that the import quantity index μ is of a stochastic nature, (4.24) is a definition of the covariance matrix in its own right, and because the vector of baseyear shares is known, the vector of coefficients α may be estimated directly from (4.14).

The possibility of having a theoretical argument to use the covariance matrix (4.18) may become of importance if the number of observations is small relative to the number of equations. The number of parameters to be estimated equals $n + \frac{1}{2}n(n-1)$ (n for the coefficients and $\frac{1}{2}n(n-1)$ for the covariance matrix, while there are $(n-1)T$ independent observations. Suppose that we require k observations for each parameter to be estimated. Then we need at least a value of the sample size T equal to $k\,[n/(n-1) + n/2]$. The following table shows, given the values of k and n, the minimum values of the sample size that is required.

Tabel 4.1 : Minimum sample size required, given the number of partners (n) and a minimum number of observations per parameter (k)

k \ n	5	10	15	20	25	30
2	8	12	17	22	27	32
3	11	18	26	33	41	48
4	15	24	34	44	54	64
5	19	31	43	55	68	80
6	23	37	51	66	81	96

If the sample size T is too small, a reduction in the number of parameters to be estimated of $\frac{1}{2}n(n-1)$ may therefore be achieved by specifying $\widetilde{H}$ to be equal to (4.18), or even (4.16) or (4.17).

6.5. STATIC MODEL WITH TIME TREND

Applying (3.9) to (3.1) the static model with time trend may be written in vector and matrix notation as

(5.1) $\qquad y_i = Z_i^\star \alpha^\star + u_i, \qquad\qquad i = 1, \ldots, n,$

where y_i and u_i were already defined in section 6.4. The definitions of $Z_i^\star$ and $\alpha^\star$ differ according to whether it concerns models I-III or model IV. For models I-III, we estimate directly the b_i from (2.6). Therefore the $Tx2n$ matrix $Z_i^\star$ has element (t,k) equal to (4.2) for $k = 1, \ldots, n$ and equal to $\delta_{i,k-n}\, T_t$ for $k = n+1, \ldots, 2n$, where δ_{ij} is the Kronecker delta. The $2n$x1 parameter vector $\alpha^\star$ is equal to $[a_1, \ldots, a_n, b_1, \ldots, b_n]'$.
For model IV we make the following transformation of the coefficients, corresponding to (2.9)

(5.2) $\qquad g_i = a_i\, \gamma_i - a_n\, \gamma_n, \qquad\qquad i = 1, \ldots, n-1.$

In this way there remain $n-1$ independent coefficients g_i to be estimated. From the estimates of the g_i and a_i the γ_i may be calculated up to a constant. If also the constraint $\Sigma_i\, w_i^o\, \gamma_i = 0$ is applied, the γ_i are all determined. The Tx$(2n-1)$ matrix $Z_i^\star$ in this case has element (t,h) equal to (4.2) for $h = 1, \ldots, n$ and equal to $\tilde{w}_{it}(\delta_{i,h-n} - \tilde{w}_{h-n,t})T_t$ for $h = n+1, \ldots, 2n-1$; the $(2n-1)$x1 parameter vector $\alpha^\star$ is now equal to $[a_1, \ldots, a_n, g_1, \ldots, g_{n-1}]'$.
This model has the same stochastic properties as the static model without time trend, therefore it should be estimated in the same way, *mutatis mutandis*. Only, the lopped model will not give an estimate for b_n, but

this may be obtained from the condition $\Sigma_i w_i^o b_i = 0$, using the estimates for $b_1, \ldots, b_{n-1}$. The latter increase the number of parameters to be estimated by $n-1$. Consequently, the requirements with respect to the sample size will also become more severe.

6.6. DYNAMIC MODEL WITHOUT TIME TREND

We obtain the dynamic model without time trend if we use (3.8) and the transformation

$$\alpha_i = (1-\lambda)\ a_i, \qquad i = 1, \ldots, n. \tag{6.1}$$

The resulting linear model, derived from (3.1), may be written in vector and matrix notation as

$$y_i = Z_i^{**}\ \alpha^{**} + u_i \qquad i = 1, \ldots, n, \tag{6.2}$$

where y_i and u_i were defined in section 6.4, Z_i^{**} is the Tx$(n+1)$ matix with element (t,h) equal to (4.2) for $h = 1, \ldots, n$ and element $(t,n+1)$ equal to s_{it-1}, while α^{**} is the $(n+1)$x1 parameter vector equal to $[\alpha_1, \ldots, \alpha_n, \lambda]'$. With respect to the static model without time trend, the number of parameters increases by one, while the α_i may now be interpreted as the short-run values of the a_i. Subsequently it is possible to calculate short-run price elasticities and elasticities of substitution. *Mutatis mutandis*, estimation of the lopped form of (6.2) may run along the same lines as for the static model without trend as described in section 6.4.

6.7 DYNAMIC MODEL WITH TIME TREND

The dynamic model with time trend is nonlinear in the parameters, even if we apply transformations such as (5.2) and (6.1). There are two ways that seem suitable to estimate (3.1). Both possibilities are extensions of the iterative maximum likelihood estimation procedure outlined in section 6.4.

A first possibility would be to replace step 2 by an iterative procedure to maximize the likelihood function conditional on $\tilde{H}$ with respect to the elements of the parameter vector, *viz.* λ, the a_i, the b_i from (2.6) for models I-III or the g_i from (5.2) for model IV. Using $\tilde{y} = g(x, \alpha)$ to denote the lopped form of the stacked model (3.1), this amounts to minimizing a function $S(\alpha)$ of the parameter vector α, defined as

$$S(\alpha) = [\tilde{y} - g(x, \alpha)]' [\tilde{H}^{-1} \otimes I_T][\tilde{y} - g(x, \alpha)]. \tag{7.1}$$

Denote the $(n-1)T\text{x}2n$ matrix of partial derivatives of the vector valued function $g(.)$ with respect to the parameter vector α by G

$$G = \partial g/\partial\alpha'. \tag{7.2}$$

The iterative procedure starts with an initial value for the parameter vector, say α^o. Then we take a linear expansion of $g(x, \alpha)$ around α^o, and substitute the resulting approximation for $g(.)$ in (7.1). Then we have to minimize with respect to α

$$[\tilde{y} - g(x,\alpha^o) - G^o(\alpha-\alpha^o)]'[\tilde{H}^{-1} \otimes I_T][\tilde{y} - g(x,\alpha^o) - G^o(\alpha-\alpha^o)] \tag{7.3}$$

where G^o is the matrix G evaluated at α^o. Setting the partial derivative of (7.3) with respect to α equal to zero, we obtain

(7.4) $$G^{o\prime}[\tilde{H}^{-1} \otimes I_T][\tilde{y} - g(x,\alpha^o) - G^o(\alpha-\alpha^o)] = 0$$

which gives as the change $d = \alpha - \alpha^o$ the generalized least squares estimator

(7.5) $$d = [G^{o\prime}(\tilde{H}^{-1} \otimes I_T)G^o]^{-1} G^{o\prime}(\tilde{H}^{-1} \otimes I_T)[\tilde{y} - g(x,\alpha^o)]$$

The next step starts from the parameter vector $\alpha^1 = \alpha^o + d$, or, as an alternative $\alpha^1 = \alpha^o + \mu d$, with $\mu > 0$ chosen such that $S(\alpha^o + \mu d) \leqslant S(\alpha^o)$. This process is repeated until the parameter vector α no longer changes. This procedure might be called *nonlinear Generalized Least Squares* [5].

Another possibility for modifying the iterative estimation procedure of section 6.4 in order to make it suitable for the dynamic model with time trend would be to iterate the procedure itself. In one step the value of λ would be fixed - at a plausible starting value or a previously estimated value -, while in the other step λ would be estimated, keeping the other parameters fixed. Several starting values should be tried to avoid the occurence of a local maximum of the likelihood function. Therefore it is useful to start to fix λ, because then only a grid search on this parameter needs to be executed.

With λ fixed, the model becomes, in matrix and vector notation,

(7.6) $$y_{i\cdot}^{\star\star\star} = Z_{i\cdot}^{\star\star\star}\,\alpha^{\star\star\star} + u_{i\cdot} \qquad i = 1, \ldots, n,$$

where $u_{i\cdot}$ was defined in section 6.4, $Z_{i\cdot}^{\star\star\star}$ is the $T\text{x}(2n-1)$ matrix with element (t,h) equal to

(7.7) $$(1-\lambda)(\omega_{ht} - \delta_{ih})[p_{ht}^{i} - \Sigma_l\, \omega_{lt}\, p_{lt}^{i}]$$

for $h = 1, \ldots, n$, and equal to

(7.8) $$\delta_{i,h-n}(T_t - \lambda T_{t-1}) - [\omega_{h-n,t} \cdot T_t - \lambda\omega_{h-n,t-1}\, T_{t-1}]$$

for $h = n+1, \ldots, 2n-1$; element t of the Tx1 vector of dependent variables y_i^{***} is equal to $s_{it} - \lambda s_{it-1}$, while the $(2n-1)$x1 parameter vector α^{***} is equal to $[a_1, \ldots, a_n, g_1, \ldots, g_{n-1}]'$, where we have used the transformation (5.2).

Keeping all coefficients but λ fixed, element t of the vector y_i^{***} becomes equal to

(7.9) $$s_{it} - (g_i - \Sigma_{h \neq n}\, \omega_{ht}\, g_h)T_t + a_i(p_{it}^i - \Sigma_l\, \omega_{lt}\, p_{lt}^i) - \Sigma_h\, \omega_{ht}\, a_h\, (p_{ht}^i - \Sigma_l\, \omega_{lt}\, p_{lt}^i),$$

element t of the Tx1 matrix Z_i^{***} the equals

(7.10) $$s_{it-1} - (g_i - \Sigma_{h \neq n}\, \omega_{ht-1}\, g_h)T_{t-1} + a_i(p_{it}^i - \Sigma_l\, \omega_{lt}\, p_{lt}^i) - \Sigma_h\, \omega_{ht}\, a_h(p_{ht}^i - \Sigma_l\, \omega_{lt}\, p_{lt}^i),$$

while the parameters vector α^{***} only contains one element, λ.

In practice, the availability of nonlinear estimation software on a sufficiently powerful computer did not confine us to this last method. The nonlinear GLS method could be used without problems in most cases.

6.8. SUMMARY AND CONCLUDING REMARKS

After the introduction of a further simplification to render the model less nonlinear, we developed in this chapter the econometric specification and estimation method for four different forms of the general specification proposed in the previous chapter to capture the models developed there. The four forms corresponded to the presence or not of trends and dynamics. For three of the four forms the resulting models were linear in the parameters, thereby proving the simplicity of estimating them. Only the model which contains trends as well as dynamics is nonlinear in its parameters. But even there a grid search on the distributed lag parameter results in repeated estimation of a linear model.

Because of this linearity, the present models may be considered as viable alternatives to the CES model presented in subsection 2.3.1, which also was linear in its parameters. Estimation of the CES model with the method of maximum likelihood, which was argued to be the least arbitrary method of estimation, amounts to the same iterative estimation procedure as for our model. In this respect the two models are therefore equivalent.

FOOTNOTES TO CHAPTER 6

1) Two positive natural numbers are equal *modulo* T, if their difference is a multiple of T and *vice versa*.

2) In practice, even condition (4.11) will only be checked *ex post*. Negative a_i will then be put equal to zero. See subsection 8.4.1.

3) KMENTA and GILBERT (1968) have shown that if this procedure converges, it converges to the maximum likelihood estimators.

4) *Cfr*. McGUIRE *et al*. (1968).

5) *Cfr*. MADDALA (1977, pp. 174-175).

CHAPTER 7 - THE DATA

7.1. INTRODUCTION

The models presented in this study so far were constructed within a given set of characteristics. The import allocation or total allocation models were assumed to be valid on a given import market or country, for a particular category of goods and with a given number of trade partners. Before we pass to actual estimation and hypothesis testing we first give a description of the available dataset. A notable feature of this dataset is that it contains *bilateral* import prices. We saw in subsection 1.4.2 that international linkage models using bilateral price data are scarce, and therefore we consider it worthwile in this chapter to pay some attention to the way in which the bilateral prices used in this study were constructed.

The international trade data that are used were originally constructed for a project for a European macro-sectoral model with national models linked at a disaggregate level [1]. The basic data from which the bilateral trade data were constructed were detailed OECD data for the period 1963-1980. The methodology used for the construction and the exact classifications are described elsewhere [2]. Here only the main features of the data construction process are given.

The final dataset contains trade data for 5 different categories of goods for 13 declaring countries with 18 trade partners.

The categories of *goods* are :

A - Agricultural, forestry and fishery products
E - Fuel and power products
Q - Manufacturing products : intermediate
K - Manufacturing products : equipment
C - Manufacturing products : consumption.

Each of these 5 categories corresponds to one or more branches as defined in the version of the General Industrial Classification of Economic

Activities in the European Communities used in the input-output tables (NACE-CLIO), as defined by the Statistical Office of the European Communities [3]. The correspondence between each category and the NACE-CLIO R44 classification [4] is given in Appendix 7.A.

The 18 *trade partners*, the first 13 of which are also *declaring countries*, are

1. Belgium-Luxembourg Economic Union (BLEU)
2. Denmark
3. Federal Republic of Germany (W.-Germany)
4. Greece
5. France
6. Ireland
7. Italy
8. Netherlands
9. United Kingdom (UK)
10. Portugal
11. Spain
12. United States of America (USA)
13. Japan
14. Rest of OECD and South Africa
15. CMEA, Mongolia and Albania
16. OPEC
17. South-East Asian fast developing countries
18. Rest of the world.

The composition of the 5 last zones is described in more detail in Appendix 7.B.

The dataset contains import data and export data, but we will only use import data, given that we estimate *import* allocation models. This has the additional advantage that the cost, insurance and freight (cif) that usually have to be paid by the importer are taken into account in the bilateral import prices. Therefore they are part of the information that may be employed by importers to make their allocation decisions.

For each bilateral import flow the dataset contains the value of that flow (in U.S. dollars), a bilateral import price index (measured cif in principle) with baseyear 1975=1, and the volume of that flow in constant 1975 U.S. dollars, obtained through deflation of the value by the price index.

For each of the 13 declaring countries the dataset contains therefore in principle (some flows may be zero) value, price index and volume of 5 (categories of goods) x 17 (partners) = 85 bilateral import flows.

The data from the OECD trade statistics, which are available on tape [5], are the *source* from which these data were constructed. These trade statistics are classified according to the Standard International Trade Classification (SITC) of the United Nations [6], either SITC, Revised or SITC, Revision 2. According to this classification, internationally traded products are classified in a 5-digit code at the most detailed level, which are called *items*. More aggregated are *subgroups* (4 digits), *groups* (3 digits), *divisions* (2 digits) and *sections* (1 digit). This system is hierarchical in the sense that items starting with the same 4 digits all belong to the same subgroup *etc.*

The SITC, Revised contains 625 *subgroups*, of which 257 are further subdivided into 944 *items* [7]. It contains therefore 1312 different *basic categories*.

The SITC, Revision 2 contains 786 *subgroups*, of which 435 are further subdivided into 1573 *items* [8]. Therefore in total 1924 *basic categories*.

The OECD data for 1963-1969 are only as detailed as the 4-digit subgroups of SITC, Revised. For the period 1970-1977 the data are classified at the most detailed 5-digit level of items (as far as the subgroups are subdivided in items) of SITC, Revised, while this is also the case for 1978-1980, using the classification of SITC, Revision 2 [9].

A bilateral trade flow at the level of an item or a subgroup is described through three elements : total value, value and quantity.

Total value is the total value of that flow in U.S. dollars irrespective of whether there is a corresponding quantity to that value.

Value corresponds to that part of total value for which there also is a *quantity* given. The quantity might be expressed in one of nine different units, such as metric tons, cubic meters, *etc.*

The three elements make it possible to calculate unit values for the flow, at the same time maintaining the total value to which the unit value is supposed to correspond.

Broadly speaking, the transformation of these basic data into the final data-set entailed the following three problems.

- the mutual compatibility of the SITC, Revised and SITC, Revision 2 classifications; correspondingly, the compatibility with the NACE-CLIO classification;
- the definition and calculation of price indices;
- the treatment of anomalies, such as non-existing unit values, SITC codes less detailed than 4 or 5 digits, negative values *etc.*

These three problems will be treated consecutively in the following three subsections.

7.2. COMPATIBILITY OF CLASSIFICATIONS

The SITC and NACE-CLIO classifications were linked to each other in the following manner. First, an intermediary classification between NACE-CLIO R25 and NACE-CLIO R44 was created for those branches which were assumed to produce internationally traded goods and for a residual to contain unclassified goods. This classification was called R23, as it contains 23 categories. As may be seen from Appendix 7.A, the aggregation of the R23 categories into the 5 classes of goods A, E, Q, K and C is straightforward.

Next, the classifications SITC, Revised and SITC, Revision 2 were merged into a classification that might be called SITC, Merged. This classification contains 1102 basic categories. Each of these basic categories contains at least one basic category of each of the two classifications. If a basic category of SITC, Revision 2 forms a subset of one single basic category of SITC, Revised [10], it was merged with that basic category to form a new basic category of SITC, Merged. If it forms a subset of more than one basic category of SITC, Revised, it was merged with all these basic categories, and possibly also with other basic categories of SITC, Revision 2 that were already merged [11]. The basic difficulty here is that the merged basic categories should each be a subset of *one* single R23 category in order to make proper aggregation possible. Otherwise expressed, if we use the symbol $\in$ to denote "is the collection of exhaustive partitions into mutually exclusive subsets of each category of", we need for proper aggregation

(2.1) $\{\mathit{SITC,\ Merged}\} \in \{R23\} \in \{A,E,Q,K,C\},$

while neither

(2.2) $\{\mathit{SITC,\ Revised}\} \in \{\mathit{SITC,\ Revision\ 2}\}$

nor

(2.3) $\{\mathit{SITC,\ Revision\ 2}\} \in \{\mathit{SITC,\ Revised}\}.$

Relationship (2.3) would seem more probable than (2.2) because SITC, Revision 2 has more basic categories (1924) than SITC, Revised (1312). Therefore the merging procedure goes more in the direction of (2.3) than (2.2). Relationship (2.1) was established in two steps using *share analysis*. *Step 1* consisted of the assignment, of each basic category of SITC, Revised, to one single basic category of the NACE-CLIO classification, and therefore to one single R23 category. This step was performed by the Statistical Office of the European Communities, using the 6-digit international trade classification NIMEXE of the European Communities [12]. This classification changes slightly from year to year, but it is more detailed than the SITC or NACE-CLIO, or

(2.4) $\{NIMEXE\} \in \{SITC,\ Revised\}$

(2.5) $\{NIMEXE\} \in \{NACE\text{-}CLIO\} \in \{R23\}$.

Therefore, if a basic category of SITC, Revised could not be assigned to one single basic category of NACE-CLIO, it was assigned to that basic category of NACE-CLIO which, over the period 1976-1978, showed the largest EEC trade (expressed as the sum - in European Currency Units - of total imports and exports of the EEC countries) for all 6-digit NIMEXE basic categories corresponding to that category. The result of Step 1 therefore establishes

(2.6) $\{SITC,\ Revised\} \in \{NACE\text{-}CLIO\} \in \{R23\}$.

Step 2 consisted of applying a similar share analysis, but for the year 1980, to merged basic categories consisting of basic categories of SITC, Revised that do not correspond to the same R23 category. Each such merged basic category was assigned to that R23 category with the largest share in total EEC trade for that merged category, again using the NIMEXE data at the 6-digit level. This guaranteed the first relationship of (2.1).

A complete list of the basic categories of SITC, Merged and their correspondences to the elements of SITC, Revised, SITC, Revision 2 and R23 may be found in ITALIANER (1982c).

The procedures followed to link the two SITC classifications to the 5 categories of goods in an unequivocal way could of course be improved upon. The shares analysis could be done for the whole sample period, while the merging of the basic categories could have been done at the level of basic categories of the NACE-CLIO classification instead of the more aggregated R23 classification. There is, however, a pay-off between the improvement of information and the amount of time needed to obtain that improvement. We feel that the present approach balances between the two, and has the merit that at least a link between the classifications has been established. Higher ambitions might even have inhibited the achievement of this primary goal.

7.3. PRICE INDICES; CURRENT AND CONSTANT PRICES

The nature of the data forced us to calculate bilateral import price indices using *unit values* for each of the 1102 basic categories of SITC, Merged. It is well known that "real" prices are to be preferred above unit values as an indicator of price movements. KRAVIS and LIPSEY (1971, pp. 4-5), *e.g.*, give two disadvantages of the use of unit values in international trade.

The first disadvantage is that unit values have to be calculated for each element of an import or export classification, and that the classifications therefore cannot be narrowly specified unless their number is increased far beyond any practical limit. Consequently, as a result of the lack of close specification, there is never any certainty that a change in the unit value represents a change in the price; the unit value of a trade classification can change, even though all prices are constant, if there is a shift from one quality or type of items to another. Given that one is obliged to use unit values, the only way to reduce the problem in this case therefore seems to be to use as many categories as possible. This is exactly what we have done, given that we had to merge a minimum of basic categories of SITC, Revised and SITC, Revision 2, such that the resulting basic categories corresponded to one single R23 category.

The second disadvantage, according to Kravis and Lipsey, is that quantities are not reported at all for many (manufactured, US-) imported and exported products, and that therefore their unit values are simply unavailable. They state that, for the United States, not more than 35 per cent (for finished manufactured imports) or 25 per cent (for finished manufactured exports) of trade was covered in unit value index calculations around 1965. In table 3.1 we show the percentages of the *value* of imports of total trade (the total of categories A, E, Q, K and C) that were covered in the unit value index calculations. For each of the 13 reporting countries we present the percentages for three reference years : 1965, 1970 and 1980.

Country	1965	1970	1980
1. BLEU	95.0	96.1	93.9
2. Denmark	99.8	99.8	99.8
3. West-Germany	99.4	99.3	99.2
4. Greece	97.3	99.7	99.6
5. France	99.3	99.3	98.9
6. Ireland	66.6	66.7	99.7
7. Italy	99.8	99.8	99.8
8. Netherlands	97.7	99.7	99.6
9. United Kingdom	86.0	82.4	88.3
10. Portugal	96.3	99.5	98.3
11. Spain	99.0	98.6	98.6
12. United States	61.4	60.8	71.8
13. Japan	92.2	96.5	96.2

Table 3.1 : Percentages of the value of imports of total trade covered in the unit value index calculations, 1965-1980.

The table shows that, except for the Anglo-Saxon countries, coverage in percentage of the total value of imports is extremely high. The results for Ireland and the United Kingdom improve after 1970 probably because of their adoption of the metric system of measurement upon their entry in the European Economic Community as of January 1st, 1973. The figures for the United States therefore are the only ones, among this sample, to remain relatively low in coverage. The second argument of Kravis and Lipsey therefore seems only valid for the United States, although the percentage coverage has increased with respect to the number they report, as well.

A general problem in the calculation of a price index according to classical formulas such as those of Paasche, Laspeyres or Fisher is that products composing the basket for which the index is calculated should be nonzero for each observation of the period over which it is calculated. Otherwise, the unit values or "real" prices for those products cannot be taken into account.

Consequently, the smaller the period, the larger in general the number of products that may be dealt with in the price index. The smallest period over which a price index may be calculated consists of *two* points of time. Therefore, the best way to take as many unit value or price movements into account is to construct the index as a *chain index number*, linking the price movements from one point in time to the next. This method has the disadvantage that over the whole sample period, the same baskets of *products* are not compared. If, however, one assumes that each basket, although composed of different products, satisfies the same *needs*, the chain index will give a correct view of the changes in the prices or unit values that have to be paid in order to satisfy those needs.

The problem of products that appear and/or disappear over the sample period becomes particularly ticklish if we consider bilateral trade flows at the level of 1102 basic categories and 29 partners (from which the 18 partners described above were derived). These detailed trade flows very often are zero for one or more years of the sample period, and therefore the chain index method seems best suited, given an interpretation of the aggregate categories in terms of needs, to retain as much information on unit values as possible.

In what follows we describe shortly the different steps in the aggregation process towards values and price indices (1975=1) for bilateral imports from 18 partners (incl. declaring country) in the categories A, E, Q, K and C, per declaring country. References to anomalies are treated more extensively in the next subsection; for the present we assume that they do not exist.

Step 1 : For each of the 1102 basic categories of SITC, Merged, the total value, value and quantity of the composing basic categories of SITC, Revised or SITC, Revision 2 are added (provided that the quantities are expressed in the same unit). Result : total value, value and quantity for :

- 1102 basic categories of SITC, Merged;
- 29 partners (incl. declaring country).

Step 2 : Calculation of unit value and unit value index with respect to previous years (if both unit values are positive) for each of the 1102 basic categories. Result : total value, unit value and unit value

index for years t with respect to year t-1 for :
- 1102 basic categories of SITC, Merged;
- 29 partners (incl. declaring country).

Step 3 : Aggregation towards R23 categories for total value and the unit values of the 1102 basic categories. Aggregation of unit values both according to Paasche and Laspeyres (which also implies the Fisher index, which is the geometric mean of the two). Result : total value and Paasche, Laspeyres and Fisher unit value index for year t with respect to year t-1 for :
- 23 categories of R23;
- 29 partners (incl. declaring country).

Step 4 : Comparison of the resulting aggregate total chain import price index with existing, published import price indices. The resulting root mean-squared percentage differences between the calculated Paasche, Laspeyres and Fisher and the published figures are given in table 3.2. From that table it appears that, over the considered period, the Fisher index is closest to the published index 10 out of 13 times. In the other three cases it is the Paasche index, with the Fisher index always close to it. This evidence provides a strong incentive to use the Fisher unit value indices to construct the chain indices (if it exists; otherwise the Paasche or Laspeyres was taken). Result : total value and Fisher unit value index for year t with respect to year t-1 for :
- 23 countries of R23;
- 29 partners (incl. declaring country).

Step 5 : Aggregation of total value and Fisher unit value index towards the 5 categories, A, E, Q, K, and C and 18 partners (incl. declaring country). Unit value index aggregation according to Paasche formula. Before aggregation, lacking unit value indices were replaced by alternative indices. Result : total value and unit value index for year t with respect to year t-1 for :
- 5 categories A, E, Q, K and C;
- 18 partners (incl. declaring country).

Country	Paasche	Laspeyres	Fisher	Period	Source(a)
1. BLEU	3.5	6.7	*3.2*	1970-1980	EEC
2. Denmark	5.7	6.5	*1.8*	1970-1980	EEC
3. West-Germany	4.3	4.0	*2.1*	1970-1980	EEC
4. Greece	17.7	13.3	*8.1*	1970-1980	EEC
5. France	*3.4*	8.6	3.8	1970-1980	EEC
6. Ireland	10.7	12.7	*3.4*	1970-1980	EEC
7. Italy	8.0	5.1	*4.4*	1970-1980	EEC
8. Netherlands	4.7	5.8	*1.2*	1970-1980	EEC
9. United Kingdom	*6.4*	11.9	7.3	1970-1980	EEC
10. Portugal	18.6	22.3	*7.6*	1963-1980	IMF
11. Spain	19.0	11.9	*5.5*	1963-1980	IMF
12. United States	*9.5*	15.3	12.3	1963-1980	IMF
13. Japan	4.4	7.8	*3.2*	1964-1980	IMF

(a) EEC : Directorate-General for Economic and Financial Affairs, Commission of the European Communities

IMF : INTERNATIONAL MONETARY FUND [1980, 1982].

Table 3.2 : Root mean-squared percentage differences between 3 types of calculated import price indices and published series. The smallest of the 3 percentages is in italics.

Step 6 : Calculation of the chain index with baseyear 1975=1 for each of the 5 categories and 18 partners. Calculation of the totals. Result : total value and chain index (1975=1) for :

- 6 categories A, E, Q, K, C and the total T;
- 19 partners (incl. declaring country and world total).

The bilateral trade flows in constant 1975 prices were obtained by simple deflation of the value figures by the chain index.

7.4. ANOMALIES

All the steps in the previous section were described as if there were no unknown codes, missing data *etc.* This situation, however, is one that is reserved for textbooks and far from reality. Consequently, this section is devoted to a description of the main obstacles that were encountered during the calculations, and the way in which they were dealt with. We will refer to the steps of the previous subsection to indicate where they occurred and were solved.

In Step 1, there are two problems which arise in practice. The first problem is that the units in which two quantities are expressed which should be added to form a basic category of SITC, Merged, are not the same. This did not happen very frequently, and in those cases the quantity which first entered into the basic category in the aggregation program got priority, while for the other(s) only the total value was used. The second problem, which occurred much more frequently, was that the SITC codes were not those of basic categories of SITC, Revised or SITC, Revision 2. That is, they started with a number of digits corresponding to a higher level of aggregation (section, division, groups, subgroups) than the basic category (subgroup, item) and ended in letters or zeros. For a detailed description of the different codes and the way they were treated we refer to ITALIANER (1982c). Let it suffice to say that if the level of aggregation was such that it corresponded to one single R23 category, the quantity and value (and therefore unit value) information was used, while otherwise only the total value was split over the corresponding R23 categories using average shares over the 29 partners at the most detailed level for the most recent years (preferably the current year).

The calculation of the unit value indices in Step 2 is only done in order to check whether the decrease or increase with respect to the previous year is not too extreme, both in absolute value and with respect to the average import unit value index over all the partners for that basic category. In the former case, the corresponding unit values for year t and years t-1 were excluded from the aggregations of Step 3 if the unit value index exceeded certain bounds (that could be different per category), while in the latter case the unit values were adjusted if the corresponding unit value index fell outside a 99.5 %-probability interval around the average import unit value index over all the partners [13]. See ITALIANER (1982c) for more details.

After Steps 3 and 4, it could turn out that some of the bilateral import unit value indices at the R23 level still did not exist, while their corresponding total value was positive. If the Fisher unit value index did not exist, but the Paasche or Laspeyres did, the latter was used as index [14]. Because the indices at that time still are for year t with respect to year t-1, a different weighting scheme will not make much difference, as the weights usually do not vary much between two years. If, however, next to the Fisher index neither the Paasche index nor the Laspeyres index existed, the missing index was replaced by an *alternative index*. This alternative was chosen out of 9 alternatives, ranging from the corresponding bilateral export unit value index to the total import unit value index of all 13 declaring countries together [15]. The first nonzero, or existing, alternative was used to replace the lacking bilateral import unit value index. All alternative indices were calculated for the same R23 category as the missing index. The alternative indices were used under the assumption that information on unit value movements for one R23 category, even at an aggregate level, would be a more accurate approximation of the lacking bilateral unit value index than similar unit value indices from other R23 categories. Because, if the lacking indices were simply not accounted for in the aggregations of the 5 categories A, E, Q, K and C and 18 partners, this would be tantamount to the assumption that they were equal to the average of the category to which they belong. Making the last assumption would furthermore entail the problem that the *order* of aggregation would become of importance. The final indices would then depend on whether the aggregation was first performed over the goods, or over the partners. Consequently, the implicitly assumed value for the missing index also depends on the order.

7.5. THE DOMESTIC AGGREGATE

In the total allocation model that was introduced in section 5.4 we assumed that all domestic products could be represented by a single domestic aggregate. The actual content of such an aggregate depends upon the context of the aggregator function from which the total allocation model is derived. In particular, we might have that the aggregator function represents a utility function or a production function. A *utility* function would typically be applicable for a branch satisfying final demand, such as the branches K and C defined in section 7.1. The domestic aggregate would then represent that part of final demand produced domestically by the branch, or its gross value added. In the context of a *production* function we would have to take into account all production factors others than imports, such as intermediary inputs, labour and capital services. The aggregate would then represent all these other production factors together. This approach would be more adequate for branches like A, E and Q defined in section 7.1.

In both cases the starting point is that one assumes weak separability between domestic elements and bilateral imports. This starting point has to be confronted with the available data series. Available are series for *gross value added* by branch for the branches A, E and the composite of branches Q, K and C (or the total manufacturing branch) for Belgium, West-Germany, France, Italy, the Netherlands and the United Kingdom. They cover the same period as the trade statistics, *viz.* 1963-1980 [16)], and were derived from the series for gross value added at market prices in current prices and as volume index (1975=100) that may be found in EUROSTAT (1980b, part II and 1983, part II), converted into U.S. dollars using the exchange rates from EUROSTAT (1983, table P).

The interpretation of the aggregator function as a utility function is only (partially) possible for the composite branch Q + K + C. Only in that case, therefore, the use of gross value added as a domestic aggregate is justified to some degree. For the other two branches there is a departure from the original weak separability hypothesis : considering gross value added as an aggregate of labour and capital services, we introduce additionally the assumption of weak separability of the production function in intermediate inputs on the one hand, and gross value added and bilateral imports on the other hand. We are forced to accept this assumption because the data did not permit the inclusion of intermediate inputs. Any test of weak separability between imports and gross value added is therefore conditional on the separability between intermediate inputs versus gross value added and bilateral imports. Intuitively one would rather have expected intermediate inputs to be in a partial aggregator funtion with bilateral imports, instead of gross value added.

7.6. SUMMARY AND CONCLUDING REMARKS

The first part of this chapter described the construction of the bilateral trade data that are going to be used for estimation and hypothesis testing in the next chapters. A notable feature of the data is the presence of bilateral import prices. They were calculated by means of a chain index linking unit value indices. Two well-known arguments against the use of unit value indices are 1) that with unit values one is never certain that one measures true prices because of the composite nature of trade categories and 2) that there are not enough observations available on values and quantities to construct unit values for all trade categories. The first argument is met by calculating the unit value indices on the largest possible number of basic trade categories. The second argument, based on observations for the United States in the 1960s, was shown to be only true for the United States data, and to a more minor extent than could be expected. There are however two additional disadvantages that remain valid. First, as was already argued in subsection 1.3.2., the unit value may not be the price at which the goods currently may be obtained but the price that was negociated at the time when the goods were contracted. This seriously hampers the interpretation of lags in a dynamic specification. Secondly, unit value series used to deflate value series in order to obtain series in constant prices imply measurement errors in the latter, assuming that the unit value series themselves contain the same measurement errors. This may result in a specification with both as dependent and independent variables series that contain measurement errors, with the resulting biases in estimation. We feel however that a bilateral import price, possibly containing a measurement error, is still a better alternative than applying the common practice in bilateral trade flow models of substituting the total export price for the bilateral price. The latter would imply even larger measurement errors.

Finally we saw that the only series available to serve as a domestic aggregate in the total allocation model was gross value added by branch. This implied for at least two branches an assumption of weak separability of the production function between intermediate inputs on the one hand, and gross value added and bilateral imports on the other hand. Instead of testing a weak separability assumption between domestic inputs and imports, one therefore will test an assumption of weak separability between gross value added and imports, conditional on the weak separability in intermediate inputs and the latter.

APPENDIX 7.A : GOODS CLASSIFICATION

This appendix provides the definition of the 5 branches A, E, Q, K and C in terms of an intermediate classification, called R23, and NACE-CLIO classification R44, *cfr*. EUROSTAT (1980a, pp. 162-166)

Branch	R23	R44	Description
A	1	01	Agricultural, forestry and fishing products
E	2	03	Coal, lignite (brown coal) and briquettes
	3	05	Products of coking
	4	07	Crude petroleum, natural gas and petroleum products
	5	09	Electric power, gas, steam and water
	6	11	Production and processing of radioactive materials and ores
Q	7	13	Ferrous and non-ferrous ores and metals, other than radioactive
	8	15	Non-metallic mineral products
	9	17	Chemical products
K	10	19	Metal products except machinery and transport equipment
	11	21	Agricultural and industrial machinery
	12	23	Office and data processing machines; precision and optical instruments
	13	25	Electrical goods
	14	27	Motor vehicles
	15	29	Other transport equipment
C	16	31	Meats, meat preparations and preserves, other products from slaughtered animals
		33	Milk and dairy products
		35	Other food products
		37	Beverages
		39	Tobacco products
	17	41	Textiles and clothing
	18	43	Leathers, leather and skin goods, footwear
	19	45	Timber, wooden products and furniture
	20	47	Paper and printing products
	21	49	Rubber and plastic products
	22	51	Other manufacturing products
	23		SITC, Revised [17)] : 93100 (special transactions not classified according to kind) SITC, Revision 2 [18)] : 93100 (special transactions and commodities not classified according to kind)

APPENDIX 7.B : COMPOSITION OF THE ZONES

This appendix gives the composition of the 5 zones that were introduced in section 7.1.

Partner	Countries
14. OR	Turkey, Yugoslavia, Austria, Finland, Iceland, Norway, Sweden, Switzerland, Australia, New Zealand, South Africa, Faeroe Islands, St. Pierre and Miquelon, Greenland.
15. SO	U.S.S.R., Mongolia, German Democratic Republic, Poland, Czechoslovakia, Hungary, Romania, Bulgaria, Albania.
16. DO	Venezuela, Ecuador, Algeria, Libya, Iraq, Saudi Arabia, North Yemen, South Yemen, Bahrain, Kuwait, Abu Dhabi, Dubai, Rasal Khaimah, Other United Arab Emirates, Qatar, Oman, Middle East not elsewhere stated(nes), Nigeria, Iran, Indonesia, Gabon.
17. DF	Singapore, Taiwan, Philippines, South Korea, Hong Kong, Malaysia.
18. DR	Rest of the world (including Mediterranean nes, Middle East nes, Europe nes, Latin America nes, Africa nes, China).

FOOTNOTES TO CHAPTER 7

1) *Cfr.* D'ALCANTARA and ITALIANER (1982).

2) *Cfr.* ITALIANER (1982c).

3) *Cfr.* EUROSTAT (1980a, pp. 162-166).

4) R44 indicates that 44 branches are distinguished; of these only the first 26 are assumed to produce internationally traded goods.

5) Part of this source appears in print in ORGANISATION FOR ECONOMIC CO-OPERATION AND DEVELOPMENT, *Statistics of foreign trade : series C*, Organisation for Economic Cooperation and Development, Paris, yearly issues.

6) *Cfr.* UNITED NATIONS (1961 and 1975).

7) *Cfr.* UNITED NATIONS (1961).

8) *Cfr.* UNITED NATIONS (1975).

9) Exceptions are Portugal, which switched to SITC, Revision 2 starting in 1979, and Spain, which did so in 1980.

10) This may be verified from the correspondences between the two classifications as given in UNITED NATIONS (1975).

11) In those cases, quantities were only added if they were expressed in the same unit. *Cfr.* section 7.4.

12) *Cfr. e.g.*, COMMISSION OF THE EUROPEAN COMMUNITIES (1980).

13) The corresponding quantity was adjusted such that the resulting unit value index became equal to the bound it exceeded.

14) There is no choice to be made among Paasche or Laspeyres, of course, because otherwise the Fisher index would exist.

15) See ITALIANER (1982c) for a complete description of the 9 alternatives. Note that the bilateral export unit value index may be used to approximate the corresponding import index under the assumption that the cif/fob ratio is constant between 2 years. This seems not too unrealistic.

16) The data for the Netherlands and the United Kingdom cover the period 1963-1978 due to lack of homogeneity of the series.

17) *Cfr.* UNITED NATIONS (1961).

18) *Cfr.* UNITED NATIONS (1975).

CHAPTER 8 - ESTIMATION

8.1. INTRODUCTION

After the groundwork laid in the previous chapters, the present chapter concerns the *estimation* of our CRESH import allocation model. It would be an impossible task to estimate all the proposed models in a way which would use the dataset that was described in the previous chapter exhaustively. Therefore we will only present relatively few estimation results as an illustration of the feasibility of the methodology and in order to deal with some specific issues.

In order to have an overview of all the possible models that may be estimated, we first recall briefly in section 8.2 the different characteristics that define the possibilities for the models to be estimated. Next, in section 8.3, we use an import allocation model for aggregate trade of analyze empirically if, given three different *a priori* covariance matrices for the disturbances, any of the three stands out among them in the sense that the corresponding loglikelihood is closest to the loglikelihood of the likelihood function when the covariance matrix is estimated subject only to the constraint of symmetry and nonsingularity. Although we use *a priori* covariance matrices only as starting matrices for our iterative estimation procedure, it may be of interest to regard the quality of *a priori* covariance matrices in case one would work, for whatever reason, with such a matrix as the true covariance matrix. In section 8.4 we demonstrate the estimation of our CRESH model on aggregate trade data for 7 importing countries. We also go into the question of the optimal functional form raised in subsection 1.3.2. Given estimated models which are in linear, loglinear or one of two different logarithmic difference forms, we try to find out if any of these four functional forms performs distinctively better than the others. Section 8.5 extends the estimation of the CRESH import allocation model to individual categories of goods, be it that we no longer regard all four different possible functional forms at a time, but rather concentrate on one of them. In section 8.6 we summarize and draw some conclusions.

8.2. MODEL CHARACTERISTICS

Before starting actual estimation, we recall briefly in this section the different characteristics of any CRESH allocation model to be estimated. It should be borne in mind that these characteristics apply equally well to estimation of the model in its CES form, because that simply is a nested case of the CRESH model, implying additional restrictions on the parameters.

A first distinction is whether we estimate the CRESH allocation model (6.3.1) as an *import* allocation model or as a *total* allocation model. We derived both models from a CRESH aggregator function, but they differ concerning the inclusion of domestic variables. Notably it is not the case that the bilateral import demand equations of the total allocation model under the assumption of weak separability between domestic variables and imports are equal to those of the import allocation model. The import allocation models were summarized concisely in section 5.5, while the interpretation of the CRESH allocation model as a total allocation model was presented in section 5.4.

A second aspect concerns the classification of *categories of goods*. For the import allocation model we may distinguish between the five categories of goods A (agricultural goods), E (energy goods), Q (intermediate goods), K (equipment goods) and C (consumption goods) that were defined in section 7.1, while the availability of data on domestic variables reduces this number to three for the total allocation model, where Q, K, and C had to be aggregated in one single category of "manufactured goods". The five (three) categories of goods may be combined in several ways, varying from five (three) separate allocation models to an allocation model for one single aggregate, the aggregate of all categories. For the import allocation model, the intermediate cases concern two, three or four models. In table 2.1 below we give the number of possibilities in each case. For instance, when there are two aggregates (and therefore two import allocation

Table 2.1 : Number of possible combinations of allocation models, given the number of aggregates

Number of aggregates (allocation models)	Categories of goods	
	Import allocation	Total allocation
	A E Q K C	A E Q + K + C
1	1	1
2	15	3
3	25	1
4	10	-
5	1	-
Total number of possibilities	52	5

models, as well as two total allocation models), the split between the number of categories of goods between the two aggregates may be 1 and 4 or 2 and 3 for the import allocation case. If the split is 1 and 4, there are five possibilities : A, E, Q, K and C each separately and the other aggregate formed by the 4 remaining categories. If the split is 2 and 3, there are $\binom{5}{2}$ = 10 combinations possible to form the aggregate containing two categories. The total number of possibilities for import allocation models with two aggregates is therefore 5 + 10 = 15. For the total allocation case there are only three possibilities of forming two aggregates.

If we allocate imports, we therefore have 52 possibilities of doing so, and if we have a total allocation model, this number reduces to 5. Hereby we assume that we have to allocate total imports (or *total* domestic expenditures). If we only look at individual allocation models, we have $2^5 - 1 = 31$ and $2^3 - 1 = 7$ possibilities, respectively. However, an individual import allocation model for, say, the aggregate Q + K + C cannot be compared with an allocation model for, say, the aggregate A + E + Q + K + C because in the former nothing is said about the allocation among trade partners of the remaining two categories of goods A and E. Because a comparison between models with different classifications interests us from the point of view of hypothesis testing in the next chapter, we will therefore always consider an *exhaustive* partition of the 5 categories of goods over a mutually exclusive set of aggregates.

A third characterization of allocation models concerns the classification of *trade partners*. For a given importing country, the data availability allows us to distinguish a maximum of 17 partners, but these may be combined into different groups, ranging in number from 2 to 17. This gives $2^{17} - \binom{17}{1} - \binom{17}{0} = 131054$ different possibilities to define trade partner groupings.

A fourth aspect is the definition of the market, or the *importing* country. Given that we have data for 13 declaring countries, we have the same number of possibilities in an import allocation model for the importing country. The limited availability of data on domestic variables reduces this number to 6 for the total allocation model, as we saw in section 7.5.

A fifth distinction concerns the CRESH *approximation* or functional form of the model that is chosen. We introduced four possibilities : an approximation in levels (Model I), a loglinear approximation (Model II), a differential approximation with homoscedastic disturbances (Model III), or a differential approximation with heteroscedastic disturbances (Model IV). The four models were derived in section 5.3 and summarized by means of one single specification in section 5.5.

A sixth characteristic is formed by the fact of whether the model is estimated in *static* or *dynamic* form and with or without *trends*. The specifications and estimation procedures for these four possibilities were given in sections 6.4-6.7.

Related to the previous aspect is the seventh and final characteristic, determined by the starting form that is chosen for the *covariance matrix* of the disturbances in the linear or nonlinear iterative estimation procedure. The three matrices were defined in equations (6.4.16)-(6.4.18). These matrices may not only be used as starting matrix, but also as *a priori* imposed "true" covariance matrices in their own right.

Summarizing, estimation of a particular allocation model derived from the CRESH aggregator function is determined by :

- import allocation or total allocation
- the definition of the aggregates of categories of goods that are allocated
- the definition of the partner groupings
- the definition of the importing country
- the CRESH approximation or functional form chosen for the derived demand equation (Models I - IV)
- the static/dynamic form and inclusion or not of trends
- the starting form of the covariance matrix.

8.3. THE COVARIANCE MATRIX

The seven characteristics presented in the previous section determine together a very large set of possible allocation models that may be estimated. If we want to test the quality of starting covariance matrices, we therefore cannot choose but a limited subset of these models, and draw inference from the results obtained for this subset for the whole set. The starting point for this section is therefore to fix such a subset. Next the following procedure is pursued. For each allocation model of the subset, we determine four values of the logarithm of the likelihood function. Each of these four values of the loglikelihood corresponds to one particular covariance matrix for the disturbances. Three of them correspond to the three different starting matrices that were proposed in section 6.4, and the fourth is the loglikelihood value obtained using the final estimate of the covariance matrix after the iterative estimation procedure as set out in section 6.4 has converged. This fourth loglikelihood value will be the highest of the 4 values because it is calculated using estimates for the model coefficients and the covariance matrix of the disturbances that correspond to a maximum of the likelihood function. Therefore the three likelihood values corresponding to the three starting covariance matrices may be expressed as a percentage of the final loglikelihood value. The highest percentage corresponds to the best approximation of the final estimate of the covariance matrix and may be therefore be classified as corresponding to the best starting matrix. *A fortiori*, if the starting matrix were to be used as the "true" covariance matrix, this procedure would give an indication as to which matrix is the best approximation of the freely estimated covariance matrix.

The model characteristics we have chosen, then, are the following :

- import allocation model
- aggregate trade (T = A + E + Q + K + C)
- trade partners (excluding importing country) : Belgium [1], West-Germany, France, Italy, Netherlands, UK, USA, Rest of the World (ROW)

- importing countries : idem, excluding ROW
- CRESH approximation : Models I - IV
- dynamic models with trends
- starting covariance matrix : all three matrices.

Because there are 7 importers and because we consider all four CRESH approximations, we may repeat the procedure outlined above for 28 models. This will be done for the CES model as well as for the CRESH model, therefore we have a comparison of the starting matrices on the basis of 56 import allocation models.

For the sake of exposition, we repeat the three forms (6.4.16)-(6.4.18) of the starting covariance matrices below. It should be remembered that it concerns the covariance matrices of the lopped import allocation models with one equation deleted. The deleted equation always corresponded to ROW.

Covariance matrix *1* corresponds to a diagonal covariance matrix for the disturbances of the equations corresponding to the first $(n-1)$ partners (if there are n partners) and nonzero covariances for the disturbances between partner n and the other partners

$$\tilde{H}_1 = \sigma^2 \hat{\tilde{r}}^{-1} , \tag{3.1}$$

where a tilde denotes the fact that it concerns a lopped model, and r is the vector of weights of the constrained model.

Covariance matrix *2* is not asymmetric in the treatment of the covariances between the residuals of the equations. It was defined as

$$\tilde{H}_2 = \sigma^2 \hat{\tilde{r}}^{-1} [I_{n-1} - (1/n)\, \iota\iota']\hat{\tilde{r}}^{-1}. \tag{3.2}$$

Covariance matrix *3* was also symmetric in the treatment of the covariances, and used additionally the vector of base year import shares w

$$\tilde{H}_3 = \sigma^2 \hat{\tilde{r}}^{-1} [\hat{\tilde{w}} - \tilde{w}\tilde{w}'] \hat{\tilde{r}}^{-1}. \tag{3.3}$$

Before we present the results, in table 3.1 for the CES model and in table 3.2 for the CRESH model, one remark concerning the estimation is in order. During estimation we did not impose the second-order sufficiency condition (6.4.11), requiring the a_i coefficients of model (6.3.1) to be non-negative. Adopting boundary solutions $a_i = 0$ would lead to decreases in the loglikelihood values that would hamper their comparability among the use of differing covariance matrices.

Let us first look at the results for the CES model in table 3.1. With 4 exceptions out of 84, all three covariance matrices imply a loglikelihood value within 10 % of the maximum attainable value. In 69 cases the likelihood value even comes as close as 5 % of the maximum. These results imply that for this set of CES import allocation models any of the three covariance matrices is in itself a good approximation of the final matrix. Additionally, however, there is a clear ranking among the three matrices. This may be seen if we look at table 3.3, which gives a summary of the best-performing covariance matrices per model. The best covariance matrix for the CES import allocation model is, uniformly over all four approximations, the first covariance matrix as defined in (3.1). This is a surprising result for two reasons. First, because $\tilde{H}_1$ is the most simple of the three covariance matrices. Secondly, because it is the only of the three matrices with an asymmetric treatment of one trade partner, in this case the ROW. Starting from the premise that a more elaborate covariance structure gives a higher value to the likelihood function than a more simple structure (in terms of the number of independent covariances), we must therefore conclude for the CES import allocation model that lack of an asymmetric treatment of the covariances of trade partners results in more loss of likelihood than lack of an elaborate covariance structure. This conclusion is affirmed by the fact that the second-best covariance matrix is the matrix (3.3), which introduces some asymmetric elements through use of the vector of weights. The asymmetric treatment of the ROW such as in (3.1) is however less outspoken. The conclusion regarding the importance of the asymmetric treatment of one partner may be conditional on the fact that it always concerned the ROW. Indeed it might be realistic to suppose that imports from the Rest of the World act as a residual in the sense that an exogenous shock in one of the other bilateral imports mostly affects

Table 3.1 : Loglikelihood values corresponding to different covariance matrices as a percentage of final loglikelihood value for the CES model (aggregate trade)

Model	Covariance matrix	Importer						
		Belgium	West-Germany	France	Italy	Netherlands	UK	USA
I	$\tilde{H}_1$	99.79	87.89	95.64	99.02	99.26	97.68	92.85
	$\tilde{H}_2$	99.84	84.75	91.08	97.42	98.18	93.76	91.82
	$\tilde{H}_3$	99.71	87.64	94.10	98.78	98.87	97.66	92.84
II	$\tilde{H}_1$	97.53	99.65	99.22	99.01	98.83	93.57	96.48
	$\tilde{H}_2$	97.69	98.65	96.29	98.16	97.90	89.99	96.06
	$\tilde{H}_3$	97.27	99.36	98.40	99.09	98.35	93.41	96.50
III	$\tilde{H}_1$	100.00	99.83	98.20	99.51	94.66	98.76	99.95
	$\tilde{H}_2$	99.91	99.91*	96.49	97.87	91.41	99.17	100.00
	$\tilde{H}_3$	100.00*	99.91	96.99	99.40	94.26	98.71	99.97
IV	$\tilde{H}_1$	99.75	99.89	99.63	99.68	99.93	99.45	99.99
	$\tilde{H}_2$	97.98	97.71	98.11	96.46	97.06	99.14	99.14
	$\tilde{H}_3$	99.67	99.92	98.85	99.58	99.87	99.33	99.99*

* Highest percentage for this model.

imports from the ROW, or at least affects those imports in a fashion asymmetrical compared to the way it affects other bilateral import flows. Therefore, if we had set any other partner than the ROW in the asymmetric position, the induced asymmetry in (3.1) would in that case be badly placed, and probably have resulted in covariance matrix (3.3) being the best matrix.

Table 3.2 : Loglikelihood values corresponding to different covariance matrices as a percentage of final loglikelihood value for the CRESH model (aggregate trade)

Model	Covariance matrix	Importer						
		Belgium	West-Germany	France	Italy	Netherlands	UK	USA
I	$\tilde{H}_1$	91.89[a]	86.41	87.60	91.35	88.84	89.71	80.61
	$\tilde{H}_2$	65.55[a]	76.45	86.53	76.51	78.53	81.60	50.89
	$\tilde{H}_3$	90.97[a]	85.20	87.05	90.51	90.67	89.21	80.15
II	$\tilde{H}_1$	93.70	90.33	94.99	94.69	96.71	95.62	90.22
	$\tilde{H}_2$	76.20	79.72	88.99	80.50	78.07	88.35	66.21
	$\tilde{H}_3$	91.37	89.16	94.50	94.00	92.65	95.23	89.92
III	$\tilde{H}_1$	95.56	91.97	94.28	93.51	91.10	96.29	94.50
	$\tilde{H}_2$	89.49	75.29	75.92	77.15	62.57	89.03	75.41
	$\tilde{H}_3$	94.70	90.29	91.56	90.89	95.83	95.56	94.74
IV	$\tilde{H}_1$	97.62	98.25	98.76	99.24	99.68	98.76	99.38
	$\tilde{H}_2$	91.48	90.46	98.14	93.38	94.53	97.90	98.70
	$\tilde{H}_3$	96.92	97.80	98.70	98.85	98.45	98.69	99.42

[a] Convergence of final model not achieved after 120 iterations.

Next we consider the results for the CRESH import allocation model as presented in table 3.2. They show that the three covariance matrices are in general less apt as an approximation for the final matrix than for the CES model. In 32 out of 84 cases the precentage covered of the maximum attainable loglikelihood value is below 90 %, and in only 24 cases above 95 %.

Table 3.3 : Number of covariance matrices with highest loglikelihood value

	Covariance matrix	Model I	Model II	Model III	Model IV	Total
CES	$\tilde{H}_1$	6	4	3	5	18
	$\tilde{H}_2$	1	1	2	0	4
	$\tilde{H}_3$	0	2	2	2	6
CRESH	$\tilde{H}_1$	6	7	5	6	24
	$\tilde{H}_2$	0	0	0	0	0
	$\tilde{H}_3$	1	0	2	1	4

The individual ranking of the three covariance matrices is however even more outspoken than for the CES model, as may be seen from table 3.3 : in 24 out of 28 cases the first covariance matrix (3.1) gives the best performance, followed by again the third matrix (3.3) on a - remote - second position. As for the CES model this points also to a predominance of the asymmetric effect contained in (3.1), with again the *proviso* that this may be due to the fact that it is the ROW which has been set in the asymmetrical position throughout.

The *conclusion* which emerges from this section is therefore that as long as the ROW is in the asymmetrical position, the best starting covariance matrix of the residuals both for the CES and the CRESH import allocation model is matrix $\tilde{H}_1$ of (3.1). The same conclusion holds, *mutatis mutandis*, if we want to use any of the three tested matrices as the "true" covariance matrix instead of estimating this matrix.

8.4. THE AGGREGATE TRADE MODEL

In this section we demonstrate the estimation of the CRESH import allocation model using the same characteristics as in the previous section, but now each time with (3.1) as starting matrix for the covariance matrix of the disturbances. The estimations have not been performed on the maximum of 17 partners per importing country for two reasons. First, we only want to use this section for a *demonstration* of the estimation of the CRESH import allocation model. Therefore we do not need to estimate a complete model as if we were linking national models for 18 countries and zones. Secondly, the estimation program at our disposal did not allow for estimation of an import allocation model of this size [2]. This does not affect the property of our CRESH model that, given adequate software, the model may be estimated for an almost unlimited number of partners because the number of parameters increases only proportionally to the number of trade partners. Furthermore, because the iterative estimation procedure of section 6.4 is applied to a *linear* model [3], there are no significant additional computational problems involved if the number of partners increases.

We start to estimate the CRESH import allocation model for all four Models I-IV as defined in section 5.5. This is done in subsection 8.4.1. In the second subsection we regard whether, on the basis of the given model characteristics, any of the four functional forms should be preferred.

8.4.1. ESTIMATION

Table 4.1 gives an impression, for our baseyear 1975, of the interdependence between the 7 importing countries and their trade partners in the form of *import shares*. It is shown, for instance, that the mutual trade integration of the countries of the European Economic Community (EEC) is much larger than with the USA. The USA imported in 1975 less than 20 % from the EEC countries displayed in the table, leading to particularly small bilateral import flows. At the level of disaggregate trade the flows may even become extremely small, as will be seen in the next section. The columns of the table form the vector of baseyear import shares w that acts as vector of weights for the constrained models formed by Models I-III (the vector of weights for Model IV is the vector of units).

In table 4.2 we give the estimates for the a_{ij} coefficients of specification (6.3.2), which we repeat here for convenience (j is the importer and i the partner country).

$$s_{ijt} = \lambda_j s_{ijt-1} + b_{ijt} T_t - \lambda_j b_{ijt-1} T_{t-1} - a_{ij}(1-\lambda_j) [p^i_{ijt} - \Sigma_h \omega_{hjt} p^i_{hjt}] + (1-\lambda_j) \Sigma_h \omega_{hjt} a_{hj} [p^i_{hjt} - \Sigma_l \omega_{ljt} p^i_{ljt}] + u_{ijt}. \tag{4.1}$$

Throughout estimation, the second-order sufficiency conditions (6.4.11), requiring all a_{ij} to be non-negative, were imposed. If negative coefficient values appeared, a number of them were fixed to be equal to zero subject to the following conditions :

- the remaining coefficients should all be nonnegative in re-estimation of the model after imposition of the zero constraints;
- the chosen combination should result in the highest (log)likelihood value, subject to the first condition.

We indicate in the table whether imposition of the constraints changes the fit of the equation significantly. This test is based on a statistic that will be presented in section 9.2 of the next chapter. It is assumed to follow the χ^2-distribution with degrees of freedom equal to the number of constraints, *i.e.* the number of coefficients which are fixed at zero. An alternative test will be discussed in Appendix 9.A.

The estimates of the a_{ij} coefficients are not of much interest themselves, but, together with the import shares, they generate the price elasticities and the substitution elasticities. It is however of some interest to see how the coefficients vary across the four functional forms of models I-IV. The estimates are in general in the same range, although with large bounds. Notably for Models III and IV, which are both differential approximations of the CRESH import allocation model, the estimated coefficients are quite close, however, as could be expected for two such similar approximations : they are both in logarithmic differences.

Note furthermore that for each of the four models about 60 % of the positive a_{ij} coefficients are significantly different from zero

Model	I	II	III	IV
Positive a_{ij} coefficients differing significantly from zero (%)	63	63	65	54

Insignificant values appear often if the coefficients reach the zero lowerbound for one or more of the models, given one particular importer and trade partner. Only for models I and II is the fit significantly changed through the imposition of the zero lowerbound for the a_{ij} coefficients

Model	I	II	III	IV
Number of constrained coefficients (%)	38	24	14	16
- of which : significant	14	10	0	0

Using formulas (5.2.22) and (5.2.23) we may calculate the own and cross-price elasticities. Instead of the optimal import share, we have used the actual import shares for 1975 from table 4.1 to calculate these elasticities for 1975 for two importing countries (as examples) : the USA,

Table 4.1 : Import shares for 1975, aggregate trade (%)

	Importer						
Partner	Belgium	West-Germany	France	Italy	Nether-lands	UK	USA
Belgium	-	8.61	9.59	3.21	12.39	3.51	1.24
West-Germany	22.38	-	18.96	17.30	25.71	8.28	5.58
France	17.72	12.15	-	13.48	7.69	6.72	2.23
Italy	3.96	9.44	8.86	-	3.56	3.36	2.53
Netherlands	17.01	14.09	6.32	4.75	-	7.58	1.12
UK	6.06	3.69	4.77	3.35	5.80	-	3.89
USA	6.43	7.75	7.61	8.77	10.09	9.61	-
ROW	26.43	44.27	43.88	49.15	34.76	60.94	83.40

as a large closed economy, in table 4.3, and the Netherlands, as a small open economy, in table 4.4. Note that as one of the properties of the CRESH model all partners are substitutes on a given import market. Again the price elasticities for the four functional forms are approximately in the same range, with Models III and IV often being closest.

The *own-price* elasticities move in general in the range 0 to -1 sometimes with outliers below -1, notably for model I. The only really small own-price elasticities (in absolute value) are for the bilateral imports by the USA from ROW and for the bilateral imports by the Netherlands from Belgium. In the former case this is not surprising given the high import share of ROW on the US market. Micro-economically the ROW must be seen as such a large monopolistic supplier that US imports are not very sensitive to price movements because there are few alternative suppliers (remember that we only consider substitution effects on the import market, and abstract from domestic import substitution because we work in the framework of an import allocation model). The low own-price elasticity for Dutch imports from Belgium is perhaps due to the fact that there are so many insitutional ties and delivery contracts between the two countries (which form together, with Luxembourg, an economic union) that this almost completely rules out price competitiveness.

Table 4.2 : Estimated a_{ij} coefficients compared over four different model specifications (aggregate trade)

		Importer j						
Partner i	Model	Belgium	West-Germany	France	Italy	Nether-lands	UK	USA
Belgium	I	-	.0^{xx}	.0	.0^{xx}	.575	.0	2.052^{x}
	II	-	.0	.0	.174	.0^{xx}	.0^{xx}	.694^{x}
	III	-	.024	.0^{xx}	.0^{xx}	.166	.243	.724^{x}
	IV	-	.0^{xx}	.0^{xx}	.0^{xx}	.062	.0^{xx}	.869^{x}
West-Germany	I	-^{a}	-	.0	1.237^{x}	.0^{xx}	.320	1.959^{x}
	II	.0^{xx}	-	.177^{x}	.965^{x}	.511^{x}	.388^{x}	.859^{x}
	III	.579	-	.178^{x}	.666^{x}	.500^{x}	.562^{x}	.656^{x}
	IV	.335	-	.171^{x}	.645^{x}	.477^{x}	.632^{x}	.708^{x}
France	I	-^{a}	1.761	-	1.562^{x}	.0^{xx}	.0	1.213^{x}
	II	.0^{xx}	1.106	-	1.140^{x}	1.017	.140	1.219^{x}
	III	.288	.556^{x}	-	.670^{x}	.671^{x}	.320	1.108^{x}
	IV	.177	.486^{x}	-	.621^{x}	.431	.237	1.167^{x}
Italy	I	-^{a}	.0^{xx}	2.752^{x}	-	.0^{xx}	6.540^{x}	.0^{xx}
	II	1.242^{x}	.0	.219	-	.386	1.252^{x}	1.410^{x}
	III	.991^{x}	.0^{xx}	.0^{xx}	-	1.299^{x}	1.477^{x}	.529
	IV	1.009^{x}	.0^{xx}	.0^{xx}	-	1.221^{x}	1.358^{x}	.732^{x}
Nether-lands	I	-^{a}	8.485^{x}	1.346^{x}	2.258^{x}	-	.329	.467^{x}
	II	1.378^{x}	9.718^{x}	1.657^{x}	2.056^{x}	-	1.060^{x}	1.053^{x}
	III	1.755^{x}	.613^{x}	.761^{x}	.653^{x}	-	.723	.550^{x}
	IV	1.651^{x}	.480	.825^{x}	.569^{x}	-	1.110	.557
UK	I	-^{a}	.0^{xx}	2.236^{x}	.335	.0^{xx}	-	1.318^{x}
	II	1.383^{x}	1.895	.981^{x}	.213	.369	-	.619^{x}
	III	1.321^{x}	1.479^{x}	.777^{x}	.745^{x}	1.038^{x}	-	.660^{x}
	IV	1.606^{x}	1.365^{x}	.849^{x}	.719^{x}	.752	-	.720^{x}

Table 4.2 : Continued

Partner i	Model	Importer j Belgium	West-Germany	France	Italy	Nether-lands	UK	USA
USA	I	-[a]	2.256	1.570^{x}	1.824^{x}	1.508^{x}	.0	-
	II	2.217^{x}	3.070^{x}	.549^{x}	1.806^{xx}	2.408^{x}	.0^{xx}	-
	III	2.421^{x}	.948^{x}	.705^{x}	1.501^{x}	.688	.564^{x}	-
	IV	2.879^{x}	.682^{x}	.666^{x}	1.347^{x}	.739	.575^{x}	-
ROW	I	-[a]	.0^{xx}	.0	.869^{x}	1.940^{x}	7.113^{x}	2.231
	II	.100	.0	.0	.0^{xx}	.843^{x}	3.772^{x}	.0^{xx}
	III	.175	.0^{xx}	.0^{xx}	.020	.781^{x}	1.933^{x}	.0^{xx}
	IV	.147	.0^{xx}	.0^{xx}	.177	.811^{x}	1.976^{x}	.101

[a] Convergence not achieved after 120 iterations

^{x} Variable exceeds more than twice its asymptotic standard error

^{xx} Constraints not rejected at 5 % level of significance

The *cross-price* elasticities are much lower in absolute value than the own-price elasticities. Save for some exceptions they are not higher than .5. The observations made on the low own-price elasticity for imports by the USA from ROW extend to the cross price elasticities for the effects of price changes in other partners on this bilateral trade flow, which are virtually zero. Except for this last column of table 4.3, the cross-price elasticities on the US market seem in general to be larger than on the Dutch market, implying more competition on the US market. On both import markets the largest cross-price effects occur upon a change in the price of the ROW. Given the diversified nature of this composite trade partner, this is an indication of a relatively large substitution that may be induced upon a change in the price of this partner.

Table 4.3 : Own and cross-price elasticities for 1975 for bilateral imports by the USA from partner i with respect to a change in the price of partner h, for four different model specifications (aggregate trade)

Price of partner h	Model	Bilateral imports of the USA from partner i						
		Belgium	West-Germany	France	Italy	Nether-lands	UK	ROW
Belgium	I	-2.027	.024	.015	.0	.006	.016	.027
	II	-.655	.048	.068	.079	.059	.035	.0
	III	-.668	.051	.086	.041	.043	.051	.0
	IV	-.825	.036	.059	.037	.028	.036	.005
West-Germany	I	.108	-1.856	.064	.0	.025	.069	.117
	II	.217	-.590	.381	.441	.329	.194	.0
	III	.229	-.448	.351	.168	.174	.209	.0
	IV	.161	-.577	.216	.136	.103	.133	.019
France	I	.027	.025	-1.197	.0	.006	.017	.029
	II	.123	.152	-1.003	.250	.187	.110	.0
	III	.155	.140	-.871	.113	.118	.141	.0
	IV	.106	.086	-1.025	.089	.068	.088	.012
Italy	I	.0	.0	.0	.0	.0	.0	.0
	II	.162	.200	.284	-1.082	.245	.144	.0
	III	.084	.076	.128	-.468	.064	.076	.0
	IV	.075	.061	.101	-.668	.048	.063	.009
Nether-lands	I	.005	.005	.003	.0	-.466	.007	.006
	II	.053	.066	.094	.109	-.972	.048	.0
	III	.039	.035	.059	.028	-.521	.035	.0
	IV	.025	.021	.034	.021	-.541	.021	.003
UK	I	.051	.048	.030	.0	.012	-1.285	.055
	II	.109	.135	.192	.222	.165	-.522	.0
	III	.161	.146	.246	.118	.122	-.513	.0
	IV	.114	.093	.153	.096	.073	-.625	.013
ROW	I	1.837	1.753	1.086	.0	.418	1.180	-.234
	II	.0	.0	.0	.0	.0	.0	.0
	III	.0	.0	.0	.0	.0	.0	.0
	IV	.343	.280	.461	.289	.220	.284	-.061

Table 4.4 : Own and cross-price elasticities for 1975 for bilateral imports by the Netherlands from partner i with respect to a change in the price of partner h, for four different model specifications (aggregate trade)

Price of partner h	Model	Bilateral imports of the Netherlands from partner i						
		Belgium	West-Germany	France	Italy	UK	USA	ROW
Belgium	I	-.529	.0	.0	.0	.0	.120	.154
	II	.0	.0	.0	.0	.0	.0	.0
	III	-.161	.016	.021	.041	.033	.022	.025
	IV	-.061	.006	.005	.015	.010	.009	.010
West-Germany	I	.0	.0	.0	.0	.0	.0	.0
	II	.0	-.425	.171	.065	.062	.405	.142
	III	.033	-.401	.133	.258	.206	.136	.155
	IV	.013	-.381	.087	.247	.152	.149	.164
France	I	.0	.0	.0	.0	.0	.0	.0
	II	.0	.051	-.915	.039	.037	.241	.084
	III	.013	.040	-.618	.103	.083	.055	.062
	IV	.003	.026	-.407	.067	.041	.040	.044
Italy	I	.0	.0	.0	.0	.0	.0	.0
	II	.0	.009	.018	-.379	.006	.042	.015
	III	.012	.036	.048	-1.206	.074	.049	.056
	IV	.004	.034	.031	-1.134	.054	.053	.058
UK	I	.0	.0	.0	.0	.0	.0	.0
	II	.0	.014	.028	.011	-.359	.066	.023
	III	.015	.046	.062	.121	-.942	.064	.073
	IV	.004	.034	.031	.088	-.698	.053	.058
USA	I	.097	.0	.0	.0	.0	-1.252	.329
	II	.0	.159	.316	.120	.115	-1.659	.262
	III	.018	.054	.072	.139	.111	-.614	.084
	IV	.008	.059	.053	.150	.092	-.648	.100
ROW	I	.432	.0	.0	.0	.0	1.133	-.483
	II	.0	.192	.382	.145	.138	.904	-.527
	III	.070	.209	.281	.544	.435	.288	-.454
	IV	.029	.222	.200	.567	.349	.343	-.434

8.4.2. FUNCTIONAL FORMS

In this subsection we try to see whether any of the models I-IV stands out among the others for the present set of import allocation models presented in the previous subsection. It will be remembered that these four models corresponded to four approximations of the original CRESH import allocation model : an approximation in levels (model I), a loglinear approximation (Model II), a differential approximation with homoscedastic disturbances (Model III) and a differential approximation with heteroscedastic disturbances (Model IV). In the discussion which we presented on functional forms in subsection 1.3.2 these functional forms also were put forward as possible alternatives in international linkage models. Because we estimate the functional forms on the same dataset and in approximation to the same model, it is an interesting empirical question whether any of the four functional forms performs the best.

The problem one faces in such an empirical comparison is the *measure* with which the different models are compared. Because the dependent variables are not the same, this measure should be defined such that its value may be compared between the different models. But even then different measures may give different outcomes. This is illustrated in tables 4.5 and 4.6. For each of the fitted values of the dependent variables of the four models, we have calculated the fitted value of the *level* of the bilateral trade flows for each import allocation model (including the fitted level for the bilateral imports corresponding to the equation which was deleted for estimation [4)]). Starting from these fitted values, we have calculated the Root Mean-Squared Percentage Errors (RMSPE) of the levels per import allocation model, as well as the Root Mean-Squared Errors (RMSE). The former are presented in table 4.5, and the latter in table 4.6. If we add up the ranks for the four models per importing country over the importing countries, we have an aggregate indication of which model performs best according to each of the two criteria. According to the RMSPE, the best model is Model III, the differential approximation with homoscedastic disturbances. But according to the RMSE the best model is Model I, the

Table 4.5 : Root Mean-Squared Percentage Errors of the four models and a comparison of their ranks (aggregate trade)

Model		Importer: Bel-gium	West-Germany	France	Italy	Nether-lands	UK	USA	Sum of ranks
I	RMSPE[a]	6.62[b]	5.19	5.89	6.84	6.37	7.38	10.72	
	Rank	1	2	4	4	2	1	4	18
II	RMSPE	7.75	4.60	5.25	5.89	6.00	9.67	9.12	
	Rank	4	1	1	3	1	4	3	17
III	RMSPE	7.05	5.74	5.56	5.63	6.81	7.46	9.01	
	Rank	2	3	2/3	1	3	2	2	15 1/2
IV	RMPSE	7.48	5.79	5.56	5.72	6.83	7.56	8.83	
	Rank	3	4	2/3	2	4	3	1	19 1/2

[a] Let $\hat{m}_{it}$ be the fitted value of the *level* of the bilateral imports m_{it} from partner $i = 1, \ldots, n$ in period $t = 1, \ldots, T$. Then the Root Mean-Squared Percentage Error (RMSPE) is calculated as RMSPE $= \{\Sigma_i \Sigma_t [(m_{it} - \hat{m}_{it})/m_{it}]^2/nT\}^{1/2} \cdot 100$.

[b] Convergence not achieved after 120 iterations; as this is the best model, this does not influence the results.

model in levels, although Model III is still second according to this criterion. Nevertheless, for both criteria the aggregate rankings are relatively close to each other, and it is therefore difficult to appoint one model, and therefore one functional form, as being outstanding compared to the others. Model III seems to be the best on average, but has in individual cases (per importing country) relatively few first ranks : in total only 3 out of 14.

Table 4.6 : Root Mean-Squared Errors of the four models and a comparison of their ranks (aggregate trade)

Model		Importer							Sum of ranks
		Belgium	West-Germany	France	Italy	Netherlands	UK	USA	
I	RMSE[a]	202.042[b]	351.873	279.422	207.961	277.914	369.315	715.937	
	Rank	1	1	1	1	4	2	4	14
II	RMSE	325.342	374.434	287.754	251.659	235.776	420.052	652.294	
	Rank	4	2	3	4	1	4	3	21
III	RMSE	214.315	480.485	291.467	215.743	246.746	368.931	562.760	
	Rank	2	4	4	2	3	1	1	17
IV	RMSE	273.837	472.454	287.023	216.765	246.297	394.318	588.447	
	Rank	3	3	2	3	2	3	2	18

[a] Let $\hat{m}_{it}$ be the fitted value of the level of the bilateral imports m_{it} from partner i in period t. Then the Root Mean-Squared Error (RMSE) is calculated as RMSE = $\{\Sigma_i \Sigma_t (m_{it} - \hat{m}_{it})^2 / nT\}^{1/2}$.

[b] Convergence not achieved after 120 iterations; as this is the best model, this does not influence the results.

As a final aid to a possible choice among functional forms we derive from table 4.2 per model and importing country the number of times that an a_{ij} coefficient attains a boundary solution $a_{ij} = 0$. This is an indication of how well a given functional form satisfies in free estimation the second-order sufficiency condition $a_{ij} \geqslant 0$ for all i, j that was derived in subsection 4.2.5. From the results, which are summarized in table 4.7, we see that here also Model III turns out to be best for satisfying the theoretical condition $a_{ij} \geqslant 0$, attaining a boundary solution in only 7 out of 56 cases. Moreover, as we saw above, this does not change the fit of the equations significantly for each of the 7 cases.

Table 4.7 : Number of a_{ij} coefficients with a boundary solution per CRESH import allocation model (aggregate trade)

Model	Importer							Total
	Belgium	West-Germany	France	Italy	Netherlands	UK	USA	
I	3[a]	4	3	1	4	3	1	19
II	2	3	2	1	1	2	1	12
III	0	2	3	1	0	0	1	7
IV	0	3	3	1	0	1	0	8

[a] Convergence not achieved after 120 iterations.

8.5. MODELS PER CATEGORY OF GOODS

The previous section presented estimation results for import allocation models of aggregate trade. There was also some evidence that the best functional form would be a model in logarithmic differences with homoscedastic disturbances (Model III). Therefore we take this particular functional form as a starting point to estimate import allocation models per category of goods. The model characteristics are :

- import allocation model
- 5 categories of trade A, E, Q, K and C and aggregate trade T = A + E + Q + K + C
- trade partners (excluding importing country) : West-Germany, France, Italy, Netherlands, UK, USA, Japan, Rest of the World (ROW)
- importing countries : idem, excluding ROW
- CRESH approximation : Model III
- dynamic models with trends
- starting covariance matrix : matrix (3.1).

We have estimated the models not only for each of the five categories of goods, but also for aggregate trade in order to compare the results for the categories with those for aggregate trade. An impression of the trade structure between the countries may be obtained if we look at the import shares for 1975 presented in table 5.1. We observe that the importance of certain trade flows for an importing market may vary from almost zero to almost 100 % (US energy imports from the ROW). The importing countries under consideration are integrated the most for equipment goods (K), and the least for energy goods (E). Also for intermediate goods (Q) there is a reasonable integration. Furthermore the table illustrates some well-known facts : the importance of West-Germany as an exporter of equipment goods, the closedness of the Japanese market for European goods, the energy dependence of all importing countries on the ROW (which includes the OPEC countries), the importance of the USA as an agricultural supplier, the mutual dependence of West-Germany and the Netherlands and so forth.

Table 5.1 : Import shares for 1975, 5 categories of goods and aggregate trade

Partner	Category	Importer						
		West-Germany	France	Italy	Nether-lands	UK	USA	Japan
West-Germany	A	-	1.93	6.82	4.89	1.99	1.04	.17
	E	-	5.40	2.36	3.29	.69	.53	.15
	Q	-	25.35	24.19	35.55	12.15	7.14	3.71
	K	-	33.18	34.47	36.35	20.39	12.93	12.93
	C	-	16.15	18.99	30.97	4.09	2.55	2.08
	T	-	18.96	17.30	25.71	8.28	5.58	1.97
France	A	7.17	-	14.57	10.33	9.48	1.98	.34
	E	2.71	-	.98	.69	2.18	.09	.01
	Q	14.09	-	19.06	9.37	6.62	4.32	1.35
	K	18.69	-	18.82	10.25	11.90	2.46	2.69
	C	13.73	-	18.83	7.42	5.05	3.17	2.66
	T	12.15	-	13.48	7.69	6.72	2.23	.87
Italy	A	9.31	10.57	-	1.63	1.93	1.94	.13
	E	2.17	.96	-	.83	1.32	.55	.04
	Q	7.31	7.83	-	2.47	2.87	2.88	.64
	K	11.61	12.53	-	4.96	6.24	3.19	2.09
	C	13.87	13.34	-	5.60	3.15	3.98	2.28
	T	9.44	8.86	-	3.56	3.36	2.53	.63
Nether-lands	A	14.14	6.80	3.47	-	13.39	.78	.04
	E	20.26	3.73	1.65	-	9.45	.36	.05
	Q	13.92	8.33	6.03	-	9.25	2.44	.71
	K	9.93	5.26	3.81	-	5.72	.75	1.05
	C	13.44	8.35	9.89	-	5.52	1.70	1.04
	T	14.09	6.32	4.75	-	7.58	1.12	.37
UK	A	1.17	1.83	1.00	2.38	-	.58	.09
	E	1.04	.66	.41	2.98	-	.17	.03
	Q	4.90	5.52	5.07	7.97	-	4.79	2.07
	K	7.09	8.50	7.21	8.65	-	6.51	7.34
	C	2.96	5.00	2.96	4.27	-	5.27	3.34
	T	3.69	4.77	3.35	5.80	-	3.89	1.40
USA	A	16.49	8.82	18.64	35.81	11.69	-	39.83
	E	2.57	2.32	3.26	2.40	1.89	-	7.85
	Q	5.89	6.27	7.75	8.98	10.14	-	17.12
	K	12.61	13.70	13.54	10.22	19.99	-	50.53
	C	5.24	6.60	5.60	5.57	6.10	-	19.39
	T	7.75	7.61	8.77	10.09	9.61	-	20.07

Table 5.1 : Continued

Partner	Category	Importer: West-Germany	France	Italy	Netherlands	UK	USA	Japan
Japan	A	.33	.27	.44	.12	.14	1.62	-
	E	.06	.06	.10	.23	.11	.02	-
	Q	2.83	15.93	2.00	1.27	3.28	21.87	-
	K	6.41	4.94	2.70	3.27	8.13	25.07	-
	C	1.22	.85	.72	1.02	11.00	5.19	-
	T	2.35	1.86	1.20	1.48	2.78	11.79	-
ROW	A	51.38	69.78	55.07	44.83	61.38	92.07	59.40
	E	71.19	86.88	91.23	89.59	84.36	98.28	91.87
	Q	51.06	45.10	35.90	34.39	55.69	56.55	74.40
	K	33.66	21.89	19.45	26.31	27.64	49.08	23.38
	C	49.54	49.71	43.01	45.15	74.99	78.15	69.21
	T	50.53	51.61	51.16	45.67	61.67	72.85	74.70

Table 5.2 contains the estimated a_{ij} coefficients from equation (4.1) for Model III, where j is the importing country and i the partner. The second-order sufficiency condition (6.4.11) was imposed on them in the same way as in subsection 8.4.1. Although the a_{ij} coefficients are not of much interest themselves, they already display a large divergence among categories, which predicts a similar divergence for the price elasticities. The coefficients are useful however in one respect : they indicate for each category of goods how well the second-order sufficiency conditions are met automatically. For agricultural goods (A) and energy (E), they attain a boundary solution $a_{ij} = 0$ 16 and 15 times respectively out of a total number of 56 constrained coefficients. The data for intermediate goods (Q) and consumption goods (C) already fit better into the CRESH model, because for them a boundary solution is only reached 10 out of 56 times. For aggregate trade (T) this is even only 5 times, while for equipment goods (K) *all* a_{ij} coefficients satisfy automatically the constraint $a_{ij} \geq 0$, which clearly is a remarkable result. Moreover, for only 8 coefficients does the imposition of the zero constraint imply a significant reduction in the fit. On average 64 % of the positive coefficients exceed twice their asymptotic standard error. For branch K (equipment goods) this is 73 % and for aggregate trade even 77 %.

Table 5.2 : Estimated a_{ij} coefficients compared for import allocation models for 5 categories of goods and aggregate trade

Partner i	Category	Importer j						
		West-Germany	France	Italy	Netherlands	UK	USA	Japan
West-Germany	A	-	1.661*	.0	1.155	.450	1.586*	2.295*
	E	-	.566*	.675	1.805*	1.391*	.859	.0**
	Q	-	.532	1.640*	.217	.0**	2.215*	.615*
	K	-	.726	.305	1.201*	.438*	.573*	1.333*
	C	-	1.749*	.0**	.274	1.115*	1.062*	1.142*
	T	-	.218	1.194*	.637*	.407*	.664*	1.063*
France	A	.586	-	.335	1.246	1.430	1.292*	2.143*
	E	1.953*	-	.0**	1.381*	.0**	2.323*	1.395*
	Q	1.105*	-	1.220*	.062	.0**	.595*	.320
	K	2.040*	-	.879*	1.435*	.134	.990*	.745*
	C	1.517*	-	.022	.173	.0**	.740*	.663*
	T	.677*	-	.993*	.766*	.479*	1.103*	.676*
Italy	A	.0**	.432	-	.247	.0**	.556*	.0**
	E	.0**	1.793*	-	2.130*	.131	.562	.0**
	Q	5.078*	.334	-	2.249*	1.147	.892*	1.070*
	K	1.406*	2.743*	-	1.558*	.655*	.673*	.883*
	C	.0**	.271	-	2.055*	2.423*	2.865*	.910*
	T	.0**	.0**	-	1.544*	1.466*	.608	1.198*
Netherlands	A	1.099*	.250	.500	-	.082	.944*	1.561*
	E	.0**	.024	1.576*	-	.0**	.0**	1.330
	Q	.723	.0**	.0**	-	.0**	1.759*	.965*
	K	.473	1.839*	.419	-	.665*	.928*	.195
	C	1.622*	.0	.349	-	.0**	.994*	.064
	T	.624*	.411	.996*	-	1.023	.715*	.487

Table 5.2 : Continued

Partner i	Category	Importer j						
		West-Germany	France	Italy	Netherlands	UK	USA	Japan
UK	A	$.0^{**}$	.226	.200	.0	-	$.620^{*}$	.387
	E	$.0^{**}$	1.153	1.944^{*}	2.804^{*}	-	$.0^{**}$	.259
	Q	1.663^{*}	.264	.351	$.0^{**}$	-	$.0^{**}$	$.0^{**}$
	K	$.832^{*}$	.290	.454	$.949^{*}$	-	$.678^{*}$	.434
	C	2.483^{*}	.427	$.667^{*}$	1.343^{*}	-	$.791^{*}$	$.729^{*}$
	T	1.875^{*}	$.816^{*}$	$.917^{*}$	1.152^{*}	-	$.683^{*}$	.245
USA	A	$.0^{**}$	$.0^{**}$	.0	.0	1.364	-	$.935^{*}$
	E	1.148^{*}	$.787^{*}$	.583	$.755^{*}$	1.991^{*}	-	$.0^{**}$
	Q	3.684^{*}	1.754^{*}	1.745^{*}	.143	.874	-	.813
	K	$.918^{*}$	1.415^{*}	$.888^{*}$	1.273	1.214^{*}	-	$.912^{*}$
	C	.525	.0	$.0^{**}$	.0	$.484^{*}$	-	1.396^{*}
	T	$.841^{*}$	$.769^{*}$	1.268^{*}	.608	$.996^{*}$	-	$.666^{*}$
Japan	A	1.214^{*}	$.0^{**}$	2.198^{*}	1.105^{*}	.094	1.252^{*}	-
	E	1.486^{*}	2.821^{*}	1.318^{*}	2.360^{*}	.594	.348	-
	Q	$.0^{**}$	.751	1.350	2.520^{*}	$.0^{**}$	1.337^{*}	
	K	.245	2.018^{*}	1.562^{*}	4.493^{*}	.496	1.542^{*}	-
	C	1.525^{*}	1.011^{*}	.795	.0	.580	.225	-
	T	.603	1.317^{*}	1.645^{*}	1.615^{*}	1.435^{*}	1.428^{*}	-
ROW	A	1.026^{*}	1.816	.0	.0	$.0^{**}$	$.0^{**}$	$.0^{**}$
	E	$.0^{**}$	$.0^{**}$	.406	9.502^{*}	$.0^{**}$	$.0^{**}$	9.458^{*}
	Q	.788	$.914^{*}$	.246	.499	3.109^{*}	.382	4.016^{*}
	K	1.176^{*}	$.833^{*}$	2.456^{*}	1.622^{*}	1.692^{*}	.843	1.166^{*}
	C	$.0^{**}$	.597	.197	2.559^{*}	3.796	.409	2.128^{*}
	T	$.0^{**}$	.180	$.0^{**}$	$.624^{*}$	1.730^{*}	$.0^{**}$	1.299

* Variable exceeds twice its asymptotic standard error

** Constraints not rejected at 5 % level of significance.

Table 5.3 : Own and cross-price elasticities for 1975 for bilateral imports by the USA from partner i with respect to a change in the price price of partner h, for 5 categories of goods and aggregate trade

Price of Partner h	Cate-gory	Bilateral imports of the USA from partner i						
		West-Germany	France	Italy	Nether-lands	UK	USA	ROW
West-Germany	A	-1.275	.253	.109	.185	.122	.246	.0
	E	-.114	2.014	.487	.0	.0	.302	.0
	Q	-1.755	.124	.185	.366	.0	.278	.079
	K	-.529	.076	.051	.071	.052	.118	.064
	C	-1.010	.036	.140	.049	.037	.011	.020
	T	-.576	.146	.080	.095	.090	.189	.0
France	A	.482	-.899	.169	.287	.189	.381	.0
	E	.342	-1.398	.224	.0	.0	.139	.0
	Q	.075	-.575	.030	.059	.0	.045	.013
	K	.014	-.965	.017	.023	.017	.039	.021
	C	.045	-.709	.122	.042	.032	.010	.017
	T	.058	-1.006	.053	.063	.060	.125	.0
Italy	A	.203	.166	-.485	.121	.080	.161	.0
	E	.506	1.367	-.231	.0	.0	.205	.0
	Q	.075	.020	-.862	.059	.0	.045	.013
	K	.013	.022	-.658	.021	.015	.034	.019
	C	.219	.153	-2.274	.205	.157	.046	.084
	T	.036	.061	-.575	.039	.038	.078	.0
Nether-lands	A	.139	.113	.049	-.861	.054	.110	.0
	E	.0	.0	.0	.0	.0	.0	.0
	Q	.125	.034	.050	-1.660	.0	.075	.022
	K	.003	.005	.004	-.921	.004	.008	.004
	C	.032	.023	.088	-.964	.023	.007	.013
	T	.019	.032	.017	-.695	.020	.041	.0
UK	A	.068	.055	.040	.027	-.593	.054	.0
	E	.0	.0	.0	.0	.0	.0	.0
	Q	.0	.0	.0	.0	.0	.0	.0
	K	.026	.045	.031	.042	-.647	.070	.038
	C	.077	.054	.208	.072	-.706	.016	.030
	T	.063	.105	.058	.068	-.618	.136	.0

Table 5.3 : Continued

Price of Partner h	Category	Bilateral imports of the USA from partner i						
		West-Germany	France	Italy	Netherlands	UK	USA	ROW
Japan	A	.382	.312	.134	.228	.150	-.950	.0
	E	.011	.031	.007	.0	.0	-.343	.0
	Q	.851	.229	.343	.676	.0	-.823	.147
	K	.228	.394	.268	.369	.270	-.928	.336
	C	.022	.016	.061	.021	.016	-.220	.009
	T	.399	.663	.366	.430	.411	-.569	.0
ROW	A	.0	.0	.0	.0	.0	.0	.0
	E	.0	.0	.0	.0	.0	.0	.0
	Q	.629	.169	.253	.499	.0	.380	-.274
	K	.244	.422	.287	.395	.289	.657	-.484
	C	.614	.428	1.656	.575	.440	.130	-.173
	T	.0	.0	.0	.0	.0	.0	.0

A final remark concerns the coefficient estimates for *aggregate trade*. In a substantial number of cases they seem to have a value lying between the minimum and maximum value of the corresponding 5 coefficients for the individual categories of goods. They therefore assume more or less automatically the role of (weighted) average of the coefficients for the individual goods. More details about the estimation results may be found in Appendix 8.A.

As in the previous section, we present in tables 5.3 and 5.4 the own and cross-price elasticities for the bilateral imports of the USA as a large, closed economy, and the Netherlands as a small, open economy. They have been calculated with formulas (5.2.22) and (5.2.23), using the shares from table 5.1 instead of the optimal shares. Also for the price elasticities we find that the elasticities for aggregate trade are often within the range of the corresponding coefficients for the 5 categories of goods, and therefore act in such cases as a kind of average.

Table 5.4 : Own and cross-price elasticities for 1975 for bilateral imports by the Netherlands from partner i with respect to a change in the price of partner h, for 5 categories of goods and aggregate trade

Price of Partner h	Cate-gory	Bilateral imports of the Netherlands from partner i						
		West-Germany	France	Italy	UK	USA	Japan	ROW
West-Germany	A	-.813	.369	.073	.0	.0	.328	.0
	E	-1.793	.009	.015	.019	.005	.016	.065
	Q	-.170	.013	.489	.0	.031	.548	.108
	K	-.839	.433	.470	.286	.384	1.356	.489
	C	-.258	.010	.122	.080	.0	.0	.152
	T	-.489	.178	.359	.268	.141	.376	.145
France	A	.780	-.404	.167	.0	.0	.746	.0
	E	.002	-1.379	.002	.003	.001	.003	.010
	Q	.004	-.061	.037	.0	.002	.041	.008
	K	.146	-1.289	.158	.096	.129	.457	.165
	C	.002	-.171	.019	.012	.0	.0	.023
	T	.053	-.702	.129	.096	.051	.135	.052
Italy	A	.024	.026	-.242	.0	.0	.023	.0
	E	.004	.003	-2.126	.006	.002	.005	.019
	Q	.034	.010	-1.897	.0	.022	.394	.078
	K	.064	.077	-1.475	.051	.068	.240	.087
	C	.022	.014	-1.889	.108	.0	.0	.207
	T	.050	.060	-1.423	.090	.047	.126	.049
UK	A	.0	.0	.0	.0	.0	.0	.0
	E	.017	.013	.020	-2.777	.007	.023	.091
	Q	.0	.0	.0	.0	.0	.0	.0
	K	.068	.081	.088	-.895	.072	.255	.092
	C	.011	.007	.083	-1.289	.0	.0	.103
	T	.060	.073	.147	-.962	.058	.153	.059
USA	A	.0	.0	.0	.0	.0	.0	.0
	E	.004	.003	.004	.006	-.753	.005	.020
	Q	.008	.002	.081	.0	-.138	.091	.018
	K	.108	.129	.140	.085	-1.159	.404	.146
	C	.0	.0	.0	.0	.0	.0	.0
	T	.056	.067	.135	.100	-.555	.141	.054

Table 5.4 : Continued

Price of Partner h	Cate-gory	Bilateral imports of the Netherlands from partner i						
		West-Germany	France	Italy	UK	USA	Japan	ROW
France	A	.008	.009	.010	.0	.0	-1.097	.0
	E	.001	.001	.001	.002	.000	-2.359	.006
	Q	.020	.006	.203	.0	.013	-2.293	.045
	K	.122	.146	.158	.096	.129	-4.037	.165
	C	.0	.0	.0	.0	.0	.0	.0
	T	.015	.018	.036	.027	.014	-1.577	.015
ROW	A	.0	.0	.0	.0	.0	.0	.0
	E	1.765	1.350	2.083	2.742	.738	2.307	-.211
	Q	.105	.030	1.087	.0	.069	1.218	-.258
	K	.354	.423	.460	.280	.375	1.325	-1.144
	C	.222	.140	1.666	1.089	.0	.0	-.485
	T	.255	.307	.618	.461	.243	.646	-.374

The *own-price* elasticities are much more volatile for individual goods than for aggregate trade. For the latter they range in general between -.5 and -1.5, while for individual categories of goods they vary between .0 and even -4, although the latter value is an exception. As in the previous section, low own-price elasticities (in absolute value) may be linked to the importance of the corresponding supplier on the import market and the related monopolistic effects. This reasoning may well explain the low own-price elasticities for imports by the Netherlands : from West-Germany for intermediate goods and consumption goods, from the USA for agricultural goods, from the ROW for agricultural goods, energy and intermediate goods, and for imports by the USA from the ROW for agricultural goods, energy, intermediate goods, consumption goods and aggregate trade.

Also the *cross-price* elasticities are much more volatile for individual categories of goods than for aggregate trade. While for the latter they stay between .0 and .7, for the former they reach values as high as 2.7. Typical examples of low cross-price elasticities appear for energy for both importing countries, notably for the Netherlands. Only a price change of the ROW on the Dutch energy import market induces large changes in the bilateral energy imports from the other partners. This is not surprising as it concerns very small trade flows in general. The differences are interesting between the cross-price elasticities for agricultural goods on the Dutch and US market. For the Netherlands they are almost uniformly very small, while for the USA they are in general more elevated. Apparently there is more competition on the US agricultural import market. From the tables it is clear that the import share plays a role in the calculation of the cross-price elasticities. For instance, Dutch imports of German equipment goods have a large share in the total Dutch import market of equipment goods. Consequently the cross-price elasticities for equipment goods involving a German price change are relatively high. This is also clear for numerous cross-price elasticities involving price changes of the ROW.

8.6. SUMMARY AND CONCLUDING REMARKS

We started this chapter with the following list of model *characteristics*, defining the whole range of allocation models that may be estimated :

- import allocation or total allocation
- definition of the aggregates of categories of goods that are allocated
- definition of the partner groupings
- definition of the importing country
- the CRESH approximation or functional form chosen for the derived demand equations : Models I-IV
- the static/dynamic form and inclusion or not of trends
- the starting form of the covariance matrix.

We conducted experiments with the starting form of the *covariance matrix* which indicated both for the CES model and the CRESH model that the best approximation of the final covariance matrix was a covariance matrix with zero covariances everywhere, save for the elements involving the partner of which the equation is deleted in order to obtain the lopped model to be estimated. Because the deleted equation always corresponded to the Rest of the World (ROW), we argued however that the asymmetric position of this trade "partner" with respect to the other partners perhaps had a stronger positive effect than the negative effect induced by the fact that the matrix allowed for very few interdependent correlations among the disturbances of the bilateral import equations. Therefore this matrix only seems a good starting matrix if the equation corresponding to the ROW is deleted.

Next, using import allocation models for *aggregate* trade, we tried to find an empirical answer to the question of which functional form should be preferred as an approximation to the CRESH import allocation model. Two criteria involving empirical fit as well as the criterion of aptness to satisfy the second-order sufficiency conditions from classical optimization seemed to indicate that the best functional form, at least on the basis of the estimated import allocation models, would be one in logarithmic differences with homoscedastic disturbances.

Starting from this functional form we finally estimated CRESH import allocation models for 7 importing countries for 5 categories of goods and aggregate trade. It was found that both the own-price elasticities and the cross-price elasticities were much more volatile for the individual categories of goods than for aggregate trade. Furthermore it was remarkable that the constraints on the coefficients implied by the second-order sufficiency conditions were satisfied automatically for all import allocation models pertaining to equipment goods. For other categories of goods and aggregate trade sometimes boundary solutions were obtained for the coefficients that were involved. In only 8 out of 56 cases did this cause a significant reduction in the fit of the model.

APPENDIX 8.A : DETAILED ESTIMATION RESULTS

Next to the estimation results already presented in section 8.5, we give in this Appendix a more complete picture of the estimations per category of goods and aggregate trade. For the sake of convenience, let us first repeat model III in the way it was estimated (*cfr.* equations (5.3.98) and (6.3.1)).

$$\text{(A.1)} \qquad \Delta ln\left(\frac{m_{ijt}}{\tilde{m}^{o}_{jt}}\right) = \lambda_j \, \Delta ln\left(\frac{m_{ijt-1}}{\tilde{m}^{o}_{jt-1}}\right) + b_{ij}(1-\lambda_j)$$

$$- a_{ij}(1-\lambda_j)\,[\Delta ln\, pm_{ijt} - \Sigma_h\, w^{o}_{hj}\, \Delta ln\, pm_{hjt}]$$

$$+ (1-\lambda_j)\, \Sigma_h\, w^{o}_{hj}\, a_{hj}\,[\Delta ln\, pm_{hjt} - \Sigma_l\, w^{o}_{lj}\, \Delta ln\, pm_{ljt}] + u_{ijt}$$

In this specification we consider bilateral imports by importer j from partner i of good k, where we have deleted the good's index. The latter concerns the five categories A, E, Q, K and C, as well as aggregate trade.

The estimation results for the a_{ij} coefficients were presented in table 5.1, together with examples of the implied price elasticities in tables 5.2 and 5.3. Next we first discuss the estimates for λ_j and b_{ij} and then some of the statistics related to the estimations.

DYNAMICS

The estimates for the λ_j coefficients are given in table A.1. Whenever λ_j became negative, it was fixed at zero. This happened in 28 out of 42 cases. In the 14 cases that λ_j was estimated to be positive, this estimate was significantly different from zero in only 6 cases. In any case, the value of .2 is only exceeded twice. We noted before that the fact that we are using unit value-based price indices could be a limiting factor when drawing conclusions about the dynamic nature of any model based on those indices. If we were to disregard this limiting factor, we would be tempted to say that from the evidence in table A.1 the mean lag $\lambda_j/(1-\lambda_j)$ does not exceed 3 months in bilateral trade in general. To the extent that unit value indices reflect prices as negotiated and not as at the time of delivery, the average lag between concluding a contract and the time of delivery should be added to the period of 3 months to have an indication of the true lag between changes in the prices and changes in the quantities.

Table A.1 : Estimated λ_j coefficients compared for import allocation models for 5 categories of goods and aggregate trade

Category	Importer j						
	West-Germany	France	Italy	Netherlands	UK	USA	Japan
A	.0	.0	.0	.0	.0	.0	.0
E	.178	.139	.0	.158*	.0	.0	.0
Q	.230*	.0	.0	.0	.161	.0	.0
K	.0	.187*	.0	.175*	.0	.0	.0
C	.347*	.043	.072	.0	.0	.0	.178*
T	.0	.084	.149	.094	.0	.0	.0

* Coefficient exceeds twice its asymptotic standard error.

TRENDS

In table A.2 we present the estimated b_{ij} coefficients that reflect trendlike changes in the bilateral import bundle. Because of the definition of the b_{ij} in equation (6.2.3), they were estimated subject to the condition

$$\text{(A.2)} \qquad \Sigma_i \, w^o_{ij} \, b_{ij} = 0.$$

The trend coefficients are significantly different from zero in only 33 out of 294 cases (11 %). Nevertheless the estimates permit one to distinguish a number of tendencies that have occurred during the second half of the sixties and the seventies. For *agricultural goods (A)* it is clear that the 5 European countries have integrated during the sample period, no doubt under

Table A.2 : Estimated b_{ij} coefficients compared for import allocation models for 5 categories of goods and aggregate trade

Partner i	Category	Importer j						
		West-Germany	France	Italy	Netherlands	UK	USA	Japan
West-Germany	A	-	2.90	4.65	-1.03	12.74*	5.27	6.00
	E	-	-7.03*	-3.29	-11.66	-1.32	-8.80	-3.54
	Q	-	-.99	.00	-.03	4.54	-.22	-1.34
	K	-	-1.60	-1.78	-.43	-1.53	-6.85*	-.15
	C	-	2.58	4.61*	2.68	5.01*	-1.52	1.95
	T	-	-.62	.89	-.17	4.88*	-1.81	-4.26
France	A	3.35	-	5.41	11.22	9.41	10.10	-.85
	E	-7.55	-	9.99	-5.15	-.33	15.74	1.08
	Q	-.72	-	1.00	2.19*	5.60*	.96	2.27
	K	1.42	-	3.62*	1.60	4.07*	-1.19	1.67
	C	-.83	-	2.57	-.86	1.86	-1.36	1.67
	T	.37	-	3.08*	2.24	4.58*	-1.51	.58
Italy	A	-1.44	5.04	-	.33	4.22	12.13*	4.29
	E	-13.00	5.06	-	-6.66	.08	6.62	-2.00
	Q	2.39	3.58	-	.86	3.33	.72	4.64
	K	-1.70	1.07	-	-.41	.34	-5.44	-.29
	C	2.62	3.57*	-	-1.73	1.45	-1.02	7.66*
	T	1.36	3.92	-	-1.08	3.12	-2.00	.20
Netherlands	A	3.83*	2.22	4.80	-	2.77	.47	-5.24
	E	5.17	1.01	9.93	-	3.68	.98	-2.66
	Q	2.37	2.97	1.70	-	3.01	5.46	-1.65
	K	-2.53	-3.21	-2.07	-	.04	-5.89	-9.01
	C	-.55	-.89	-.05	-	1.47	-1.80	-2.68
	T	1.65	.73	1.63	-	2.05	-1.59	-4.55

Table A.2 : Continued

Partner i	Category	Importer j						
		West-Germany	France	Italy	Netherlands	UK	US	Japan
UK	A	4.34	9.74	.35	-3.02	-	.67	-1.22
	E	10.01	3.06	-4.77	-1.27	-	41.91*	-2.49
	Q	.60	-.34	-2.38	.57	-	1.43	-.59
	K	-2.49	-3.52	-2.02	.25	-	-5.61*	-1.97
	C	.63	1.59	-1.52	-.25	-	-2.94*	-2.14
	T	2.79	.08	-.15	1.16	-	-1.18	-2.40
USA	A	.45	1.16	.46	-.88	-1.16	-	1.72
	E	-10.48	-2.90	-9.08	-10.44	-12.18	-	-7.26
	Q	-.19	-2.24	-4.06	2.62*	-2.95	-	-.85
	K	-3.32	-2.78	-3.63	.14	-4.61	-	-.10
	C	1.84	-1.48	-1.10	-2.35	.02	-	-.73
	T	-2.27	-1.87	-3.89	-.53	-1.38	-	-2.94
Japan	A	-2.84	5.58	1.55	-.12	-5.90	.61	-
	E	-4.24	-14.40	-7.82	-4.36	-12.93	.33	-
	Q	5.35	8.49	-3.08	2.54	6.40	2.25	-
	K	10.49*	11.66*	9.66*	7.33	5.41	3.73	-
	C	.28	-.94	-1.22	-2.63	-4.15	-9.02*	-
	T	7.00*	8.54*	1.96	5.01	5.24	2.41	-
ROW	A	-1.49	-1.48	-2.48	-1.62	-2.37*	-.55	-1.17
	E	-.55	.40	.15	.96	-.10	-.08	.66
	Q	-1.12	-.56	.57	-1.54	-2.17*	-1.31	.21
	K	.32	3.06*	1.99	-1.48	1.03	1.15	1.17
	C	-.59	-1.59*	-2.88	-1.11	-.51	.99*	-.03
	T	-.98	-.57	-.69	-.39	-1.60*	-.05	.96

x 100

* Coefficient exceeds twice its asymmptotic standard error.

the influence of the Common Agricultural Policy. For all 5 countries this was at the expense of the ROW.

For *energy goods (E)*, the Netherlands has strengthened its position on the markets of the other European countries and the USA. The penetration of the UK on the American market is remarkable. Although this is not shown in the tables, this due to the fact that the UK market share has started to rise from virtually nothing to 2.5 % of the American import market in 1980. The coefficients for ROW show that the dependency from the Oil Producing Exporting Countries is still present, and even significantly increasing in the Netherlands. The USA is losing market shares in all the six countries considered in the tables as is Germany.

For *equipment goods (K)*, there is a loss of market shares over the sample period in virtually all markets considered in the table for Germany, Italy, the Netherlands, the UK and the USA. This happens to the advantage of France but most of all Japan, with trends reaching 10 % per year on several markets for this last country.

For *intermediate goods (Q), consumption goods (C) and aggregate trade (T)* the tendencies are less clearly marked, save for the general gain on the six markets for aggregate trade for Japan, and the loss for the USA and the ROW (except in Japan).

The conclusion for the trend coefficients is that although few of them are significantly different from zero, their inclusion is in general needed because otherwise some very strong trend effects might not be captured, which would be at the expense of the other estimated coefficients.

AUTOCORRELATION

In table A.3 we give the Durbin-Watson (DW) statistics for the individual bilateral import equations [5)]. This statistic provides a valid test for autocorrelation if no lagged dependent variable is present in the equations. As we know from table A.1, this is the case in 28 out of 42 cases for our estimations, so there the DW test is strictly applicable if we disregard the fact that we work in a multivariate context. In the other cases the test may not be applied, and we should use other tests, such as the *h*-statistic

Table A.3 : Durbin-Watson statistics for individual equations of import allocation models for 5 categories of goods and aggregate trade

Partner i	Category	Importer j						
		West-Germany	France	Italy	Netherlands	UK	USA	Japan
West-Germany	A	-	2.524	1.797	2.487	2.172	2.335	3.026
	E	-	2.145[a]	2.394	1.975[a]	1.825	1.342	2.290
	Q	-	1.624	2.027	2.666	1.641[a]	2.062	2.039
	K	-	2.464[a]	2.637	1.857[a]	1.925	2.113	1.714
	C	-	.996[a]	2.235[a]	1.078	.963	2.222	2.513[a]
	T	-	2.263[a]	1.610[a]	1.771[a]	1.450	1.875	1.427
France	A	2.806	-	1.974	2.250	1.452	2.311	2.448
	E	2.538[a]	-	2.037	2.502[a]	2.851	2.034	2.657
	Q	1.069[a]	-	2.274	1.592	1.645[a]	2.401	1.768
	K	2.868	-	1.391	2.510[a]	1.480	1.183	2.234
	C	2.898[a]	-	1.727[a]	2.824	2.333	1.476	1.796[a]
	T	1.528	-	1.377[a]	1.937[a]	2.151	1.691	1.253
Italy	A	1.653	2.415	-	2.091	2.229	2.100	2.484
	E	1.528[a]	1.555[a]	-	1.506[a]	1.020	1.207	2.757
	Q	1.824[a]	1.566	-	1.570	2.191[a]	2.526	2.190
	K	1.745	2.219[a]	-	2.638[a]	2.078	2.172	3.152
	C	2.233[a]	1.774[a]	-	1.974	1.347	1.897	2.058[a]
	T	1.662	1.901[a]	-	1.415[a]	1.462	1.414	1.640
Netherlands	A	1.901	1.854	2.337	-	.993	2.866	2.264
	E	1.771[a]	1.811[a]	1.576	-	2.674	2.278	3.134
	Q	1.579[a]	1.246	1.953	-	2.627[a]	1.913	1.805
	K	1.796	1.662[a]	2.749	-	2.573	1.288	1.950
	C	1.808[a]	2.005[a]	1.786[a]	-	1.166	2.680	1.722[a]
	T	.407	2.123[a]	2.097[a]	-	1.616	1.948	1.969

Table A.3 : Continued

Partner i	Category	Importer j						
		West-Germany	France	Italy	Netherlands	UK	USA	Japan
UK	A	2.857	2.558	2.306	3.058	-	1.674	2.453
	E	1.039[a]	1.954[a]	1.346	2.516[a]	-	.636	1.831
	Q	1.940[a]	1.140	1.444	1.780	-	.784	1.856
	K	1.169	1.812[a]	1.955	1.985[a]	-	.968	2.399
	C	2.051[a]	2.193[a]	1.261[a]	1.400	-	1.809	1.118[a]
	T	.626	1.309[a]	.984[a]	1.116[a]	-	1.346	2.049
USA	A	2.686	2.228	2.723	2.580	1.783	-	2.371
	E	2.409[a]	2.024[a]	2.286	2.375[a]	2.271	-	1.394
	Q	1.109[a]	2.155	1.377	2.438	2.061[a]	-	2.084
	K	2.219	2.240[a]	1.324	2.920[a]	1.416	-	1.654
	C	2.610[a]	1.488[a]	2.097[a]	1.599	2.020	-	2.324[a]
	T	2.138	2.444[a]	2.022[a]	2.500[a]	1.548	-	2.478
Japan	A	2.097	2.416	2.707	1.970	3.158	2.223	-
	E	2.430[a]	1.863[a]	1.732	1.864[a]	2.648	2.063	-
	Q	1.869[a]	1.620	2.234	2.128	1.744[a]	1.544	-
	K	1.841	2.426[a]	1.876	2.315[a]	1.192	1.907	-
	C	1.905[a]	2.525[a]	2.307[a]	2.373	2.177	1.392	-
	T	1.986	1.947[a]	2.668[a]	1.610[a]	1.932	1.555	-
ROW	A	not available						
	E							
	Q							
	K							
	C							
	T							

[a] Equation contains a lagged dependent variable.

of DURBIN (1970). Nevertheless, for the cases where a lagged dependent variable is present, we still use the DW as a crude indicator for the presence of possible autocorrelation in the residuals as transformed through the Koyck transformation.

Let d_L be the lowerbound for the rejection of autocorrelation [6]: if $DW < d_L$ the hypothesis of no autocorrelation is rejected. Similarly, let d_U be the upperbound : if $DW > d_U$, we do not reject the null hypothesis of no autocorrelation. If $D_L < DW < d_U$, the test is inconclusive. Because we estimate per importer j (with n partners) $2n$ parameters (the a_{ij} and b_{ij}) for n equations in the case of no dynamics, we take for the 5 % significance points of d_L and d_U the values corresponding to an equation with $2n/n = 2$ explanatory variables and 16 observations (1965-1980). These values are $d_L = .98$ and $d_U = 1.54$. On the basis of these values the hypothesis of no autocorrelation has to be rejected 11 times : 6 times in favour of positive autocorrelation, and 5 times in favour of negative autocorrelation. Otherwise the hypothesis is not rejected or the test is inconclusive. Compared to a total of 252 DW statistics, there is a rejection of 4.4 %, which is close to the 5 % we had chosen for our significance points, of course not taking account of the inconclusive region.

GOODNESS OF FIT

The goodness of fit of the estimations is summarized in two tables. Table A.4 presents standard errors for the individual bilateral import equations, while table A.5 summarizes per importer and category of goods the goodness of fit through Root Mean-Squared Percentage Errors (RMSPEs).

A comparison between table 5.1 (with the baseyear import shares) and table A.4 (with the standard errors per bilateral import equation) shows that there is an inverse relationship between the value of the 1975 import share w^o_{ij} and the value of the standard error : the lower the share, the higher in general the standard error. This may be illustrated if we calculate for three classes of shares the - simple - averages for the standard errors of the corresponding equations.

Table A.4 : Standard errors for individual equations of import allocation models for 5 categories of goods and aggregate trade

Partner i	Category	Importer j						
		West-Germany	France	Italy	Netherlands	UK	USA	Japan
West-Germany	A	-	13.40	20.69	15.92	14.50	18.48	55.85
	E	-	9.65	25.02	31.44	26.76	100.27	163.55
	Q	-	2.82	4.44	3.16	9.08	11.77	12.39
	K	-	3.55	3.79	3.73	5.43	9.17	9.09
	C	-	6.55	6.01	5.43	8.85	5.50	10.99
	T	-	3.32	4.53	3.18	5.41	9.77	14.63
France	A	20.90	-	12.77	36.97	19.03	37.19	84.11
	E	11.90	-	46.98	38.66	30.91	65.22	82.90
	Q	3.07	-	4.06	4.25	8.85	8.73	13.06
	K	4.50	-	3.67	9.36	7.60	13.16	13.36
	C	6.25	-	7.67	6.32	13.32	6.81	15.22
	T	3.45	-	3.52	7.43	6.66	4.95	14.01
Italy	A	5.38	25.90	-	13.15	9.87	21.10	47.87
	E	37.92	32.92	-	44.05	28.52	70.91	313.45
	Q	14.10	8.96	-	10.13	12.30	13.42	13.92
	K	6.70	4.80	-	10.84	6.95	12.36	15.73
	C	5.49	6.77	-	10.93	12.71	15.52	11.81
	T	5.39	7.44	-	8.66	9.07	8.56	15.77
Netherlands	A	6.95	12.07	11.82	-	19.33	10.73	20.87
	E	12.70	17.17	47.45	-	17.86	79.76	129.68
	Q	4.02	6.44	5.36	-	10.54	19.38	24.71
	K	6.83	8.78	8.39	-	5.68	11.73	42.04
	C	5.10	6.41	8.48	-	7.74	8.81	15.32
	T	4.59	6.14	4.86	-	7.87	11.00	15.96
UK	A	6.02	28.07	26.61	44.43	-	14.27	36.66
	E	27.11	31.10	53.49	36.25	-	78.13	73.69
	Q	9.62	7.57	8.46	5.92	-	11.99	16.98
	K	6.87	5.96	7.44	6.46	-	10.04	16.52
	C	6.99	7.61	8.17	13.43	-	3.96	10.23
	T	10.07	4.49	6.63	6.55	-	6.01	7.03
USA	A	9.94	11.49	19.10	11.28	14.57	-	5.90
	E	30.13	22.46	22.74	24.02	49.20	-	17.67
	Q	9.85	11.01	9.54	4.13	11.68	-	12.04
	K	7.89	8.74	8.85	14.92	12.68	-	5.10
	C	28.10	9.10	10.57	10.03	7.38	-	11.30
	T	8.39	8.01	8.18	7.87	6.83	-	6.18

Table A.4 : Continued

Partner i	Cate-gory	Importer j						
		West-Germany	France	Italy	Nether-lands	UK	USA	Japan
Japan	A	12.63	35.66	38.25	22.12	25.50	25.16	-
	E	72.93	155.60	71.36	143.92	172.71	127.43	-
	Q	29.20	25.39	42.32	12.35	27.24	10.33	-
	K	8.37	14.99	15.00	19.14	18.64	8.66	-
	C	6.39	10.04	16.64	10.42	11.90	9.55	-
	T	10.08	7.71	18.84	13.49	13.82	10.44	-
ROW	A	3.43	4.00	6.25	4.98	3.41	1.47	4.03
	E	4.26	1.29	2.06	1.52	3.49	1.08	1.55
	Q	2.46	2.52	2.63	3.53	3.23	4.99	3.32
	K	3.51	3.92	5.66	4.76	4.27	5.89	11.27
	C	3.37	3.03	5.70	4.18	1.95	1.06	2.53
	T	2.21	1.91	2.48	2.85	1.94	2.43	2.11

x 100

Class	Number	Average standard error	Standard deviation
$w^o_{ij} < 1$ %	43 (15 %)	62.86	58.93
$1\ \% \leqslant w^o_{ij} < 5$ %	86 (29 %)	11.97	10.54
$5\ \% \leqslant w^o_{ij}$	165 (56 %)	7.69	5.43
TOTAL	294(100 %)	18.47	30.18

The average standard error for all 294 equations is 18.47 %, but it is clear that this is due to the equations for small bilateral trade flows. Notably the flows which had an import share smaller than 1 % in 1975 account to a large extent for this high average. For the 56 % of the bilateral trade-flows for which this share was greater than or equal to 5 %, the average standard error is 7.69 %. Given the fact that we apply a uniform approach *without any modification* (such as through dummies or additional explanatory variables) to a detailed aspect of international trade this may be considered as a satisfactory fit. Moreover, in a simulation excercise one will usually judge the fit of the model from the total trade variables that result through identities from the bilateral trade flows, and through the aggregation process that is applied to obtain these variables, errors will tend to cancel out (as long as they are random).

Nevertheless there remains the problem of the large standard errors for the small flows. In actual practice, one might take two approaches to this problem. In the first place one might try to find additional explanations that would improve the estimations for the small flows. There is a large probability, however, that this would be at the expense of the internal coherency of each import allocation model that would be concerned, for instance because the adding-up condition would be violated. The second approach would be to accept as such the bad goodness of fit of the equations for the small bilateral trade flows because large errors in small values would affect only marginally the fitted value of the total trade variables from which they are part. If there is lack of information on specific bilateral trade flows, the second approach is the only remaining possibility.

Table A.5 : Root Mean-Squared Percentage Errors for the levels of all bilateral imports in import allocation models for 5 categories of goods and aggregate trade

Category	Importer j							Total
	West-Germany	France	Italy	Netherlands	UK	USA	Japan	
A	27.55	21.59	21.58	26.77	16.72	19.96	45.49	27.14
E	47.67	245.34	54.06	103.48	313.54	155.41	1478.64	583.70
Q	13.29	11.39	19.41	7.01	14.47	12.34	16.05	13.90
K	6.64	8.36	8.33	11.56	10.03	10.55	21.35	12.51
C	12.75	7.36	9.95	9.46	9.89	8.87	11.90	10.17
T	7.00	5.97	8.84	7.98	8.21	8.30	12.29	8.57

Calculated as in table 4.5

Finally we present in table A.5 RMSPEs for the *levels* of the bilateral trade flows per importer and category of goods. As it concerns *unweighted* averages, the RMSPEs for categories of goods containing small bilateral trade flows may become extremely large. An example are the energy imports of Japan : for each of the 5 European countries the import share on the Japanese energy import market did not exceed .15 % in 1975. This problem occurs in general for all importers for the categories agricultural goods (A) and energy (E). The lowest total RMSPE is for aggregate trade (T) with 8.57 %. Of the individual categories of goods, the best result is obtained for consumption goods (C), followed by equipment goods (K) and intermediate goods (Q).

FOOTNOTES TO CHAPTER 8

1) Throughout this chapter and the following, Belgium stands for the Belgium-Luxembourg Economic Union (BLEU).

2) The estimations were performed using the TSP 3.4 programme, *cfr.* HALL and HALL (1978).

3) That is, if we assume for the dynamic model with time trends that it is estimated using a grid search over the distributed lag parameter λ, *cfr.* Section 6.7.

4) In doing so, we have taken the *actual* values for the lagged dependent variables. An alternative would be to calculate the fitted levels by means of a dynamic simulation.

5) We interpret the DW statistics like for single equations, despite the fact that we estimate a multivariate model. Furthermore, the DW statistics for ROW are missing because this equation was excluded in all estimations in order to obtain the model in lopped form.

6) In the following, DW should be replaced by 4-DW if $DW > 2$. In that case we test for negative autocorrelation, if $DW < 2$, we test for positive autocorrelation.

CHAPTER 9 - HYPOTHESIS TESTING

9.1. INTRODUCTION

The present chapter will deal with two kinds of hypotheses to be tested. The first kind is a test of the hypothesis of weak separability of the aggregator function in domestic products and imports. The second kind involves testing the CES import allocation model against the CRESH import allocation model developed in Chapters 5 and 6 and estimated in the previous Chapter.

The hypothesis of weak separability is a very crucial one, because it acts as a *conditio sine qua non* for the derivation of any import allocation model. In section 5.4 we re-interpreted the CRESH import allocation model as a total allocation model and we derived the conditions under which weak separability holds in the context of this model. Depending on the category of goods for which the allocation model is estimated, the underlying aggregator function may be interpreted as a production function or a utility function. In the case where one interprets the aggregator function as a production function, one should test the weak separability between (an aggregate of) *all* domestic production factors and imports. In section 7.5 we saw however that the available data did not permit us to include all production factors, notably intermediate inputs, in the domestic aggregate. In fact, only data concerning *gross value added* per branch were available, representing an aggregate of capital services and labour, therefore. Instead of testing weak separability between (an aggregate of) *all* production factors we therefore test, within a partial aggregator function of labour, capital services and bilateral imports, the weak separability between an aggregate of the first two production factors versus imports. This test is therefore conditional on the assumption that the production function is weakly separable in intermediate inputs and a partial aggregator function of labour, capital services and bilateral imports. The outcomes of the tests of weak separability should therefore be carefully interpreted : if the hypothesis of weak separability is not rejected in the case where we use gross value added, we do not know whether it would be rejected either for a production function *including* intermediate inputs. If, on the other hand, the hypothesis is rejected in the case of value added, we know that this also rejects weak separability of the complete production function. The outcomes of the tests are presented in section 9.3.

Testing the CES import allocation model against the CRESH import allocation model amounts to a test of the hypothesis that the more complex CRESH model does not alter significantly the explanatory power of a less complex model such as the CES import allocation model. It is therefore a test of the question whether we need import allocation models containing more or less constraints among the price effects. The CES model, implying equality between all Allen Elasticities of Substitution, Direct Elasticities of Substitution and Shadow Elasticities of Substitution as defined in subsection 3.2.3. is clearly more restrictive in this respect than the CRESH model. The question to be tested is whether the more general CRESH model is a *significant* improvement over the CES model. If not, the CES model dispenses with the need for the CRESH model upon application of the principle of "Occam's razor".

We defined in section 8.2 seven characteristics with which we could identify any allocation model to be estimated. We also argued in subsection 1.5.3 that the outcome of any test, be it a test of weak separability or a test of the CES import allocation model against the CRESH model, was in a sense "local". This local nature was due to the fact that it is only valid for the specific model characteristics for which the test was performed. Notably for the test of the CES versus the CRESH model, we argued that a change in two kinds of model characteristics could be of influence. The first factor which could influence the outcome of the test was the *classification of the partner countries*. Interpreting the CES versus CRESH test as a test of the hypothesis that all elasticities of substitution are equal versus an alternative that they are not equal, we argued that this hypothesis would be more significantly rejected if the number of partners increased. This meta-hypothesis will be tested, together with the ordinary test of the CES versus the CRESH model, in section 9.4. The second model characteristic which, if changed, may modify the outcome of the test is the *classification of goods*. Again in the framework of a hypothesis of equal elasticities of substitution against an alternative hypothesis of unequal elasticities of substitution we argued that we could expect *a priori* two, though opposite, effects. It was posited that increased *product homogeneity* would cause the hypothesis of equal elasticities of substitution to be less firmly rejected, while on the other hand the increased *specialization* going along with increased product homogeneity would exert an opposite influence. Consequently we were unable to define *a priori* a meta-hypothesis like for the partner classification, and decided to let the facts speak for themselves. The results of these tests are presented in section 9.5.

Before we present the individual tests, however, we treat in section 9.2 that part of the test procedure which is common to all tests. The distribution of the main test statistic which we will use is only known asymptotically, nevertheless we try to correct the statistic for small-sample bias in Appendix 9.A. We conclude the chapter with a summary and some remarks in section 9.6.

9.2. THE GENERAL TEST PROCEDURE

This section describes how we test the ordinary hypothesis of weak separability and the ordinary hypothesis of the CES import allocation model against the CRESH model. That is, we do not discuss here the procedures followed for the meta-hypotheses.

Keeping the model characteristics fixed, we estimate the model under consideration twice for each test of a hypothesis : once with the model coefficients estimated freely, and once with the restrictions on the coefficients implied by the null hypothesis. The "free" estimation should of course happen under the restrictions on the coefficients implied by the theory, such as a Koyck lag parameter between zero and one in (5.3.25) and non-negative a_i coefficients in (6.3.1) as a second-order sufficient condition. Because we estimate with the method of maximum likelihood we obtain as a byproduct the values of the likelihood function in the maximum or their logarithms (loglikelihood). Because we will estimate model III as defined in section 5.5, which is a constrained model with as vector of weights the vector of baseyear import shares, we know from Corollary 4.3.1 that we have to delete for each of the two estimations the equation corresponding to the *same* partner, because otherwise the loglikelihood values are no longer comparable.

Then, because we know from sections 5.3 and 5.4 that the restrictions on the coefficients that are implied by the null hypotheses are nested in the free estimation, we may apply the *Likelihood Ratio Test*. This test is based on the ratio of the values of the maximum of the likelihood function under restricted and unrestricted estimation of parameters of some (not necessarily normal) distribution, where the values of the restricted parameters are implied by a (null) hypothesis that is nested within the unrestricted case. Let L_1 be the value of the likelihood function as it attains its maximum for unrestricted estimation. Let L_0 be the maximum value of the likelihood function under restricted estimation, where it is assumed that there are k restrictions. Then the likelihood ratio l is defined as

$$l = L_0/L_1 \; . \qquad (2.1)$$

If the restrictions implied by the null hypothesis for the parameter values differ substantially from the unrestricted estimates, the value of the restricted likelihood function L_0 will also be considerably smaller than that of the unrestricted function L_1. The Likelihood Ratio Test consists therefore of rejection of the null hypothesis if $l \leqslant L_\beta$, where L_β is a constant defined such that the probability to reject the null hypothesis when it is true (the so-called type I error) is β %.

The actual value of L_β depends on the distribution of the likelihood ratio l. The small-sample distribution of this criterion is however not always known, and in that case we have to rely on asymptotic results. This is also the case for our model. The test results in this chapter (as well as the tests made with regard to the imposition of non-negativity contraints on the coefficient estimates for a_{ij} in the previous chapter) will be based on the asymptotic distribution of the criterion. From cases where the finite sample distribution of the criterion is known, we know however that the use of asymptotic distributions may induce a strong bias towards rejection [1]. Therefore we try to apply at least a small-sample correction to the test statistic in Appendix 9.A; this correction is derived from the one that applies to a particular form of the multivariate linear model. Although it does not eliminate the bias completely, there is at least a substantial reduction in the value of the test statistic.

The well-known asymptotic result which we will use for the likelihood ratio test is the following. In accordance with Chapter 6, let α be the parameter vector of the model to be estimated. Partition α into two subvectors α_1 and α_2, and suppose that we want to test the null hypothesis $\alpha_1 = \bar{\alpha}$ versus the alternative hypothesis $\alpha_1 \neq \bar{\alpha}$, where we assume that α_1 has k elements. Then it is well known, that asymptotically

$$(2.2) \qquad C = -2 \ln l \sim \chi^2_k,$$

in other words : minus twice the logarithms of the likelihood ratio follows asymptotically a chi-square distribution with k degrees of freedom [2]. Given a significance level β, the null hypothesis will therefore be rejected if $-2 \ln l \geq \chi^2_k(\beta)$, the upper β % point of the Chi-square distribution with k degrees of freedom. It may then be calculated that the critical value for the Likelihood Ratio Test equals

$$(2.3) \qquad L_\beta = exp\ \{-\tfrac{1}{2}\ \chi^2_k(\beta)\}\ .$$

In actual practice it is more convenient to work with the C-statistic $-2 \ln l$, because the values of L_β become small for large k and small β.

The form of the test as described above may be applied directly to the situation where we test non-negativity constraints on the a_i coefficients in (6.3.1). Putting negative coefficients equal to zero is tantamount to $\alpha_1 = 0$ in the null hypothesis. For weak separability and the testing of the CES versus the CRESH model we impose equality constraints on the coefficients of the type

$$(2.4) \qquad a_1 = \ldots = a_n,$$

where n is the number of trade partners.

These constraints may be cast in the form of the null hypothesis if we make the following one-to-one transformation of the coefficients

$$(2.5) \qquad \begin{aligned} a_i^\star &= a_1 - a_n \qquad\qquad i = 1, \ldots, n-1,\\ a_n^\star &= a_n, \end{aligned}$$

and test $a_i^\star = 0$ for $i = 1, \ldots, n - 1$, implying $k = n - 1$ restrictions.

Before we pass to the actual tests, two more remarks are in order.

We saw in table 8.2.1 that the composition of our dataset allows us to estimate 52 different import allocation models and 5 different total allocation models by varying the classification of goods alone. Generally speaking, these allocation models are *composite* allocation models *i.e.* they comprise one or more different *individual* allocation models. For instance, because we distinguish 5 different categories of goods, we may estimate a composite import allocation model that consists of 5 individual import allocation models. We argued that it was important to consider these composite models because an individual allocation model does not describe the allocation over trade partners for all categories of goods, unless the individual model concerns aggregate trade. Consequently, if we test the CES model against the CRESH model or weak separability against non weak separability, we may do so for an individual model following the procedure outlined above, but the procedure should also be extended to make it fit for application to a composite allocation model. This extension is relatively straightforward if we assume, when there are g aggregates, and therefore g individual allocation models, that their disturbances each are distributed *independently*. In that case the value of the likelihood function of the composite allocation model is nothing but the product of the likelihood functions of the g individual allocation models. Denote by $L_0(\gamma)$ and $L_1(\gamma)$ the values of the likelihood function of individual model $\gamma = 1, \ldots, g$ corresponding to restricted and unrestricted estimation, then the values of L_0 and L_1 for the composite allocation model are obtained as

$$(2.6) \qquad L_0 = \Pi_\gamma L_0(\gamma) \ ,$$

$$(2.7) \qquad L_1 = \Pi_\gamma L_1(\gamma) \ .$$

Next the same test procedure as before may be applied to these two likelihood values, albeit that the degrees of freedom of the individual allocation models should be added to obtain the degrees of freedom for the composite test.

The second remark anticipates the testing of the meta-hypotheses. Suppose we are given the C-statistics of two composite allocation models with different degrees of freedom k_1 and k_2, and suppose that we want to know in which case the CES hypothesis or hypothesis of weak separability is rejected most strongly. In that case we cannot rely on a comparison of the value of the C-statistics, because they are statistics following two different (chi-square) distributions. The solution to this problem would be to calculate, for each C-statistic, the corresponding cumulative density or probability value, and to compare the two values of the cumulative densities : the statistic corresponding to a higher cumulative density indicates the strongest rejection of the null hypothesis, because that value has the lowest probability, of the two, to result under the null hypothesis. Let a C-statistic which follows the chi-square distribution with k degrees of freedom have the value $C^{\star}$. Then the corresponding cumulative density $G(C^{\star})$ may be calculated as [3] :

$$G(C^{\star}) = \int_{0}^{C^{\star}} \frac{x^{(k-2)/2}\, e^{-x/2}}{2^{k/2}\, \Gamma(k/2)}\, dx, \tag{2.7}$$

where $\Gamma(y)$ is the gamma function

$$\Gamma(y) = \int_{0}^{\infty} x^{y-1}\, e^{-x}\, dx, \qquad \text{for } y > 0. \tag{2.8}$$

9.3. WEAK SEPARABILITY

We already noted in section 9.1 that due to lack of data we are not able to test the hypothesis of weak separability as it should be tested. Because gross value added per branch and imports together form final demand, we rather test in a *final demand* framework the weak separability between gross value added and imports. Nevertheless one may draw conclusions concerning the true weak separability hypothesis on the basis of this partial evidence. Suppose the aggregator function for which we would like to test the assumption of weak separability contains as elements bilateral imports, gross value added and other domestic factors (for instance intermediate inputs in the case of a production function). The assumption of weak separability then amounts to the condition that the partial derivative of the marginal rate of substitution between any two bilateral imports with respect to gross value added or any of the other domestic factors equals zero. If therefore any of these derivatives is not zero, the assumption of weak separability will be rejected. What we are testing is only one of these partial derivatives, namely the one with respect to gross value added. If the hypothesis that the partial derivative of the marginal rate of substitution with respect to gross value added equals zero is rejected, this therefore seems a sufficient condition for the true weak separability assumption to be rejected. If the former is not rejected, the result is inconclusive, and does not necessarily need to lead to acceptance of the true weak separability hypothesis.

Let us first present the characteristics of the model which we estimate for the tests

- total allocation model (final demand allocation)
- aggregates of goods : A, E, M, $A+E$, $A+M$, $E+M$, $A+E+M$ for individual allocation models (+ resulting composite allocation models), where M is the aggregate $Q + K + C$
- partner countries (next to gross value added as "partner" and excluding the importing country) : Belgium, West-Germany, France, Italy, Netherlands, UK, USA, Rest of the World (ROW)

- importing countries : Belgium, West-Germany, France, Italy, Netherlands, UK
- CRESH approximation : Model III
- dynamic models with trends
- starting form of the covariance matrix : matrix (8.3.1).

The models are estimated for 1965-1980 for Belgium, West-Germany, France and Italy, and for 1965-1978 for the Netherlands and the UK. We have chosen Model III and the starting covariance matrix on the evidence of the previous chapter.

We present in table 3.1 first the cumulative densities for the 7 individual allocation models. Note that 100.0000 is not a cumulative density of 100 % but one which is greater than or equal to 99.99995 %.

Aggregate	Importer					
	Belgium	West-Germany	France	Italy	Netherlands	UK
A	99.9783	99.8029	98.8194	20.9739	22.9326	47.8503
E	99.9124	99.3688	100.0000	99.8065	77.8958	98.3986
M	99.9198	95.8000	99.0308	69.4571	80.0642	99.9986
A+E	97.4211	99.9880	99.8678	64.1396	99.7683	37.4308
A+M	87.1177	38.3955	99.5963	96.3200	93.7709	99.9949
E+M	100.0000	99.9937	99.3275	84.6975	99.9235	100.0000
A+E+M	99.9999	99.9999	99.8223	96.4536	99.2718	100.0000

Table 3.1 : Cumulative densities (%) for the weak separability hypothesis in seven individual final demand allocation models

The cumulative densities of aggregates consisting of two or three individual categories do not seem to be related to the cumulative densities of these individual categories of goods. For West-Germany for instance, the weak separability hypothesis is rejected at the level of 1 % for agricultural goods A and at the level of 5 % for manufactured goods M, while for the aggregate A+M the cumulative density is 38 %, indicating a rejection only at a significance level of about 62 %.

For aggregate trade A+E+M the weak separability hypothesis is rejected at a significance level of 1 % for Belgium, West-Germany, France, the Netherlands and the UK, and at a level of 5 % for Italy. For aggregate trade there is therefore a clear tendency towards rejection of the weak separability hypothesis, at least from the partial evidence of our final demand allocation model. For the other aggregates the evidence is more mixed. For agricultural goods A the hypothesis is only rejected at a 1 % or 5 % level of significance for 3 countries, while this is the case for 4 countries for manufacturing goods M. For energy goods, on the other hand, the only country for which the weak separability is not rejected at any of these two significance levels is the Netherlands. This is undoubtedly the result of the fact that there is considerable domestic energy production in the Netherlands; consequently the composition of its foreign energy supplies will hardly be affected through changes in the value added of the energy branch, and will mainly be determined through relative prices and trends. For the aggregates consisting of two individual categories of goods, there is a rejection of the weak separability hypothesis at a significance level of 1 % or 5 % in 12 out of 18 cases.

Next we pass to the cumulative densities of the 5 composite models that may be formed from the 7 individual models. These are presented in table 3.2. For the composite models consisting of 2 aggregates we have also presented the cumulative density corresponding to the average of the C-statistics of the three composite models that fall into this category. In this way we may analyze whether there is a trend in the cumulative densities and therefore in the strength of rejection of the weak separability hypothesis if the classification becomes more detailed.

Number of aggregates	Importer					
	Belgium	West-Germany	France	Italy	Nether-lands	UK
1. A+E+M	99.9999	99.9999	99.8223	96.4536	99.2718	100.0000
2. A E+M	100.0000	99.9998	99.9373	59.6047	99.0558	100.0000
E A+M	99.8913	93.3126	100.0000	99.9394	93.7063	99.9990
M A+E	99.9804	99.9941	99.9881	68.4891	99.6064	99.9745
Average[a]	99.9994	99.9755	99.9995	93.6626	98.6127	99.9998
3. A E M	100.0000	99.9909	100.0000	97.2617	67.3105	99.9974

[a] Cumulative density corresponding to the average of the C-statistics of these three composite models.

Table 3.2 : Cumulative densities (%) for the weak separability hypothesis of five composite final demand allocation models

If for the composite models containing two aggregates we only consider the average, then we may state that *all* composite models for Belgium, West-Germany, France and the UK reject the hypothesis of weak separability of the final demand aggregator function in gross value added and imports at a 1 % level of significance. For Italy we have rejection at a level of 5 % for aggregate trade and the composite of the three individual categories A, E and M, and one rejection at 1 % for one of the three composite models consisting of two aggregates. For the Netherlands there is rejection at a 1 % level of significance for aggregate trade and at 5 % for the average of the composite models containing two aggregates. The general picture therefore is a predominant *rejection of the weak separability hypothesis* for composite models.

Finally we may look at the presence of effects of product homogeneity or specialization as set out in subsection 1.5.3, but then applied to the weak separability hypothesis. Because the composite models corresponding to the three groups of table 3.2 are comparable as defined in Defintion 1.5.1, we may analyze the direction of the change in the cumulative densities if the degree of detail, as defined in Definition 1.5.2., increases, going from aggregate trade A+E+M to the composite of the individual models for A, E and M. There are monotone movements only for France, the Netherlands and the UK. For France the cumulative density and therefore the firmness of rejection increases monotonically with the degree of detail (using the average for group 2). This is therefore an indication of a predominant effect of specialization on rejection of the hypothesis of weak separability. In the Netherlands and the UK, there is an opposite monotone movement downwards of the cumulative densities. Here an increased product homogeneity causes the weak separability hypothesis to be rejected less firmly, although the effect is only really outspoken in the Netherlands. For the other three countries we must conclude that there is a mixture of the two effects.

9.4. CLASSIFICATION OF PARTNERS

This section deals with a test of the CES import allocation model against the CRESH import allocation model, and the influences on the outcome of this test of the classification of trade partners, and more specifically of the *number* of trade partners. We already presented an argument concerning these influences in subsection 1.5.3. It was brought forward there that a decrease in the number of trade partners would reduce the inequality between the elasticities of substitution. We will illustrate this hypothesis with an analytical example using variances as a measure of inequality between the elasticities of substitution in subsection 9.4.1.

A test of the CES versus the CRESH import allocation model may be considered as a test of the hypothesis that the elasticities of substitution (Allen partial Elasticity of Substitution, Direct Elasticity of Substitution, Shadow Elasticity of Substitution) are equal. The equivalent of the hypothesis that the elasticities of substitution become more equal if the number of trade partners is reduced would therefore be the *meta-hypothesis* that the CES import allocation model becomes less significantly rejected against the CRESH model if the number of trade partners is reduced. In other words, we would expect the cumulative densities corresponding to the C-statistic (2.2) to become smaller in that case.

If the meta hypothesis were to prove true, it would imply that for an international linkage model with relatively few partners the CES model would be sufficient in order to give an adequate description of the price effects on the bilateral import flows. A more elaborate model such as the CRESH import allocation model would then only be necessary with an increasing number of trade partners.

9.4.1. AN ANALYTICAL EXAMPLE

The starting point for this example is to assume that some concept of elasticity of substitution *(ES)* may be considered as a measure of the physical substitution possibilities between the goods supplied by any two trade partners. Starting from a model with n trade partners we assume that this model is reduced to a model with $n-1$ trade partners, obtained by "merging" two different trade partners. We will then assume that the *ES* involving this merged trade partner are approximately equal to some weighted average of the *ES* involving the two merged trade partners individually, with weights depending on the import share of each of these two trade partners. We therefore assume that the physical substitution possibilities between the goods supplied by the merged partner and any other partner are an average of those between this other partner and the two merged partners separately We will then show that it is likely that the variability of the *ES* in the case with $n-1$ partners is smaller than with n partners. *A fortiori*, an assumption of equal *ES* - the case of zero variability - such as in the CES model becomes less invalid if the number of trade partners is reduced.

Let $E_{ih} = E_{hi}$ be the *ES* between the goods supplied by partners i and h on a particular import market, where for convenience it has been assumed that the *ES* are symmetric. The value shares of partners i and h in total imports at a certain point in time will be denoted by $\bar{w}_i$ and $\bar{w}_h$ respectively. To distinguish between *ES* in the model with n partners and in the model with $n-1$ partners, those for the former will be denoted by E_{ih} and those for the latter by $\tilde{E}_{ih}$.

If we can ascribe a mean and a variance to the *ES* in the two models, their variability may be compared in terms of their *variances*. Let us suppose without loss of generality that partners number $n-1$ and n are merged in the model with n partners in order to obtain the model with $n-1$ partners. If we compare the variability of *ES* between the two models, two kinds of *ES* should be left out of consideration. The first are the "own" *ES* or E_{ii} and $\tilde{E}_{ii}$ for all i, because they do not convey information on the substitution *between* partners directly. The second are the *ES* between partners

$n-1$ and n in the model with n partners or $E_{n-1,n} = E_{n,n-1}$. They have no analogue in the model with $n-1$ partners and are therefore superfluous in the calculations of mean and variance in view of comparability with the model with $n-1$ partners.

Therefore, the calculations of the mean and variance for the model with n partners should include all E_{ih} only for $i \neq h = 1, \ldots, n$, while excluding $E_{n-1,n} = E_{n,n-1}$. One way to describe mean and variance is to assume that the *ES* belong to a discrete probability distribution, with each *ES* having a certain probability, defined as a function of the shares. This approach will then take into account the importance of each partner on the import market, given the import shares. Because we exclude some E_{ih}, we will redefine the shares such that the probabilities of the distribution add up to one. To that order, define the modified import share w_i as

$$(4.1) \qquad w_i = \bar{w}_i \left[1 - \Sigma_{h=1}^{n} \bar{w}_h^2 - 2\, \bar{w}_{n-1}\, \bar{w}_n \right]^{-1/2}, \qquad i = 1, \ldots, n.$$

The probability associated with each of the "allowed" E_{ih} may then be defined as $w_i w_h$, and it may be seen that these probabilities add up to one as follows

$$(4.2) \qquad \Sigma_{i=1}^{n-1} \Sigma_{h\neq i}^{n-1} w_i w_h + w_n \Sigma_{h=1}^{n-2} w_h + w_n \Sigma_{i=1}^{n-2} w_i$$

$$= \Sigma_{i=1}^{n} \Sigma_{h=1}^{n} w_i w_h - \Sigma_{i=1}^{n} w_i^2 - 2\, w_{n-1}\, w_n$$

$$= 1.$$

Using the modified shares w_i, we obtain the mean μ_n (not to be confused with the import quantity index μ) of the model with n partners as

$$(4.3) \qquad \mu_n = \Sigma_{i=1}^{n-1} \Sigma_{h\neq i}^{n-1} w_i w_h E_{ih} + 2 w_n \Sigma_{h=1}^{n-2} w_h E_{nh},$$

while the variance σ_n^2 may be calculated as

(4.4) $$\sigma_n^2 = \Sigma_{i=1}^{n-1} \Sigma_{h\neq i}^{n-1} w_i w_h (E_{ih} - \mu_n)^2 + 2w_n \Sigma_{h=1}^{n-2} w_h (E_{nh} - \mu_n)^2 .$$

Next we consider the model with *n-1* partners, whose ES are indicated by $\tilde{E}_{ih}$. Above we already argued that it would be reasonable to assume that the *ES* involving the merged trade partner would be approximately equal to a weighted average of the corresponding *ES* of each merged partner individually. Therefore $\tilde{E}_{n-1,h} = \tilde{E}_{h,n-1}$ would be a weighted average of $E_{n-1,h} = E_{h,n-1}$ and $E_{nh} = E_{hn}$, with as weights the (modified) normalized imports shares $\bar{w}_{n-1}(w_{n-1})$ and $\bar{w}_n(w_n)$

(4.5) $$\tilde{E}_{n-1,h} \approx (\bar{w}_{n-1} E_{n-1,h} + \bar{w}_n E_{nh})/(\bar{w}_{n-1} + \bar{w}_n)$$

$$= (w_{n-1} E_{n-1,h} + w_n E_{nh})/(w_{n-1} + w_n), \quad \text{all } h < n-1.$$

For the other *ES* of the model with *n-1* partners we introduce the following *ceteris paribus* assumption

(4.6) $$\tilde{E}_{ih} \approx E_{ih}, \qquad i,h = 1, \ldots, n-2, \quad i \neq h.$$

From assumptions (4.5) and (4.6) we are now able to calculate the mean μ_{n-1} of the model with *n-1* partners as being approximately equal to the mean μ_n of the model with *n* partners (where it should be realized that the import share of the merged trade partner equals $\bar{w}_{n-1} + \bar{w}_n$, or $w_{n-1} + w_n$, if it is modified).

(4.7) $$\mu_{n-1} = \Sigma_{i=1}^{n-2} \Sigma_{h\neq i}^{n-2} w_i w_h \tilde{E}_{ih} + 2(w_{n-1} + w_n) \Sigma_{h=1}^{n-2} w_h \tilde{E}_{n-1,h}$$

$$\approx \Sigma_{i=1}^{n-2} \Sigma_{h\neq i}^{n-2} w_i w_h E_{ih} + 2 \Sigma_{h=1}^{n-2} w_h (w_{n-1} E_{n-1,h} + w_n E_{nh})$$

$$= \Sigma_{i=1}^{n-1} \Sigma_{h\neq i}^{n-1} w_i w_h E_{ih} + 2 w_n \Sigma_{h=1}^{n-2} w_h E_{nh}$$

$$= \mu_n.$$

Using this result, and again (4.5) and (4.6) the difference $\sigma_n^2 - \sigma_{n-1}^2$ between the variances of the two models may after some calculations be seen to be nonnegative as follows

$$(4.8) \qquad \sigma_n^2 - \sigma_{n-1}^2 =$$

$$\Sigma_{i=1}^{n-1} \Sigma_{h\neq i}^{n-1} w_i w_h (E_{ih} - \mu_n)^2 + 2w_n \Sigma_{h=1}^{n-2} w_h (E_{nh} - \mu_n)^2$$

$$- [\Sigma_{i=1}^{n-2} \Sigma_{h\neq i}^{n-2} w_i w_h (\tilde{E}_{ih} - \mu_{n-1})^2$$

$$+ 2(w_{n-1} + w_n) \Sigma_{h=1}^{n-2} w_h (\tilde{E}_{n-1,h} - \mu_{n-1})^2]$$

$$\approx 2w_{n-1} \Sigma_{h=1}^{n-2} w_h (E_{n-1,h} - \mu_n)^2 + 2w_n \Sigma_{h=1}^{n-2} w_h (E_{nh} - \mu_n)^2$$

$$- 2(w_{n-1} + w_n) \Sigma_{h=1}^{n-2} w_h [(w_{n-1} E_{n-1,h} + w_n E_{nh})/(w_{n-1} + w_n) - \mu_n]^2$$

$$= 2 w_n \cdot w_{n-1}/(w_{n-1} + w_n) \Sigma_{h=1}^{n-2} w_h (E_{n-1,h} - E_{nh})^2 \geqslant 0.$$

The interpretation of (4.8) is clear : the variability, as measured by the variances, of the *ES* in the model with n partners is approximately at least as great as in the model with $n-1$ partners. This conclusion is of course subject to a number of abstractions made in order to derive the result, but it gives at least an analytical illustration of the intuitive expectation that the variability of the *ES* is influenced by the number of partners of the model. *A fortiori*, the results of a test of the CES model will also undergo this influence, and we are led to the *ex ante* expectation or meta-hypothesis that the CES model will be less significantly rejected if the number of trade partners in the model decreases, because the more general model then becomes closer to the CES model because the variability of its *ES* decreases. The empirical verification of this meta-hypothesis will be carried out in subsection 9.4.3.

9.4.2. TEST PROCEDURE

The test procedure runs as follows. For each importing country we estimate the CES import allocation model and the CRESH model for a given set of model characteristics with, say, n trade partners. From these two estimations per importing country we calculate the cumulative density corresponding to the C-statistic (2.2). Next we "merge" two of the trade partners and, keeping the other model characteristics fixed, we estimate the resulting CES and CRESH import allocation models for $n-1$ trade partners, which gives us a second cumulative density corresponding to the C-statistic (2.2). This procedure is repeated until the number of trade partners is reduced to three [4)]. On the resulting series of cumulative densities per importing country we may then perform a test of the meta-hypothesis that this series is decreasing if the number of trade partners is reduced.

This test procedure imposes two problems. The first is the choice of the two trade partners which should be merged in each step, and the second is which test we should perform to verify our meta-hypothesis.

The choice of the two trade partners to be merged will be determined as follows. We know that the CES model implies that all a_i coefficients of model (6.3.1) are equal. If we have (asymptotic) estimates for the variances and covariances of these coefficients, we may determine which of any pair of two coefficients is closest in a statistical sense. We propose to merge then the two partners whose corresponding a_i coefficients are closest in a statistical sense. Under a *ceteris paribus* assumption we create in this way the largest possible inequality between the a_i coefficients of the merged import allocation model, and therefore we expect *a priori* to generate the largest possible cumulative density. This implies that we reduce as far as possible the possibility that, if we reduce the number of trade partners by one, the cumulative density decreases. In other words, this practice obstructs as much as possible the creation of a series of cumulative densities which would be in line with our meta-hypothesis. If the meta-hypothesis nevertheless still cannot be rejected, this enforces the evidence in favour of the meta-hypothesis.

The pair of a_i coefficients which is closest in a statistical sense is determined as follows. Let $var(a_i)$ denote an (asymptotic) estimate of the variance of coefficient a_i, and $cov(a_i, a_k)$ a similar estimate of the corresponding covariance between coefficients a_i and a_k. Then the estimated variance of the difference between the coefficients a_i and a_k will equal

$$(4.9) \qquad var(a_i - a_k) = var(a_i) + var(a_k) - 2cov(a_i, a_k).$$

The difference $a_i - a_k$ is closest to zero for those two partners i and k for which the distance of $a_i - a_k$ to zero in terms of standard errors is smallest in absolute value

$$(4.10) \qquad \min_{\substack{i,k \\ i \neq k}} \frac{|(a_i - a_k) - 0|}{[var(a_i - a_k)]^{1/2}},$$

with $var(a_i - a_k)$ calculated from (4.9).

The second problem concerning the test procedure was the choice of the test to be performed in order to test the meta-hypothesis. Let $G_n, \ldots, G_3$ be the series of cumulative densities corresponding to the C-statistics of estimation of the CES and CRESH import allocation model for a given importer as the number of partners decreases from n to 3. Our expectation is that the series $G_n, \ldots, G_3$ is decreasing or $G_n > G_{n-1} > \ldots > G_3$. This is, however, not an operational meta-hypothesis. Instead we will reverse the null hypothesis and the alternative hypothesis, and posit

META-HYPOTHESIS 4.1 : The order of $G_n, \ldots, G_3$ is random.

The alternative hypothesis is then that the series $G_n, \ldots, G_3$ is decreasing.

This formulation of the meta-hypothesis leads to meaningful statistical tests. Because the measurement scale of $G_n, \ldots, G_3$ is at least ordinal, at least three nonparametric tests are possible in order to test Meta-Hypothesis 4.1. The first is the *trend test* of COX and STUARD [1955] , the other two are tests based on *rank correlation, viz.* Spearman's rank correlation coefficient or Kendall's rank correlation coefficient [5]. The last two tests should then be interpreted as tests of randomness. The first test, when applied to random variables which are known to be normally distributed, has an asymptotic relative efficiency [6] of about .79 with respect to both the last two tests [7], and therefore seems to be less useful, given the fact that our sample is small. The Spearman and Kendall rank correlation coefficients, in their turn, are known to have an asymptotic relative efficiency of about .91 with respect to the best parametric test, the Pearson correlation coefficient [8]. Because of this property we will only use the Spearman rank correlation coefficient, as it is easier to calculate.

Let $r(p) = n+1-p$ be the rank associated with a number of partners p (the maximum of p, or n gets rank 1), while $r(G_p)$ is the rank of G_p from the series of cumulative densities $G_n, \ldots, G_3$ (the largest G_p gets rank 1). If we define d_p as $r(p) - r(G_p)$, Spearman's rank correlation coefficient ρ may be obtained from the formula

$$(4.11) \qquad \rho = 1 - \frac{6\ \Sigma_{p=3}^{n}\ d_p^2}{(n-2)^3 - (n-2)} ,$$

which may be seen to be equal to the Pearson correlation coefficient between the ranks $r(p)$ and $r(G_p)$, *cfr.* SIEGEL (1956, pp. 203-204).

The value of the ρ thus obtained may be compared with the critical value of the distribution of ρ under the null hypothesis at a level of significance α. Call this critical value r_α, then Meta-Hypothesis 4.1 will be rejected if $\rho \geqslant r_\alpha$, and in that case we must conclude that a larger number of trading partners indeed rejects the CES import allocation model more firmly against the CRESH model, or that the assumption of equal elasticities of substitution is less valid in that case. Note that this is a one-tailed test because we exclude, through the alternative hypothesis, the possibility that the series $G_n, \ldots, G_3$ is increasing. In that case one would test whether $-\rho \geqslant r_\alpha$.

9.4.3. TEST RESULTS

The characteristics of the starting models with *n* partners were the following :

- import allocation model
- import allocation of aggregate trade T = A + E + Q + K + C
- partner countries (excluding importing country) : Belgium, Denmark, West-Germany, France, Ireland, Italy, Netherlands, UK, USA, Japan, Rest of the World (ROW)
- Importing countries : idem, excluding ROW
- CRESH approximation : Model III
- dynamic models with trends
- starting form of the covariance matrix : matrix (8.3.1).

As in the previous section, we have chosen Model III and the starting form of the covariance matrix on the basis of the empirical evidence of Chapter 8. The experiments, which required the estimation of 80 pairs of CES and CRESH import allocation models, were only performed for *aggregate trade*.

The resulting cumulative densities and Spearman rank correlation coefficients ρ are presented in table 4.1. For Belgium, West-Germany, Ireland, the UK, the USA and Japan Meta-Hypothesis 4.1 is rejected, in favour of the alternative hypothesis of positive correlation, at a significance level of 5 % if we compare ρ to $r_{.05}$. For 4 out of the 10 importing countries the meta-hypothesis cannot be rejected. Because all the rank correlations are *positive*, our initial meta-hypothesis that the CES import allocation model is less firmly rejected against the CRESH model if the number of partners decreases is generally confirmed, and this confirmation is significant in a majority of cases.

Number of partners	Importer									
	Belgium	Denmark	West-Germany	France	Ireland	Italy	Nether-lands	UK	USA	Japan
10	–[a]	–[a]	99.9981	100.0000	94.1883	96.1065	79.4515	100.0000	99.9998	99.9829
9	99.9903	99.8921	99.9545	95.1500	92.0121	79.6405	94.1089	100.0000	99.3785	99.9647
8	99.2465	–[a]	99.7790	99.2485	99.6917	98.3490	96.2941	99.9999	99.6365	94.8557
7	99.9229	99.9259	91.1388	98.7361	83.0610	55.7739	86.4718	99.9996	97.3891	95.9806
6	99.5335	99.6836	95.7300	98.8102	59.2737	57.9295	64.3323	73.7521	95.0842	83.3703
5	96.6139	99.9789	86.9759	99.7134	65.9863	80.8186	22.2396	41.1503	63.0181	60.0774
4	84.0390	99.3532	–[a]	96.7847	32.5560	66.4817	63.6645	22.7099	82.8960	56.1219
3	99.0889	99.6701	–[a]	75.2916	54.5098	74.0326	82.9162	69.2725	80.8973	18.9662
ρ	.786	.543	.943	.476	.881	.429	.500	.923	.905	.976
$r_{.05}$	.714	.829	.829	.643	.643	.643	.643	.643	.643	.643

[a] CRESH model not converged after 120 iterations

Table 4.1 : Cumulative densities (%) and Spearman rank correlation coefficients ρ *starting from 10 trade partners (aggregate trade)*

Additionally we may perform a test that encompasses at the same time the results for all importing countries. This is done as follows. Calculate, for any given level of significance α and a given number of trade partners $p = 3, \ldots, n$, the percentage of import allocation models for which the CES model is rejected against the CRESH model at that level of significance. Next calculate the Spearman rank correlation coefficient for the resulting series of percentages as the number of trade partners decreases. A value of the Spearman rank correlation coefficient greater than or equal to the critical value corresponding to a given level of significance then indicates *global* rejection of Meta-Hypothesis 4.1 (at least for our given sample of import allocation models). The results for this test are given in table 4.2, and clearly indicate a global rejection of Meta-Hypothesis 4.1 in favour of a positive rank correlation for all three displayed levels of significance. The results from the analytical example of subsection 9.4.1 are therefore confirmed empirically on the basis of a global test.

Number of partners p	Level of significance α		
	10 %	5 %	1 %
10	87.5	75	62.5
9	90	70	60
8	100	88.9	66.7
7	70	60	30
6	50	50	20
5	30	30	20
4	22.2	22.2	11.1
3	22.2	22.2	22.2
ρ	.899	.923	.780
$r_{.05}$	.643	.643	.643

Table 4.2 : Percentage of rejections of the CES model at a level of significance α, given a number of trade partners p, and Spearman rank correlation coefficients

9.5. CLASSIFICATION OF GOODS

The last tests which we will perform concern the influence of the classification of goods on the outcome of a test of the CES import allocation model against the CRESH model. We presented arguments on this influence in subsection 1.5.3. It was argued there, in terms of elasticities of substitution, that an increase in the detail of the classification of goods could *a priori* be expected to exert two, opposite, influences on the equality of elasticities of substitution. It was posited that the concomitant increase of the *product homogeneity* would not only increase the substitution possibilities and therefore the elasticities of substitution, but also make the elasticities of substitution converge. An adverse effect, however, is caused by the fact that an increased degree of detail of the classification entails more *specialization* in certain products among the supplying countries. This specialization effect will induce the elasticities of substitution to diverge as the classification of goods becomes more detailed. The combined result for the equality of elasticities of substitution may therefore be mixed, and we are not led to any *a priori* meta-hypothesis about which effect will dominate.

As in the previous section, we may transpose the above discussion into the framework of testing the CES import allocation model against the CRESH model. Again this may be done through interpretation of the CES model as the model in which different types of elasticities of substitution are equal. An increase in the inequality of the elasticities of substitution is then translated as an increase in the cumulative density that corresponds to the C-statistic (2.2) that may be calculated for the test of the CES versus the CRESH model. An increased cumulative density implies rejection of the hypothesis that all elasticities of substitution are equal at a lower level of significance.

If the test results show the predominance of either of the two effects, this has important implications for empirical modelbuilding. If, for instance, the effect of product homogeneity prevails, the conclusion of the tests which we may draw is that an increased degree of detail of the classification of goods requires import allocation models which are less elaborate in their price effects than conversely. A more elaborate model like the CRESH import allocation model would then only be required for classifications with a low degree of detail, such as for aggregate trade. Of course, if the specialization effect is predominant, the reasoning should be inverted : in that case the CES model suffices for classifications of low degree of detail, but more elaborate models such as the CRESH model are required as soon as the degree of detail increases. Given the results of the previous section, the choice between the CES model and, say, the CRESH model should however additionally be determined taking the number of trade partners into account.

9.5.1. TEST PROCEDURE

The test procedure is as follows. Keeping the model characteristics fixed except for the classification of goods, we estimate per importing country the 31 pairs of individual CES and CRESH import allocation models which the data allow us to estimate. The number 31 arises from the fact that we distinguish 5 individual categories of trade. This gives $2^5 - 1 = 31$ possible combinations. As we saw in table 8.2.1, these 31 individual import allocation models may be combined into 52 different composite import allocation models, each containing between 1 and 5 aggregates of categories of goods. Therefore we may calculate for each of the 52 different composite import allocation models the C-statistic (2.1) for the test of the CES import allocation model against the CRESH model. The effect of an increased degree of detail may then be analyzed by comparing the cumulative density corresponding to the C-statistic of a composite model with g aggregates, $g = 1, \ldots, 5$, with the cumulative density corresponding to the C-statistic of a composite model with $g+i$ aggregates, $g+i \leq 5$, whose classification is *comparable* with that of the model with g aggregates according to Definition

1.5.1. If the second cumulative density is higher, the specialization effect prevails, otherwise the effect of product homogeneity is predominant. The problem with this practice is that we create a number of "chains" of 5 cumulative densities in this way which is far too large to analyze. Therefore we apply the following method. For each category of composite import allocation models containing g aggregates we calculate the simple average of the C-statistics in that category (which may be done because they all follow per category the same chi-square distribution), and next we calculate the cumulative density corresponding to this average C-statistic. In this way we obtain per importing country 5 cumulative densities G_g as the number of aggregates g contained in the composite models increases from 1 to 5. Under the assumption that the "average" classifications corresponding to two cumulative densities associated with a different number of aggregates are comparable, we obtain in this way a measure of the influence of the degree of detail on the outcome of the test of the CES versus the CRESH import allocation model. We even may posit a meta-hypothesis similar to Meta-Hypothesis 4.1 stating that the order of the cumulative densities $G_1, \ldots, G_5$ is random, and calculate Spearman's rank correlation coefficients to test this hypothesis. If the meta-hypothesis is not rejected at a given level of significance, there is no effect that prevails. If it is rejected, one of the effects is apparently significantly stronger than the other.

9.5.2. TEST RESULTS

The estimates for the 31 individual import allocation models were performed with the following model characteristics :

- import allocation model
- classification of goods : all 31 possible non-empty subsets to be formed from the 5 categories A, E, Q, K and C

- partner countries (excluding importing country) : West-Germany, France, Italy, the Netherlands, UK, USA, Japan, Rest of the World (ROW)
- importing countries : idem, excluding ROW
- CRESH approximation : Model III
- dynamic models with trends
- starting form of the covariance matrix : matrix (8.3.1)

As in the previous section we again have chosen Model III and the starting form of the covariance matrix on the basis of the empirical evidence of Chapter 8. The 31 possible individual import allocation models range from models for the individual categories of goods A, E, Q, K and C to aggregate trade A + E + Q + K + C.

In table 5.1 we first present for a selected sample of the 31 pairs of estimations of individual CES and CRESH import allocation models the cumulative densities corresponding to the C-statistics that may be calculated for each pair. For agricultural goods and energy goods the CES model is rejected twice and once respectively for each category at a level of significance of 5 %. This might be due to the relative homogeneity of these product groupings compared to others, as may be seen from Appendix 7.A.

Type of aggregate	Importer						
	West-Germany	France	Italy	Nether-lands	UK	US	Japan
A	92.2862	68.5396	80.9614	98.1884	39.2661	93.5081	96.5085
E	94.3750	87.0578	97.8216	84.4966	84.9876	40.3033	24.7801
Q	80.1135	97.0149	98.8584	99.9988	91.4851	99.1225	99.2581
K	91.5749	99.9646	92.4890	99.8423	99.4466	70.2966	75.5255
C	93.5933	41.4804	29.9953	99.3203	95.9415	99.9699	85.7195
Q+K+C	32.9197	89.8411	98.7250	82.1619	99.2223	70.8235	99.8672
A+E+Q+K+C	98.9213	99.2599	80.8602	68.8627	89.7184	94.8383	97.4095

Table 5.1 : Cumulative densities (%) for individual import allocation models of seven importing countries for seven selected aggregates of goods

For intermediate goods and equipment goods we may expect a strong effect of specialization : for intermediate goods this largely follows from the availability of natural resources, while for equipment goods the industrial specialization plays a role. It is therefore not surprising that the CES model is rejected five times for intermediate goods and three times for equipment goods. This tendency is also present for the aggregate Q+K+C of manufacturing products. Because we have seven trading partners, the results for aggregate trade may be compared to those for seven trade partners in table 4.2. At a significance level of 10 %, this table indicates for 7 partners a rejection of the CES import allocation model in 70 % of all cases. For table 5.1 this percentage is 4/7 x 100 = 57 %. At a level of significance of 5 % these percentages are, respectively, 60 % and 43 %, and for a level of significance of 1 %, respectively 30 % and 14 %. The results for aggregate trade in table 5.1 are therefore only broadly in line with those of table 4.2, the absolute level of the percentage of rejections being lower.

Next we present in table 5.2 the cumulative densities G_g that correspond to the average C-statistics per group of composite import allocation models containing a specific number of aggregates g. If there is only one aggregate or if there are 5 aggregates, there is only one composite model, as we know from table 8.2.1. The first line of table 5.2 therefore corresponds to the last line of table 5.1. The meta hypothesis that the order of the cumulative densities is random as the number of aggregates increases is rejected at a significance level of 5 % for West-Germany, France, Italy, the Netherlands, the UK and the USA in favour of a positive influence on the cumulative densities. For Japan, the order indeed seems to be random. This evidence therefore points significantly for 6 out of 7 countries to a predominance of the *specialization effect*. An increase in the degree of detail of a composite import allocation model will therefore reject the CES model more significantly against the CRESH model. Interpreted in terms of elasticities of substitution : a higher degree of detail implies more inequality of the elasticities of substitution.

Number of aggregates g	Importer						
	West-Germany	France	Italy	Nether-lands	UK	US	Japan
1	98.9213	99.2599	80.8602	68.8627	89.7184	94.8383	97.4095
2	97.7814	99.3932	96.7748	98.7798	99.1892	99.5737	99.8873
3	99.0823	99.6712	99.0199	99.9891	99.6135	99.9004	99.9121
4	99.5380	99.8424	99.5546	99.9999	99.7345	99.9650	99.7973
5	99.6696	99.9208	99.6707	100.0000	99.7621	99.9845	99.1772
ρ	.900	1.000	1.000	1.000	1.000	1.000	0.100
$r_{.05}$	.900	.900	.900	.900	.900	.900	.900

Table 5.2 : Cumulative densities (%) G_g corresponding to the average C-statistic of composite models containing g aggregates for seven importing countries, and Spearman rank correlation coefficients

To see if the specialization effect has a significant effect if we take all the importing countries of table 5.2 together, we may calculate, per level of significance α, the percentage of models per number of aggregates g that are rejected at this level of significance. These results, which are comparable to those of table 4.2, are presented in table 5.3. The only difference with table 4.2 is that we now look at other levels of significance because the cumulative densities are so close to 100 %. For the significance levels 1 % and .5 % the specialization effect is significantly present according to the Spearman rank correlation coefficient, at a level of significance of 5 %. When the level of significance is .1 % the positive effect of the specialization is still very strong, and almost significant.

Number of aggregates g	Level of significance α		
	1 %	.5 %	.1 %
1	14	0	0
2	57	29	0
3	100	71	43
4	100	100	29
5	100	86	43
ρ	.900	.900	.800
$r_{.05}$	.900	.900	.900

Table 5.3 : Percentage of rejections of the CES model at a level of significance α given a number of aggregates g, and Spearman rank correlation coefficients

The *conclusion* of this section is therefore that on the basis of our empirical evidence elasticities of substitution tend to diverge if the degree of detail of the classification of goods increases. If one is not satisfied with this interpretation of the fact that the CES import allocation model is rejected more firmly against the CRESH model with an increasing degree of detail, the empirical implication that the CES model is only a sufficient description of the relative price effects for classifications of goods which have a relatively low degree of detail, such as aggregate trade may suffice. Otherwise a more elaborate model, such as the CRESH import allocation model, should be employed.

9.6. SUMMARY AND CONCLUDING REMARKS

In this chapter, three hypotheses have been tested : 1) is the aggregator function weakly separable in imports and domestic factors ?, 2) does the number of trade partners in an import allocation model influence the inequality of elasticities of substitution ?, and 3) does the classification of goods in an import allocation model influence the inequality of elasticities of substitution ?

The evidence relating to the *first* hypothesis was only partial in the sense that lack of data on intermediate inputs prevented the use of a complete aggregator function. The tests were performed for six countries and composite total allocation models containing one, two or three aggregates of goods. For four of the six countries the hypothesis of weak separability was rejected for all three levels of aggregation at a significance level of 1 %. For one of the other two countries the hypothesis was rejected for the three levels of aggregation at a level of significance of 10 % while for the last country there was rejection for two of the levels of aggregation at a significance level of 5 %. Given the particular model and data with which the hypothesis was tested, we must therefore conclude that the hypothesis of weak separability of the aggregator function in imports and domestic factors in general is not realistic at all the levels of aggregation that were considered.

The implications which emerge upon the basis of our evidence for the first hypothesis for empirical international linkage modelling are quite drastic : the major result is that the weak separability hypothesis, which is needed in order to be allowed to work with an import allocation model, seems to be rejected for anything but small international linkage models, say with 8 countries or less [9)]. In actual practice, however, the circumstances may force the modelbuilder to disregard the consequences which this result would entail. The sample period may be too small, for instance, such that the inclusion of domestic variables causes a loss of degrees of freedom that makes estimation impossible. Moreover, information on domestic variables may be missing as in our own experience or in the case where the linkage part of the international linkage model is constructed independently of the national models [10]. From a practical point of view one might therefore neglect the fact that the weak separability hypothesis might not be true. As long as one is aware of this fact this is not a serious error, but it should be taken into account for the analysis of any results which are based on it.

For the second and third hypotheses, a specific measure of inequality of elasticities of substitution was used. It was defined as the level of significance at which the CES import allocation model would be rejected against the CRESH import allocation model. The lower this level of significance (or the higher the corresponding cumulative density), the more unequal the elasticities of substitution were assumed to be. This interpretation is possible because the CES model is a special, nested, case of the CRESH model when all elasticities of substitution (Allen partial Elasticity of Substitution, Direct Elasticity of Substitution, Shadow Elasticity of Substitution) are assumed to be equal. The advantage of this method of testing is that it does not require one to specify *which* elasticities of substitution are equal. It therefore prevents one having to make a choice among the possible alternatives.

The *second* hypothesis was tested on aggregate trade for ten importing countries. All ten countries showed the behaviour that an increase of the number of trade partners in the import allocation models increased the inequality between the elasticities of substitution among the trade partners, while the effect was significant in six countries. In other words, an increase in the number of trade partners rejected the CES import allocation model more firmly against the CRESH model for these countries. When we performed an aggregate test for all ten countries together, this behaviour was confirmed as being significant. For actual modelbuilding this implies that relatively simple import allocation models such as the CES model suffice only when the number of trade partners is small, say seven or smaller. Otherwise there is a need for a more elaborate model such as the proposed CRESH model.

The *third* hypothesis used the same notion of inequality of elasticities of substitution as the second. *A priori* we distinguished two effects that could possibly influence the inequality of the elasticities of substitution. The first was the effect of *product homogeneity*. An incrased product homogeneity, corresponding to an increased degree of detail of the classification of goods, was assumed to reduce the inequality between the elasticities of substitution. An opposite influence with an increased degree of detail was taken to come from the effect of *specialization* that takes place in that case. From the sample, which included seven importing countries and per importing country 52 classifications of goods at 5 levels of aggregation, the effect of specialization was found to be significantly present for six of the seven countries. Also an aggregate test for all seven importing countries showed that the CES model was more firmly rejected against the CRESH model when the degree of detail was increased. On the basis of this evidence, the CES model is therefore only an adequate model for the description of bilateral trade flows at a low degree of detail such as for aggregate trade. A more detailed classification of goods requires more complex import allocation models such as the CRESH model.

The conclusions of this chapter regarding the appropriateness of the CES import allocation model have to be drawn conditionally upon the strong assumption of weak separability of the aggregator function in imports and domestic factors, which we showed to be rejected in a majority of cases. If we accept the weak separability assumption, however, we see that the CES model, and with it an assumption of equal elasticities of substitution, is only justified for import allocation models with a small number of trade partners and a relatively low degree of detail, such as aggregate trade.

APPENDIX 9.A : A SMALL-SAMPLE CORRECTION FOR THE LIKELIHOOD RATIO TEST

DERIVATION

In statistical testing, notably for allocation models, one often has to rely on asymptotic distributions for the test statistics. An example of this practice was the C-statistic (2.2), which is asymptotically distributed as chi-square with degrees of freedom equal to the number of constraints that are being tested. All the test results presented as far in this chapter were based on this asymptotic property. The major drawback if one applies such an asymptotic result to small samples is that there may be a considerable bias in the outcome of the tests. The desirable cure for this deficiency would of course be to use a distribution which is also valid for small samples, or otherwise to apply at least a small-sample correction to the test statistic which is used. Unfortunately the availability of these methods depends strongly on the kind of model one uses, and on the restrictions one wishes to test. The purpose of this appendix is to derive an approximative small-sample correction for our likelihood ratio test. The correction is approximative because we cannot derive the asymptotic expansion from which one usually may distil the small-sample correction.

Empirical evidence on the small-sample bias of asymptotic tests has been provided for the Rotterdam model by LAITINEN (1978) and MEISNER (1979). Laitinen tested homogeneity and Meisner symmetry. They both found on the basis of Monte Carlo experiments that with a given sample size there was a bias towards rejection that increased with the number of goods that were distinguished. The latter is not surprising : as the sample size is fixed and as the number of parameters to be estimated in the Rotterdam model increases about quadratically with the number of goods, one may expect a considerable loss of degrees of freedom and consequently an increasing bias when the number of goods becomes larger. Moreover, Laitinen was also able to derive the small-sample distribution for his test statistic and was therefore able to test correctly. He could, however, only derive the small-sample distribution because of the special form in which the homogeneity tests may be cast. For the testing of symmetry, Meisner did not derive a small-sample distribution, which seems a hard task because the symmetry conditions do not fit into the Laitinen framework. These two examples show how important it is to have at least a small-sample correction of the test statistic.

The basis for our approximative small-sample correction is the multivariate linear model of ANDERSON (1958, Ch. 8). Let $y_1, \ldots, y_T$ be a set of T observations on the $n\text{x}1$ vector y, y_t being drawn from $N(Bx_t, \Sigma)$. The $q\text{x}1$ vectors x_t are known, and the symmetric $n\text{x}n$ matrix Σ and the $n\text{x}q$ matrix B are unknown. Σ and B are estimated by the method of maximum likelihood. We assume that $T \geqslant n+q$ and the rank of $X = [x_1, \ldots, x_T]$ is q. Suppose we partition $B = [B_1\ B_2]$ such that B_1 has q_1 columns and B_2 has q_2 columns. Anderson then derives an asymptotic expansion for the distribution of a transformation of the likelihood ratio l for testing the hypothesis

$$H_o : B_1 = B_1^{\star}, \tag{A.1}$$

where $B_1^{\star}$ is a given matrix.

If we denote *"Pr"* for *"Probability"*, we may write the result of ANDERSON (1958, p. 208) as

$$\begin{aligned} Pr\,\{-\,2\,\tfrac{m}{T}\,ln\,l \leqslant z\} = {} & Pr\,\{\chi^2_{nq_1} \leqslant z\} \\ & + \frac{\gamma_1}{m^2}\,(Pr\,\{\chi^2_{nq_1+4} \leqslant z\} - Pr\,\{\chi^2_{nq_1} \leqslant z\}\,) \\ & + \frac{1}{m^4}\,[\,\gamma_2(Pr\,\{\chi^2_{nq_1+8} \leqslant z\} - Pr\,\{\chi^2_{nq_1} \leqslant z\} \\ & - \gamma_1^2(Pr\,\{\chi^2_{nq_1+4} \leqslant z\} - Pr\,\{\chi^2_{nq_1} \leqslant z\})] + O(T^{-6}), \end{aligned} \tag{A.2}$$

with $m = T - q_2 - \frac{1}{2}(n+q_1+1)$, $\gamma_1 = nq_1(n^2+q_1^2-5)/48$ and

$$\gamma_2 = \gamma_1^2/2 + nq_1\,[\,3n^4 + 3q_1^4 + 10n^2q_1^2 - 50(n^2 + q_1^2) + 159]/1920.$$

From (A.2) it is clear that as $T \to \infty$, the C-statistic $-2\ ln\ l$ is distributed as chi-square with nq_1 degrees of freedom. The number of restrictions per equation is q_1, therefore nq_1 is the total number of restrictions for the complete model.

If our model could be cast into the form of Anderson's model, we could directly apply (A.2) and we would have cumulative densities which would be correct up to an error of the order T^{-6}. Even if we were only to use the first term on the right-hand side of (A.2), the error would only be of the order T^{-2}. Anderson's model is however not of the form of our model III which we estimated in this chapter, as may be seen from equation (6.7.6). Whereas Anderson has the same explanatory variables, but different coefficients per equation, our model has opposite characteristics : we have the same coefficients for each equation but different explanatory variables.

Anderson's model may however be applied to the Rotterdam model, for instance. If we use only the first term on the right-hand side, (A.2) amounts to a small-sample correction of m/T to the value of the C-statistic (2.2). Let us apply this correction to an example, for instance the estimates of the Rotterdam model by BARTEN (1969). Barten used a sample of 30 observations $(T = 30)$, and his lopped model (with one equation deleted) consisted of 15 equations $(n = 15)$. With intercepts and no constraints imposed, each equation contained 18 coefficients $(q = 18)$ to be estimated. If we consider testing for homogeneity, we test one restriction per equation $(q_1 = 1,$ $q_2 = 17)$. Therefore $m/T = .15$. In this case the small-sample correction would therefore amount to 15 % of the actual value of the C-statistic. The value of Barten's C-statistic in this case therefore reduces from 436.5 to 65.6, *cfr.* BARTEN (1969, p. 67). As the 5 % significance level for χ^2_{15} is equal to 25.0, homogeneity is still rejected, but the bias has been strongly reduced.

We will next give an interpretation to the correction factor m/T in order to be able to apply it to our model. Multiply both denominator and numerator by n, the number of equations, to obtain

$$\text{(A.3)} \qquad \frac{mn}{nT} = \frac{nT - nq_2 - \frac{1}{2}n\,(n+q_1+1)}{nT}$$

$$= \frac{nT - nq - \frac{1}{2}n(n+1)}{2nT} + \frac{nT - nq_2 - \frac{1}{2}n(n+1)}{2nT}$$

where it should be remembered that $q = q_1 + q_2$. The numerator of the first term in (A.3) gives the degrees of freedom for *unrestricted* estimation of Anderson's model : the total number of observations is nT, the number of coefficients in the B matrix to be estimated equals nq, while for the symmetric matrix Σ one estimates $\frac{1}{2}n(n+1)$ elements. If one applies nq_1 restrictions, these may be added to the degrees of freedom. The numerator of the second term therefore gives the degrees of freedom for *restricted* estimation of Anderson's model. Equation (A.3) therefore gives as correction factor for the C-statistic *the average of two correction factors for degrees of freedom without and with restrictions respectively*. Therefore, if we use only the first term of (A.2), we may use this interpretation of Anderson's correction factor to calculate such a factor for other types of models, such as ours, or Anderson-type models with restrictions that do not fit in his framework (such as symmetry for the Rotterdam model). It should however be borne in mind that this extension of the use of Anderson's correction factor is highly speculative, and that any results based on it are therefore surrounded with a certain amount of uncertainty. This uncertainty should of course be compared to the bias that one is likely to obtain if one does not make any correction at all. We have chosen to present both results : the asymptotic results in the main body of this chapter, and the results based on the approximative correction factor in this appendix.

Before we present the results based on the use of the correction factor, we first define it explicitly for our model as :

$$\text{(A.4)} \qquad \psi = \frac{1}{2}\,\frac{gnT - q^{\star} - \frac{g}{2}n(n+1)}{gnT} + \frac{1}{2}\,\frac{gnT - q_2^{\star} - \frac{g}{2}n(n+1)}{gnT}$$

Here T is the same as with Anderson, and n is the number of equations per allocation model, but $q^{\star}$ now represents the total number of coefficients to be estimated for *all* equations, $q_2^{\star}$ equals $q^{\star}$ minus the total number of restrictions imposed on the coefficients, and g represents the number of allocation models that are estimated. Suppose we test the CES import allocation model against the CRESH import allocation model for $n+1$ partners and for g composite models in the framework of model III with a dynamic specification and including trend coefficients. Then $q^{\star} = 2(n+1)\ g$ $q_2^{\star} = 2(n+1)\ g - ng$, because the CES model implies ng restrictions on the a_i coefficient in (6.3.1). Then we find

$$\text{(A.5)} \qquad \psi = \frac{nT - \frac{1}{2}(n+2)^2}{nT} ,$$

which is independent of the number of composite import allocation models g. As long as we test the same kind of restrictions per composite model, this property is maintained. For example, for $T = 16$ and $n = 7$, (A.5) gives a correction factor of $\psi = .638$.

RESULTS

In tables A.1 - A.7 we have gathered the results of tables 3.1, 3.2, 4.1, 4.2, 5.1, 5.2 and 5.3 when calculated with the first term of (A.2), using (A.4) as correction factor m/T. Next to these results we have also recalculated the test statistics corresponding to the tests of significance in tables 8.4.2 and 9.5.2. each time when coefficients were fixed to zero in order to meet the second-order sufficient conditions. In table 8.4.2, the rejection of this constraint is no longer valid at a 5 % level of significance (after application of the small-sample correction) for Model II for West-Germany, all other rejections are maintained. For table 8.5.2 the only coefficients whose restriction induces a significant change become those for the import allocation model for consumer goods (C) for the Netherlands, that is only 2 out of 56 restricted coefficients.

Aggregate	Importer					
	Belgium	West-Germany	France	Italy	Nether-lands	UK
A	98.8792	96.0065	89.0848	7.9805	7.2916	19.2447
E	97.4885	86.9538	99.9966	96.0487	42.9331	83.0800
M	97.6119	78.1899	90.2162	39.6675	45.4075	99.5427
A+E	83.2407	99.2053	96.8207	34.8900	95.5423	13.6746
A+M	60.7158	16.9028	94.0073	79.6850	67.6483	99.1081
E+M	99.9864	99.4562	92.0191	57.1163	96.3342	99.9997
A+E+M	99.9669	99.9499	96.2361	80.0857	88.5220	99.9721

Table A.1 : Cumulative densities (%) for the weak separability hypothesis in seven individual final demand allocation models (with small-sample correction)

Number of aggregates	Importer					
	Belgium	West-Germany	France	Italy	Nether-lands	UK
1. A+E+M	99.9669	99.9499	96.2361	80.0857	88.5220	99.9721
2. A E+M	99.9983	99.8372	95.8739	21.0539	77.7177	99.9889
E A+M	93.5283	60.7705	99.9972	95.9456	53.5174	98.9878
M A+E	97.7507	98.8069	98.2738	27.4556	84.5403	95.4041
Average[a]	99.6507	97.4720	99.6722	61.6711	73.9505	99.5755
3. A E M	99.9653	97.3784	99.9954	65.4117	13.7383	97.0100

[a] Cumulative density corresponding to the average of the C-statistics of these three composite models

Table A.2 : Cumulative densities (%) for the weak separability hypothesis of five composite final demand allocation models (with small-sample correction)

Comparison of tables A.1 and A.2 with tables 3.1 and 3.2 shows that the decrease in cumulative density for the *weak separability* hypothesis brought about by the small-sample correction is more drastic for lower densities than for higher densities. This is logical because the chi-square distribution is fatter near the origin than further to the right where it approaches the x-axis. For aggregate trade A+E+M, the number of rejections at a 1 % level of significance reduces from five to three, while there remains one rejection at a level of 5 %. If we consider only the average for the composite models containing two aggregates, we see from table A.2 that instead of four countries, now only one country, Belgium, rejects weak separability at a level of significance of 1 % for all three composite models. For West-Germany, France and the UK this assertion only holds at a level of 5 %. Save for one exception, Italy and the Netherlands no longer show any rejection at 5 %. The overwhelming evidence from table 3.2 against weak separability is therefore now reduced to four of the six countries under consideration.

In tables A.3 and A.4 we present the results for the influence of the *number of trade partners* on the rejection of the CES model against the CRESH model, when we apply the small-sample correction. These tables should be compared to tables 4.1 and 4.2 of this chapter. If we compare the Spearman rank correlation coefficient ρ to its 5 % critical value $r_{.05}$, we note that Meta-Hypothesis 4.1 of no correlation is rejected against a positive correlation between rank and cumulative density for five countries : West-Germany, Ireland, the UK, USA and Japan. Compared to table 4.1, the hypothesis is therefore no longer rejected for Belgium, although Belgium has a positive, but insignificant, correlation, together with France and Italy. For two countries, Denmark and the Netherlands, the rank correlation now becomes negative but insignificant. Table A.4 gives the aggregate test for three levels of significance. Compared to table 4.2, the percentage of rejections for a given level of significance and number of trade partners is of course lower due to the small-sample correction. Nevertheless the Meta-Hypothesis of no correlation is rejected in favour of a positive correlation between number of trade partners and percentage of rejection for all three levels of significance. This result corresponds to the conclusions of table 4.2, therefore.

Number of partners	Importer									
	Belgium	Denmark	West-Germany	France	Ireland	Italy	Nether-lands	UK	US	Japan
10	-[a]	-[a]	99.0954	99.9276	61.0739	67.0010	36.7046	99.9945	99.7383	97.2875
9	98.7349	95.4708	97.1173	69.8528	62.0668	42.8792	67.0034	99.9955	88.9022	97.4800
8	90.7912	-[a]	95.3393	90.8046	94.3855	85.8856	78.2800	99.9545	93.8452	74.2143
7	98.2539	98.2956	70.8446	90.5598	58.2406	30.8178	63.0886	99.9308	85.5396	81.4253
6	96.1384	96.9962	81.1670	92.9527	37.9347	36.7732	42.4927	51.9290	82.7079	63.3962
5	88.7947	99.6597	72.3761	97.9271	48.2951	64.3508	13.4164	26.9098	45.4492	42.7212
4	71.9044	97.1829	-[a]	91.0503	23.1256	52.6133	49.8636	15.6841	70.4939	42.8253
3	97.0511	98.6235	-[a]	64.9544	44.6091	63.6234	73.4271	58.7290	71.1051	14.5918
ρ	.500	-.600	.829	.262	.786	.167	-.024	.833	.881	.929
$r_{.05}$	.714	.829	.829	.643	.643	.643	.643	.643	.643	.643

[a] CRESH model not converged after 120 iterations.

Table A.3 : Cumulative densities (%) and Spearman rank correlation coefficients ρ *starting from 10 trade partners (aggregate trade and with small-sample correction)*

Number of partners p	Level of significance α		
	10 %	5 %	1 %
10	62.5	62.5	50
9	50	50	10
8	66.7	22.2	11.1
7	40	30	10
6	30	20	0
5	20	20	10
4	22.2	11.1	0
3	22.2	22.2	0
ρ	.851	.774	.833
$r_{.05}$	.643	.643	.643

Table A.4. : Percentage of rejections of the CES model at a level of significance α, given a number of trade partners p, and Spearman rank correlation coefficients (with small-sample correction)

Finally we come to the effects of the application of the small-sample correction to the test results for the influence of the *classification of goods*. Table A.5, which is the equivalent of table 5.1, gives cumulative densities for seven selected aggregates of goods. For agricultural goods and energy goods, there is now no longer any rejection of the CES model at the level of 10 % or lower. As we argued before, this is possibly due to the product homogeneity of these two categories of goods. For intermediate goods, equipment goods and consumption goods, which are assumed to be less homogeneous product groupings, it is therefore not surprising to find four, three and two rejections, respectively, at a significance level of 10 %. Table A.6 is the equivalent of table 5.2, and gives the cumulative densities for different numbers of aggregates. In table 5.2 we found a significant positive correlation between the number of aggregates involved and the

Type of aggregate	Importer						
	West-Germany	France	Italy	Nether-lands	UK	US	Japan
A	73.0381	41.8755	55.5023	88.3262	19.2409	75.5508	82.8778
E	77.4696	63.9810	86.9923	60.2147	60.9110	19.8974	10.9019
Q	54.4412	84.3662	91.1124	99.8684	71.4916	92.3988	93.1224
K	71.6615	98.9182	73.4414	97.2971	94.2289	43.5942	45.8596
C	75.7339	20.6529	13.7336	93.4731	81.3211	99.0200	61.9707
Q+K+C	15.4033	68.5213	90.5110	57.0477	92.9263	44.1208	97.5653
A+E+Q+K+C	91.4061	93.1325	55.3744	42.1874	68.3093	78.5512	85.6058

Table A.5 : Cumulative densities (%) for individual import allocation models of seven importing countries for seven selected aggregates of goods (with small-sample correction)

Number of aggregates g	Importer						
	West-Germany	France	Italy	Nether-lands	UK	US	Japan
1	91.4061	93.1325	55.3744	42.1874	68.3093	78.5512	85.6058
2	80.0127	89.8213	75.8680	85.3022	88.1334	91.5708	95.9192
3	82.4365	89.2943	81.8835	98.1464	88.4111	94.1166	94.4803
4	83.3240	89.7797	83.5928	99.7856	87.0057	95.0103	88.5167
5	81.8433	90.1898	81.8701	99.9732	84.1846	95.3392	73.7126
ρ	-.300	-.300	.700	1.000	.100	1.000	-.400
$r_{.05}$	.900	.900	.900	.900	.900	.900	.900

Table A.6 : Cumulative densities (%) G_g corresponding to the average C-statistics of composite models containing g aggregates for seven importing countries, and Spearman rank correlation coefficients (with small-sample correction)

cumulative density for six of the seven importers, which we ascribed to the effect of *product specialization*. This result is strongly modified upon application of the small-sample correction : the specialization effect is only present for four countries, where significant for two of them. In each of the three other countries we find a negative correlation which is not significant, but points nevertheless to the effect of product homogeneity in some importing countries. Table 5.3 presented an aggregate test for significance levels of 1 %, .5 % and .1 %. Because the level of the cumulative densities has been generally reduced through the small-sample correction, these levels would produce rather meaningless results in the present circumstances. Therefore we have made an aggregate test with significance levels of 10 %, 5 % and 1 %, the results of which are presented in table A.7. Despite positive correlations in all three cases, the only significant case is for a significance level of 5 %. Therefore, although the evidence is slightly less significant, we still find in the aggregate an effect of product specialization on the equality among elasticities of substitution : they will tend to diverge if the product classification becomes more detailed.

Number of aggregates g	Level of significance α		
	10 %	5 %	1 %
1	29	0	0
2	29	14	0
3	43	14	0
4	29	29	14
5	43	29	14
ρ	.625	.950	.875
$r_{.05}$	.900	.900	.900

Table A.7 : Percentage of rejections of the CES model at a level of significance α given a number of aggregates g, and Spearman rank correlation coefficients (with small-sample correction)

CONCLUSION

The small-sample correction that has been employed in this appendix to correct the results of the main body of this chapter is intuitively appealing, being an average of correction factors for degrees of freedom in restricted and unrestricted estimation. Nevertheless it should be kept in mind that its derivation originates in a model other than the one to which it is applied, so that it seems to be at most an *approximation* of the "true" correction factor, if it exists. The correction generally lowers the cumulative densities and therefore increases the levels of significance that are required to reject the hypotheses. This affects the conclusions of this chapter in the sense that the statistical basis on which they were drawn is weakened, but not to an extent that would lead us to revise them.

FOOTNOTES TO CHAPTER 9

1) *Cfr.* LAITINEN (1978) and MEISNER (1979).

2) *Cfr. e.g.* MOOD *et al.* (1974, pp. 440-441).

3) For our calculations we have used the function PROBCHI of the SAS programme, *SAS Institute Inc., SAS Circle, P.O. Box 8000, Cary, North Carolina, U.S.A. 27511-8000.*

4) It may be verified that estimation of (6.3.1) for Model III with 2 trade partners amounts to a specification with perfectly multi-collinear explanatory prices.

5) *Cfr. e.g.* SIEGEL (1956, pp. 202-223).

6) The *asymptotic relative efficiency* or *power efficiency* of test A with respect to test B is the ratio of the sample sizes of test B and test A needed to obtain the same power for both tests as the sample size goes to infinity.

7) *Cfr.* CONOVER (1971, p. 135).

8) *Cfr.* SIEGEL (1956, p. 223).

9) This evidence is confirmed in studies by WINTERS (1984a, 1984b) for British imports of manufactures from 10 partners, using the Almost Ideal Demand System of DEATON and MUELLBAUER (1980). He rejects weak separability for this case.

10) The most well-known example being project LINK, *cfr.* BALL (1973), WAELBROECK (1976) and SAWYER (1979).

CHAPTER 10 - CONCLUSION

The purpose of our study was to analyze the interactions between trade linkage models in practice and the economic and econometric theory that relates to them. This last chapter gives an overview of the results that have been obtained in this respect, and finishes with some suggestions for further research.

10.1. THEORY

The number of existing international trade linkage models has been growing over the last 15 years due to the increasing importance of international trade in the world economy. Conceptually they may differ according to their size, their treatment of demand and supply on the international goods markets, their degree of disaggregation, their treatment of dynamics and their functional form. Regardless of these conceptual elements, they could be classified according to the following dichotomous characteristics :

- global versus bilateral linkage;
- total versus import/export allocation;
- consistent versus inconsistent linkage;
- estimation-consistent versus simulation-consistent linkage.

It was argued that the class of *estimation-consistent import allocation models* should be preferred among the possible classes of trade linkage models.

Next the theory was developed which is needed in order to derive estimation-consistent import allocation models in a framework of neoclassical optimization. Hereby we discussed the aggregator function, different definitions of separability, the aggregation problem and the adding-up condition. The major prerequisite for the existence of import allocation models is the *weak separability* of the aggregator function in imports and domestic inputs. In many empirical applications this condition is a maintained hypothesis; we however tested it in our empirical part. The estimation-consistency of import allocation models is closely related to the *adding-up condition*, requiring bilateral imports to add up to total imports in value and volume. We showed however in the context of linear homogenous import quantity indices that the adding-up condition may be fallacious and that several alternative solutions exist to guarantee its validity.

The adding-up condition usually implies that the system of bilateral import equations in an import allocation model should be estimated subject to a *linear constraint* in order to remain estimation-consistent. The resulting dependency between the equations implies that the covariance matrix of the disturbances becomes singular. The solution to this problem is to delete one equation, or, more generally : to delete as many equations as there are independent constraints. This creates the problem of whether the estimation results depend on the identity of the deleted equations. It was argued, in the context of maximum likelihood estimation, that there are actually two problems : 1) the dependency of the maximum likelihood estimates (of the coefficients and the covariance matrix) on the set of equations which is deleted and 2) the dependency of the value of the likelihood function on which equations are deleted. It was shown that the conditions required to make the maximum likelihood estimates independent of the identity of the deleted equations are weaker than for independency of the value of the likelihood function.

The major determinant of the substitution possibilities between the goods supplied by different trade partners on the same import market in an import allocation model is the functional form of the partial aggregator function from which the bilateral import equations are derived under cost minimization. As soon as more than two partners are distinguished there does no longer exist a unique concept of *elasticity of substitution* to describe the substitution possibilities. When we analyze the different definitions for multifactor elasticities of substitution in a coherent framework, we find that the Allen partial Elasticity of Substitution is closest to the elements of the Hessian matrix (and therefore closest to the functional form of the partial aggregator function), although it is far from a generalization of the unique two-factor concept of elasticity of substitution. Even closer are the price elasticities, although they can hardly be called elasticities of substitution.

10.2. PRACTICE

A substantial number of empirical estimation-consistent import allocation models is based on a *CES* partial aggregator function. The Allen partial Elasticities of Substitution, Direct Elasticities of Substitution and Shadow Elasticities of Substitution between any pair of goods supplied by two different partners are all equal and constant in this model. This implies one and the same relative price effect in each bilateral import demand equation. Despite the fact that the CES model is therefore quite simple, it is frequently used in empirical studies because it may easily be applied to a large number of trade partners and requires a method of estimation that is also simple, given the circumstances. We showed however that this estimation method contains contradictory elements and delivers inefficient estimators. The method of maximum likelihood would alternatively be the most appropriate estimator.

We next developed an estimation-consistent import allocation model with a less simple structure of price effects based on the *CRESH* partial aggregator function. Although this model has to be estimated with maximum likelihood methods, as the CES model should, it may easily be applied to a large number of trade partners. Therefore it participates in the advantages of the CES model, with the additional advantage that it is a more general model. In the elaboration of the CRESH model we were able to apply our alternative solutions for the adding-up problem, while the model could also be re-interpreted as a total allocation model that could serve to test the hypothesis of weak separability.

The CRESH model contains the CES model as a special case, and given maximum likelihood estimation we may use the likelihood ratio test to detect whether the CRESH model is a significant improvement compared to the CES model.

We argued however that the outcome of such a test would depend on two dimensions of the import allocation model : the number of *trade partners* and the *classification of goods*. It was posited that the significance of the improvement of the CRESH model over the CES model would decrease with the number of trade partners. As regards the influence of the classification of goods, two opposite effects were discerned that would be exerted by a more detailed classification on the significance of the CRESH model over the CES model : it was assumed that the corresponding increase in *product homogeneity* would decrease the significance, while the concomitant increase in *product specialization* would have an opposite effect. These two influences were couched in terms of more or less equality between elasticities of substitution and could therefore be applied directly to the CES-CRESH dichotomy.

The estimations of the CRESH model and of the CES model were performed on a dataset containing yearly, disaggregate bilateral trade data (including bilateral prices based on unit values) for five categories of goods for 1963-1980. Among the empirical findings, the following are conspicuous :

- Instead of estimating the covariance matrix of the disturbances, one may impose an *a priori covariance matrix*. Of the three forms that were tested, the most simple form gave the highest likelihood value both for the CES and the CRESH model. With this form there are no contemporaneous correlations between the disturbances of pairs of trade partners, except for the pair where the Rest of the World is one of the two partners. The Rest of the World is therefore a residual partner which catches all shocks in bilateral imports from other partners, in that case.
- Four approximations of the CRESH model were estimated for seven importers and aggregate trade : a linear one, a loglinear one and two approximations in logarithmic differences. In order to detect if any of these *functional forms* should be preferred, we compared the Root Mean-Squared Percentage Errors and Root Mean-Squared Errors among the four approximations. On the basis of ranks there is no clearcut choice to be made as to the best type of functional form. If we compare among the approximations how well the estimated coefficients respect automatically the constraints implied by the theory (i.e. the second-order sufficiency condition), the approximations in *logarithmic differences* both stand out.
- Estimations of one of the CRESH approximations in logarithmic differences for seven importers, distinguishing five categories of goods but also aggregate trade, confirmed the *a priori* expectation that *own-price* and

cross-price elasticities are much more volatile for individual categories of goods than for aggregate trade. Whereas for the latter they vary from -.5 to -1.5, this range is extended for the former category to the bounds 0 and -4.

- The hypothesis of *weak separability* was tested for six importers and three levels of disaggregation on the basis of a final demand CRESH partial aggregator function. The hypothesis is rejected at all three levels for four countries at a significance level of 1 % if we use the asymptotic distribution of the likelihood ratio criterion. For one country this is the case at a level of 10 % while for the last country the hypothesis is rejected at a significance level of 5 % for two of the three levels of disaggregation. The rejection of the weak separability hypothesis is therefore preponderant. We argued however that the strong consequence for empirical linkage models of this conclusion, *i.e.* the switch from *import* allocation models to *total* allocation models, could be challenged in view of a number of practical arguments.
- Two influences on the test of the CES versus the CRESH models were analyzed: the number of trade partners and the classification of goods. The influence of the *number of trade partners* was tested by estimating CES and CRESH import allocation models for ten importers and letting the number of trade partners decrease. It was then analyzed whether the cumulative density associated with the value of the likelihood ratio criterion for a test of the CES against the CRESH model decreased if the number of trade partners decreased. If so, this would imply that the smaller the number of trade partners, the smaller the improvement of the CRESH model over the CES model. This tendency was present for all ten importers, and significant for six of them. An aggregate test for all ten importers together also showed this tendency to be significant at levels of significance of 10 %, 5 % and 1 %.
- The influence of the *classification of goods* on the test of the CES versus the CRESH import allocation model was analyzed through estimation of the two models for seven importers at five levels of disaggregation. In six of the seven cases, an increasing degree of detail implied significantly an increase in the cumulative density associated with the likelihood ratio test for the CES versus the CRESH model. In these cases there is therefore a

predominant influence of the *specialization effect*, which causes a greater disparity of elasticities of substitution and consequently a decrease in the validity of the CES model which states that all elasticities of substitution are equal (and constant).

- The findings on the weak separability hypothesis and the influences of the number of trade partners and the classification of goods were all reached using the asymptotic distribution of the likelihood ratio criterion. It is well known that application of an asymptotic result to a small sample may cause considerable bias. In the absence of knowledge of the finite-sample distribution one could at least apply a small-sample correction to the test statistic of which one knows the asymptotic distribution. Unfortunately, obtaining an asymptotic expansion (and whence a small-sample correction) for the likelihood ratio criterion for the type of models we estimated was not evident. Therefore we have only been able to apply an *approximation* to the *small-sample correction factor* based on an interpretation of such a factor for the multivariate linear model. Upon application of this correction factor (which corrects a bias towards rejection) the results for the weak separability hypothesis and the influence of the number of trade partners remain upright, though they are slightly weakened. For the influence of the classification of goods the results change more : the specialization effect, which was significant in six out of seven cases, is now only significant in two of the seven importing countries. Its opponent, the effect of product homogeneity, is, though present in three cases, significant nowhere. Also an aggregate test for all seven importers still confirms the predominant role of specialization, although it is less important than without correction factors.

10.3. SUGGESTIONS FOR FURTHER RESEARCH

The general purpose of econometric modelbuilding may be described as providing mathematical and statistical methods for the analysis of economic phenomena. This study has been an attempt at doing so for international trade linkages. However, one can never say that the process of improvement has ended, as there always remain open ends and indeed new phenomena to be analyzed. In this final section we indicate some ways which, in our opinion, need further exploration in the field of international linkage models, and with respect to our own results.

Other linkages

We started this study by restraining ourself to international *trade* lingages. From a historical point of view, trade has certainly been a major factor linking national economies during the period 1960-1980. But, in the meantime, halfway through the eighties, trade has been joined by other factors. The increased mobility of capital and the debt problem, the consequences of considerable movements of immigrant workers and the internationalization of transport and communication are events that have acquired such importance that they require adequate individual representation in international linkage models. Trade linkages should therefore be supplemented with linkages through *capital, services* and *people*.

Conceptual elements

The CRESH import allocation model which we estimated was derived from neoclassical cost minimization, in which there was no room for supply elements. Nevertheless it is clear that these elements play an important role in international trade. The neoclassical optimization framework should therefore be extended to include *supply elements*, if not explicit supply equations. With the introduction of supply elements, one may also think of an extension in the direction of models for temporary equilibria. The resulting models should be estimation-consistent, however. Furthermore, although the CRESH model was already more general than the CES model, it is not the most *general form* of import allocation model that may be derived without reverting to systems where the number of coefficients increases quadratically with the number of trade partners, such as the Rotterdam model or flexible functional forms. For instance, the CRESH partial aggregator function which we used was linear homogeneous, which implies a unit elasticity of bilateral imports with respect to the import quantity index. This is a maintained hypothesis which requires further testing.

Next to supply elements and a more general partial aggregator function, one may also think of improving the explanatory power through the inclusion of *additional explanatory variables*, such as variables pertaining to one particular bilateral trade flow. This enhances however the possibility that estimation-consistency and the conditions for weak separability are violated. Estimation-consistency may also be threatened if we allow for a different scheme of *dynamics* per bilateral trade flow equation. Nevertheless it is not *a priori* obvious why each importer would have equal (partial) information concerning each trade partner at his disposal, as we assumed for the bilateral import prices.

Data

The majority of presently existing international linkage models use trade data for one category (either manufactures or aggregate trade) and make the (implicit) assumption that a bilateral trade flow price may be identified with the total export price of the exporter which is involved. This study departed from this practice through the use of *disaggregate* bilateral trade data and *bilateral* import prices. Nevertheless one may imagine improvements to this dataset : we only analyzed trade data from OECD declarants, while the bilateral trade prices were calculated on the basis of unit value indices with their corresponding disadvantages. The dataset should be extended to cover the world trade completely, while bilateral prices should preferably be calculated using actual price movements instead of unit values.

Testing

Due to limited data availability we tested the weak separability hypothesis starting from an aggregator function for final demand. This implies the maintained hypothesis that intermediate inputs are weakly separable from the components of final demand. On the other hand this may also be interpreted as weak separability between intermediate inputs and the aggregate of the production factors labour, capital and imports. Because several categories of import goods are used as inputs in the production process, one may expect that the composition of the trade partners for those goods may be influenced by the amount of corresponding intermediate inputs. In those cases the maintained hypothesis would be violated and we should test the weak separability hypothesis starting from an aggregator function *including intermediate inputs*.

In order to correct our likelihood ratio criterion for small-sample bias, we used a correction factor which was derived intuitively from the one that is used in the multivariate linear model with equal explanatory variables and different coefficients among equations. The models we estimated are just the opposite : among equations there are different explanatory variables, but the same coefficients. To obtain an optimal test procedure for this type of model, one would need to derive a finite sample distribution for the likelihood ratio criterion. As this seems a remote objective, one should in a first instance at least try to derive analytically a small-sample correction factor from an asymptotic expansion of the criterion.

REFERENCES

AITKEN, N.D. (1973), "The effect of the EEC and EFTA on European trade : a temporal cross-section analysis", *American Economic Review,* 63 : 881-892.

d'ALCANTARA, G. and A. ITALIANER (1981), *Bilateral trade flows in the COMET model,* Paper presented at the world meeting of project LINK, August 31 - September 4, La Hulpe, Belgium.

d'ALCANTARA, G. and A. ITALIANER (1982), *European project for a multinational macrosectoral model,* Report MS 11 to the Commission of the European Communities, Directorate-General for Science, Research and Development, Brussels.

d'ALCANTARA, G. and J. THEEUWES (1981), "Specification of equations for international bilateral trade flows", in COURBIS, R. (ed.), *International trade and multicountry models,* Economica, Paris, 105-109.

ALLEN, R.G.D. (1938), *Mathematical analysis for economists,* St. Martin's Press, London. Reprinted by Macmillan, London.

ALLEN, R.G.D. and J.R. HICKS (1934), "A reconsideration of the theory of value, II", *Economica,* 1 (new series) : 196-219.

AMANO, A., E. KURIHARA and L. SAMUELSON (1980), "Trade linkage sub-model in the EPA World Economic Model", *Economic Bulletin,* 19, Economic Research Institute, Economic Planning Agency, Tokyo.

AMANO, A., A. MARUYAMA and M. YOSHITOMI (eds.) (1981a), *A three-country linkage model,* Economic Research Institute, Economic Planning Agency, Tokyo.

AMANO, A., A. MARUYAMA and M. YOSHITOMI (eds.), (1982), *EPA World Economic Model, Vols. I and II,* Economic Research Institute, Economic Planning Agency, Tokyo.

AMANO, A., A. SADAHIRO and T. SASAKI (1981b), "Structure and application of the EPA World Economic Model", *Discussion Paper,* 22, Economic Research Institute, Economic Planning Agency, Tokyo.

ANDERSON, T.W. (1958), *An introduction to multivariate statistical analysis,* Wiley & Sons, New York.

ANDO, A., R. HERRING and R. MARSTON (eds.), (1974), *International aspects of stabilization policies,* Proceedings of a conference held at Williamstown, Massachusetts, June 1974, Conference series no. 12, Federal Reserve Bank of Boston, Boston.

ARMINGTON, P.S. (1969a), "A theory of demand for products distinguished by place of production", *International Monetary Fund Staff Papers,* 16 : 159-178.

ARMINGTON, P.S. (1969b), "The geographic pattern of trade and the effects of price changes", *International Monetary Fund Staff Papers,* 16 : 179-201.

ARMINGTON, P.S. (1970a), "A many-country model of equilibrating adjustments in prices and spending", appendix to RHOMBERG, R.R., "Possible approaches to a model of world trade and payments", *International Monetary Fund Staff Papers,* 17 : 23-26.

ARMINGTON, P.S. (1970b), "Adjustments of trade balances : some experiments with a model of trade among many countries", *International Monetary Fund Staff Papers,* 17 : 488-523.

ARMINGTON, P.S. (1973), "A note on the income-compensated price elasticities of demand used in the Multilateral Exchange Rate Model", appendix to ARTUS, J.R. and R.R. RHOMBERG, "A Multilateral Exchange Rate Model", *International Monetary Fund Staff Papers,* 20 : 608-611.

ARROW, K.J., B.H. CHENERY, B.S. MINHAS and R.M. SOLOW (1961), "Capital-labour substitution and economic efficiency", *Review of Economics and Statistics,* 43 : 225-250.

ARTUS, J.R. (1973), "The short-run effects of domestic demand pressure on export delivery delays for machinery", *Journal of International Economics,* 3 : 21-36.

ARTUS, J.R. and A.K. McGUIRK (1981), "A revised version of the Multilateral Exchange Rate Model", *International Monetary Fund Staff Papers,* 28 : 275-309.

ARTUS, J.R. and R.R. RHOMBERG (1973), "A Multilateral Exchange Rate Model", *International Monetary Fund Staff Papers,* 20 : 591-611.

BACHARACH, M. (1965), "Estimating nonnegative matrices from marginal data", *International Economic Review,* 6 : 294-310.

BALL, R.J. (ed.) (1973), *The international linkage of national economic models,* North-Holland Publishing Company, Amsterdam.

BARTEN, A.P. (1966), *Theorie en empirie van een volledig stelsel van vraagvergelijkingen* (theory and empirism of a complete system of demand equa tions), Doctoral dissertation, Netherlands School of Economics, Rotterdam.

BARTEN, A.P. (1967), "Evidence on the Slutsky conditions for demand equations", *Review of Economics and Statistics,* 49 : 77-84.

BARTEN, A.P. (1968), "Estimating demand equations", *Econometrica,* 36 : 213-251.

BARTEN, A.P. (1969), "Maximum likelihood estimation of a complete system of demand equations", *European Economic Review,* 1 : 7-73.

BARTEN, A.P. (1970), "Réflexions sur la construction d'un système empirique des fonctions de demande", *Cahiers du Séminaire d'Econométrie,* 12 : 67-80.

BARTEN, A.P. (1971), "An import allocation model for the Common Market", *Cahiers Economiques de Bruxelles,* 50 : 153-164.

BARTEN, A.P. (1981), "COMET in a nutshell", in COURBIS, R. (ed.), *International trade and multicountry models,* Economica, Paris, 211-219.

BARTEN, A.P. and G. d'ALCANTARA (1976), "The linkage of models of the EEC countries", in GLEJSER, H. (ed.), *Quantitative studies of international economic relations,* North-Holland Publishing Company, Amsterdam, 25-73.

BARTEN, A.P., G. d'ALCANTARA and G.J. CARRIN (1976), "COMET : a medium term macro economic model for the European Economic Community", *European Economic Review,* 7 : 63-115.

BARTEN, A.P. and G. d'ALCANTARA (1977), "Models of bilateral trade flows", in ALBACH, H., E. HELMSTÄDTER and R. HENN (eds.), *Quantitative Wirtschaftsforschung. Wilhelm Krelle zum 60. Geburtstag,* J.C.B. Mohr, Tübingen, 43-57.

BARTEN, A.P. and S. TURNOVSKY (1966), "Some aspects of the aggregation problem for composite demand equations", *International Economic Review,* 7 : 231-259.

BECKERMAN, W. (1956), "The world trade multiplier and the stability of world trade 1938 to 1953", *Econometrica,* 24 : 239-252.

BERNDT, E.R. and L.R. CHRISTENSEN (1973), "The internal structure of functional relationships : separability, substitution and aggregation", *Review of Economic Studies,* 40 : 403-410.

BERNDT, E.R. and D.O. WOOD (1977), "Engineering and econometric approaches to industrial energy conservation and capital formation : a reconciliation", *Working Paper,* no. MIT-EL-77-040 WP, MIT, Energy Laboratory, Cambridge, Massachusetts.

BIANCHI, C. and P. RANUZZI (1981), "Some problems related to the construction of linkage models", in COURBIS, R. (ed.), *International trade and multicountry models,* Economica, Paris, 185-196.

BLACKORBY, C., G. LADY, D. NISSEN and R.R. RUSSEL (1970), "Homothetic separability and consumer budgeting", *Econometrica,* 48 : 468-472.

BLACKORBY, C., D. PRIMONT and R.R. RUSSEL (1975), "Budgeting, decentralization and aggregation", *Annals of Economic and Social Measurement,* 4 : 23-44.

BLACKORBY, C., D. PRIMONT and R.R. RUSSEL (1978), *Duality, separability and functional structure : theory and economic applications*, North-Holland Publishing Company, New York.

BOND, M.E. (1979), "The world trade model : invisibles", *International Monetary Fund Staff Papers*, 26 : 257-333.

BRANSON, W.H. (1972), "The trade effects of the 1971 currency realignments", *Brookings Papers on Economic Activity*, 1 : 15-69.

CARRIN, G.J., J.W. GUNNING and J. WAELBROECK (1980), *A general equilibrium model for the world economy : some preliminary results*, Paper presented at the 8th IIASA Global Modelling Conference, July 22-25, Laxenburg, Austria.

CHRISTENSEN, L.R., D.W. JORGENSON and L.J. LAU (1973), "Transcedental logarithmic production frontiers", *Review of Economics and Statistics*, 55 : 28-45.

CHRISTENSEN, L.R., D.W. JORGENSON and L.J. LAU (1975), "Transcedental logarithmic utility functions", *American Economic Review*, 65 : 367-383.

CLEMENTS, K.W. and H. THEIL (1978), "A simple method of estimating price elasticities in international trade", *Economics Letters*, 1 : 133-137.

COMMISSION OF THE EUROPEAN COMMUNITIES (1980), "Règlement (CEE) n° 3285/80 de la Commission, du 19 décembre 1980, modifiant la nomenclature des marchandises pour les statistiques du commerce extérieur de la Communauté et du commerce entre ses Etats membres (Nimexe)", *Journal Officiel des Communautés Européennes*, L 346 : 1-529.

CONOVER, W.J. (1971), *Practical nonparametric statistics*, Wiley, New York.

COURBIS, R. (1981a), "Introduction", in COURBIS, R. (ed.), *International trade and multicountry models*, Economica, Paris, 21-38.

COURBIS, R. (1981b), "La construction de modèles multinationaux : problèmes methodologiques", in COURBIS, R. (ed.), *International trade and multicountry models*, Economica, Paris, 243-247.

COURBIS, R. (ed.) (1981c), *International Trade and multicountry models*, Economica, Paris.

COX, D.R. and A. STUART (1955), "Some quick tests for trend in location and dispersion", *Biometrika*, 42 : 80-95.

CRAMER, H. (1946), *Mathematical methods of statistics*, Princeton University Press, Princeton.

DAVIDSON, J.E.H., D.F. HENDRY, F. SRBA and S. YEO (1978), "Econometric modelling of the aggregate time-series relationship between consumers' expenditure and income in the United Kingdom", *Economic Journal*, 88 : 661-692.

DEATON, A.S. and J. MUELLBAUER (1980), "An almost ideal demand system", *American Economic Review*, 70 : 312-326.

DEPPLER, M.C. and D.M. RIPLEY (1978), "The world trade model : merchandise trade", *International Monetary Fund Staff Papers*, 25 : 147-206.

DHRYMES, P.J. (1971), *Distributed lags : problems of estimation and formulation*, Holden Day, San Francisco.

DIEWERT, W.E. (1973), "Functional forms for profit and transformation functions", *Journal of Economic Theory*, 6 : 284-316.

DIEWERT, W.E. (1974), "Application of duality theory", in INTRILIGATOR, M. and D. KENDRICK (eds.), *Frontiers of quantitative economics*, Vol. II, North-Holland Publishing Company, Amsterdam, 106-171.

DIEWERT, W.E. (1976), "Exact and superlative index numbers", *Journal of Econometrics*, 4 : 115-146.

DIEWERT, W.E. (1982), "Duality approaches to microeconomic theory", in ARROW, K.J. and M.D. INTRILIGATOR (eds.), *Handbook of mathematical economics, Vol. II*, North-Holland Publishing Company, Amsterdam, 535-599.

DON, F.J.H. (1982), "Restrictions on variables", *Journal of Econometrics*, 18 : 369-393.

DRAMAIS, A. (1974/1975), "DESMOS III - Neuf modèles nationaux liés pour l'étude des mesures de politique économique entre les pays members du Marché Commun", *Cahiers Economiques de Bruxelles*, 64 : 473-514, 65 : 53-108, 66 : 201-260.

DRAMAIS, A. (1977), "Transmission of inflationary pressures between the EEC members", *European Economic Review*, 9 : 21-42.

DRAMAIS, A. (1981), "Le modèle DESMOS", in COURBIS, R. (ed.), *International trade and multicountry models*, Economica, Paris, 221-234.

DURBIN, J. (1970), "Testing for serial correlation in least squares regression when some of the regressors are lagged dependent variables", *Econometrica*, 38 : 410-421.

EUROSTAT (1980a), *European system of integrated economic accounts ESA, second edition*, Office for Official Publications of the European Communities, Luxembourg.

EUROSTAT (1980b), *National Accounts ESA. Detailed tables by branches 1970-1978*, Office for Official Publications of the European Communities, Luxembourg.

EUROSTAT (1982), *National accounts ESA. Aggregates*, Office for Official Publications of the European Communities, Luxembourg.

EUROSTAT (1983), *National accounts ESA. Detailed tables by branch 1970-1981*, Office for Official Publications of the European Communities, Luxembourg.

EZAKI, M. (1978), "Linking national econometric models of Japan, U.S.A., and the East and Southeast Asian countries : a pilot study", *Discussion Paper 101*, Center for Southeast Asian Studies, Kyoto University, Kyoto.

FAIR, R.C. (1981), "A multicountry economic model", *N.B.E.R. Working Paper No. 414 R*, National Bureau for Economic Research, Cambridge, Massachusetts.

FLEMING, J.M. and S.C. TSIANG (1956/1957), "Changes in competitive strength and export shares of major industrial countries", *International Monetary Fund Staff Papers*, 5 : 218-248.

FONTELA, E. and M. LO CASCIO (1983), *Interdependence : a system of models and a general concept for the world economy*, Paper presented at the 4th International Workshop of the Applied Econometric Association, December 8-9, Brussels.

FRENGER, P. (1978), "Factor substitution in the interindustry model and the use of inconsistent aggregation", in FUSS, M. and D. McFADDEN (eds.), *Production economics : a dual approach to theory and applications, Vol. 2*, North-Holland Publishing Company, Amsterdam, 269-310.

FUSS, M. and D. McFADDEN (eds.) (1978), *Production economics : a dual approach to theory and application, 2 Vols.*, North-Holland Publishing Company, Amsterdam.

GANA, J.L., B.G. HICKMAN, L.J. LAU and L.R. JACOBSON (1979), "Alternative approaches to linkage of national econometric models", in SAWYER, J.A. (ed.), *Modelling the international transmission mechanism*, North-Holland Publishing Company, Amsterdam, 9-43.

GERACI, V. and W. PREWO (1982), "An empirical demand and supply model of multilateral trade", *Review of Economics and Statistics*, 64 : 432-441.

GOLDSTEIN, M. and M. KHAN (1978), "The supply and demand for exports : a simultaneous approach", *Review of Economics and Statistics*, 60 : 275-286.

GOLDMAN, S.M. and H. UZAWA (1964), "A note on separability in demand analysis", *Econometrica*, 32 : 387-398.

GORMAN, W.M. (1959), "Separable utility and aggregation", *Econometrica*, 27 : 469-481.

GORMAN, W.M. (1965), "Production functions in which the elasticities of substitution stand in fixed proportion to each other", *Review of Economic Studies*, 32 : 217-224.

GORMAN, W.M. (1971), *Two stage budgeting*, Unpublished paper, London School of Economics and Political Science, London.

GREEN, H.A.J. (1964), *Aggregation in economic analysis*, Princeton University Press, Princeton.

GREEN, H.A.J. (1976), *Consumer theory, revised edition*, Macmillan, London.

GREGORY, R.G. (1971), "United States imports and internal pressure of demand : 1948-1968", *American Economic Review*, 61 : 28-47.

GUILLAUME, Y. (1981), "MARCO II, un modèle structure-conjoncture de l'économie mondiale", in COURBIS, R. (ed.), *International trade and multi-country models*, Economica, Paris.

HALL, B.H. and R.E. HALL (1978), *Time Series Processor. Version 3.4. User's Manual*, Stanford University, Stanford.

HALTTUNEN, H. and D. WARNER (1979a), "A model of trade and exchange rate projections", *N.B.E.R. Working Paper No. 389*, National Bureau of Economic Research, Cambridge, Massachusetts.

HALTTUNEN, H. and D. WARNER (1979b), "A model of trade and exchange rate projections : equations and parameters", *N.B.E.R. Working Paper No. 390*, National Bureau of Economic Research, Cambridge, Massachusetts.

HANOCH, G. (1971), "CRESH production functions", *Econometrica*, 39 : 695-712.

HANOCH, G. (1975), "Production and demand models with direct and indirect implicit additivity", *Econometrica*, 43 : 395-419.

HANOCH, G. (1978a), "Symmetric duality and polar production functions", in FUSS, M. and D. McFADDEN (eds.), *Production economics : a dual approach to theory and applications, Vol. 1*, North-Holland Publishing Company, Amsterdam, 111-131.

HANOCH, G. (1978b), "Polar functions with constant Two Factors-Two Price elasticities", in FUSS, M. and D. McFADDEN (eds.), *Production economics : a dual approach to theory and applications, Vol. 1*, North-Holland Publishing Company, 287-309.

HECKSCHER, E.F. (1919), "The effect of foreign trade on the distribution of income", *Ekonomisk Tidskrift*, 21 : 497-512. Reprinted in ELLIS, H.S. and L.A. METZLER (eds.), *Readings in the theory of international trade*, Blakiston, London, 1949, 272-300.

HELLIWELL, J.F. (1974), "Trade, capital flows, and migration as channels for international transmission of stabilization policies", in ANDO, A., R. HERRING and R. MARSTON, *International aspects of stabilization policies*, Proceedings of a conference held at Williamstown, Massachusetts, June 1974, Conference series No. 12, Federal Reserve Bank of Boston, Boston, 241-278.

HELLIWELL, J.F., F.W. GORBER, G.R. SPARKS and I.A. STEWART (1973), "Comprehensive linkage of large models : Canada and the United States", in BALL, R.J. (ed.), *The international linkage of national economic models,* North-Holland Publishing Company, Amsterdam, 395-425.

HELLIWELL, J.F. and T. PADMORE (1984), "Empirical studies of macroeconomic interdependence", forthcoming in KENEN, P.B. (ed.), *Handbook of International economics, Chapter 21,* North-Holland Publishing Company, Amsterdam.

HEMPHILL, W.L. (1980), "Estimation of the timing asymmetry in international trade", *International Monetary Fund Staff Papers,* 27 : 135-160.

HICKMAN, B.G. (1973), "A general linear model of world trade", in BALL, R.J., (ed.), *The international linkage of national economic models,* North-Holland Publishing Company, 21-43.

HICKMAN, B.G. (ed.) (1982), *Global international economic models,* Proceedings of the 8th IIASA Symposium of Global Modelling, IIASA, Laxenburg, Austria.

HICKMAN, B.G. and L.J. LAU (1973), "Elasticities of substitution and export demands in a world trade model", *European Economic Review,* 4 : 347-380.

HICKS, J.R. (1932), *The theory of wages,* Macmillan,London, Second edition, 1963.

HICKS, N.L. (1976), "A model of trade and growth for the developing world", *European Economic Review,* 7 : 239-255.

HIERONYMI, O. (1983), *The balance-of-payments model in the interdependence system,* Paper presented at the 4th International Workshop of the Applied Econometric Association, December 8-9, Brussels.

HOGAN, W.W. (1979), "Capital-energy complementarity in aggregate energy-economic analysis", *Resources and Energy,* 2 : 201-220.

HOLTHAM, G. (1984), "Multinational modelling of financial linkages and exchange rates", *OECD Economic Studies,* 2 : 51-92.

HOWE, H., E. HERNANDEZ-CATA, G. STEVENS, R. BERNER, P. CLARK and S.Y. KWACK (1981), "Assessing international interdependence with a multi-country model", *Journal of Econometrics,* 15 : 65-92.

IMF (1980), *International Financial Statistics. Yearbook 1980,* International Monetary Fund, Washington, D.C.

IMF (1982), *International Financial Statistics, February 1982,* International Monetary Fund, Washington, D.C.

ITALIANER, A. (1982a), "An evaluation of the bilateral trade flows in the COMET model", *Discussion Paper D/1982/2020/15,* Catholic University of Louvain, Centre for Economic Studies, Louvain.

ITALIANER, A. (1982b), *Towards a disaggregate bilateral trade flow model,* Report MS 14 to the Commission of the European Communities, Directorate-General for Science, Research and Development, Brussels.

ITALIANER, A. (1982c), *Bilateral trade data for the European project for a multinational macrosectoral model,* Report MS 13 to the Commission of the European Communities, Directorate-General for Science, Research and Development, Brussels.

ITALIANER, A. and G. d'ALCANTARA (1983), *Modelling bilateral sectoral trade flows,* Paper presented at the 4th International Workshop of the Applied Econometric Association, December 8-9, Brussels.

JOHNSON, K.N. (1978), *Balance of payments equilibrium and equilibrating exchange rates in a world econometric model,* unpublished Ph.D. Dissertation.

JUNIUS, Th. (1977), *Shepard technologies and neoclassical production functions,* Doctoral dissertation, Stenfert Kroese, Leiden.

JUNZ, H.B. and R.R. RHOMBERG (1965), "Prices and export performance of industrial countries 1953-1965", *International Monetary Fund Staff Papers,* 12 : 224-271.

JUNZ, H.B. and R.R. RHOMBERG (1973), "Price competitiveness in export trade among industrial countries", *American Economic Association, Papers and Proceedings,* 63 : 412-418.

KELLER, W.J. and J. VAN DRIEL (1981), "A new class of consumer demand differential systems", *Internal CBS report,* Netherlands Central Bureau of Statistics, Voorburg.

KEMP, M.C. (1962), "Errors of measurement and bias in estimates of import demand parameters", *Economic Record,* 38 : 369-372.

KHAN, M.S. (1974), "Import and export demand in developing countries", *International Monetary Fund Staff Papers,* 21 : 678-693.

KHAN, M.S. and K.Z. ROSS (1975), "Cyclical and secular income elasticities of the demand for imports", *Review of Economics and Statistics,* 57 : 357-361.

KHAN, M.S. and K.Z. ROSS (1977), "The functional form of the import demand equation", *Journal of International Economics,* 7 : 149-160.

KIRKPATRICK, G. (1983), *A multi country OECD/Comecon simulation model*, Paper presented at the 4th International Workshop of the Applied Econometric Association, December 8-9, Brussels.

KLEIN, L.R. (1976), "Five-year experience of linking national econometric models and of forecasting international trade", in GLEJSER, H. (ed.), *Quantitative Studies of international economic relations*, North-Holland Publishing Company, Amsterdam, 1-24.

KLEIN, L.R. (1981), "The LINK project", in COURBIS, R. (ed.), *International trade and multicountry models*, Economica, Paris, 197-209.

KLEIN, L.R., C. MORIGUCHI and A. VAN PEETERSSEN (1975), "The LINK model of world trade, with applications to 1972-73", in KENEN, P.B. (ed.), *International trade and finance : frontiers for research*, Cambridge University Press, Cambridge, 453-483.

KLEIN, L.R. and A. VAN PEETERSSEN (1973), "Forecasting world trade within project LINK", in BALL, R.J. (ed.), *The international linkage of national economic models*, North-Holland Publishing Company, Amsterdam.

KMENTA, J. and R.F. GILBERT (1968), "Small sample properties of alternative estimators of seemingly unrelated regressions", *Journal of the American Statistical Association*, 63 : 1180-2000.

KOOYMAN, J. (1981), "The METEOR model", in COURBIS, R. (ed.), *International trade and multicountry models*, Economica, Paris, 235-242.

KOOYMAN, J., J.J. POST and A.N.R. SCHWARZ (1977), "National impulses and their impact on the world, an example", *CPB reprint series no. 163*, Central Planning Bureau, The Hague.

KOYCK, L.M. (1954), *Distributed lags and investment analysis*, North-Holland Publishing Company, Amsterdam.

KRAVIS, I.B. and R.E. LIPSEY (1971), *Price competitiveness in world trade*, Studies in International Economic Relations No. 6, National Bureau of Economic Research, New York.

KUZNETS, S. (1964), "Quantitative aspects of the economic growth of nations: IX. Level and structure of foreign trade : comparison for recent years", in *Economic Development and Cultural Change*, Vol. XIII, Part II.

LAITINEN, K. (1978), "Why is demand homogeneity so often rejected ?", *Economics Letters*, 1 : 187-191.

LAU, L.J. (1969), "Budgeting and decentralization of allocation decisions, *Memorandum No. 89*, Center for Research in Economic Growth, Stanford University, Stanford.

LAU, L.J. (1976), "A note on the elasticity of substitution functions", *Review of Economic Studies,* 43 : 353-358.

LAU, L.J. (1978), "Applications of profit functions", in FUSS, M. and D. McFADDEN (eds.), *Production economics : a dual approach to theory and applications Vol. 1,* North-Holland Publishing Company, Amsterdam, 133-216.

LEAGUE OF NATIONS (1942), *The network of world trade,* Princeton, New Jersey.

LEAMER, E.A. and R.M. STERN (1970), *Quantitative international economics,* Allyn and Bacon, Boston.

LEONTIEF, W.W. (1947), "A note on the interrelation of subsets of independent variables of a continuous function with continuous first derivatives", *Bulletin of the American Mathematical Society,* 53 : 343-350.

LINNEMAN, H. (1966), *An econometric study of international trade flows,* North-Holland Publishing Company, Amsterdam.

MADDALA, G.S. (1977), *Econometrics,* McGraw Hill, Tokyo.

MAGEE, S.P. (1975), "Prices, incomes and foreign trade", in KENEN, P.B. (ed.), *International trade and finance : frontiers for research,* Cambridge University Press, Cambridge, 175-252.

MAKS, J.A.H. (1980), *Empirical preference orderings and applied demand analysis,* Doctoral dissertation, University of Groningen, Groningen.

MALINVAUD, E. (1980), *Statistical methods of econometrics,* third revised edition, North-Holland Publishing Company, Amsterdam.

MARWAH, K. (1976), "A world model of international trade : forecasting market shares and trade flows", *Empirical Economics,* 1 : 1-39.

McFADDEN, D. (1963), "(Further results on) Constant Elasticity of Substitution Production functions", *Review of Economic Studies,* 30 : 73-83.

McGUIRE, T.W., J.K. FARLEY, R.E. LUCAS Jr. and L.W. RING (1968), "Estimation and inference in which subsets of the dependent variable are constrained", *Journal of the American Statistical Association,* 63 : 1201-1213.

MEADE, J.E. (1962), *A neoclassical theory of economic growth, revised second edition,* Allen & Unwin, London.

MEISNER, J.F. (1979), "The sad fate of the asymptotic Slutsky symmetry test for large systems", *Economics Letters,* 2 : 231-233.

MENNES, L.B.M. (1967), "A world trade model for 1970", *Weltwirtschaftliches Archiv,* 99 : 225-255.

METZLER, L.A. (1950), "A multiple region theory of income and trade", *Econometrica,* 18 : 329-354.

MINTZ, I. (1967), *Cyclical fluctuations in the exports of the United States since 1879,* Studies in Business Cycles No. 15, National Bureau of Economic Research, New York.

MOOD, A.M., F.A. GRAYBILL and D.C. BOES (1974), *Introduction to the theory of statistics,* McGraw-Hill, Tokyo.

MORIGUCHI, C. (1973), "Forecasting and simulation analysis of the world economy", *American Economic Review,* 63 : 402-409.

MORISHIMA, M. and Y. MURATA (1972), "An estimation of the international trade multiplier, 1954-1965", in MORISHIMA, M., Y. MURATA, Y. NOSSE and T. SAITO (eds.), *The working of econometric models,* Cambridge University Press, Cambridge, 303-329.

MUKERJI, V. (1963), "A generalized S.M.A.C. function with constant ratios of elasticities of substitution", *Review of Economic Studies,* 30 : 233-236.

MUNDLAK, Y. (1968), "Elasticities of substitution and the theory of derived demand", *Review of Economic Studies,* 35 : 225-236.

NEISSER, H. and F. MODIGLIANI (1953), *National incomes and international trade : a quantitative analysis,* University of Illinois Press, Urbana.

NYHUS, D. (1978), "A detailed model of bilateral commodity trade and the effects of exchange rate changes", in STONE, R. and W. PETERSON (eds.), *Econometric contribution to public policy,* Macmillan, London, 130-150.

OECD, *Statistics of foreign trade : series C,* yearly issues, Organisation for Economic Co-operation and Development, Paris.

OECD (1979), "The OECD international linkage model", *OECD Economic Outlook, Occasional Studies,* Organisation for Economic Co-Operation and Development, 3-33.

OECD (1984), *National Accounts Vol. I. Main aggreagates 1953-1982,* Organisation for Economic Co-operation and Development, Paris.

OHLIN, B. (1933), *Interregional and international trade,* Harvard University Press, Cambridge, Massachusetts.

OLSEN, E. (1971), *International trade theory and regional income differences, United States 1880-1950,* North-Holland Publishing Company, Amsterdam.

ORCUTT, G.H. (1950), "Measurement of price elasticities in international trade", *Review of Economics and Statistics,* 32 : 117-132.

PHAN, D.L. (1965), "La position concurrentielle de la France sur le marché mondial 1953-1962", *Bulletin du Ceprel No. 5,* 121-168.

PLASMANS, J.E.J. (1982), "Interplay, a linked model for economic policy in the EEC, a modified version, 1953-1975", in PLASMANS, J.E.J. (ed.), *Econometric modelling in theory and practice,* Martinus Nijhoff Publishers, The Hague, 181-232.

PLASMANS, J.E.J. (1984), *Specification and estimation of the linkage block of Interplay II (1953-1984),* Mimeographed, University of Tilburg, Tilburg, May.

POLAK, J.J. (1953), *An international economic system,* University of Chicago Press, Chicago.

POLAK, J.J. and R.R. RHOMBERG (1962), "Economic instability in an international setting", *American Economic Review,* 52 : 160-218.

POWELL, A.A. (1969), "Aitken estimators as a tool in allocating predetermined aggregates", *Journal of the American Statistical Association,* 64 : 913-922.

PÖYHÖNEN, P. (1963a), "A tentative model for the volume of trade between countries", *Weltwirtschaftliches Archiv,* 90 : 93-99.

PÖYHÖNEN, P. (1963b), "Towards a general theory of international trade", *Ekonomiska Samfundets Tidskrift,* 2 : 69-77.

PULLIAINEN, K. (1963), "A world trade study : an econometric model of the pattern of the commodity flows in international trade in 1948-1960", *Ekonomiska Samfundets Tidskrift,* 2 : 78-91.

RANUZZI, P. (1981), "The experience of the EEC Eurolink project in modeling bilateral trade linkage equations", *Journal of Policy Modeling,* 3 : 153-173.

RAO, P. and R.L. MILLER (1971), *Applied econometrics,* Wadsworth Publishing Company, Belmont, California.

RESNICK, S. (1968), "An empirical study of economic policy in the Common Market", in ANDO, A., E.C. BROWN and A.F. FRIEDLAENDER (eds.), *Studies in economic stabilization,* The Brookings Institution, Washington, D.C., 184-214.

RESNICK, S.A. and E.M. TRUMAN (1975), "An empirical examination of bilateral trade in Western Europe", in BALASSA, B. (ed.), *European Economic Integration,* North-Holland Publishing Company, Amsterdam, 41-78.

RHOMBERG, R.R. (1968), "Transmission of business fluctuations from developed to developing countries", *International Monetary Fund Staff Papers,* 15 : 1-29.

RHOMBERG, R.R. (1970), "Possible approaches to a model of world trade and payments", *International Monetary Fund Staff Papers*, 17 : 1-26.

RHOMBERG, R.R. (1973), "Towards a general trade model", in BALL, R.J. (ed.), *The international linkage of national economic models*, North-Holland Publishing Company, Amsterdam 9-20.

RHOMBERG, R.R. and L. BOISSONNEAULT (1964), "Effects of income and price changes on the U.S. balance of payments", *International Monetary Fund Staff Papers*, 11 : 59-124.

RHOMBERG, R.R. and P. FORTUCCI (1964), "Projections of U.S. current account balances for 1964 from a world trade model", *International Monetary Fund Staff Papers*, 11 : 414-433.

RICARDO, D. (1817), *Principles of political economy*, London.

RIPLEY, D.M. (1980), "The world model of merchandise trade : simulation applications", *International Monetary Fund Staff Papers*, 27 : 285-319.

RIPLEY, D.M. (1981), "The IMF world trade model : a progress report", in COURBIS, R. (ed.), *International trade and multicountry models*, Economica, Paris, 123-136.

ROY, R. (1942), *De l'utilité*, Hermann et cie., Paris.

SALLIN-KORNBERG, E. and E. FONTELA (1981), "Scenarios building with the Explor-Multitrade 85 model", in COURBIS, R. (ed.), *International trade and multicountry models*, Economica, Paris, 309-325.

SAMUELSON, L.W. (1973), "A new model of world trade", *OECD Economic Outlook, Occasional Studies*, Organisation for Economic Co-operation and Development, Paris, 3-22.

SAMUELSON, L.W. (1978), "International transmission of economic fluctuations : simulations with a model of OECD short-term economic prospects", in STONE, R. and W. PETERSON (eds.), *Econometric contributions to public policy*, Macmillan, London, 111-126.

SAMUELSON, L.W. and E. KURIHARA (1980), "OECD trade linkage methods applied to the EPA world economic model", *Economic Bulletin No. 8*, Economic Research Institute, Economic Planning Agency, Tokyo.

SARMA, K.S. (1983), *Alternative methods of trade linkage*, Paper presented to the 4th International Workshop of the Applied Econometric Association, December 8-9, Brussels.

SATO, K. (1967), "A two-level constant-elasticity-of-substitution production function", *Review of Economic Studies*, 34 : 201-218.

SAVAGE, I.R. and K.W. DEUTSCH (1960), "A statistical model of the gross analysis of transaction flows", *Econometrica,* 28 : 551-572.

SAWYER, J.A. (ed.) (1979), *Modelling the international transmission mechanism,* North-Holland Publishing Company, Amsterdam.

SHEPARD, R.W. (1953), *Cost and production functions,* Princeton University Press, Princeton. Reprinted by Springer-Verlag, Berlin, 1981.

SHISHIDO, S. et al. (1980), "A model for the coordination of recovery policies in the OECD region", *Journal of Policy Modeling,* 2 : 33-55.

SHISHIDO, S., M. AISE, H. FUJIWERA and T. FUKUCHI (1981), *Revised version of Tsukuba-FAIS world econometric model (T-FAIS V),* Paper presented at the world meeting of project LINK, August 31-September 4, La Hulpe, Belgium.

SIEBRAND, J.C. (1972), "Potential demand and external trade", *De Economist,* 120 : 260-295.

SIEBRAND, J.C. (1979), *Towards operational disequilibrium macro economics,* Martinus Nijhoff, The Hague.

SIEGEL, S. (1956), *Nonparametric statistics for the behavioural sciences,* McGraw-Hill, Tokyo.

SIGNORA, A. (1981), "Les leçons d'une expérience d'application de modèles mondiaux au niveau sectoriel", in COURBIS, R. (ed.), *International trade and multicountry models,* Economica, Paris, 163-170.

SNELLA, J.J. (1979), *An econometric model of international trade,* Paper presented at the Seventh International Conference on Input-Output techniques, April 9-13, Innsbruck, Austria.

SOLOW, R.M. (1955/1956), "The production function and the theory of capital", *Review of Economic Studies,* 23 : 101-108.

SONO, M. (1945), "The effect of price changes on the demand and supply of separable goods (in Japanese)", *Kokumin Keisai Zasshi,* 74 : 1-51. Translated in *International Economic Review* (1961), 2 : 239-271.

STEUER, M.D., R.J. BALL and J.R. EATON (1966), "The effect of waiting times on foreign orders for machine tools", *Economica,* 33 : 387-403.

STONE, J.R.N. (1954), "Linear expenditure systems and demand analysis : an application to the pattern of British demand", *Economic Journal,* 64 : 511-527.

STONE, J.R.N. and A. BROWN (1964), *A computable model for economic growth,* Chapman and Hall, London.

STROTZ, R.H. (1957), "The empirical implications of a utility tree", *Econometrica*, 25 : 269-280.

STROTZ, R.H. (1959), "The utility tree - a correction and further appraisal", *Econometrica*, 27 : 482-488.

TAKAYAMA, A. (1974), *Mathematical economics*, The Dryden Press, Hinsdale.

TAPLIN, G.B. (1967), "Models of world trade", *International Monetary Fund Staff Papers*, 14 : 433-455.

TAPLIN, G.B. (1973), "A model of world trade", in BALL, R.J. (ed.), *The international linkage of national economic models"*, North-Holland Publishing Company, Amsterdam, 177-223.

THEIL, H. (1965), "The information approach to demand analysis", *Econometrica*, 33 : 67-87.

THEIL, H. (1971), *Principles of econometrics*, Wiley & Sons, New York.

THEIL, H. (1975/1976), *Theory and measurement of consumer demand, 2 Vols.*, North-Holland Publishing Company, Amsterdam.

THORBECKE, E. and A.J. FIELD (1974), "A ten-region model of world trade", in SELLEKAERTS, W. (ed.), *International trade and finance, Essays in honor of Jan Tinbergen*, Macmillan, London, 221-261.

TIMS, W. and F.J.M. MEYER-zu-SCHLOCHTERN (1962), "Foreign demand and the development of Dutch exports", *Cahiers Economiques de Bruxelles*, 15 : 389-395.

TINBERGEN, J. (1962), *Shaping the world economy : suggestions for an international economic policy*, The Twentieth Century Fund, New York.

TYSZINSKI, H. (1951), "World trade in manufactured commodities 1889-1950", *Manchester School of Economic and Social Studies*, 19 : 272-304.

UNITED NATIONS (1961), "Standard international trade classification, revised", *Statistical Papers series M No. 34*, United Nations, New York.

UNITED NATIONS (1975), "Standard international trade classification revision 2", *Statistical Papers series M No. 34/Rev. 2*, United Nations, New York.

UZAWA, H. (1962), "Production functions with constant elasticities of substitution", *Review of Economic Studies*, 29 : 291-299.

VAN POECK, A. (1979), *World price trends and price and wage developments in Belgium*, Doctoral dissertation, Catholic University of Louvain, Louvain.

VEIL, E. (1982), "The world current account discrepancies", *OECD Economic Outlook, Occasional Studies*, Organisation for Economic Co-Operation and Development, Paris, 46-63.

VIAENE, J.M. (1982), "A customs union between Spain and the EEC", *European Economic Review,* 18 : 345-368.

VIAENE, J.M. (1983), "Product availability, price discrimination and interdependent import flows", *Discussion Paper 8317/G,* Institute for Economic Research, Erasmus University, Rotterdam.

VOS, A.F. de, and J.A. BIKKER (1982), "Interdependent multiplication models for allocation and aggregates : a generalization of gravity models", *Research Paper No. 80,* Interfaculty of Actuarial Sciences and Econometrics, Free University, Amsterdam.

WAELBROECK, J. (1962), "La demande extérieure et l'évolution des exportations Belges", *Cahiers Economiques de Bruxelles,* 15 : 397-412.

WAELBROECK, J. (1967), "On the structure of international trade interdependence", *Cahiers Economiques de Bruxelles,* 36 : 495-511.

WAELBROECK, J. (1973), "The methodology of linkage", in BALL, R.J. (ed.), *The international linkage of national economic models,* North-Holland Publishing Company, Amsterdam, 45-61.

WAELBROECK, J.L. (ed.) (1976), *The models of project LINK,* North-Holland Publishing Company, Amsterdam.

WAELBROECK, J. and A. DRAMAIS (1974), "Desmos : a model for the coordination of economic policies in the EEC countries", in ANDO, A., R. HERRING and R. MARSTON (eds.), *International aspects of stabilisation policies,* Proceedings of a conference held at Williamstown, Massachusetts, June 1974, Conference series no. 12, Federal Reserve Bank of Boston, Boston.

WAELBROECK, J. and V. GINSBURGH (1981), "Some calculations of the impact of tariffs on world trade and welfare with a general equilibrium model of the world economy", in COURBIS, R. (ed.), *International trade and multicountry models,* Economica, Paris, 279-294.

WILKS, S. (1962), *Mathematical Statistics,* Wiley, New York.

WINTERS, L.A. (1984a), "British imports of manufactures and the Common Market", *Oxford Economic Papers,* 36 : 103-118.

WINTERS, L.A. (1984b), "Separability and the specification of foreign trade", *Journal of International Economics,* forthcoming.

WOODLAND, A.D. (1979), "Stochastic specification and the estimation of share equations", *Journal of Econometrics,* 10 : 361-383.

WOOLLEY, H.B. (1965), *Measuring transactions between world areas,* Studies in International Economic Relations No. 3, National Bureau of Economic Research, New York.

YEATS, A.J. (1981), "On the accuracy of partner trade statistics", *Oxford Bulletin of Economics and Statistics*, 40 : 341-361.

ZELLNER, A. (1962), "An efficient method of estimating seemingly unrelated regressions and tests for aggregation bias", *Journal of the American Statistical Association*, 57 : 348-368.

AUTHOR INDEX

SUBJECT INDEX

D

ADVANCED STUDIES IN THEORETICAL AND APPLIED ECONOMETRICS
VOLUME 9

---

1. Paelinck J.H.P. (ed.): Qualitative and Quantitative Mathematical Economics, 1982.
   ISBN 90 247 2623 9.
2. Ancot J.P. (ed.): Analysing the Structure of Economic Models, 1984.
   ISBN 90 247 2894 0.
3. Hughes Hallett A.J. (ed.): Applied Decision Analysis and Economic Behaviour, 1984.
   ISBN 90 247 2968 8.
4. Sengupta J.K.: Information and Efficiency in Economic Decision, 1985.
   ISBN 90 247 3072 4.
5. Artus P. and Guvenen O., in collaboration with Gagey F. (eds.): International Macroeconomic Modelling for Policy Decisions, 1986.
   ISBN 90 247 3201 8.
6. Vilares M.J.: Structural Change in Macroeconomic Models, 1986.
   ISBN 90 247 3277 8.
7. Carraro C. and Sartore D. (eds.): Developments of Control Theory for Economic Analysis.
   ISBN 90 247 3345 6.
8. Broer D.P.: Neoclassical Theory and Empirical Models of Aggregate Firm Behaviour.
   ISBN 90 247 3412 6.
9. Italianer A.: Theory and Practice of International Trade Linkage Models, 1986.
   ISBN 90 247 3407 X.